**W9-CTR-920**

Special thanks to all the souls whose time, patience and resources helped to make this edition possible. We all returned to the shores of California, didn't we? May we bless and love all life in this sacred garden.

To Jenifer whose sharp eyes and inner and outer beauty inspired me to stay on track and create in spiritual partnership. To my Angel Dog Karma who taught me unconditional love and to her beloved pack, Panda, Sammy, Meesha and Sheba, now reunited in spirit. To the community - one for all and all for one.

**20 YEARS of QUALITY:** Since 1976 Robert W. Matson has been publishing regional travel books of exceptional quality. "Everything I write about I experience first hand." The Sonoma Coast, Wine Country and Redwood Forests is the 3rd edition of his 2nd of 5 titles. See page 317.

Whenever an illustration or photograph is integrated into the text of an individual destination, there was a fee charged. In order to participate in a paid feature in this book, each destination had to pass specific criteria established by the author, Robert W. Matson. Each destination is exceptional in one way or another, insuring the traveler a top notch guide to the best, whether moderate or expensive accommodations, restaurants, galleries, general stores and recreational transformation destinations North of San Francisco.

COVER PHOTOGRAPHS: "Turtle Rock" at Salt Point was captured by Jack Haley, a veteran photographer of the Sonoma Coast and American West. Jack's instincts are intimately in tune with the flow of life at shores edge. Back cover photograph of "Millennium Sunset" by restaurateur Wolfgang Gramatzki won Sunset Magazine's 1998 Grand Prize. Unfortunately Wolfgang transitioned before he knew of his award. It is in the spirit of his creativity that we dedicated this photo at River's End in Jenner. Oak tree and vineyards by Richard Gillette is a "Mystical Moment in the Garden". Spirit fashions the elements of the Universe to create the tiny acorn from which springs the mighty oak!

North of San Francisco Guide Book ™
Sonoma Coast — Wine Country and Redwood Forests
First Printing: Winter of 1986
Second Printing: Winter of 1991
Third Printing: Spring of 2000
Manufactured in the United States of America   ISBN: 0-916310-05-1

# SONOMA COAST,
# Wine Country & Redwood Forests
## *The Guide to Conscious Tourism*

To All The Animals Who Live
In The Garden of Eden
North of San Francisco

And To All The Caretakers
Who Really Care

To All the Farmers and
Gardeners Who Create Foods
That Nourish and Heal Us.
May More of Us
Enter Their Field of Dreams.

To All the Healers and
Spiritual Teachers Who Are
Leading Us Through
The Next Millennium

Conscious tourism embraces life and the love of it. It takes the well-being of the whole planet into consideration; plants, animals, people - all living things. It brings to it a sacredness and reverence for all the elements - earth, air, fire and water. Day and night, sun and moon, stars and planets - we witness and experience all this and more when we travel and explore other cultures and ways of life.

Conscious tourism embraces small mom and pop businesses - the backbone of America. It avoids unconscious and irresponsible corporations. Conscious tourism means personal intervention and contribution to aid fellow humans, plants and animals along the roadways and paths that we travel. Consuming renewable resources by using non-throw away items such as traveling with a handcrafted coffee mug and recycling whenever possible. Leaving the environment cleaner than you found it, by picking up trash and properly disposing of it wherever you go. Conscious tourism means spreading good will and good cheer, building bridges between people and places, extending kindness to those you meet along your way and engaging in a healthy partnership between you and the planet.

# WELCOME To The Sonoma Coast!
## HOW TO USE THIS BOOK

Over two decades of travel and contact with knowledgeable residents and curious visitors to the north coast helped to field test and engineer this practical, unpretentious and easy-to-use guide book. The Sonoma Coast, Wine Country and Redwood Forests book is divided into three chapters - the Coast, the Inland Valleys and Recreational Transformation. It thoroughly covers a slice of paradise along State Highway 1 between Tomales in northwestern Marin County; all along the Sonoma County coastline, to Point Arena in southwestern Mendocino County. Then moves inland to cover the Highway 101 corridor (The Redwood Highway) beginning with Petaluma and traveling north to Hopland which lies just over the Mendocino County border.

The centerfold maps beginning on Page 154 are laid out to help you locate cities, landmarks and destinations. The alphabetized index beginning on Page 310 lists destinations by page number. For example, in the Coastal Communities Index (page 310), the fishing village of Bodega Bay is listed on Page 20. Individual destinations are placed in this book to follow the highways in geological order, usually from south to north and/or east to west.

## PRICES and HOURS of OPERATION

All listings in the various sections of this book were cross-checked for accuracy. Prices mentioned in the features are subject to change due to fluctuations in the economy and management. Operating hours are also subject to change, especially on a seasonal basis in rural areas. As a rule of thumb, room rates usually increase $5 - $10 per room per year. So what costs $70 in 1999 will probably cost $80 in 2000, $90 in 2001, $100 in 2002 and so on. Menu prices usually increase about 10% to 20% per year. The following price rating symbols accompany each restaurant in the **DINERS CHOICE** selections at the beginning of each community.

**($) Inexpensive to Moderate: Meals under $10, Lodging under $75/2**
**($$) Moderate to Expensive: Meals $10-$20, Lodging $75-$200/2**
**($$$) Very Expensive: Meals over $20, Lodging over $300/2**

## A WORD ABOUT THE REVIEWS

Because I am a resident author of Northern California I have the opportunity to frequent the coastline, wine country, redwoods and mountains. These roads and the people who live here are well known to me and the reviews are accurately written with a depth of first hand experience few travel writers ever achieve.

Each restaurant, accommodation, general store and winery is personally inspected and the proprietors interviewed. Each restaurant has been dined at 2 to 3 times prior to being written up. I have always personally inspected each accommodation and interviewed the proprietors for their amenities. I always pay my way, accepting little more than a cup of coffee on the house. However, on occasion I have sampled certain dishes to give the innkeeper or chef feed-back.

# TABLE OF CONTENTS

**NOTE:** The various destinations in the Sonoma Coast book appear in the order in which they are located along the highways; from south to north and east to west.

## CHAPTER ONE - THE COAST

## CHAPTER TWO - THE INLAND VALLEYS

# FARMS, GARDENS and RANCHES

# SONOMA COUNTY WINE and REDWOOD COUNTRY
## Russian River Redwoods, Dry Creek Valley and Alexander Valley

# CHAPTER THREE - RECREATIONAL TRANSFORMATION

# INDEXES and CREDITS

Photo by Jan Alexander

## TOMALES-DILLON BEACH
**DINER'S CHOICE:**   Area Code (707)
**Angel's Cafe** ($$) 26950 Shoreline Hwy 1 878-9909; **Country Delights** ($), 27000 Hwy 1. 878-2732; **Diekmann's Store** ($) Hwy 1, Tomales 878-2384; **Lawson's Resort Cafe** ($$) #1 Beach Rd. 878-2505; **Nicks Cove** - a great stop for BBQ'd oysters, located 5 miles south of Tomales ($$) 23000 Hwy 1 (415) 663-1033; **Tomales Bakery** ($) 27000 Hwy 1 878-2429; **Tomales Pizza** ($-$$) State Route 1 @ Dillon Beach Rd. 878-2222; **William Tell Hotel** ($$) 26955 Hwy 1 878-2403.

## TOMALES-DILLON BEACH LODGING
**Lawson's Landing** ($) 137 Marine View Dr 878-2443;. **Lawson's Resort** ($$-$$$) Dillon Beach Rd. 878-2204;    **Shoreline House** ($$-$$$), (415) 663-1943 Fax: 663-1944; **U.S. Hotel** ($$) 26985 Hwy 1 878-2742.

## ANGEL'S CAFE

Some of the most successful travelers ask for divine guidance to keep them safe and on the proper path. Angel's Cafe in the tiny community of Tomales is one of the perfect starting points. You will enjoy the hearty country cuisine chef/proprietors Kathleen and Bill Crayne and staff prepare for breakfast, lunch and weekend dinners. You will absolutely adore her collection of Angels adorning the walls and counter which Kathleen has been collecting for the past 20 years.

You'll also enjoy Kathleen's generous portions of biscuits & gravy, pancakes, Belgian waffles, hot cereal, the Country breakfast (2 eggs any style, hash browns, toast and choice of linguisa, ham, sausage or bacon) or the Rancher's breakfast (with 3 eggs, extra potatoes, toast & meat). For lunch (from $6.00) you can enjoy a variety of hot or grilled sandwiches, delicious homemade soups, homemade salads, daily specials, or choose from a variety of toppings, meats, vegetables and cheeses on a tasty and filling deli sandwich. The fresh cut flowers, candlelight, soft background music and occassional Pacific fog that silently drifts in makes dining with the angels at Angels Cafe a heavenly experience.

*$-$$ ANGEL'S CAFE American Country Cuisine*
*26950 Shoreline Hwy 1, Tomales, CA. 94971*    *Open 6:30am to 4pm*
*Fri & Sat dinner till 9:30*    *AE, MC & Visa*    *(707) 878-9909*

## WILLIAM TELL HOUSE

"We don't tell at the William Tell," state the proprietors to this colorful Tomales saloon and restaurant. The William Tell House is a popular stop where locals and tourists sit elbow-to-elbow at the long bar to wash down their cares with a cool beer or cocktail. The stories are flavored with truths and yarns spun by people who are tied to the land: local ranchers, Basque sheepherders, fishermen and farmers. A juke box provides music and before the night is over, the small dance floor might be packed with old and new-found acquaintances from near and far.

Most people walk away full, after putting away a family-style feast in the William Tell's dining room (seating for 60). The talented chef prepares pasta, beef, chicken, prime rib and seafood dinners, which are served with soup or salad. Before or after dinner you can catch the sunset at the beach which is but a short drive west.

*$$ WILLIAM TELL HOUSE* *26955 State Hwy 1, Tomales, CA. 94971*
*Steaks, Seafood & Pasta Entrees* *(707) 878-2403  Reservations*

## U.S. HOTEL

Rarely do you find such devotion to replicating a historic landmark as the Davis family of Tomales have shown in recreating the U.S. Hotel, which opened in 1990. According to local historians, at least 3 hotels have stood at this location. Today the hotel is under the ownership of Kate Foist and her faithful mascot "Mate", an Australian Sheppard. Eight upstairs rooms await discerning travelers visiting this coastal showplace. Each room is named after an early Tomales pioneer. All have private baths, century-old antique oak beds, armoires, dressers with mirrors, potted plants and fresh cut flowers. Rates for two are from $75 weekdays, $85 weekends (subject to changes & tax) and include a continental breakfast.

*$$ U.S. HOTEL* *P.O. Box 34, 26985 State Hwy 1, Tomales, CA. 94971*
*Bed & Breakfast* *Gifts, Antiques, Art Gallery, Video Store & VCR Rentals*
*AE, MC & Visa* *(707) 878-2742  Reservations Necessary*

## DIEKMANN'S GENERAL STORE

Today's visitor to Tomales would be surprised to know that at one time this tiny community boasted four hotels, nine saloons and two general stores. The present Tomales general store and post office opened in April of 1875 with the philosophy to "carry anything for the daily needs of life." After World War II, Iowa banker Walter Diekmann came to Tomales and purchased the store which has stayed in the family since 1948. Today Diekmann's General Store is under the direction of Kristin Lawson and Bill Diekmann.

A split level hardwood floor and banister divides the store into two sections. Dairy products, juices, canned goods, picnic supplies, film, toilet items, beer, wine and liquor are stocked up front. On the upper level you'll find work clothes, tools, hardware, camping and cooking utensils, fishing gear, towels, beach items and video rentals.  Hunting and fishing licenses are also available. In 1998 the Diekmanns added a new front porch balcony and coat of paint to the 100-year-old building. The community and visitors alike are fortunate that the Diekmann family had the vision and faith to refurbish the building and carry on the general merchandising philosophy.

$ DIEKMANN'S GENERAL STORE        *Open daily, 9 a.m. to 6 p.m.*
Hwy 1, Tomales 94971         *Closed major holidays  (707) 878-2384*

## TOMALES PIZZA

In the back of historic Diekmann's General Store is Tomales Pizza.  Fit into a small space, this tiny galley kitchen is a source of wonderful pizza made from scratch. "Gastronomical Delights to pick up and eat," is proprietor Michael Bambach's motto.  He and his staff do a really good job on the pizzas they serve.  The produce, Kieth Guisto's milled organic flour, dairy from the Straus Family Creamery and tomato products are local and mostly organic.  Verni's "California Gold" extra virgin olive oil from Clovis, California is key to taste and flavor.  The 500 degree F+ tile oven yields pizza with a moist, light, crispy yet robust crust.  The menu is simple and to the point.  Choose from 22 combinations - individual servings, deep dish, medium and large.  Garden fresh Caesar, daily specials and real Biscotti, chocolate too.  These matched with iced tea, and fountain sodas or rich coffee do satisfy.  All orders are to go only. Michael is a busy entrepreneur - a realtor for Pepperwood Properties in Marin and San Francisco (415) 563-1943; a sometimes innkeeper booking 30 days in advance (415) 663-1943 and pizza maker.  Kind of reminds me of the innkeeper in the film "Local Hero."  Open Thur - Sun from 4-8pm and until 9pm weekends.

$$ TOMALES PIZZA    *Route 1 @ Dillon Beach Rd., Tomales, CA. 94971*
*Gourmet Pizza Tonite!*                    *(707) 878-2222 Strictly to go*

## LAWSON'S RESORT

A twisting country lane winding over rural hillsides leads down from several hundred feet to Dillon Beach, a small, almost forgotten coastal town just north of San Francisco.

In the lofty hillside oceanview Patio Cafe of Lawson's Resort, with indoor / outdoor dining, guests can feast on clam fritters, BBQ'd oysters, deep fried fish & chips, beef burgers, vegetarian garden burgers, vegetarian pita sandwiches, shrimp Louie's, Caesar salads and homemade clam chowder; plus coffee, cappucino, lattes, chilled mineral water, beer and wine. For dinner (from $11.95) you can fill up on porter house steak, broiled salmon, or calamari calebresa served with choice of soup or salad. You can watch migrating whales with your binoculars or see the surf break on the pristine beach below.

Simple oceanview cottages to elegant vacation homes are available all year, so bring the whole family (no pets allowed). You can run for miles on unspoiled beaches with the resort offering a mile of private beachfront. At Lawson's General Store guests can stock up on fresh produce, meats, fish, wine, beer, canned goods, coffee, hardware, firewood, ice, fishing gear, tourist information and souvenirs.

$-$$$ *LAWSONS' RESORT and PATIO CAFE*
*Continental Cuisine & Vacation Rentals    P.O. Box 97, Dillon Beach, CA 94929  Open daily Jun-Aug, wknds off season.    Oceanviews, kitchens, beaches.    Restaurant: (707) 878-2505   General Store: (707) 878-2094*

## LAWSON'S LANDING

Located at the mouth of Tomales Bay on the northwest shoreline is Lawson's Landing. Campers and RVer's by the hundreds find this 1,000 acre ranch just what the doctor ordered. During summer and fall Lawson's Landing is a bee-hive of activity, but with the first winter rains the campground is reduced to a whisper in the wind. People come here to fish, swim, surf, kayak, beachcomb, count birds and the stars. Fishing and crabbing is often excellent.

Clam diggers and abalone divers often get their legal catch, and rock and surf fishermen reel them in. The Lawson family and their experienced staff take guests out on the "Clam Clipper", a 42 foot ferry boat ideally suited to excursions on Tomales Bay for wildlife viewing and fishing. Pier fishing for perch and smelt and crabbing the wharf (daylight hours only) is fun. Rock fish and salmon fishing is nearby. In the boat house campers can purchase bait (bait shop closed Dec & Jan) tackle, weights, gas, oil, ice and firewood. Open year around.

$ *LAWSON'S LANDING  Box 67, 137 Marine View Drive, Dillon Beach,*
*Camping, RV Sites, Clamming & Fishing     Email:N347CV@aol.com*
*www.lawsonslanding.com          MC & Visa      (707) 878-2443*

Photo by Jan Alexander

The pristine Estero Americano is closed to all but kayakers who can put in at the bridge just south of Valley Ford. Turn off State Hwy 1 at Dinucci's Italian Restaurant in Valley Ford and go south 1/2 mile on Valley Ford Estero Road. Visitors can bicycle or walk this road to bird watch, but be careful of speeding traffic. The daily fluctuations of the tides and spring floods are an awesome sight to behold. Pastures with early morning mist resemble Irish Bogs.

## COUNTRY DELIGHTS

The Country Delights delicatessen, at the corner of Hwy. 1 and Dillon Beach Road, offers a delicious assortment of meats, cheeses, breads and salads, states owner Ilene Matthews. Open daily, Country Delights also specializes in hot, cold, vegetarian and meat sandwiches featuring the California lamb sandwich for lunch and the answer to any visitor's questions about the area. The full service deli is enhanced by a fine selection of salads, ice creams, as well as chilled juices, fresh brewed coffee and espresso. The corner bakery has quite a reputation for fresh baked breads and desserts.

*$ COUNTRY DELIGHTS*          *27000 Hwy 1, Tomales, Ca. 94971*
*Delicatessen & Catering*       *(707) 878-2732 Sit down & to go.*

## TOMALES REALESTATE - Sharon Vallej'o

Those seeking coastal propriety or a business opportunity in paradise should give real estate broker Sharon Vallej'o a call. She has showcased homes, ranches, land and opportunities from West Marin to West Sonoma and beyond since 1980. With the millennium knocking at our door maybe its time for a change in your life.
*$ - $$$ Real Estate & Business Opportunities  27000 Hwy 1, Tomales, CA. 94971  http://listinglink.com  Fax: 878-2755 or (707) 878-2700 Ext #6*

# SONOMA COAST
# Valley Ford to the Sea Ranch

ROUTE 1 winds its way through river valleys and creek watersheds, up steep ridgelines and through verdant redwood forests, and at times crowds the edge of 1,000 foot cliffs.

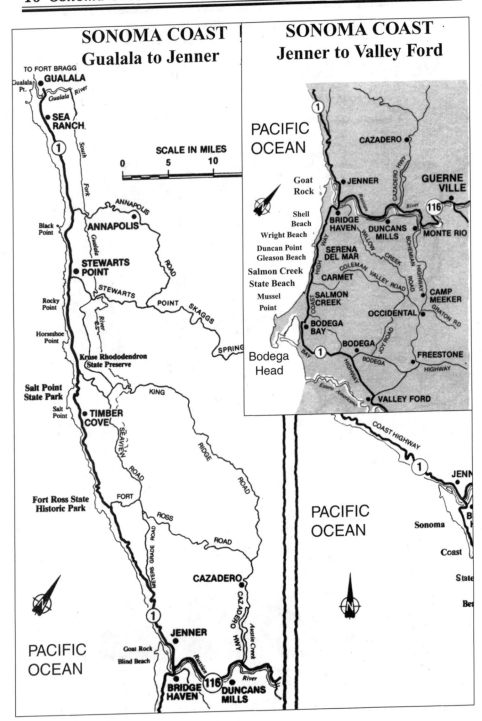

## SONOMA COAST
### Gualala to Jenner

## SONOMA COAST
### Jenner to Valley Ford

TO FORT BRAGG

Gualala Pt.

**GUALALA**

Gualala River

**SEA RANCH**

SCALE IN MILES

0     5     10

Black Point

ANNAPOLIS

**ANNAPOLIS**

ROAD

Gualala River

**STEWARTS POINT**

Rocky Point

STEWARTS

POINT

SKAGGS

Horseshoe Point

River

SPRING

Kruse Rhododendron State Preserve

**Salt Point State Park**

Salt Point

KING

**TIMBER COVE**

SEAVIEW

ROAD

RIDGE

ROAD

**Fort Ross State Historic Park**

FORT

ROSS

ROAD

MEYERS GRADE ROAD

**CAZADERO**

CAZADERO HWY

Austin Creek

**JENNER**

Goat Rock

Blind Beach

Russian River

River

**116**

**BRIDGE HAVEN**

**DUNCANS MILLS**

PACIFIC OCEAN

PACIFIC OCEAN

**1**

**PACIFIC OCEAN**

Goat Rock

Shell Beach

Wright Beach

Duncan Point

Gleason Beach

**Salmon Creek State Beach**

Mussel Point

Bodega Head

**CAZADERO**

**JENNER**

CAZADERO HWY

Russian River

**GUERNE VILLE**

**116**

**BRIDGE HAVEN**

**DUNCANS MILLS**

**MONTE RIO**

WILLOW CREEK

**SERENA DEL MAR**

COLEMAN VALLEY ROAD

BOHEMIAN HIGHWAY

COAST HIGHWAY

**CARMET**

**SALMON CREEK**

**OCCIDENTAL**

**CAMP MEEKER**

GRATON RD

**BODEGA BAY**

**BODEGA**

JOY ROAD

**FREESTONE**

BAY

**1**

BODEGA

HIGHWAY

HIGHWAY

Estero Americano

**VALLEY FORD**

COAST HIGHWAY

**1**

**JENN**

Sonoma

Coast

State

Be

B

H

# Route 1 Travel Advisory

The Sonoma County is a fabulous place to visit.  Any month of the year, nature orchestrates one of the greatest shows on earth!  You can stroll expansive, driftwood scattered beaches; watch the drama of a fresh water river meeting the ocean; hike through a verdant coastal forest to the ledge between land and sea; explore eerie Moonrock State Park; go tide pooling or rock fishing; or watch the California gray whale migrations from a ringside seat at one of our fine coastal accommodations.  The meaning of recreation often changes to re-creation.

During the summer, California State Highway 1 is the busiest two-lane state highway in California.  Wintertime is the best time to vacation here.  The highway often slows to a trickle of traffic and you can practically have the whole north coast to yourself.  At cheery resorts in front of a crackling fire or from cozy rooms priced at special off-season rates you can revel in the security of riding out the wild Pacific Coast storms with their twenty foot breakers.  A visit to the Sonoma Coast is more than a vacation—it's an adventure!

As a travel author I feel a responsibility for the safety of those encouraged by my book to travel to this special part of California.  Drownings, falls, collisions with other vehicles, livestock, or wildlife, and the possibility of having your dog shot by a sheep rancher are a few of the things that can and have happened to travelers and residents along the North Coast.  The days are gone when a resort owner could say, "Don't tell 'em that.  They might not come."  Today's traveler expects and deserves to be told the truth.  Here are a few ground rules for those who will be exploring the beaches and woods along California's North Coast.

# Roads, Traffic, and Driving:

The amount of traffic along Route 1 has increased dramatically over the past few decades.  Old-timers may still remember the days when they would go to their window to see who was passing by on the highway, but the times are long gone when four or five cars a day used the road.  Now, on a summer weekend it's more like four or five cars a minute.  Whether these coastal roads are adequate to the demand being placed on them is a serious question.

The important thing to remember is that it takes a different attitude to drive these roads.  You are not on a freeway.  Some of the locals have a harder time remembering that than the visitors.  Some "poke along" and try to control others who are in a hurry and become nothing more than an obstacle and safety hazard.  Still others speed along for the sheer pleasure of trying out their driving skills and the performance of their vehicle.  Differing intentions make safe driving a special challenge on coastal roads.  The usual rules and common courtesies are all the more required under these conditions.  Pull over if you are holding up someone else. Expect the unexpected around every blind curve.  Expect an oncoming vehicle on your side of the road when you go around a curve and you will be ready for it if it happens.

The traffic on Route 1 is very diversified ranging from log trucks (usually April 1 through October 1), RV motorhomes, large delivery trucks, high speed sports cars, café motorbikes, 4-wheel drive trucks, family cars and 10-speed bicyclists in their Pacific Coast bicycle lanes.  Accidents are inevitable, all are unnecessary.  The log trucks usually run with the most frequency along Route 1 in the summer and fall.  They also use River Road in Sonoma County.  The drivers of heavy rigs are usually excellent, but sometimes they get *pushy* beyond good highway safety etiquette and follow too close.  If this happens, then pull over and wave them by to defuse the situation.

*Continued to Page 45*

Photo by David Althen

Valley Ford's population hasn't changed much in 100 years. The wide open space of ranches and stands of eucalyptse makes it a scenic stop for meals or a overnight rest.

## VALLEY FORD, BODEGA & FREESTONE DINING   Area Code (707)
**Bodega Road House** ($$) Downtown Bodega 876-1810; **Casino Bar & Grill** ($$) Bodega Hwy 876-3185; **Dinucci's Italian Dinners** ($$) Hwy 1 876-3260; **Java the Hut** ($) 500 Bohemian Hwy 1 874-2436; **Sonoma Coast Villa** ($$$) 16702 Hwy 1 876-9818; **Valley Ford Grill** ($$) Hwy 1 876-9860; **Valley Ford Hotel** ($$) 14415 Hwy 1. 876-3600.

## VALLEY FORD, BODEGA & FREESTONE LODGING:
**Big Trees Llama Farm** ($$) 14430 Hwy 1 795-5726; **Bodega Estero Bed & Breakfast** ($$) 17699 Hwy 1 876-3300; **Green Apple Inn** ($$) 520 Bohemian Hwy 874-2526; **Inn @ Valley Ford** ($$) 14395 Hwy 1 876-3182; **Sonoma Coast Villa** ($$-$$$) 16702 Hwy 1 876-9818; **Valley Ford Hotel** ($$) 14415 Hwy 1 876-3600.

## BOOKSTORES, GENERAL STORES, GIFT SHOPS and the ARTS:
**Bodega Country Store** ($-$$) 17190 Bodega Hwy 876-3191; **Bodega Landmark Studio** ($-$$$) 17255 Bodega Hwy 876-3477; **Collector's Depot Antiques** ($-$$) 17135 Bodega Hwy 876-3035; **Freestone Country Store** ($$) 500 Bohemian Hwy 874-1417; **Freestone House & Gardens** ($$) 306 Bohemian Hwy 823-3710; **Gourmet Goat** ($$) 17190 Bodega Hwy 876-9686; **Pastorale** ($$) 12779 Bodega Hwy 823-0640; **Penny Whistle Antiques** ($-$$) 17135 Bodega Hwy 876-9670; **Seagull Antiques** ($-$$) 17190 Bodega Hwy 876-3229; **Valley Ford Market** ($$) 14400 Hwy 1 876-3245; **Wooden Duck Antiques** ($$) 132 Bodega Lane 876-3176.

## SURF SHOP: Northern Light Surf ($$) 17191 Bodega Hwy 876-3032.
*FREE SURF REPORT (Updated Daily) (707) 876-3110*

## VALLEY FORD MARKET

The Valley Ford Market successfully promotes an old-fashioned general store atmosphere. "We encourage a friendly community shopping experience for locals and tourists to enjoy," state proprietors Steve and Karri Miller. "Because the community and tourist needs are so diversified, we stock anything from road flares to diapers. This large market has a full selection of canned foods, baked goods, seasonings, desserts, beverages, premium wine and beer. In the deli you can order a made from scratch sandwich from a selection of dozens of cheeses and meats. Light hot entrees and salads are also available.

The late 1800's ethic of "everything for the everyday needs" has been applied here. To begin with: candles, firewood, hardware, tools, some automotive supplies (fix-a-flat, oil & transmission fluid), fishing tackle & bait, some canning equipment, light clothing for summer wear at the beach, books and magazines, VCR & video rentals, gives one a glimpse of the stock. Open rain or shine 365 days of the year, the Valley Ford Market is a lifeline you can count on.

*$-$$ VALLEY FORD MARKET*
*Food and Provisions    Open 7 days a week year around. Local & Travelers*
*14400 Coast Hwy 1, Valley Ford, CA 94972    Checks  (707) 876-3245*

## LILLY of the VALLEY FORD GRILLE

Beginning at 6:30am daily, the Lilly of the Valley Ford Grill begins to fill up with members of the local ranching and dairy community. Owner Lilly Filipow has transformed this cafe into a pleasurable destination for locals and visitors. Breakfast entrees (served all day) range from a thick slice of ham and eggs with breakfast potatoes to scrambled eggs with smoked salmon or delicious French toast marinated in orange rind. For lunch try the whole grilled Portabella mushroom, grilled chicken pesto or the gorgonzola cheese burger or veggie burger. Light eaters can dine on garden fresh salads and sumptuous homemade soups. Lilly's menu offers locals traditional foods with the exciting addition of gourmet home cooked meals, which can also be prepared to go.

The authentic character of Valley Ford is evident in the faces of the long time ranchers who line the counter early in the morning. By lunch time later risers, entrepreneurs, tourists and bicyclists begin to stop by.

*$ LILLY of the VALLEY FORD GRILLE    14450 Hwy 1, Valley Ford, CA.*
*Eclectic Comfort Cuisine                (707) 876-9860 Sit down or to go*

## DINUCCI'S ITALIAN RESTAURANT

Since 1968 the Wagner family has been serving big hearted Italian meals for the big hearted people who live or visit rural Sonoma County. Over the years Gene, Betty, daughters Dolores and Jeanne, husband Enrique and grandsons Joel and Jon have brought many smiles to the faces of bar and dinner guests.

If the receptionist or a family member tells you to have a seat in the bar, don't be offended, for Gene, or daughter Jeanne and husband Enrique (who makes the homemade fettucini) cook each entrée to order. Everybody comes out pleased and contented. Daughter Dolores, who is in charge of the full bar, will make almost any drink in the world as well as introduce you to her own original "jello shots".

Dinner begins with a loaf of sourdough bread and a large tray of antipasta. Next, comes a meal in itself—a tureen of Gene's famous minestrone soup, which is so delicious that folks buy it by the gallon to take home for those special occasions. Both Bon Appetite and Gourmet Magazine have requested the secret recipe for Gene's minestrone soup. After you have had time to savor the soup, a salad and choice of dressing arrives. Pasta (a choice of spaghetti or ravioli) arrives next and you begin to wonder if your stomach has enough room for the main course! Folks, this is no "Hollywood by the Sea" where you leave broke and hungry! Next up is the cooked-to-order main entrée, served with a baked potato and sour cream or vegetables. You can choose between a variety of Italian or American entrées such as baked lasagna, chicken cacciatore, porterhouse or New York steaks, and prawns or scallops. Don't overlook the Bodega Bay fresh fish catches (in season) such as grilled salmon steak or snapper as well as sauteed shellfish and seafood crepe's. If you have any room left, there is ice cream or chocolate mousse for dessert. And how much do you think such a large five course dinner will cost? From $8.95 to $13.95 at the most with soup and salad priced at only $8.00. Gene states, "Excellence without extravagance is our motto." At Dinucci's you can count on consistent quality and you leave with a full stomach and a contented feeling.

Besides reasonable prices, Dinucci's is famous for Thanksgiving dinners. Gene arrives at daybreak to put ten tom turkeys in the oven. By noon, guests are enjoying fresh, roasted turkey and stuffing, homemade gravy, mashed potatoes, cranberry dressing and pumpkin pie.

*$-$$ DINUCCI'S FAMILY STYLE DINING*
*Italian, Seafood, & Steaks*      *14485 Valley Ford Rd @ Hwy 1, Valley Ford,*
*Dinner: 4pm Thurs.-Mon.*      *Sunday from 12:30 (hours vary seasonally),*
*Closed Tues. and Wed.*      *Full bar.*      *AE, MC, & VISA.*      *(707) 876-3260*

## FREESTONE HOUSE and GARDENS

Prominently set in Freestone (6 miles west of Sebastopol), and in Sonoma County's First Historic District, is the 2-story century old hotel building which houses the Freestone House and Gardens plus a Fine Art Gallery. Many call the nursery "a farm" with its abundance of rare, exotic and domestic animals and birds. There are Colonial fountains, Maybeck statuary from the Palace of Fine Arts in San Francisco, as well as a Statue of Liberty on the pond (1/19th scale). Often overheard is the exclamation, "It's like heaven on earth!"

Well known for its variety of plant material, garden statuary, unusual trees, perennials, ornamentals; the nursery includes roses, fuchsias, vines, camellias, rhododendron's and water plants. The new office has seasonal items, house plants, bulbs, gifts, planters and you name it!

Art collectors will love to explore the treasures to be found in the Fine Art Gallery. The setting of the Freestone valley is wonderful for a break, and there are excellent restaurants, and lodging nearby.

*$$ FREESTONE HOUSE & GARDENS Open 9am--5pm ./Clsd Tues & Wed.*
*306 Bohemian Hwy. Freestone, CA 95472     Information: (707) 823-3710*

## FREESTONE COUNTRY STORE

A pleasant early morning stop for coffee, fresh fruit and pastries can be found at the historic Freestone Country Store. Built in 1872, the store retains a presence and charm all to it's own. All year long locals and those traveling the backroads of Western Sonoma County visit for provisions, snacks or to simply pause and refresh on a bench beneath the old fashioned front porch.

Next door is **JAVA the HUT** ice cream parlor and coffee shop for that cool sweet taste of ice cream or jolt of caffeine - almost a necessity for early morning workers or mid day bicycle tour groups passing by the creeks, apple orchards and meadows of picturesque Freestone Valley. The proprietors know how to charge you up and will also give you travel tips to the Sonoma Coast. Java The Hut's high powered organic coffee, protein bars, smoothies and pastries really hit the spot. Stop buy!

| | |
|---|---|
| *$ JAVA the HUT* | *$ FREESTONE COUNTRY STORE* |
| *Coffee House & Ice Cream Parlor* | *Groceries, Gifts and Merchandise* |
| *500 Bohemian Hwy, Freestone,* | *500 Bohemian Hwy, Freestone,* |
| *CA. 95472   (707) 874-2436* | *CA. 95472  (707) 874-1417 Info* |

## SONOMA COAST VILLA

This rather large and elegant 60 acre coastal estate, the Sonoma Coast Villa and restaurant, is located just north of tiny Valley Ford on California State Highway 1. This fully equipped destination sits like a gemstone in a landscaped valley of rural ranch land. Here you can feel free to take off your shoes and kick up your heels by the in-suite fireplace with your sweetheart in one hand and a glass of good spirits in the other. Proprietors Cyrus and Susan Griffin trust you'll find the hospitality cordial and the whole family will feel at home.

Terraced grounds, terra-cotta stucco, red tiled roofs and an expansive veranda give the inn the architectural qualities of a Mediterranean villa. Just outside your accommodations is the private landscaped courtyard with a swimming pool and a large indoor jacuzzi spa. Twelve private guest rooms have their own distinct style, with slate floors, beamed ceilings, and wood burning fireplaces. Each room features elegant yet comfortable furnishings, a full bath, television, refrigerator, coffee machine and complimentary bottles of premium Villa wine. Come morning a full country breakfast is served in the dining room. Rates for two begin at $225 weekends with special rates available off-season.

Fresh seasonal food from the Sonoma Coast Villa's on-site organic gardens, fresh seafood from Bodega Bay, local ranch meats are combined with subtle blends of herbs and seasonings to create a stimulating dining experience. The Prix Fixe menu varies each week and includes appetizers such as smoked salmon quesedillas, crab cakes with fresh Remoulade, the Asian sampler or Yucatan lime soup. The house Caesar or garden mix are absolutely fresh and crisp. Entrees include Sonoma Coast lamb with fresh mint, vegetarian wild mushroom ravioli, Southwestern style Sonoma chicken or halibut steak with lime caper butter. Desserts include profiteroles, chocolate mousse torte and maple cheese cake. The fragrance of fresh cut flowers, a crackling fire and herbed creations from the kitchen casts a spell, reminding us of our higher human qualities.

The Sonoma Coast Villa is a wonderful location for weddings and receptions, (up to 150) corporate retreats or special events marking the rights of passage of our lives. Explorers are welcome to stop by for a tour or a sensational dining experience which often leads to an overnight stay.

*$$-$$$ SONOMA COAST VILLA*

*Lodging, Breakfast & Dinner    Box 236, 16072 Coast Hwy One,  Bodega, CA. 94922    http://www.scvilla.com   1-888-404-2255 or (707) 876-9818*

Saint Teresa's Catholic Church and the historic Potter school house sits on the hill above the tiny community of Bodega. Bodega lays a few miles inland from the lapping waters and fishing boats of Bodega Bay. Bodega is home to several antique shops, Northern Light Surf shop, a fabulous art gallery, Bodega Road House Coffee Shop, a general store and the historic Casino Bar & Grill. Hitchcock's movie "The Birds" was filmed here.

## CASINO BAR & GRILL

Two landmarks in Bodega are famous. The historic Potter Schoolhouse where the Alfred Hitchcock movie "The Birds" was filmed and the historic Casino Bar and Grill. Evelyn Casini's roadhouse is a favorite hang-out for West County ranchers with roots to the late 1800's as well as newcomers of the 60's thru 90's. The pool tables and long bar is a friendly environment for a glass of wine, mineral water, beer or cocktail. The Casino is locally famous for its mouth watering burgers (quality and quantity at a fair price) and summertime BBQ oyster feeds. Historic memorabilia lines the walls including mechanical Ravens from Hitchcock's movie set. Open 9am till?

$ CASINO BAR & GRILL     17050 Bodega Hwy (Hwy 12), Bodega, CA. 94922
Full Bar, Burgers, Hot Dogs BBQ Oysters    Cash Only    (707) 876-3185 Info.

## BODEGA LANDMARK STUDIO COLLECTION   While touring the West

Sonoma and Marin Counties be sure to stop by the Bodega Landmark Studio and stock up on the latest in travel guides, maps and local publications. Along with an excellent selection of post cards, note cards and books, you'll find one of the north coasts largest selections of amateur and professional films and supplies. Vintage maps and photographica are a specialty, but be sure to allow yourself enough time to enjoy the beautiful exhibition of local fine arts and crafts. The Bodega Landmark Studio (est 1978) is open from 10am to 6pm, closed Tuesday and Wednesday.

$-$$ BODEGA LANDMARK STUDIO   17255 Bodega Hwy, Bodega, CA. 94922
Regional Fine Art & Craft Gallery     (707) 876-3477 Regarding Info & Shows

## BODEGA COUNTRY STORE   Bodega Country Store, located just 1 mile east of

Route 1 on Bodega Highway, is a landmark locals and tourists can count on. Contemporary thinker Helen Bonfigli is no stranger to assisting coastal explorers in getting more out of their vacations. Locals know last minute ingredients for that all-important daily dinner, end-of-the-day drink or deliciious fresh made deli sandwich can be purchased here. Store shelves are lined with all manor of canned goods, health food, fresh produce, beer, wine, liquor, ice cream, chilled juices, gourmet coffee and cooking utensils. Flashey T-shirts, tourist souveniers, movie rentals and post cards are displayed. ATM and Lotto / open daily from 9am - 6pm.

$ BODEGA COUNTRY STORE     17190 Bodega Hwy, Bodega, CA. 94922
General Store - Groceries & Gifts      (707) 876-3026 Info

## BODEGA ESTERO Bed and Breakfast

An energy efficient geodesic dome with modern day farm located amid the rolling hills of Bodega sets this coastal bed and breakfast inn apart. Wildflowers, fruit trees, towering eucalyptse, sheep, llamas, and goats guarded by the inn mascot provides a wonderful setting. Outside the large picture window a balmy summer breeze holds a red tailed hawk in place. Wintertime Pacific coast storms howl and buffet the dome, peeking one's appetite for the cheery security of a gourmet breakfast by the snug wood stove.

Four spacious and tastefully appointed rooms with private baths with tubs await, (from $90/2). The following morning a gourmet breakfast of fresh baked scones, muffins, apple Betty's or quiche with fresh fruit salad, oat meal, juice, coffee or tea is served by Innkeeper Edgar Furlong. Innkeeper Michael O'Brien will gladly give you a tour of the farm as well as point out the award winning mohair, alpaca and wool he spins. Sorry, no TV, radio or ringing telephones, but guests can relax with the morning paper or greet the goats, chickens and exotic birds, and help make their day happy with a handful of grain and a pat on the head.

*$$ BODEGA ESTERO BED and BREAKFAST    Box 362, 17699 Hwy 1, Bodega, CA. 94922   MC & Visa,     (707) 876-3300 / 1-800-422-6321*

## BODEGA HARBOUR GOLF

One of the finest seaside golf courses in America with panoramic oceanviews is located at Bodega Harbour just 65 miles north of San Francisco and 2 hours west of Sacramento. Designed by Robert Trent Jones Jr., this challenging 18 hole golf course with an oceanview from every tee offers the finest golfing experience "west of Scotland and north of Pebble Beach."

Resident golf pros can assist newcomers in the fully equipped pro shop or out on the Par 70, 6,220 yard championship tee course or 5,630 yard regular tee course.

After the game in the oceanview lounge golfers can swap tales. Lunch & dinner menus feature a variety of meals including steak sandwich, burrito special, king salmon, rack of lamb or the special of the day.

Special Bodega Harbour golf packages are available. Be it a fund raiser, organized tournament, or group outing; Bodega Harbour Golf Links and Club House Restaurant takes pride in providing gracious and professional service to all golfers fortunate enough to play our links. Banquet and event catering is also available at our yacht club which seats up to 165 persons for buffet dinner or 200 persons for passed horsd'oeuvres and cocktail packages. This waters edge yacht club is an impressive and romantic location for special gatherings.

*$$ BODEGA HARBOUR GOLF LINKS      Box 368, 21301 Heron Dr., Golf Links, Pro Shop & Clubhouse  Bodega Bay, CA. 94923. (707) 875-3538 WEBSITE: wwwbodegaharbourgolf.com   Rest. & Catering: (707) 875-3513*

# LUCAS WHARF, RESTAURANT & FISH DELICATESSEN

Fishing boat docks have always held a special fasination. Fishermen, having braved a completely unpredictable sea, often for days at a time, put in for safe harbor here. Bone tired and proud, they march off their boats to unload their catch and rest a few days or hours before returning to the open sea. Things have changed a bit over the years and you'll hear the fishermen grumble about this and that, but the desirability of fresh fish from sea to stomach hasn't changed a bit. One of the nicest things about Lucas Wharf is there is usually no middle man between fisherman and market. The fresh caught fish are unloaded at the wharf, fillet'd out, iced down, and nicely displayed in the delicatessen case. A few items like prawns, scallops, lobster, snow crab, shrimp and squid are shipped in. Local catches of fresh ling cod, rock cod, petrale sole, rex sole, English sole, sand dabs, Pacific red snapper, thresher shark, flounder, albacore, Pacific coast oysters, and cabazone are usually available year-round. Dungeness crab (Nov-June), halibut (late summer - fall), and salmon (sporadically May-Sept) are available seasonally. Dry smoked or lox salmon is also carried.

Lucas Wharf Restaurant opened in October of 1984. This spacious dinner house was built over the water amid a working fishing village. Rich redwood grains, a fireplace, long bar and dinner room with lots of natural light filtering in the windows, makes for a pleasant setting to savor premium wines & spirits or fresh fish and gourmet dinners. Guests love dining over the water with picture window views of the fishing fleet, aquatic life and placid Bodega Bay. Besides the fixed menu, there are also white boards which list daily specials such as wine by the glass, innovative entrees and desserts. Fresh shucked oysters, smoked local salmon, steamed Eastern mussels, fresh broiled Petaluma chicken, char-broiled New York steak, and a spectrum of common to unusual fish which the fishermen bring in are served daily. The Lucas family really went all out to provide a total dining experience for locals and tourists.

In the full service delicatessen next door, over 20 varieties of cheese, 10 kinds of sandwich meats, breads or rolls, salads, desserts, soft drinks, fruit juices and many gourmet goodies are stocked. Sound like its time for a picnic or luau on the beach? Family owned and operated and in the fish business as commercial fishermen since the 40's - the Lucas Family can usually be found on premises and eager to meet with the public. Also on premises is a fresh Seafood Snack Bar serving fried take out meals of fish & chips, shrimp, clams, calamari & oysters. Deli catering is also available.

The Lucas Wharf is located in the south Bodega Bay Harbor. You can't miss it!

*$-$$ LUCAS WHARF, RESTAURANT & FISH DELICATESSEN*
*Fresh Fish & Gourmet Dinners   Dining: 11:30am-9:00pm Wknds 11:30am-9:30pm*
*599 Hwy 1, Bodega Bay,         Full Bar till? Deli: 10am - 6pm winters, 10am to*
*P.O. Box 667, Bodega Bay,       8pm summers. Restaurant: (707) 875-3522 Res.*
*California  94923            not accepted. Delicatessen: 875-3562 Seafood to go.*

# BODEGA BAY

The Bodega Bay of today looks much different than the Bodega Bay of 200 years ago. Runoff from development around its edges fills it in each spring. Consequently, dredging is required from time to time. The protected sand spit to the south is a county park and home to the U.S Coast Guard. An earthquake generating a tidal wave of

Photo Courtesy Bodega Landmark Studio ©TVI

30 feet or more would lick the beaches clean of visitors and their recreational vehicles, but the crisp clean air, breaking surf and open beach make it worth the risk. Why live in fear of such a rare event? Why not go into town and celebrate at one of the fine restaurants Bodega Bay is famous for! Yes! That's a good idea! Check out the nautical shops, explore the art galleries, heal in one of the local hot tubs and spend the evening under the stars.

**BODEGA BAY DINING ESTABLISHMENTS: Telephone Area Code is (707)**
**Bay View Room** ($$) 800 Hwy 1  875-2751;  **Boat House** ($) 1445 Hwy 1  875-3495;  **Bodega Bay Grill** ($$)  2001 Hwy 1  875-9190; **Bodega Harbour Golf Course** ($), 21301 Heron Dr.  875-3538;  **Breaker's Cafe**  ($$)  1400 Hwy 1  875-2513;  **Crab Pot Fish Market** ($$)  1750 Hwy 1  875-9970;  **Diekmann's Bodega Bay Store** ($) 1275 Hwy 1  875-3517;   **Duck Club, The** ($$$) 103 Hwy 1  875-3525;  **Inn at the Tides** ($$$) 800 Hwy 1  875-2750;  **Lucas Wharf** ($$) 599 Hwy 1 / Deli 875-3562, Restaurant 875-3522;  **McCaughey Bros. Store Deli** ($)  1850 Bay Flat Rd.  875-3935;  **Pelican Plaza Grocery & Deli** ($)  1400 Hwy 1  875-2522; **Pelican Plaza Pizza & Video** ($$)  1400 Hwy 1  875-3245;  **Sandpiper Dockside Cafe** ($$) 1410 Bay Flat Rd., 875-2278;  **Sushi Osaka** ($$) 2001 Hwy 1  875-2550; **Three Daughter's Deli & Seafood** ($)  1850 Bay Flat Rd. 875-8883; **Tides Wharf Restaurant** ($$)  835 Hwy 1  875-3652;  **Whaler's Inn** ($$) 1805 Hwy 1  875-2829.

**BODEGA BAY LODGING:**
**Bay Hill Mansion** ($$$) 3919 Bay Hill Rd. 800-526-5927;  **Bodega Bay & Beyond** ($$$) 1400 Hwy 1  875-3942;  **Bodega Harbor Inn** ($$) 1345 Bodega Ave. 875-3594;   **Bodega Bay Lodge Resort & Conference Center** ($$$) 103 Hwy 1 875-3525;  **Chanselor Guest Ranch** ($$) 2660 Hwy 1  875-2721; **Inn at the Tides** ($$$)  800 Hwy 1  800-541-7788;  **Porto Bodega Campground** ($) 1500 Bay Flat Rd.  875-2354;  **Vacation Rentals USA** ($$$) 555 Hwy 1  800-548-7631

**GAS & PROPANE:  Mason's Bodega Bay Marina Store** ($)  1820 Westshore Rd., 875-3811;  **Tides Texaco Gas & Store** ($)  900 Hwy 1., 875-9868.

**SONOMA COAST THINGS TO DO:**
**Fishing and Whale Watching:**
Bodega Bay Sport Fishing Center / 875-3344  Challenger Sport Fishing / 875-2474.
**Surf Shops:**  Northern Light, Bodega  876-3032;  Surf Shack, Bodega Bay  875-3944.
**Science & Research Facilities:**  Bodega Bay Marine Laboratory, 875-2211.
*FREE SURF REPORT*   *(Updated Daily)*   *(707) 876-3110*

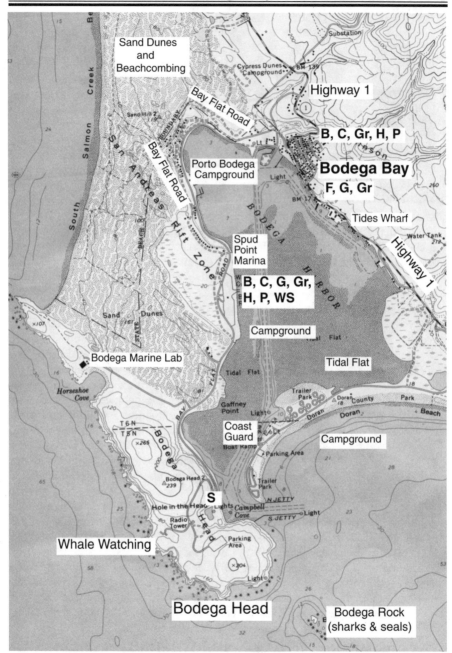

Sand Dunes and Beachcombing

Highway 1

**B, C, Gr, H, P**

Porto Bodega Campground

**Bodega Bay**
**F, G, Gr**

Tides Wharf

Spud Point Marina

**B, C, G, Gr, H, P, WS**

Campground

Bodega Marine Lab

Tidal Flat

Coast Guard

Campground

**S**

Whale Watching

**Bodega Head**

Bodega Rock (sharks & seals)

MAP of BODEGA BAY

| | | |
|---|---|---|
| | Boat Launch **B** | Camping **C** |
| Fish Market **F** | Gasoline **G** | Golfing **Go** | Groceries **Gr** |
| Hot Shower **H** | Propane **P** | Swimming **S** | Wind Surfing **WS** |

## TIDES WHARF RESTAURANT

Photo by Jan Alexander

Since 1930, the setting at the Tides Restaurant has been a wonderful introduction to life in a small California fishing village. There are few places where you can dine on the sea's bounty while watching fishermen unload their daily catch from bobbing boats beneath a sky full of seagulls. It's no wonder the motion picture "The Birds" was filmed here. Remolded in 1997, breakfast, lunch and dinner is served year round.

An extensive selection of seafood awaits you. Steaming bowls of crab cioppino and clam chowder, oysters, fresh filet of salmon, snapper, ling cod, albacore and sole are served. In the bar you can hear the men . . . and lady fisherpersons swapping tales of the sea. After drinks in the bar you can retire to one of the luxurious suites a short walk across the street at The Inn at the Tides.

### THE INN AT THE TIDES

Neatly terraced on a coastal slope overlooking Bodega Bay Harbor are the 12 lodges of The Inn at the Tides. Eighty-six rooms await those who want to get away from it all. The rooms & suites are light and airy, decorated with pleasant earth tones, most with fireplaces and patios. Lots of windows and skylights let in the sun and give each room sweeping views of the fishing harbor and bay. Amenities are numerous and include king or queen beds, sofa beds, tables and chairs, remote controlled color cable TV, direct dial phones, AM/FM clock radios, in room coffee brewers, refrigerators, snack bars, original art, hair dryers and full private baths. In the Spa, you might want to swim a few laps in the 50 foot, T-shaped pool or enjoy the clear bubbling waters of the whirlpool, and afterwards, take a sauna or use the exercise room. Breakfast and dinner room service is also available. The morning paper at your doorstep and a continental breakfast at the new Tides Wharf Restaurant across the street is a great way to start the day. You can relax knowing that every detail has been thought of to make your stay at The Inn At The Tides a pleasant and memorable experience.

*$$ TIDES WHARF RESTAURANT*
*Fresh right off the boat Seafood*
*835 Coast Hwy 1, Bodega Bay, CA*
*94923 Open Daily 7:30am-10 pm.*
*(707) 875-3652 Reservations*

*$$-$$$ THE INN at the TIDES*
*Bay View Lodging*
*800 Coast Hwy 1, Bodega Bay, CA. 94923*
*Fireplaces, Rm Service, Pool, Spa, Sauna.*
*www.innatthetides.com*
*(800) 541-7788 / (707) 875-2751 Res.*

## BODEGA BAY & BEYOND VACATION HOME RENTALS

Discover the pleasures and treasures of the Sonoma Coast. Choose from our unique, 1 to 5 bedroom, completely furnished, water view homes, many with hot tub/spas and fireplaces located along the beautiful Sonoma Coast, just 65 miles north of San Francisco.

Select from luxury homes to quaint cottages that are located in several diversified micro-climates. You can take your pick of homes from the hills overlooking the Pacific Ocean at the Bodega Harbour Golf Course community at Doran Beach, the homes "around and on the Bay" at Bodega Harbor, the homes at the delicate marshland and dunes of Salmon Creek, the homes at Carmet and Sereno Del Mar at Carmet, Schoolhouse and Portuguese Beaches, nestled along the rugged coastline and rocky cliff areas, or the coastal river town of Jenner where the Russian River flows into the Ocean. Rental rates are from $250-$880 for two nights and $625-$2,175 per week.. Monthly rates available upon request.

$-$$$ *BODEGA BAY & BEYOND*     575 *Hwy 1, Box 129, Bodega Bay, CA*
    *Vacation Home Rentals   email: reservations@ap.net     (707) 875-3942*
    *www.sonomacoast.com                        Nationwide: 800-888-3565*

## VACATION RENTALS USA

Thanks to family owned and operated companies like Vacation Rentals USA, many people who can't afford to own a luxurious Bodega Bay home can still vacation in one. Steve Carpenter and his staff roll out the carpet to locals and world

travelers who stay with them on the Sonoma Coast. Whether it's for a long awaited family get-together or a romantic getaway, you'll find just what you're looking for with over 80 properties to choose from. Enjoy sitting in a hot tub and watching the sunset from a beautiful ocean front home or watching golfers from a luxury home on the Bodega Harbour Golf Links. Each vacation retreat is an easy drive, in some cases a short walk, to gourmet restaurants, galleries and markets.

$$$ *VACATION RENTALS USA*     555 *Hwy 1, Bodega Bay, CA 94923*
    *Vacation Rental Homes   email: vacation@monitor.net     (707) 875-4000*
    *www.vacationsrentalsusa.com                Nationwide: 800-548-7631*

# Gourmet au bay

Perched right on the water's edge of the beautiful Bodega Bay Harbor, a classic gift gallery and wine boutique basks in the clean sea air of the Sonoma Coast. This unique gathering place for romantic explorers and the eclectic traveler boasts close up views of the colorful local fishing fleet.

For the wine enthusiast there are over 1,000 award winning California wines "laying" in wait with prices starting at $7.00. Collectors from the city rejoice when finding classic vintage wines no longer available - - - and at discount prices!

The artisan "Galerie" pieces, which proprietors Ken and Connie Mansfield have carefully selected, are a reflection of their personal taste after 30 years of travel around the world. At one time Ken was U.S. Manager for the Beatles' Apple Records as well as a Grammy Winning Record Producer.

Gourmet au bay features ambient accessories for the dwelling place plus CD's and cassettes, wine accessories, crafted candelabra, romantic artisan pieces, glassware, functional sculpture and things for your mouth.

*$$ Gourmet au bay          913 Coast Hwy 1, Bodega Bay, CA 94923*
*Wine Boutique and Artisan Gift "Galerie"          Open 7 days a week*
*Sun 12 - 8pm     AE, MC & Visa.  Fax: (707) 875-9800     (707) 875-9875*
*email: gourmet@monitor.net    http://www.bodegabay.com/business/gourmet*

## HARBOR VIEW GIFTS

This bay view shop located right on the waterfront is literally a one stop shopping experience. Unbelievable, well stocked with souvenirs, T-shirts, jewelry, shells, flags, windsocks, kites, sea life figures, chimes, cards, books, mugs and magnets to name just a few. There is an incredible selection of every item.

Owners Lowell and Sandy will be glad to satisfy your sweet tooth too, with gourmet candy and salt water taffy. They are also happy to help guide you along your coastal travels and share a fish story or two. As a matter of fact, Lowell is an eye witness to a large mystery fish spotted off the north coast several years ago. He is not alone. Several State Highway 1 road workers observed it near Stinson Beach after the Loma Prieta earthquake. National Fisheries Magazine even did a feature on this "mystery sea serpent." Easy parking and easy on the wallet, Harbor View Gifts is open daily from 10am to 6pm.

*$ HARBOR VIEW GIFTS & GOODIES  935 Coast Highway 1, Bodega Bay*
*Tourist Information & Giftshop     Discover, MC & Visa    (707) 875-3221*

## DIEKMANN'S BODEGA BAY STORE

Since 1946 the Diekmann family have provided for the basic everyday needs of their friends and neighbors. Those in a hurry can get a quick cup of fresh brewed coffee, mocha, espresso or an olde fashioned sandwich with all the fixins from the delicatessen. Enchiladas, burritos, homemade soup, potato or seafood salad and chunks of in-season smoked salmon are also available.  In their community oriented grocery store you can purchase dairy products, juices, canned goods, picnic supplies, film, toilet items, beer, wine, camping and cooking utensils, first aid supplies, towels and beach items. Gift items such as trendy T-shirts, post cards, maps, and guide books are also sold.

If we were lucky to have been raised by the sea as fisherman and diver Jim Diekmann was,  we would have experienced the hidden world at our feet.   Jim is an excellent source of fishing and diving information.   A full line of fishing tackle, dive gear, wet suits, spear guns, tanks, and underwater accessories are stocked next door at Bodega Bay Pro Dive Center (875-3054).   Diekmann's Bodega Bay Store is open daily (but Christmas) from 7am to 8pm, Friday & Saturday till 9pm.

*$ DIEKMANN'S BODEGA BAY STORE     1275 Coast Hwy1, Bodega Bay*
*Delicatessen, Groceries & Merchandise    MC & Visa     (707) 875-3517*

## CANDY and KITES

One would not believe how complex and sophisticated kites have become since the dawn of Space Age Technology.  The only well stocked full service kite shop in several counties is located in Bodega Bay. Dragons, diamonds, parafoils, deltas, boxes, sleds and eight different types of stunt kites as well as parts are in stock.  Candy and Kites provides an introduction to a low cost sport the whole family can enjoy.   Kite flying helps develop strength, agility, speed, hand-eye coordination, increased reaction time and is an ideal sport for a developing child.  There are even special illuminated and lighted kites for nite flights beneath the stars (sounds romantic). Kites sell from a few cents to hundreds of dollars.  Ask to see the videos on kite flying. Your hosts, Barbara Price and Roma Robbins welcome you to their happy store where they specialize in being nice since 1983.

Of course, what goes up must come down; and when it does, you might decide to purchase some sweets.  The shop boasts a Salt Water Taffy Boat (there are over 200 constantly changing varieties available), as well as premium and novelty candies. There is also an innovative selection of unusual action toys, flags, windsocks, air toys and books.  Lots of fun!

*$-$$ CANDY & KITES     1415 Hwy 1, Bodega Bay,  94923    MC & Visa*
*Open Seasonally from 11am to 5pm.          http://www.candkite@mch.org*
*Telephone Orders are accepted and shipped by UPS.          (707) 875-3777*

## BREAKER'S CAFE

The Breaker's Cafe is a California surfer's dream come true for Sally Sumner and Joy Dixon. This popular Bodega Bay cafe has established quite a following. The owners have created a distinct surfing personality through the use of a redwood surf board and incredibly realistic paintings of shore breaks and secret surfing spots. The cuisine reflects the high standards of the owners and staff.

Appetizers include crab corncakes, BBQ'd oysters and baked brie. Grilled veggie burgers, ground beef, chicken, steak, the fresh catch-of-the-day, bouillabaisse, jambalaya and several pasta and vegetarian entrees complete the menu. The house salad is one of the best north of San Francisco. It is an earthy garden of fresh Sonoma County greens delicately flavored with flowers and herbs. The homemade chowder or soup of the day is not to be missed. Sonoma County vintages and desserts made-on-the-premises are a plus.

Breakfast (served from 9am to 11:30am) is a delight, especially when the fog lifts to reveal the fishing fleet anchored in the bay directly below the picture windows and outdoor dining area. Belgian waffles, baked polenta, biscuits & gravy, oven roasted potatoes and omelettes give coastal explorers the energy to hike the Sonoma Coast. Sunset is a special time to prepare the soul for the tapestry of stars that will soon reveal themselves above Bodega Bay.

*$-$$ BREAKER'S CAFE*          1400 Hwy 1, Bodega Bay, CA. 94923
*Seafood / Continental*     MC & Visa      (707) 875-2513 Reservations

## PELICAN PLAZA GROCERY & DELI

The most complete shopping center plaza (built in 1983) on the Sonoma County coastline occupies a eucalyptus topped hillside overlooking the Bodega Bay fishing fleet. Built like a U-shaped fort, sheltering cars and tourists from the westerly prevailing winds and winter rains, the plaza is home for the town's laundromat, office supply center with copy & fax, video store, pizzeria, surf shop and the Pelican Plaza Grocery and Deli.

Vacationers can rest assured that whatever they mirror to the staff at Pelican Plaza Grocery will be reflected back - whether hurried or relaxed. You can get a fast cup of morning coffee to go or take a long tour along shopping isles overflowing with goodies. Indeed, waves of coffee are served each morning from 6:30am to wake Bodega Bay up and help get the town on its feet. From the deli section you can purchase a freshly made sandwich with choice of 2 dozen ingredients, homemade macaroni, tuna or potato salad, piroskis or mini pizzas. Pelican Plaza store is large as stores go on the coast - 2,800 square feet. You'll find a good selection of canned and packaged produce, dairy products, meat and fish, fresh fruits & vegetables, baby food, firewood, road flares, some hardware, fishing gear, cooking utinsels, rope, books, magazines and if you are feeling lucky - Lotto. The grocery & deli is open from 6:30am - 10pm daily year around.

*$ PELICAN PLAZA GROCERY & DELI  Box 966, 1400 Hwy 1, Bodega Bay,*
*Full Service Grocery Store & Deli, ATM & LOTTO*        (707) 875-2522

### THE BOAT HOUSE

Poised above a verdant valley on Highway 1 at the north end of Bodega Bay is the Boat House Restaurant. Here, Sophie and Rick Power book those magical journeys out to sea to visit migrating gray whales, sea lion colonies, bird sanctuaries and do a little salmon and rock cod fishing. Rick runs charters for himself and other skippers 4 blocks down the hill in Porto Bodega. Sophie books passengers, sells bait and tackle and runs the fish & chips restaurant. Patrons can dine indoors or out on fish & chips (fresh local cod when available or Icelandic cod), prawns, calamari, burgers, cole slaw, potato salad, onion rings, mineral water, coffee, sodas, beer and wine. "During the summer we grill the best BBQ'd oysters in town," she states. Daily fishing reports and the best strategy to land a salmon are given.

*$ THE BOAT HOUSE     Box 1148, 1445 Hwy 1, Bodega Bay, CA. 94923*
*Off-Shore Charters and Fish & Chips  (707) 875-3495 To go & Fishing Info*

### BODEGA HARBOR INN

At the top of the slope above Porto Bodega Marina, yet set a "country block" off busy Route 1, is the Bodega Harbor Inn. Built on quiet Bodega Avenue, the 16 cozy cottage rooms provide solitude for weary north coast explorers. Spotless rooms and suites include amenities such as antique furnishings, sundecks, sofa/hide-a-beds, king and queen beds with harbor views, and all rooms have private baths and cable color TV with rates from $50/2 plus tax. There are also vacation homes with numerous amenities. Within walking distance are fine restaurants, stores, a laundromat, and the colorful fishing fleet.

*$$ BODEGA HARBOR INN    at 1345 Bodega Ave. adjacent Pelican Plaza.*
*Rooms, Suites and Vacation Homes      P.O. Box 161, Bodega Bay 94923*
*Located at the north end of the Bay         (707) 875-3594 Reservations*

### THE CRAB POT FISH MARKET

Located on a curvey stretch of Highway 1 just north of Bodega Bay is The Crab Pot Fish Market, a colorful and authentic outlet for the finest of fresh smoked Pacific coast products. The Crab Pot is easily recognizable by its international orange and white color scheme and nautical exterior. Billie or Lynn are easy to talk to, and fill you in on the daily fresh catch. The quality of the Crab Pot's fresh in-season crab, smoked salmon, tuna, lox, kippered cod, sword fish, kippered salmon is superb. My personal favorite is the smoked & peppered salmon (delicious but red hot!). Beer, wine and soda are available. You can purchase oysters in the shell, prawns, clams, scallops, fresh frozen abalone & lobster tails. The Crab Pot's fresh smoked products keep well for the trip home and create wonderful memories.

*$$ THE CRAB POT FISH MARKET  1750 Hwy 1, Bodega Bay, CA. 94923*
*Fresh Smoked Fish                        (707) 875-9970 Information*

### The REN BROWN COLLECTION

The drive to The Ren Brown Collection is itself a changing tapestry of hillsides turned a golden brown in the summer, and emerald green after winter rains. Pelicans and egrets glide effortlessly in crystal clear air, above sandy beaches or rocky outcrops along the shore. In the fishing village of Bodega Bay, amid such an appealing coastal setting, is a particularly wonderful discovery - the Ren Brown Collection.

The gallery is located right on Highway 1, at the northern end of Bodega Bay. An enchanting world awaits the visitor just inside the door. Trickling water and a small Japanese garden create a special setting, where you can discover a wide variety of contemporary art from both sides of the Pacific, to enrich either a home or office setting.

The Ren Brown Collection has unique rotating exhibits of fine art, and is dedicated to representing both contemporary Japanese printmakers and artists of Northern California. Included are a wide selection of original etchings, woodblocks, and serigraphs, by artists such as Toko Shinoda, Micah Schwaberow, Mayumi Oda and Ryohei Tanaka, as well as sculpture and paintings by Sharon Spencer, Robert DeVee, Ron Megorden and others. Over eighty world renowned and newer artists offer works that are both representational and abstract in design. The Ren Brown Collection provides a unique, serene environment on the Sonoma County Coast, where you can also discover fine handcrafted gifts, jewelry,ceramics and Japanese antique furnishings.

*Photographs by Bodega Bay Photography*

*$$-$$$ The REN BROWN COLLECTION       Box 156, 1781 Highway One,*
*A Fine Art Gallery          AE, MC & Visa          Bodega Bay, CA. 94923*
*Open 10am - 5pm Thurs thru Mon and by appointment.*
*Representing Japanese Printmakers  &  the works of North Coast Artists*
*(707) 875-2922        1-800-585-2921*

## BLUE WHALE CENTER

At the Blue Whale Center, located on the north end of Bodega Bay and at the upper harbor entrance off Highway 1 at Eastshore Road, is a one stop destination for ocean fishing, dining, accommodations, art and body work.

You can share a thrill with Wil's Fishing Adventures by booking one of his deep-sea rock fishing, salmon and sightseeing tours on the Tracer, Aggressor or Payback. A knowledgeable crew equips the novice fisher person and takes you out to the Cordell Banks for King Neptune's treasures. "Sugar", Wil's African gray parrot sometimes talks non-stop for a 1/2 hour - spouting out every imaginable language and sound affect she has heard in the past week. The bait and tackle shop is well stocked. Next door is the Sea Gull Deli where George Wells does breakfast and lunch. Eggs any style with breakfast meats, gourmet coffee drinks, super sandwiches, fish chowder, salad and desserts will fill you up. You can rent a vacation rental home (for 2-8 by the day or week) from Coastal Vistas. Homes are located between the harbor at the south to the mouth of the Russian River to the north. A visual feast is Local Color Art Gallery where six Sonoma County artists and one framer hang or showcase their contemporary art treasures. They also exhibit consignment art from other Sonoma County artists. For that new look and optimal health you can make an appointment with Donna Dellepere at Ocean Wave Styling Salon or relax and unwind in the dry heat of the soft cedar sauna; then receive a Swedish/Esalen massage and deep relaxation body work at Bodega Bay Body Works.

Drive through Bodega Bay to the north end of town at Eastshore Road and take a left. You'll spot the Blue Whale Center straight-ahead on the right.

*BLUE WHALE CENTER          1580 Eastshore Road, Bodega Bay, 94923*
*#A  WIL'S Fishing Adventures    Open 6:30am-6pm  www.bodegabayfishing.com*
*(707) 875-2323; #B  SEA GULL Deli  Open 7am-4pm, phone/fax (707) 875-8871;*
*#C COASTAL VISTAS  Call for Appt., www.coastalvistas.com 1-800-78VISTA;*
*#D  LOCAL COLOR Art Gallery L.L.C.  Open 10am-5pm daily  (707) 875-2744;*
*#E OCEAN WAVE Salon  Open by Appt.,  (707) 875-2291;  #H Bodega Bay*
*BODY WORKS Open by Appt.  Located on 2nd floor  (707) 875-2362.*

## BRANSCOMB GALLERY

The large and luxurious three story Branscomb Gallery sets on the northeast side of Bodega Bay, offering distant harbor views from showrooms lined with inspirational works of art. Exhibits include bronze sculptures, oils, watercolors, etchings, tapestries, pastels, photography and a gift shop featuring high quality unusual gifts.  Guests will also want to sign up for the newsletter/calendar of events or call for information at (707) 875-3388 or FAX 1-(707)-875-2905. The owner also wants to remind art collectors that her gallery mats and frames art work, gift wraps and ships. Art lovers can stop by the Branscomb Gallery for an audio-visual feast of inspirational works and even spend the night in lovely upstairs accommodations. Open 7 daily 10am-4pm.

*$$-$$$ BRANSCOMB GALLERY*
*Fine art, custom framing &unique gifts    1588 Eastshore Rd., Bodega Bay,*
*CA. 94923    FAX (707) 875-2905 or   (707) 875-3388 Shows & Information*

### BODEGA BAY SPORT FISHING CENTER

Those seeking to experience the open sea, whale watching or sport fishing can rest assured that the Bodega Bay Sportfishing Center can accommodate them. Proprietor Rick Power and a hearty crew of veteran Bodega Bay skippers and boat owners will take you where the fish are. Helpful deck hands will help the novice fisherman get started. Sightseers often get close enough to get a good picture of the seasonally migrating California Grey Whales or perhaps watch a great white shark hunt an elephant seal off Seal Rock or the mouth of Tomales Bay where they breed. There is always fishing (weather permitting) along the Cordell Banks, one of the richest marine eco-systems on the West Coast.

A rare treat is to charter one of the 2 to 3 albacore trips each year to catch this truly delicious game fish (wonderful smoked or grilled over an open pit fire with wild mushrooms, fresh rosemary or perhaps brushed with a marinade). Fishing boats depart early at 2:30am and return at 7pm the same evening. These 50 to 100 mile round trip journeys are a wonderful adventure at sea.

All the charters assemble early from 5:30am to 6:30am for departure at 7am from the Bodega Bay Sport Fishing Center in Porto Bodega fishing village. Rick and crew want to be sure everyone is prepared whether sightseeing or fishing. Everything you need to purchase is in the general store as well as loads of fishing tips from experts. Fishing licenses, every type of bait you can imagine - squid, anchovies, herring, night crawlers, grass shrimp, ghost shrimp, pile worms, crab bait, pink shrimp and even "prehistoric yuppie bait."

There is a large assortment of tackle for surf or boat fishing and crab pots. Rubber boats, fuel tanks, fuel lines, hardware and fittings are stocked. Last minute needs for your charter include wind breakers, snack food and beverages. There is also a giftshop in the store to purchase a memory of your visit to Bodega Bay. There is a tremendous joy in seeing a whale close-up in its natural environment or catching and dining on a big fish which _you caught_ for yourself or your loved ones!

*$$ BODEGA BAY SPORT FISHING CENTER*       *1500 Bay Flat Rd.,*
*Sport Fishing & Whale Watching Charters*       *Bodega Bay, CA. 94923*
*A full line of fishing tackle and bait  MC & Visa  (707) 875-3495 Res. & Info*

## MASON'S BODEGA BAY MARINA and DAVE'S PIT STOP

Whether you are driving a big diesel truck, RV, or car and need gasoline, air, water, propane, or diesel fuel, you'll find **Dave's Pit Stop** a welcome sight.   Prices are kept reasonable at this small chain of four gas stations and convenience stores located in Bodega Bay, Forestville, Sebastopol and at the Todd Road exit on Highway 101 on the south side of Santa Rosa.   For the best fuel prices on the Sonoma Coast you'll want to note the location of **Mason's Marina** in Bodega Bay. On the north end of town take the Bay Flat Road exit off Route 1 and go down the hill into the harbor and follow the road 1 1/2 miles around the north side of the harbor to Mason's Marina.   The station is open daily till 8pm and serves the needs of locals, smart travelers and fishing boat skippers.

$ *MASON'S MARINA, 1820 Westshore Rd., Bodega Bay, 94923  (707) 875-3811*
$ *DAVE'S PIT STOP,   55 Todd Road,       Santa Rosa, 95407  (707) 584-9610*
$ *DAVE'S PIT STOP, 7200 Healdsburg Ave., Sebastopol, 95472 (707) 823-6283*
$ *DAVE'S PIT STOP,   7001 Hwy 116,       Forestville, 95436 (707) 887-7665*

### McCAUGHEY BROS. GENERAL STORE

The General Merchandise Store with the oldest established name on the coast is now situated in a new building at Spud Point Marina in Bodega Bay.  Formerly located amid the pastureland of Bodega, then to Porto Bodega; the store now occupies a site adjacent the lapping waters of Bodega Bay's main fishing fleet off Bay Flat Road.   Under the proprietorship of Ned Mantua, today the store supplies the daily needs of fishermen, campers and many locals.   The McCaughey Brothers Store is a real general store, not a gourmet imitation.  The aisles are lined with practical goods for practical working people.  Domestic & marine plumbing, electrical & nautical fittings, turnbuckles, rope, tools & convenience groceries are stocked as well as hooks, lines and sinkers.   There is also a good selection of imported & domestic beers as well as premium California wines.  Time permitting, minor repairs can be made for the coastal adventurer who puts into port in this part of Bodega Bay.

$-$$ *McCAUGHEY BROS. GEN. STORE*
*General Merchandise & Groceries*
*1850 Bay Flat Rd., Bodega Bay, Calif.*
*94923. (707) 875-3935 Information*

The Bodega Marine Laboratory is located on Bodega Head. Turn off State Highway 1 and drive 3 miles west down Bay Flat Road to Westside Road and turn right into the marine preserve. For current tour times it's best to call 875-2211.

There are numerous exhibits at the Bodega Marine Lab. This is the skeleton of the fin of a sperm whale. The bone structure is very similar to the human hand. The sperm whale is a mammal and no doubt our distant evolutionary relative.

## UNIVERSITY of CALIFORNIA
## BODEGA MARINE LABORATORY

Passengers in a parked car atop a Sonoma Coast bluff wonder what it looks like beneath the waves of the surface of the sea. A peek into this world can be enjoyed at the Bodega Marine Lab (BML), which is located off Bay Flat Road just north of Horseshoe Cove on the Bodega Marine Reserve. This is an extremely serious research facility producing reports and findings of global impact. There are tours of the facilities (as of this writing / Fridays 2pm - 4pm), a marvelous library of books and reports, and the scientists who participate in the lecture series are among the most intelligent and environmentally sensitive on the planet. For many, pure research and a genuine concern for all life, without the manipulative strings of politics and economics, is their reason to work here. For others there is a sincere attempt to employ science and business to work hand in hand for everyone's benefit. Salmon, crab, oyster, sea urchin, sea weed, great white shark and other residents of the sea present opportunities for sea farmers, fishermen, suppliers, retail markets, health food stores, medicine suppliers and restaurants.

A visit here can reveal more than a few imprisoned salmon and red snapper swishing their tails around in aquatic wall tanks. In back are lobsters who fearfully raise their claws in response to the silhouette of a human towering above them. What to eat? Who eats who? A visit to the Bodega Marine Lab will help you answer these timeless questions since the first fish slithered up on shore and asked the same question.

*$ University of California Bodega Marine Laboratory*
*Sealife Exhibits, Tours, Lectures & Library*     *2099 Westside Road,*
*Box 247,  Bodega Bay, CA. 94923*                    *(707) 875-2211*

## SANDPIPER DOCKSIDE CAFE

Located in Bodega Bay and just down the hill from Route 1 in the Porto Bodega fishing harbor at the north end of town is the Sandpiper Dockside Cafe. This restaurant is a favorite among locals, with its commitment to exceptional service and excellent food utilizing the freshest farm produce and dockside catches of fresh fish and crab.

The cozy artistic and nautical-themed cafe is a popular breakfast destination for eggs and homefries, omellettes, huevos rancheros, French toast, Belgian waffles or the famous homemade country sausage gravy served over oven fresh bisquits (from $3.50). Lite eaters can enjoy the "veggie Benedict." Lunch features a large variety of sandwiches, burgers, fresh seafood entrees, shrimp or crab Louies, wonderful homemade chowder or daily soup and daily specials. Premium wine and beer, herbal teas, espresso and cappucino are available.

You can relax by candlelight while outside the big picture windows, the coastal sun sets the bay and intertidal zone on fire. Silouettes of fishing boats floating on the glassy waters brings one an inner peace. Nightly specials include calamari saute, prawn scampi and snapper stuffed with crab & shrimp served with French fries, new red potatoes or rice pilaf, choice of soup or salad and fresh baked sourdough bread (from $12.95). Sumptuous desserts include cheesecake topped with fresh berries, fruit tortes and chocolate delights.

*$-$$ SANDPIPER DOCKSIDE CAFE*  Brkfast from 7am, Lunch from 11:30
*Seafood and American*                    Dinner from 5pm. Approved cks ok.
*1410 Bay Flat Rd, Bodega Bay, CA. 94923 Dis, MC & Visa (707) 875-2278*

## BODEGA BAY GRILL, SUSHI OSAKA and BAY HILL MANSION

If you are coming down State Highway 1 from the north, then the first opportunity you'll have to enjoy really delicious fish in Bodega Bay is at the Bodega Bay Grill in the Ocean View Center. You can also arrange for accommodations at the luxurious Bay Hill Mansion Bed and Breakfast Inn just across Highway 1, RV or camp at the Bodega Bay RV Park behind the restaurants and enjoy a mocha or espresso at the Roadhouse. At Bodega Bay Gifts you can pick up a post card, T-shirt or handcrafted Sonoma coast treasure.

*($$) BODEGA BAY GRILL*        2001 Hwy 1, Bodega Bay  (707) 875-9190;
*($$) BODEGA BAY RV PARK*     2001 Hwy 1, Bodega Bay  (707) 875-3701
*($$) BODEGA BAY GIFTS*        2001 Hwy 1, Bodega Bay  (707) 875-2449
*($$$) ADAM'S REALTY*          2001 Hwy 1, Bodega Bay  (707) 875-3200
*($) ROADHOUSE CAFE*          2001 Hwy 1, Bodega Bay  (707) 876-1810
*($$$) BAY HILL MANSION 3919 Bay Hill Rd., Bodega Bay (707) 875-3577*

Communion with nature can be enjoyed by horseback at Chanslor Guest Ranch which is located just north of Bodega Bay. The historic Chanslor Ranch has been operated as a cattle and horse ranch since the 1850's. The power and grace of a horse, gentle sandy beach, the pounding surf and pristine air acts as an elixir to longevity.

## CHANSLOR GUEST RANCH

Located 2 miles north of Bodega Bay, bordering Salmon Creek on the Sonoma County coast is the Chanslor Guest Ranch. In the main Ranch House are three comfortable rooms with private baths. The common living room with it's scenic ocean view invites stimulating conversation with new found friends.

The Loft Suite (for 1 or 2 couples) offers a fireplace, whirlpool tub and balconies facing the beach or hills. The moonrise is spectacular. The knotty pine Bunk House, built in the late 1870's, has lovely ocean vistas. Two bedrooms with a third room available to groups, 2 baths, a large fully equipped kitchen and eating alcove and large furnished living room make the Bunk House perfect for groups (sleeps up to 12 with third room, linens included). Rates for 2 from $75 include a full ranch style breakfast.

Of special note are the trail rides on this 700 acre working horse, sheep and cattle ranch. Chanslor Ranch Stables offer Guided Trail Rides along the beach or

on the ranch which are filled with visions of wildlife and natural California coastal beauty. The ranch offers hay wagon rides and Bar B Q's during the summer season. Guests also have fun hiking, rock climbing, fishing and camping. Chanslor Guest Ranch is an opportunity for parents to introduce their children to ranch life as well as the Pacific shoreline.

*$$ CHANSLOR GUEST RANCH*          *Bed and Breakfast Ranch*
*Box 1510, 2660 Hwy 1, Bodega Bay, CA. 94923.     (707) 875-2721 Res.*

# SURFING on the SONOMA COAST

Salmon Creek Beach is a popular surf spot for beginners and professional surfers.

## NORTHERN LIGHT SURF SHOP

Situated in the town of Bodega is a surf shop many local soul-surfers feel is the world's finest surf shop. Always stocked with the highest caliber surf gear available, one can find rental wetsuits & boards, new & used surf boards, skate boards, long boards, fun boards, short boards & boogie boards. A true hardcore surf shop, Northern Light carries Rusty, Local Motion, Rip Curl, Hotline, BZ, Roxy, Robert August and fresh threads for North Coast Surfers who challenge the power and majesty of the cold northern Pacific waves. The shop specializes in cold water gear and custom surfboards designed and built on the Sonoma Coast by lifetime local shaper Mitch Palmer.

However, one need not be a true hardcore to appreciate the essence of surfing, and visitors are always welcome to browse or reminisce in the always friendly atmosphere of this unique setting where "Surf Free" is the philosophy!

Visitors to the North Coast are reminded that this is one of the last frontiers where adventure can be found so close to the comforts of modern civilization so please, pack your trash and help keep the beaches clean and free.

*$-$$$ NORTHERN LIGHT SURF SHOP*
*Surfware, Revolutionary Boards and Surfer Gifts.*
*17191 Bodega Hwy., Box 138, Bodega, CA. 94922　(707) 876-3032*

Waves of the North Coast.  Oil Pastel paintings by George Smith on display at the Breaker's Cafe in Bodega Bay.  George (707) 632-5806.

## HIGH TIDE SURF SHOP

The California surf shop is one of the best places for the next generation to begin their education from one of the greatest teachers - the Pacific Ocean. Located just 2 blocks off Bodega Highway in the historic "walking tour" region of Petaluma, the High Tide Surf Shop is at the crossroads to several famous north coast beaches at Bodega Bay, Salmon Creek, Jenner, Dillons Beach and Stinson Beach.  Proprietors and All-American native Californians, Lynda and Leonard Crain, grew up on the beach and now share their California lifestyles with 2nd generation surfing son Ross as well as visitors to their High Tide Surf Shop. All sizes of surfboards, wet suits, fins and body boards can be purchased.  High Tide is currently the only Sonoma County surf shop to sell Clark foam blanks with complete fin and finishing kits. Custom designed beach and casual ware, T-shirts, sweat shirts, shorts, pants, hats, sandals, tote bags, beach accessories and Grateful Dead merchandise are stocked.  Don't forget to ask about the surf report and check out the books and magazines.

Surfs UP!
$-$$ HIGH TIDE SURF SHOP    9 Fourth Street, Petaluma, CA. 94952
Surf Boards & Beach Ware    www.waveslave.com    (707) 763-3860

## SURF SHACK BIKE, BOARD and KAYAK RENTALS

This tiny California surf shop is big on heart. A family man, owner Bob Miller makes it a priority that the whole family enjoy communion with the big blue and has turned the Surf Shack into the unofficial Sonoma County surfer headquarters. Inside you'll find a nice selection of hardcore surf clothing, bikinis, wet suits, surfboards and accessories, boogie boards, T-shirts, trunks, sunglasses and hats, shoes and sandals, surfing magazines, books and videos at easy on the wallet prices. Outside are bike, surf board and kayak rentals ($5/hr - $23 per day). Bob offers a 24 hour Sonoma Coast Surf & Weather report - just pick up the phone and call. He also helps to sponsor annual surf contests. The surf contests are often followed by a "bong fire" celebration and tribal drumming.

Surfing has become a family oriented sport where the motto "families that surf together stay together" certainly applies. Low cost surf lessons are available for beginners and there is a selection of consignment used wet suits and boards. Remember - *Live to Surf - Surf to Live!*

*$-$$ SURF SHACK   1400 Hwy 1 in the Pelican Plaza, Bodega Bay, CA.*
*Surf Shop and Bike, Board & Kayak Rentals  MC & Visa   (707) 875-3944*

## GOLD COAST COFFEE & KAYAKS

For over a decade locals and visitors have enjoyed the mondo surf family environment at Gold Coast Coffee. Established by surfers and local java legend Patrick Jenning, Gold Coast has locally roasted their beans in Duncans Mills since 1990. They now feature only organically grown coffee beans including Cyclops (a real eye opener), Jump-Up, and Coast Roast which are marketed throughout the north bay. Today the upbeat family energy created by new owner Patrick Parks carries Gold Coast into the Millennium in style. The outdoor garden patio is divine and the

original art, fresh baked goods, bagel sandwiches, fresh fruit smoothies and gourmet coffee drinks are the best.

You can rent a new top of the line Aquaterra kayak and explore the lower Russian River to the mouth using Gold Coast as your headquarters. Breathtaking scenery rolls out like a fine tapestry with seals, sea otters, osprey, hawks and sea gulls your traveling companions ($10 per hour and $25 sunset specials).

*$-$$ GOLD COAST COFFEE & KAYAKS*
*Box 100, Jenner, CA. 95450 Steelhead Blvd., Duncans Mills, CA 95430*
*Gourmet Snacks, Espresso, Kayaks & Entertainment       (707) 865-1441*

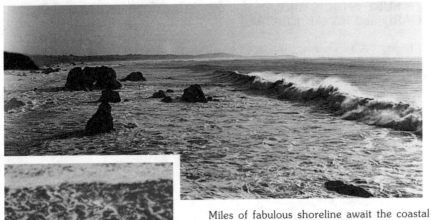

Miles of fabulous shoreline await the coastal explorer of the Sonoma Coast State Beaches. Remember to never turn your back on the ocean and when climbing or exploring tide pools and cliff lines, use the "partnership system". Top: Combers flying rooster tails during a break in a winter storm at sunset north of Salmon Creek Beach. Left: Sharing your beach walk with a friend makes it memorable..

## SONOMA COAST STATE BEACHES

Broad, shining beaches, secluded coves, rugged headlands, natural arches and a craggy coastline with tidal pools and reefs characterize one of California's most scenic attractions - Sonoma Coast State Beach. The Beach, actually a series of beaches separated by rocky bluffs, extends 13 miles between Bodega Head and the Russian River in Sonoma County. It is accessible to beachcombers, fishermen, sunbathers and picnickers from more than a dozen points along Coast Highway 1. Sonoma Coast is a fisherman's paradise and picnicking is a popular pastime. There are some picnic tables at a few of the beach access points such as Wright's Beach and Rock Point, but generally people like to settle down directly on the sand and use the fire rings provided for cooking. There are 30 developed campsites (no showers) around the edge of Wright's Beach. Bodega Dunes, a hundred-site developed campground with hot showers, restrooms, a trailer sanitation station and a campfire center is located half a mile south of Salmon Creek. The campgrounds are very popular, and it is a good idea to make reservations in advance, especially in summer. Reservations may be made at any of the MISTIX outlets in stores and businesses throughout the state. During the summer camping stays are limited to 7 days. At other times the limit is 30 days. *A word of caution - be careful of the bluffs and the rocks. These shale formations are unstable and unsafe for climbing. Stay on the trails and heed warning signs and fences.*

At Salmon Creek Beach a lagoon forms when sand and wave action closes the mouth of Salmon Creek.  This is a well used area, with surf fishing and beachcombing the most popular activities.  Deep green eel grass waves in the current of the creek and birds overhead make near prehistoric sounds.  The park headquarters and information center are located at the northwest corner of the Highway 1 bridge over Salmon Creek.

Salmon Creek Beach is a dune stabilization area.  In 1951, a program was begun to control drifting sand and keep it from filling in the bay.  The dunes between Bodega Bay and Salmon Creek were planted with various specialized grasses including European beach grass, used to protect dikes in the Netherlands.  In the 1980's a United Nations report concluded that the biggest threat to humanity by the end of the next century would be the desertification of the planet.  Unfortunately fire hazard along the replanted dunes is high.

Like most north coast beaches, Sonoma Coast is not for swimming, and lifeguard service is not provided.  Strong undertow, heavy surf, and sudden ground swells make even surf play dangerous.  Duncan's Landing, also called **DEATH ROCK**, is famous for two things: it was used as an early day landing for loading small coastal ships with lumber and food products; and its rocky headland is the most dangerous point along the beach, claiming almost 100 known people in drownings and God only knows how many more.  Goat Rock, at the northern end of the park near the mouth of the Russian River is another spot known for drownings (averaging 1/month).  The scenic shoreline, sandy beach, and fresh and saltwater fishing make this one of the more popular day-use areas, but watch out for the **SLEEPER WAVES.**  Sleeper waves are larger than normal waves than appear with no warning and can pull you, your child or dog under and outside the break.  Rescue is hard - drowning is common.

If you bring your dog, make sure he is leashed and not allowed to run loose.  There is an additional charge for each dog brought camping with you.  Dogs are usually not allowed on State Beaches except for Salmon Creek.  Be sure to keep a close eye on your dog.  Years ago dogs picked up by the Sonoma County Humane Society were unfairly suffocated (murdered) - or sold to Medical Laboratories (a fate worse than death).  The leash law is a good excuse to pick loose dogs up.  Unfortunately many of the sheep ranchers shoot first and ask questions later - even if your dog is just walking down the road or ditch.  Having felt increased population pressure and loss of thousands of head of sheep to stray dogs, the rancher feels a justifiable anger.  I feel it is time for a few free-run beaches along the Sonoma Coast and for ranchers to get off it and install dog proof fences in high traffic areas.

If you exercise a little caution when appropriate, you'll no doubt have a wonderful time at Sonoma Coast State Beach.  Have fun - you are literally in a Garden of Eden setting, but remember to never turn your back on the ocean, She is quick to take the unsuspecting (small child, dog or adult) on a ride for their life.  I'll repeat that one more time: **NEVER TURN YOUR BACK ON THE OCEAN!**

Above:  Cowboy turned mariner, Thomas rows his skiff to Jenner.  Nearby Willow Creek Road is a delightful bicycle ride or hike.  Pomo Campground with wilderness campsites is located 2 miles off State Highway 1.  Willow Creek is an active restoration site for Trout Unlimited and the meandering road becomes a dirt trail flanked by ancient redwood trees with mystical trunks.

## BRIDGEHAVEN CAMPGROUND

Located on State Highway 1 at the southern anchor point of a large bridge that crosses the Russian River is the sheltered B r i d g e h a v e n Campground.  The lush valley the campground sits in reminds me of a sleepy-hollow-by-the-sea.  The proprietors keep the campground quiet, so please don't come here expecting to party loud.  The family pet is more than welcome, but please bring a leash for your dog.  Twenty three campsites await - sites 1-17 have fire pits, water and electric and are ok for tents, trailers and RV's (sorry - no pull through sites).  Sites 18-23 are a real score for those seeking a secluded tent or sleeping bag setting with grassy floor that stays green year around, walls of thick vegetation and a low canopy of tree limbs.  There are hot showers, a reading library, animals for the children to get acquainted with and a private beach where canoes and kayaks can be launched into the river (Note: campground flooding occurs in the winter).  A restaurant which is open year around is just up the hill.  Rates for two are $20 per night, $120 per week and extended stays are ok.  Numerous amenities are in Bodega Bay ten miles south or Jenner cafe's and stores are two miles to the north.

$-$$  *BRIDGEHAVEN CAMPGROUND*    *Box 59, Jenner, CA. 95450*
*Camping, Trailer & RV sites*            *(707) 865-2473 Reservations*

## SIZZLING TANDOOR

The cuisine of the gentle and enchanted land of India can now be enjoyed in a spectacular setting in Sonoma County amid sweeping river valley views adjacent the Pacific Ocean. Guests can be served on the lofty outdoor patio kissed by the crystal clear ocean breeze and sweet smell of grass covered hillsides.  Far below, the Russian River exits the wine country on its seaward journey as red tailed hawks hover above a landscape of grazing sheep and cattle.

Lunch and dinner is served outdoors (weather permitting) or inside the richly decorated dining room with large picture windows.  The chef skillfully combines the spices of India in the time honored art of cooking in the famous tandoor. The huge clay oven fueled to intense heat by mesquite charcoal came to India by way of ancient Persia.  It is the center piece in Tandoori cooking.

The menu of this award winning Sonoma County restaurant is divided into appetizers, soups & salads, Tandoori (cooked Western BBQ style on skewers, and served on the sizzler), lamb curry, chicken curry, seafood, vegetarian specialties, rice specialties, tid bits, Tandoori bread, Western entries, seafood specialties, desserts, tea and coffee.  Western and Tandoori luncheons feature fresh fish, lamb, and chicken.  The appetizer of assorted Indian snacks is a nice introduction to Tandoori cuisine, which can be enjoyed on the premises or ordered to go for at-the-beach or late night snack in your room.  A full course dinner for two might include Mulligatawny soup, chef salad, Tandoori mixed grill (Tandoori chicken, chicken tikka, seekh kabob and fish), lamb or chicken saag (cooked in a spinach curry with spices and cilantro), Aloo Gobi Masala (cauliflower and potatoes cooked in Indian spices) and delicious Tandoori bread freshly baked to order.  Be sure to try the Indian Masala tea which looks and tastes like coffee but is caffeine free. Those traveling inland can dine at the Sizzling Tandoor at 409 Mendocino Avenue in Santa Rosa.

*$$ SIZZLING TANDOOR*
*Northern India Cuisine*
*9960 Hwy One, Jenner, CA. 95450*
*India & California Beer & Wine,*
*AE, MC & Visa.  Summertime seating till 10pm*
*Orders to go or Elegant River View Dining:  (707) 865-0625*

Mouth of the Russian River: The rising tide and surge of waves has broken through the berm of sand built up by the lazy summertime river flow. Up to 300 seals live at the mouth.

J enner, a little known corner of the Universe, holds much charm and natural wonder to explore. It is here that the Russian River empties itself into the Pacific Ocean. The river's beginnings are 90 some miles north where numerous creeks and tributaries merge in the ranchland and wine country of Mendocino and northern Sonoma Counties. By the time the river reaches the bridge over Coast Highway 1 at Bridgehaven, it is a swollen torrent of water ready to do combat with the river eater, the Pacific Ocean. During the dramatic winter storms, the battle to claim land at the mouth is at full height. Huge breakers and river currents smack into each other at locomotive forces. Sometimes the river wins a battle, but the ocean always wins the war. Several months later (during summer) the tides and waves pile up sand and the mouth is sealed by a smooth berm. This natural land bridge enables tourists to walk all the way from Goat Rock to the north shore. Throughout the natural history of the planet such natural land bridges have enabled migrations of animals and people to move into new hunting grounds. It is this ongoing drama that makes visiting the mouth of the Russian River so interesting.

With the winter rains, the biological time clocks in the salmon and steelhead trout trigger and they enter the river's mouth. This attracts the seals who have mated earlier in the year (August - October) on the rocky islands offshore and in secluded coves away from humans and great white sharks. They first shoot out into the mouth of the river and swim into the current, allowing it to carry them slowly out to sea from fresh to salt water, often no more than a hundred yards or so. Occasionally you'll see an explosion of blood

The pounding of waves against the shore have closed the mouth of the Russian River. Land bridges such as this enables humans and animals to explore new territory.

as a 300 pound seal snaps a death grip on a 30 pound fish. Other seals charge in to catch the fragments.

A large clockwise whirlpool sometimes forms at the mouth. Once at sea the seals jockey for position and line up like a flight of fighter planes about to dive. They peel off one or two at a time to catch waves which will place them close enough to shore to be able to shake flippers with. They may snag another fish on the way in and repeat the cycle a few more times. Eventually they will beach themselves up river away from predators and sightseers to sunbathe and digest their fresh catch of the day. Overhead flights of sea gulls and terns envy the lounging seals and occasionally a pelican takes a dive to try his luck. The mouth of the Russian River is definitely the hunger zone for a lot of critters. By late April and May the pregnant cows give birth to one pup and the river's mouth becomes a nursery, safe from great white sharks and killer whales which occasionally ply the surface near the rocky outcroppings to the West. The newborn pups play and romp in the surf and then you can see them catch sight of something on the cliffs above. They pause and ponder the silhouette - the silhouette of a human - and no doubt wonder what this two legged creature is all about and what effect it will have on their environment.

The State Rangers conduct narrative excursions to within safe viewing distance of the seals during good weather. It's a critical time for the pregnant cows and they should not be disturbed. Both the cows and bulls will protect the pups from intruders. One of the most magnificent vantage points to observe a West Coast river flowing into the Pacific is from the dining room of River's End Restaurant, which is perched high above the north bank of the Russian River. Another place is land's end where Highway 1 turns north above the mouth of the river. Day's end is the time to be here to toast the fireball with it's golden skirt shimmering over the placid water of the river. Just before it descends into the wave tossed Pacific and beneath the curvature of the Earth gather the energy of the moment in the palms of your hands and make a heartfelt wish. Perhaps you'll witness the "Green Flash", a rare phenomenon which occurs just as the orangish sun descends beneath the horizon.

Another mystical phenomenon to witness is when the red tide comes in. At night the waves at the mouth glow an erie phospherescent green in the mist and

A lone fisherman is outnumbered by a hungry pod of 200 harbor seals at the mouth of the Russian River. Large protected seal populations, logging, vineyards and urban pollution are blamed for the depletion of salmon and steel head runs. Fishermen sometimes watch seals rip out the belly of migrating salmon and toss the dying fish into the air; leaving the rest for gulls. Great white sharks, the seals natural predator, have been over fished.

Visitors can view the spring births of harbor seals from a distance. State park rangers keep a watchful eye. Dogs are allowed on leash only.

In the bottom photo the spring tide is going out and the river is a dangerous rapids. Parents and caretakers should keep a watchful eye on their children and dogs.

fog.  Go to the river mouth.  Now is the time for a light show, the likes of which few have ever seen, but be careful you don't get carried away.  As you walk on the sand along the shore tiny pressure sensitive micro organisms called dyno-flatuates explode emitting a green burst of luminescence.  All around your feet and in the water are emerald green flashes of light.  As the sea lions dive into the water there are explosions of green brilliance.  You can see green comets and skyrockets in the brackish water just upriver from the mouth as seals chase fish.  Its unforgettable.  Its a crystal dream come true.

There are few places on California's West Coast where the sights and smells between land and sea are so crisp and clear.  Such is the case of the unspoiled view facing westward from the beach at the mouth of the river.  Relax and rid your mind of human made worries.  Do you feel it?  Perhaps memories stir of a time more familiar to the genes in your bone marrow; to the soles of your bare feet pressed against the sand.  Perhaps a whale will spout just off-shore in the brackish currents where water from the mountains mixes with the sea.  Relax, the Spirit of the Soul takes over here, and when you shed the more formal clutter of the conscious mind, the more primitive animal brain surfaces and with it ancient memories.  The waves represent the continuum of the life experience on this planet.  Each wave began in the center of the Universe and is manifested by the solar winds.  Cryptic messages are picked up by the subconscious mind of those who know how to read the currents - surfers, divers fishermen and ancient explorers - perhaps even you.  Our genetic memory even recalls past life events.  With each wave beat is the assurance and security that Mother Nature will provide for us as long as we stay within her natural checks and balances.  This show goes on every day of the year, rain or shine.  It's the Greatest Show on Earth - and it's Free!

**ROUTE 1 TRAVEL ADVISORY:**          *Continued from Page 11*
If the truck driver is unreasonable then take the truck company name and number and call the dispatcher or the California Highway Patrol and report the incident.  Remember, because these 18-wheel trucks and trailers are so long and heavy it takes them longer to brake and slow down, and they need much larger turning areas around corners than a standard car.  RV motorhomes are exceptionally slow.  There are numerous pull-offs for vehicles to stop and ponder the natural beauty of our unspoiled coast—use them!  It's a California law for slower moving vehicles with five or more cars behind them to pull over to the right and allow traffic to safely pass.  It is usually safe for RV's, vans, or cars to spend the night in pull-offs along Route 1.  Be sure to set the brake!  Also keep track of where the next gas station is and how much gas you have on board.  Rural coastal service stations close at 6 pm winters, 9 pm in the summer).

**Open Range:**  The fifteen miles between Jenner and Fort Ross marks the most unforgivable coastal stretch of highway in Northern California.  Besides the diversity of traffic, there are sheer cliffs with few guard rails, and in some places it's 900 feet down a near vertical cliff to crashing waves and boulder-strewn beaches.  Many have been severely injured or killed and some have never been found.  As if that's not bad enough, it's still under open range law, which means unpredictable sheep and cattle can lay in the road or sporadically *mosey* across in front of your vehicle day or night,

*Continued to Page 47*

**JENNER to SEA RANCH DINER'S CHOICE: Telephone Area Code (707)**
**Jenner by the Sea** ($$) Hwy 1 downtown Jenner 865-1192; **Jenner "C"**
**Store** ($) Hwy 1 downtown Jenner 865-2906; **Fort Ross Store** ($) 12 miles
north of Jenner at 20705 Hwy 1 847-3414; **River's End Resort** ($$$) Hwy 1
north end of Jenner 865-2484; **Salt Point Bar & Grille** ($$ 17 miles north
of Jenner at 23255 Hwy 1 847-3234; **Sea Gull Espresso Bar** ($) 10439 Hwy
1 865-2594; **Sea Ranch Lodge** ($$) Hwy 1, Sea Ranch 785-2371; **Sizzling**
**Tandoor** ($$) 9960 Hwy 1, 865-0625; **Stewart's Point Store** ($) 32000 Hwy
1, 785-2406; **Timber Cove Inn** ($$) 21780 Hwy 1, 847-3231; **Timber Hill**
**Ranch** ($$$) 35755 Hauser Bridge Rd. on the ridge above Timber Cove 847-
3258.

**JENNER to SEA RANCH LODGING:**
**Fort Ross Lodge** ($$-$$$) 12 miles north of Jenner at 20705 Hwy 1 847-
3414; **Heaven's Edge** ($$) 10425 Hwy 1 865-1409; **Jenner Inn &**
**Cottages** ($$-$$$) Hwy 1 downtown Jenner 865-2377 800-732-2377;
**Ocean Cove Campground** ($) 23125 Hwy 1 847-3422; **Pomo State Park**
**Campgrond** ($) 2 miles east of Bridgehaven on Willow Creek Rd.; **Ram's**
**Head Realty Vacation Homes** ($$$) 1000 Annapolis Rd. 785-2427 / 800-
785-3455; **River's End Resort** ($$-$$$) Hwy 1 north end of Jenner 865-
2484; **Salt Point Lodge** ($$) 17 miles north of Jenner at 23255 Hwy 1 847-
3234; **Salt Point State Park** ($) 25050 Hwy 1 847-3221; **Sea Coast**
**Hideaways** ($$-$$$) 13 miles north of Jenner at 21350 Hwy 1 847-3278;
**Sea Ranch Escapes** ($$$) 60 Sea Walk Drive 785-2426; **Sea Ranch Lodge**
($$) Hwy 1, Sea Ranch 785-2371; **Sea Ranch Vacation Rentals** ($$$) Box
88, Sea Ranch 785-2579; **Stillwater Cove Ranch** ($) 16 miles north of
Jenner at 22555 Hwy 1 847-3227; **Timber Cove Boat Landing** ($) 13 miles
north of Jenner at 21350 Hwy 1 847-3278; **Timber Cove Inn** ($$-$$$)
21780 Hwy 1 847-3231; **Timber Hill Ranch** ($$$) 35755 Hauser Bridge Rd.
on the ridge above Timber Cove 847-3258.

**GENERAL STORES, GIFT SHOPS and the ARTS:**
**Fort Ross Store** ($-$$) 20705 Hwy 1 847-3414; **Jenner "C" Store** ($-$$)
Hwy 1 - Jenner 865-2906; **Ocean Cove Store** ($) 23125 Hwy 1 847-3422;
**Racoon Cove Giftshop @ Timber Cove Inn** ($-$$$) 21780 Hwy 1 847-
3231; **Seagull Giftshop & Deli** ($-$$) 10439 Hwy 1 865-2594; **Seaview**
**Art Glass** ($-$$$) 27780 Seaview Rd. 847-3443; **Sea Ranch Store** ($-$$ )
Sea Walk Dr. 785-2371; **Stewarts Point Store** ($-$$) 32000 Hwy 1 785-
2406.

**SONOMA COAST THINGS TO DO:**
**Bicycling, Fishing, Diving, Hiking, Rock Climbing, Surfing, Seal and**
**Whale Watching:** At the mouth of the Russian River access through Goat Rock
State Beach and hike 1 mile to river mouth or drive north of River's End to the
point for cliffside observation.
**Surf Shops: Northern Light**, Bodega 876-3032; **Surf Shack,** Bodega Bay
875-3944; **FREE SURF REPORT (Updated Daily) (707) 876-3110.**

## JENNER "C" STORE

After fighting the treacherous curves of Coast Highway 1, you round a sharp corner and there it is, the spacious tree lined parking lot of the Jenner "C" Store - plenty of room for big RV's, sports cars and groups of bicyclists. Gas pumps, water hose, air line, bathrooms and pay telephones are outside. Inside is hot coffee, a espresso /

cappuccino machine, chilled beverages and a deli where you can purchase sandwiches, apples and pastries. Groceries, canned produce, motor oil, fishing gear, toiletries, T-shirts, hats and other travel necessities are stocked. Daily newspapers, road maps, post cards, guide books and a bulletin board of information is also on display. The Jenner "C" Store is open 365 days of the year from 7am to 9pm (summers), 8am to 8pm (winters) and is a regular life-line for locals and tourists.

*$-$$ JENNER "C" STORE*     *Coast Highway 1, Jenner, CA. 95450*
*Deli, Groceries & Gasoline*     *MC & Visa  (707) 865-2906 Information*

**ROUTE 1 TRAVEL ADVISORY:***from Page 45* rain or shine, foggy, or clear. If you hit one of these poor animals, then you must pay for it's death or injury, plus the damages to your vehicle and occupants. It doesn't matter if you or a loved one are seriously injured—the rancher still expects to collect. To allow open range on a lonely or little traveled stretch of highway is one thing, but to allow it on Route 1, one of the busiest two-lane state highways in California, is a

Watch out for sheep or cattle on the road as well as winter time wash-outs.

blatant and inexcusable disregard for public safety and animal welfare. Furthermore, the grazing by sheep along Route 1 has reduced the ability of a traditionally unstable soil base to retain water which has contributed to highway washouts costing the taxpayers thousands of dollars in upkeep and repairs.

The greatest factor to all this lies silently in the ocean trenches awaiting God's command. A major *shake* would shave these slopes down to the shoreline, permanently removing this stretch of Route 1 from the guidebooks. The slopes need to be reforested or the highway will no doubt permanently wash out as it did at Boiler Gulch (just north of Jenner) in March of 1983. Drive safely & happy trails.

## JENNER INN and COTTAGES

California's Route 1 snakes its way for miles along the rugged and breathtaking coastlines of Marin, Sonoma and Mendocino. Midway along this stretch is a charming and unusual bed and breakfast inn where you can have one of those fabulous experiences in life you owe to yourself. The setting is both romantic and inspirational - where the Russian River meets the sea.

The landmark Jenner by the Sea Lodge is the headquarters for the Jenner Inn, a one of a kind redwood structure with a nautical flavor where receptions and meetings of up to 150 people can be accommodated. The Lodge's peaceful view of the river's broad estuary and pristine hills is shared by most of the inn's private rooms and cottages.

Eight early village homes throughout the town have been converted to bed and breakfast rooms, suites and individual cottages. All have private baths and separate entrances, and several have fireplaces or spas. Most have private decks where you can relax and enjoy the view. More than half of the inn's 21 rooms and cottages are right at the water's edge, and one scrumptious waterfront room has a marble bathroom with jacuzzi tub for two. . . and, of course, a fireplace, huge deck and fabulous view!

Each of the inn's cozy accommodations has a charm and personality all its own, whether on the waterfront or across the road closer to the lodge and the meadow, where there is a year round creek and a bocci ball court.

An abundant buffet breakfast of fresh fruit, fresh ground coffee and warm muffins and pastries start off your morning in the cozy parlor of the main lodge. With it's crackling fireplace, deep Chesterfield couches and selection of books and games, the parlor is also a warm and inviting living room where guests can refresh themselves with complimentary teas or aperitifs.

The Jenner Inn offers a peaceful and romantic setting for lovers, and is also an ideal location for corporate meetings and retreats, enhanced by the natural vortex of energy created by the blending of river and ocean. There is a unique and beautiful serenity here in which to recharge the human spirit.

*$$-$$$ JENNER INN and COTTAGES   Coast Hwy 1, Box 69, Jenner, CA. Lodging available year-around      Fireplaces, spas, kitchens, river and oceanviews. AX, MC & Visa. Special Events, Banquets, Weddings by the Sea*
*www. jennerinn.com     (707) 865-2377     1-800-732-2377 Res. Advised*

## SEAGULL GIFTSHOP DELI & ESPRESSO

There was a time (1955) when maybe 2 or 3 cars a day passed through Jenner. But times have changed and on weekends it's now 2 to 3 cars a minute pass by. Todays visitor will be delighted by the Seagull Giftshop run by Joel Martin along with his capable staff. After years of being in the giftshop business on the California North Coast, Joel has turned his shop into a showplace of locally crafted and imported keepsakes. Rare and unusual hand-crafted art from Pacific Northwest artists is also highlighted. You'll soon discover all sizes and personalities of seagulls, brass nautical fixtures, native redwood burl, reproductions of sealife in marble, silver and gold, abalone jewelry, wind chimes, cards, candles, film, stationary and an excellent array of guide books. A nice selection of premium wine is also available.

There is a coffee espresso bar and deli featuring coffee drinks, hot dogs, clam chowder, gourmet desserts and sandwiches which can be enjoyed on the riverside outdoor deck. With a backdrop of the Russian River flowing into the sea, the air at times is filled with birds and you can see powerful harbor seals cruising the waters just outside the shop. As Osprey dive and fish the river you can be picnicking or sunning yourself on the Seagull's deck, savoring premium wine or a fresh brewed espresso and enjoying that last look at the California coast, taking your time to ponder the nature of it all.

*$-$$ SEAGULL GIFTSHOP DELI/ESPRESSO Summers: 8:30am - 6pm daily,*
*Gifts and Food To Go       Winters: 9am - 4pm, weekends 9am - 5pm.*
*10439 Hwy 1 at Jenner, CA. 95450     MC & Visa.     (707) 865-2594*

Harbor Seals near the mouth of the Russian River.

## RIVER'S END RESORT and RESTAURANT

You can scan the banks of the mouths of north coast rivers that flow into the sea between the Golden Gate Bridge and the Lost Coast and find few dining establishments.  At the River's End Restaurant and Inn, you will encounter a landmark restaurant on the very cutting edge between a fresh water river and the open sea.

In a secluded hollow below the highway and restaurant, the cabins and rooms at the River's End provide a restful escape from the outside world with an ocean and river view.  Rustic cabins with redwood exteriors and pine interiors, private baths, special amenities such as cozy down comforters and gas fireplaces provide a perfect setting for romance.  All rooms and cabins offer majestic views, have private balconies and access to River's End own river beachfront.  The following morning you'll awake refreshed to the call of seagulls and terns or perhaps the splash of a pelican or playful harbor seal.

Many agree, the crowning touch at River's End is the dining experience.  The creator of this incredible restaurant, Wolfgang Gramatzki, spent 25 years perfecting the creative menu.  He passed his culinary magic to the River's End Executive Chef, David Dahlquist, so future generations could enjoy the uncommon blending of spices and herbs into international dishes, which tantalize the taste buds.  Stephanie and Bert Rangel, owners/operators, are working together to carry-on the traditions of River's End. . .  The restaurant features Sonoma County and Russian River Valley wines, with over 100 selections.  As dusk approaches, you can't miss the sunset!

House specialties include Bahmie Goreng (chicken, shrimp, scallop, beef and Indonesian vegetable noodles with Gramatizki's famous peach chutney).  Boneless quail, medallions of venison, the catch of the day and crispy duck, served with fresh vegetables, potato pancake & almond croquettes.  House specials with complete dinner include raw vegetables & dipping sauce, crispy hot French bread, soup du jour or ceviche of octopus, scallops & shrimp.  A favorite entree is the coconut fried shrimps with orange rum sauce. Dinners are from $12 to $27.  It is sheer magic when your senses are allowed the raw blending of the cuisine with such a stimulating and splendid overnight setting as you'll find at River's End.

*$$-$$$  RIVER'S END*
*Website: www.rivers-end.com                    Email: info@rivers-end.com*
*Restaurant & Lodging        MC & Visa      Full Bar, Beach & Ocean Access*
*Coast Hwy 1, Jenner, CA. 95450   (707) 865-2484 Res. Strongly Advised*

## FORT ROSS STATE PARK

On a lonely promontory overlooking the Sonoma Coast is the restored Russian settlement known as Ross Village, now a part of the California State Park System. In 1812 approximately 95 Russian explorers and 40 Aleut sea otter hunters came ashore to establish a self-sufficient colony as part of the irresistible expansion by Russian interests to the East. It was their desire to establish an agricultural settlement to feed outposts farther to the north. The well-manned and vigilant fortress was said to have "at least 20 - some say as many as 40 cannons mounted in the blockhouses and elsewhere around the fort, including sentinels at night and small arms practice on holidays;" something the park rangers enjoy mimicking today. On Living History Day rangers dress up in authentic costumes, prance around and shoot off muskets and cannons. Its a fun day for all as rangers and numerous volunteers and guests from near and far get to see a wonderful re-creation of early life on the Sonoma Coast.

It would have been a different story indeed if a Russian Count had not been killed when his mount fell in Siberia while he was on his way back to Fort Ross to marry a Mexican senorita at the Mission de la San Francisco. Russian would have been spoken on the streets of San Francisco today instead of English. Coastal gophers had their way with Russian crops, grizzlies preyed upon livestock and the fur trade dwindled nearly to extinction due to exploitation of the California sea otter and fur seal. The Russians were forced to sell the fort. After the Mexicans declined, John Sutter of Sutter's Fort in Sacramento purchased Fort Ross in December 1841. Sutter's mountain men ousted General Vallejo from Sonoma and with the Mexican contingency out of California the coast became American.

There were good moments over the years at Fort Ross as travelers from across the world visited the impeccably run Russian fortress. French diplomat Eugene Duflat de Mofras, who visited in 1841 commented that "the Commandant's house was better furnished than the Mexican Governor's house in Monterey." He was especially delighted by Commandant Rotchev's library, the supply of French wines, and the excellent piano on which the Princess Helena, acclaimed for her beauty, charm and wit, played Mozart and other favorites of that era.

The Fort Ross Historic Park is open to tour every day but Christmas, New Years Day and Thanksgiving from 10am to 4:30pm. There is a well-planned visitor's center at the entrance highlighting what you'll see at the historically rebuilt fortress and a nice collection of books and brochures. The rangers on duty will answer any of your questions. The names Russian River and the Napa Valley's Mount Saint Helena hint at Russia's influence here, and restaurants all along the coast are still serving delicious Gravenstein Apple pie derived from the seed stock which the Russians originally planted above the fort.

*$ FORT ROSS STATE PARK   19005 Coast Hwy 1, 10 miles north of Jenner*
*Historic & Contemporary Visitors Center      (707) 847-3286 Admission fee*

*JESSE LONGACRE'S*
*The WEB of*  $LIFE$

## A Children's Story about the Patterns of Nature

*Finitude, Circularity, Diversity, Interconnectedness and Stability*

The **Patterns of Nature** sounds like it is going to be very hard to understand. I mean, all those big words. The truth is that learning about the Patterns of Nature is really very easy. The best place to start is to think of nature as one big round spider web. All the patterns are right there. Now, keep that image of the spider web in your mind while I throw some of these big words at you; and remember, I am going to go through each pattern and explain it in simple "spider web" terms:

**Finitude, Circularity, Diversity, Interconnectedness and Stability.**

How is that for a mouthful? If you want, you can just call it the **Web of Life.** These big words help us describe the Patterns of Nature. Just keep the idea of the Web of Life in your mind, and I'll go through each of these words and explain them in simple terms.

Let's start with **Finitude**. What finitude means in regards to the Patterns of Nature is that the Earth is a planet, a round ball floating in space. Earth is sort of like an island surrounded by an ocean of space.

This planet Earth is the only place that we know of that has Life on it. Finitude means that there are limits. **This Earth is self contained.** We don't get loads of new animals and candy bars delivered to us from outer space on a weekly

> Paste or draw a picture
> here that illustrates FINITUDE

basis. **What is here now has always been here.** That is, the basic materials that make up all of the Life on this Earth have always been here. Here are some more big words for you that will further explain this idea of "Finitude": The first law of energy, **Thermodynamics,** states that "Nothing is created and nothing is destroyed." The only things the Earth gets from the outside is an occasional meteorite and a supply of sunlight which supplies our energy. Finitude is a little hard to relate to the Web, but if you think of the Web as earth, round, with nothing coming into or out of it, then you will begin to see how the Earth is like a big round web floating in space.

The importance of Finitude for me is this: **the Earth is our home.** It is the only place that we have Life. In that sense this planet Earth is very special. This is the Home of all Life that we know of, be it people from China, California, or Siberia, a tiny shrimp in Alaska, or an elephant from Africa. Perhaps someday we will find Life somewhere else out there in the great universe, but for now we are the only ones we know of who are lucky enough to listen to the gurgling of a creek or the breath of a whale, or feel the warmth of sunlight or the glow of a loved one's touch.

The next Pattern of Nature, **Circularity,** is a bit easier to envision. Just like the spider web, nature is also round. "Circularity" refers not to the shapes of things in nature that are round, but to the fact that everything in nature moves in circles; that is, the Galaxy (which is all the stars and planets that you can see in the sky at night), moves in a circle, completing a big circle once every 150 - 200 million years around the center of the galaxy. The earth itself travels in an elliptical orbit around the sun at 18 1/2 miles per second or 67,000 mph. At its equator the earth is round and rotates on its axis at 1,000 miles per hour and at its poles zero mph. Almost enough to make you dizzy, isn't it? The earth is round. A circle is natures most efficient way of storing stuff, even the cells that make up all of Life are round. So, you see, in nature things work in circles. This is one of nature's patterns.

Paste or draw a picture
here that illustrates CIRCULARITY

An old log is lying on the forest floor. What becomes of it? Does it die and become nothing? No. First a woodpecker will drill holes in it. Then bugs come and eat the sap. Then birds come and eat the bugs. Mushrooms start living on the older log as it starts to look more like soil and wood. Young trees start to absorb some of the nutrients that once provided life for this tree when it was growing. What was once a living tree has now given it's Life to the life forms that used it for food. **Just as those life forms will give Life to others when their bodies are ready to be recycled. Life becomes death. Death becomes life.** Where is the beginning and where is the end in a circle? LIFE - DEATH - LIFE !

Remember the law of energy that says "Nothing is created and nothing is destroyed?" If Life didn't work in circles then long ago we would have run out of materials to continue Life with. It may seem that life forms die, but that is only a little bit true. You see, one of the things that is true in Life is that death gives life. In nature death is what makes food for new life to be able to grow. What was once wolf bones is now part of the roots of a redwood tree. What was once a redwood tree is now soil for a garden of rose bushes. From wolf to rose or rose to wolf, the cycle is never ending.

Another pattern that we can perceive in the Web of Life is that of **Diversity.** Diversity means variety or difference. Notice all the strands that go into making up this web. Each strand is as important as all the others. Each of these strands contribute to the overall strength of the web. In nature diversity is one of the great instruments that helps create the Music of Life.

The key aspect of diversity to keep in mind is this: everything that you see living anywhere is incredibly well-suited to living there. The truth of the matter is that everything we see living is really sort of a miracle. We may think that a cactus is just some old dumb plant with nasty stickers on it. The truth is that a cactus is a miracle in that it has responded to Life and found a way to live in a place where it may not get water for several years. The cactus can live in heat over 110 degrees F. A cactus can shrink and expand with the amount of water it gets so that it can store water in rainy times and slowly use it during dry times. And those nasty stickers are yet another of nature's miracles. They help the cactus not to be eaten and not to lose water.

Diversity is the appropriate technology of nature. Whatever is best for that situation is what will be found there. Diversity is in many ways what makes this world so very alive. Imagine yourself standing from afar and looking at this planet; seeing that in every crevice and crack there is another form of life; that as all the conditions of earth, air, fire and water change, so do all of life's responses. In each situation another way of living is developed. The strands of the Web of Life are many indeed!

Diversity is not only a beautiful principle to observe outside of us, but also among us and inside of our own selves. We all have something to add to Life. Perhaps we are bigger or smaller than many others. Or perhaps we are not as "good looking" as what we think we are "supposed" to be. Whatever our differences are, outside or inside, it is all just part of the great Diversity of Life. It is what makes us strong. Nobody can be just like us, nor can we be like anybody else. We have to make peace with the diversity among each other by allowing each other to be who they are, not by being who we think they ought to be.

I firmly believe in the truth and power of Love. I firmly believe that as we treat ourselves, so we treat each other. I believe that each person has a voice in them that knows what they need and want. In some it may have gotten covered over; something else has blocked it out, usually because of deep pain from having that deeper love blocked. Yet, I still believe that most people are really good, that when we listen to ourselves, we want to do good, we want to love, we want to contribute.

Paste or draw a picture
here that illustrates DIVERSITY

```
┌───────────────────────────────────────┐
│                                        │
│                                        │
│                                        │
│                                        │
│                                        │
│                                        │
│                                        │
│                                        │
│                                        │
│                                        │
│                                        │
│                                        │
│                                        │
│                                        │
│                                        │
│                                        │
│                                        │
│          Paste or draw a picture       │
│           here that illustrates        │
│          INTERCONNECTEDNESS            │
└───────────────────────────────────────┘
```

**Interconnectedness** is another Pattern of Nature. This concept states that all things, living and non-living, are in one way or another connected to each other. Maybe directly, maybe not so directly, but in the end all of Life touches and affects something else in Life. You may have heard this stated as, "Life is all One." Looking at our Web of Life you can also understand this principle. Notice how there is the round web with all the strands. Then notice how each of the strands in one way or another is adding strength to the others. It is this connecting of strands that gives the web its overall endurance.

Interconnectedness can be demonstrated in many ways. One example I can see as I look out my window is the formation of fog. But first, in order to understand, we have to back up a bit. Back way up to the very beginning. Like back to the **Big Bang.** The big bang is what got the earth rotating around the sun. It is that rotation around the sun that winds up causing fog. You remember how the earth is traveling around the sun at about 67,000 miles an hour, and around on it's own axis, once a day, at 1,000 miles an hour. This creates wind. This wind comes across the ocean surface off our northern Pacific coast and moves some of the top water. As this top water is moved, water from the bottom of the ocean is moved up to the top to replace it. This water is cold. It also brings with it many nutrients which help support much of the Life found in our rich coastal waters. So, when this cold water reaches the surface it often meets air that is warmer. This causes evaporation. Thus we have fog. Now this fog tends to move towards warmer areas on shore. As it does it carries its moisture inland. That is why when I look out my window I can see redwood trees. The fog is collected by the special shape of the redwood needles and thus provides redwoods with water. This is especially important during the summer months, when there is no rainfall. The redwoods, as well as Bishop pines, could not live without the fog. The redwood forest then supports the growth of certain ferns that feed certain bugs which are needed by different species of birds. Thus the presence of a banana slug winds up being connected to the rotation of the earth, the winds, the ocean, evaporation, fog, and redwood trees. As John Muir said, "When you trace anything in nature back to it's roots, you find it hitched to everything else in the Universe.

When one backs away from this earth and looks at it, what one sees is

Paste or draw a picture

that **Life has achieved a balance.** This balance may appear harsh at times, but when viewed over a long time, it is perfect. This "Interconnectedness" has allowed for new species to evolve and adapt. It has allowed for the billions and billions of organisms on this planet to live together. It has provided a network of feedback systems that allows for Life to proceed and grow. Through Life's Interconnectedness, the many strands in the Web of Life are tied together and the Web becomes One.

The last Pattern of Nature that I want to mention here is that of **Stability.** All the preceding patterns have led up to this strength. **This principle is my ultimate reason for optimism.** I believe way down to my very cells that Life is far greater than all of us, that we are just one part. Life will find a way to keep living.

An example of nature's stability pattern can be seen in the following example. Let's say you take a piece of barren land with nothing on it. Now begin looking at this land for years. At first you may only see some rain and wind slowly decomposing the rock. Then the first plants appear; those of a very basic nature such as lichens and then some mosses. Eventually some weeds and then some grasses move in after the soil has become rich enough to support these plants. Then after the weeds and grasses have had their roots digging the soil, adding their old leaves to it and in general enriching it, some shrubs will move in. The soil becomes richer. The moisture-holding ability becomes greater. More species begin living in this land. In the shade of the shrubs some young trees begin to grow. Soon they begin to shade out the shrubs, which have since shaded out most of the grasses and weeds. Now within the shade of those trees come the pines. Up they come until they now shade out the trees that once grew over them. The casual observer will notice that tree limbs that want to live will grow upward pointing toward the sun. Tree limbs that want to die will sag downward and point toward the ground. Now with the pines coming into full maturity, the forest will continue to change, but not as visually dramatic as it has been up to this point. This is what we call a **climax community** or the mature forest. This process is called **succession.**

A very interesting aspect of this forest is that up until the time when the forest reached its maturity it was spending most of its energy by concentrating on growth. Now the energy starts to be directed towards stability. That is, the number of species usually becomes greater. The interactions or interconnectedness between the living and non-living aspects of the forest become much greater. The energy is not so much put into growing new material as it is in creating more strands to connect the web with, making the web all that much stronger. Maintenance, quality, perfection, become the rules. Efficiency and quality, not quantity, become the driving goals of a mature system.

Perhaps the greatest thing one can say about the earth's stability is that of time and longevity. For hundreds of millions of years this earth has taken these principles or Patterns of Nature and flowed on and around. Personally, I have no doubt as to the long-term survival of this planet. People and societies who choose to ignore the basic reality of living on a planet in space may have to learn some hard lessons, but I truly believe it will be Nature teaching them a lesson as opposed to people teaching the earth a lesson.

One last concept to keep in mind while talking about the earth's stability is to remember that the earth is very much like a living organism itself. Looking at individual plants, knowing names and distributions and things like that, are fun and often interesting, but to be able to look at nature as whole and realize how alive it all is, well, that is a much deeper feeling. The way this earth is able to maintain its balances of temperature, of gasses and nutrients, how our atmosphere is so much like that of a semi-permeable membrane, allowing only certain things in and out - - when you add to this the earth's ability to recycle, to have its great diversity of Life in every situation, to tie all this together in an intricate interconnected web that has been going on for some five billion years, one can begin to grasp the idea of how very much alive this magnificent planet Earth is.

Just as early explorers, such as the Vikings at sea navigated by the Mother Current, so can you navigate in the ocean of life around you. When one becomes aware of the **Mother Current** we can realize that there is no shortage of abundance on the planet. We can manifest as much abundance into our lives as we want. Our thoughts will manifest our material comfort zone.

**Finitude, Circularity, Diversity, Interconnectedness, and Stability: these are the Patterns of Nature.** These are concepts that I hope will make your relationship with nature a bit deeper. They really are not difficult. They can be seen and observed by almost anyone, anywhere. Yet as simple as they are, they are also ideas that we can always come to understand, feel and appreciate more deeply. Simple, yet profound, as are many of the great truths in this great and wonderful **Web of Life.**

## *EPILOG*

Each of you can develop some hobbies or interests that are healthy for you. Of course, I really encourage ones that involve nature. Hiking, fishing, diving, bird or star watching, just observing. There are lots of groups that do all these things and much more listed at any Chamber of Commerce. Take time out for things and get off by yourself, or with a good friend, and just observe Life sometimes. You will be amazed how powerful just sitting in one spot quietly and observing nature can be. It is among the most beneficial things I know of. Fly a kite, go camping, take pictures, draw, make up stories. If you find some kind of activity that involves being outdoors you will have added an ingredient to your life that will make it higher in many important ways. You meet good people, you participate with nature and you increase your health, to name a few. You are what you think, speak and do.

Another thing I want to say to you is that there are some ways to make your Life much better or much harder. I know I do not really have much influence on most of you, but maybe even one of you will hear me. So here is my bit of advice for helping you have a better life: **Stay away from mean-spirited people. Find kind people. Keep drugs out of your life.** They may seem sort of glamorous and fun, but they have a way of pushing happiness out of your life. **Put good things in your life, and keep bad things out of your life and remember that Love is positiveness and it is the most powerful force of all.**

*For Further Reference see Re-Creational Transformation on page 246.*

Jesse Longacre was the Eule Gibbons of Sonoma County - taking small groups of children and adults out to the seashore and wild forests above Jenner to discover their hidden strengths and help build a nature crafting community. He went into classrooms where he lit children's eyes up with a dazzling slide show and narration about the Web of Life. He led groups on wild foraging expeditions into their backyards and nearby meadows and forests. They returned to prepare their sacred harvest and share a wonderful meal by candlelight. Of the many he shared his life with, there are countless others who could have benefitted. Jesse transitioned on May 15, 1993 at the age of 41 .

Those who want to donate to the Jesse Longacre Memorial Fund may write Box G, Santa Rosa, CA. 95402. (enclose your phone # or S.A.S.E. and the appropriate people will get back to you). It is hoped that a film called "The Web of Life" and a Workbook with questions and answers for children and adults can be funded. The film and workbook will be accompanied by a Course and Field Trip into the "Web of Life".

## IDEAS FOR NATURE CRAFTERS

*The Prehistory diet meant connecting with living plants and wild and domestic animals on a daily basis. This natural interaction strengthened our immune system, making it resistant to anything nature threw at us from our local environment. This natural daily interaction is one of the key ingredients missing from our lifestyles today.  So take a hike and plant a secret victory garden.*

### SECRET VICTORY GARDENS:

Planting vegetable gardens for future survival needs in remote high quality environments is a vital activity to insure a natural and diversified source of food and seeds for replanting.   A wild vegetable garden is a wonderful greeting party for any campers.  If you are serious about your life, then you are going to need a seed bank, super soil, a pristine environment and the vision and iron will to think the unthinkable *and GO FOR IT!*

### SEED BANKS:

The best diet is composed of foods that are grown organically whereby soil is renewed and fertility sustained, without using synthetically compounded petroleum based fertilizers, pesticides and other materials.   Foods grown where you live and eaten fresh within minutes of picking them contain the life force energy or prana of Mother Earth and are charged with live amino acids, undamaged natural vitamins and minerals which promote healing, regeneration, vitality and longevity for the body.

The best plants are grown from seeds that were created by plants that were grown in living soil which received natural sunshine and "living water" from rainfall, a natural spring or well, an unpolluted creek, river or lake (as opposed to water with additives, chlorine or fluoride from a water treatment plant).   Seeds that were harvested from where you live contain genetic codes that strengthen your immune system.  It is good to always keep a seed bank capable of producing 2 to 3 years of gardens.

**SOURCES of SEEDS see Herbs & Natural Medicine Section on page 264**

### SEA POWER:  Harvesting Seaweed

Seaweed is a Super Survival Food loaded with vitamins and minerals.  The finest chefs know that when the tide is out the table is set!  Seaweed is edible and can be prepared to taste delicious.  It is a miraculous source of vitamins and trace elements.  It even possesses the quality of removing radioactive strontium 90 (from acid rain) from our bodies.  Algenic acid in seaweed acts as a binding agent to remove radiation from our digestive tract.  It detoxes the body of caffeine, nicotine and many drugs.   Native Americans used seaweed to comfort tooth aches by wrapping it around their gums.

You can gather seaweed at low tide off the rocks in unpolluted areas of the coastline. Remove as many critters (periwinkles, bugs and shrimp) as you can off the fronds and return them to the sea.  Flush the remaining seaweed in *fresh water* for 15 minutes at shores edge, then dump the water which puts the rest of the critters back into the ocean.  Next, place the seaweed on racks for drying.  Use the sun, a campfire or your oven.  You can crinkle the dried fronds into small particles and place in a seasoning jar. Sprinkle at will on soups and salads or bake in breads or entries.  All year long you can be benefiting from the medicinal qualities of seaweed!

## FORT ROSS LODGE

One of the nicest lodging facilities on the magnificent Sonoma Coast, offers 22 tastefully decorated units on 37 acres. Sixteen units are located just 500 yards off the coastline with unsurpassed ocean views & coastal access.

An additional 6 units are located approximately 1,000 feet above the main lodge with panoramic ocean and forest views. These modern rooms include king size beds, fireplaces, wet bars, in-room hot tubs and saunas. A large Executive/Bridal suite with a king size bed, fireplace, wet bar, in-room hot tub, sauna, and a large private covered deck, is romantic for any special occasion.

Fort Ross Lodge offers many amenities including barbecues on a private patio, spacious tubs and showers, king and queen size beds, refrigerators, wet bars, microwaves and VCRs. Across the street is the Fort Ross Store and Deli where guests are assured of groceries, drinks, fresh coffee, sandwiches and gasoline.

Fort Ross Lodge, a nature lovers retreat, a perfect place to enjoy the summer sunshine or the wild winter storms. You can get close...close to nature and to each other. Rates are $78 to $200/2. Year-around mid-week rates available.

*$$-$$$ FORT ROSS LODGE       22 cozy rooms, oceanviews, fireplaces,*
*Seaside Accommodations       hot tubs, saunas, General Store and Deli.*
*20705 Coast Hwy. 1, Jenner, CA 95450   AE, MC, Visa (707) 847-3333*

**TIMBER COVE BOAT LANDING** At Timber Cove Boat Landing you can rock fish, dive for abalone, or explore the rugged cliffs and fragile tide pool life of the wild Pacific Coast. Day use, overnight camping, picnic tables, boat rentals, scuba tank rentals and trailer spaces are a few of the amenities. The Timber Cove Boat Landing is one of the few boat launching campgrounds to be found on the north coast where aluminum or light car top boats can be sling-launched. There are also hot showers, a hot tub, bait, tackle, propane, fishing licenses and information. Vacation rentals are available for the whole family, with amenities such as fireplaces, kitchens and hot tubs. The proprietor also has the Anchor Bay Lodge, a 4-unit motel 2 miles north of Anchor Bay on Hwy. 1 with a year-around brook and waterfall in a grove of redwoods at 884-1079. It's convenient for Bay Area sportsmen and radio commentators to call owner David Verno at 847-3278 for fishing, weather and diving conditions along the Sonoma Coast.

*$ TIMBER COVE BOAT LANDING    The Boat Landing is located about*
*Diving, Boat Launching and Vacation Rentals.   13 miles north of Jenner.*
*21350 N. Coast Hwy. 1, Jenner, CA. 95450       (707) 847-3278 for Res.*

### SEA COAST HIDEAWAYS

When you arrive from your magnificent ride up the coast from Jenner-by-the-sea, you'll be greeted by the on-duty host or proprietor of Sea Coast Hideaways, often a real information center unto themselves and a jack-of-all-trades, who also runs Timber Cove Boat Landing and Campground. Don't be fooled by the unpretentious appearance of this working fishing village and seaside trailer court, for the proprietors hold the keys to luxury homes occupying some of the most fabulous oceanview and ridgeline settings in northern California.

Settings include beach, cliffline, redwood forest, high ridge, creekside and meadow in a variety of microclimates teaming with vibrant and diversified wildlife ranging from wild boar and bobcat to osprey and eagle. Relax for hours watching large waves and migrating whales just off-shore. Choose from several vacation home rentals, including a redwood cabin on the cliff with beach access and a hot tub; a meadow house surrounded by pine trees with 3 bedrooms, large fireplace, stereo and TV and several decks; a cozy studio cabin on the hillside overlooking the ocean; the "Sea Eagle's Nest", a 3,000 square foot group meeting retreat with many amenities, hidden in the redwoods; with large parking area and almost total hot tub privacy; a cabin befitting the captain and first mate, rustic and perched on a rocky cliff with incredible views and next to a fern-filled forest; and a 2 bedroom chalet on 5 acres enveloped by tall pines. Linens and firewood furnished to all rentals. Rates: $110-$400 for 2 nights and payment in full is due within 10 days. To the north in Anchor Bay is a motel lodge close to the beach with a live creek and forest setting.

Enjoy boat, fishing tackle and scuba gear rentals, beachcombing and picnicking; observe fishermen and divers returning with their catch-of-the-day, and you'll realize why a two day minimum stay is necessary on the Sonoma Coast!

*$$ - $$$ SEA COAST HIDEAWAYS*
*Vacation Rentals & Boat Landing*
*21350 North Coast Hwy 1, Jenner, CA. 95450*
*(707) 847-3278 Reservations Advised*

# Fishing in the Presence of the Dragon King

Timber Cove is one of the most pristine fishing spots along the Sonoma Coast. Located 17 miles north of Jenner, Timber Cove has become a popular destination for fishermen, abalone divers and coastal explorers seeking a wild and spectacular setting to explore and be in love with each other and the elements. During the winter months fresh water creeks cascade down sheer cliffs into the cove's turbulent emerald green waters.   The forces of nature are very strong here, as is the will of residents of Timber Cove.  This small region is an extremely dynamic area both on-shore and off-shore.  I have always felt it would be a wonderful area to construct a small underwater community of transparent shelters just above the ocean floor, so that humans could live and love underwater completely surrounded by the sea and in plain sight of all the beautiful and mysterious underwater creatures.

Buddhists say The Dragon King lives here. The dragon's tail is off Mexico with it's head off Washington. At the north end of the cove is the totem pole sculpture by Benjamin Bufano, which is dedicated to world peace.  Buddhist monks come here several times during the year to make offerings by dropping sacred urns into the cove.  They also save the lives of super market lobsters they rescue and release into the invigorating waters of Timber Cove.  David Verno, the proprietor of Timber Cove Boat Landing, takes the monks out in his 14 foot fishing boat to a place over the Dragon's Palace so the kindred spirits of the dead can enter the Karmic doorway of their next life.  Verno came to the cove 20 years ago to raise his family and live the life of a fisherman.  Today he and a crew of self reliant helpers run the campground and Sea Coast Hideaways, a vacation home rental agency.

Weekends, the boat landing takes on the appearance of a carnival of reincarnated pirates harvesting the treasures of the sea - namely abalone, salmon, Pacific Coast snapper, ling cod, rock cod, sea urchin (for uni roe), mussels and seaweed.  Divers make the plunge after the increasingly elusive abalone, go spear fishing or photograph the spectacular underwater garden of eden around Timber Cove.

## TIMBER COVE

## THE KELP FOREST

*Undersea Garden of Eden:  The majestic kelp forests provide shelter for snapper, ling cod, abalone and divers.*

This draws out another player at the cove whose ego finds the theatrical energy an irresistible stage for himself to exhibit his prowess and uncanny abilities to reel in pound after pound and inch after inch of the delicious king of the cove - the ling cod.  When Ross S. Smith, the proverbial rock fish king and red neck hound dog of the depths lowers his 22 foot panga, christened the "Rock Fish Guru" into the waters of Timber Cove to conduct a fishing seminar, it is guaranteed he and novice fishermen will return with their limit.  When the three kings are in the cove at the same time, you know something will be offered up.

Native Oklahoman, Ross Smith exclaims, "I was born with a shotgun in one hand and a fishing pole in the other!"  More likely he has the hands of a gorilla attached to the cool - common sense mind of an "Okie".  He's one of the best rock fish boys to ever fish the Sonoma Coast and his seminars will prove it.  Ross can hold his breath underwater for over a minute and can free dive over 60 feet.  He is so tough that when once bit on the head by a shark, he didn't loose a drop of blood! Could it be the rock fish king has salt water running through his veins?  He has caught four fish at once on one line with two hooks! Two rock fish took the bait and hooks and two ling cod mouthed over them! He quickly put a net under all four and lifted them aboard!

Ross's handyman ethic and inventive mind give him the luxury to create his own nautical gear, lures, flies and fishing weights at his coastal retreat above Timber Cove. Ross has fun building the fishing gear for himself and his students and then having it work the way it's supposed to. Seminars cost $75 per person (more than 1 person) and $100 for a private lesson. Weather permitting the boat leaves Timber Cove with safety always coming first. Graduates claim they

The old fashioned boat sling at Timber Cove Boat Landing. Do you see "Frankenstein Rock"? Now all boats are trailer launched off the beach.

have never had more fun fishing after they take Ross's class. He has taught hundreds his secrets.

Decades of fishing experience both on top and diving under the sea has enabled Ross to read the surface like a book. But what's his secret? We'll let him tell you in his own words. "I use custom light tackle to jig for rock fish in 10 to 90 feet of water above rocky coves and undersea grottos at the edge of the kelp forest. The bait comprises a lead jig with triple hook and 15 inches above this I tie a buck tail jig (fly) to a dropper loop so it will hang naturally under water. I prefer 25 pound test P line. A small level - wind saltwater reel with a star drag completes my custom rock fish lander package. I use a certain rhythm of jigging with light whippy rods (as opposed to heavier gear) in a natural sort of way. I have found the best time to fish is when the barometric pressure is rising, so I always check my barometer just before we go out which is equally important with the ebb and flow of the tides - full moon / new moon. All that translates into a nice big rock fish on the dinner table. The sensitivity of light line and light weight translate every tug and vibration directly into my hand. So I can feel the big ling cod mouthing my lure with it's extra piece of squid or small bait fish as I jig it a few reel cranks above the bottom. Ling cod find the helpless spastic motion of a wounded or dying fish irresistible. They twitch up with desperate flips of their tail as they swim up and then sink a few feet. The ling cod and the shark are the janitors of the sea, cleaning up the weak, wounded or dead from the water."

"With the clutch released and one of my thumbs clamped onto the reel to act as a sensitive alternate drag I begin jigging the set up from a point 5 feet under the surface (there I pick up the live blues I use as bait on the lings). I then continue to drop the rig in 5 to 15 foot increments, jigging until the bottom is reached and until it's time to test for hungry lings."

"When a strike happens, I snap the clutch home, or close it after I hit bottom and pull the lure up a few cranks. If I don't get any bites then I move to another site or favorite fishing hole. I always get my limit and so do my students. Fun is the key word here."

*Continued from Page 65*

Occasionally on weekends Ross and best friend Cookie share their catch with local inhabitants and guests at the Timber Cove Boat Landing. The biggest cast iron skillet you ever saw sits atop a gas burner at cliffs' edge. Drenched in a top secret batter and deep fried in corn oil amid the cleanest air in America, fish filets and strips of abalone steak are piled high sizzling for finger, fork or knife to retrieve. Plates are loaded with a smorgasbord of goodies fellow diners bring for a primal feast few will ever forget. Even feuding locals put aside their differences at times like these to renew their bodies and make new friends and allies or plan strategies for future "ass kickin's". It's a friendly insurance policy that bonds Smith to the people who live and work here and it's better than *any* insurance policy you could ever buy. A community fish fry created from clean healthy fish where all eat their fill is the best insurance policy for the future generation.

**ROSS SMITH OCEAN ROCK FISHING SEMINARS    *Classes at Timber Cove Boat Landing are $100 Private Lesson; $150/2 21350 N. Coast Highway 1, Jenner, CA. 95450 Lodging: (707) 847-3278 Fishing: (415) 456-0629 or (707) 847-3671 Lodging for small groups is available at the Sea Wolf Lodge, (707) 522-0550, Write: Box G, Santas Rosa, CA. 95402***

### DIAS del MAR

Wilderness Family Robinson never had it so good than at Dias del Mar. This homey all natural two story log cabin is bright and cheery with forest and oceanviews set on the ridge above State Highway 1 and the open sea. Hosts Ann and Bob Dias have created quite the love nest or group get-away depending upon your needs.

The open upstairs loft sleeps 6 with a king, queen and hideabed, private bath with hydrotherapy jet tub and large picture window views of forest and sea. Downstairs is a private bedroom with queen bed. A fully equipped gourmet kitchen, bath with ornate claw foot Victorian tub / shower, spacious dining room and majestic moss rock hearth with couches and hideabeds for additional explorers. Large decks wrap completely around the log home. The views, ocean air and evening starlit skies are exceptional. Rates begin at $200/night with weekly rates at $1,050.

*$$ DIAS del MAR    Fax: (510) 680-5667    (510) 685-2656  Res. Nec.*

## TIMBER COVE INN

Timber Cove Inn is situated on a 26-acre, cliff-top promontory, commanding an unobstructed view of the sea and Timber Cove. This dramatic setting is complimented by the rustic yet sophisticated architecture of the Inn.

Each of the Inn's 49 rooms has its own unique character, and nearly every room offers either a private hot tub or a giant Roman tub, plus a fireplace and deck with either a view of the ocean, the cove, or the Inn's Japanese pond. The Inn also offers several suites, one with a sauna, wet bar, stone fireplace, and a solarium with a breathtaking view of the cliffs and the sea.

The Inn's great lobby features a massive, three-story stone fIreplace. Abundant use of glass provides expansive views of the ever changing sea, as well as the quiet serenity of the Japanese pond, with its exotic bird inhabitants. Guests can watch the ocean from the bar, or from the Inn's intimate and romantic dining room. Dining at the Inn is always a pleasure. The varied menu offers continental cuisine and the widest variety of fine wines on the Sonoma Coast.

Wildlife abounds at Timber Cove. Raccoons provide nightly entertainment with their playful antics, and the Inn is an ideal spot for seasonal whale watching. The wild bird pond has been added to the grounds to provide a rest stop for migratory birds and a special viewing treat for guests. Be sure to visit the Raccoon Cove Giftshop which is stocked with art, crafts, jewelry and chocolate treats,

Favored by naturalist photographer Ansel Adams and artist Benjamin Bufano, whose works grace the grounds at the Inn, Timber Cove has long inspired artists, writers, lovers and adventurers. The absence of artificial distractions at the Inn also make it an ideal place to find quiet solitude or to hold an important team-building retreat or conference. Special mid-week rates are available year around.

Located just three miles north of historic Fort Ross, 14 miles north of Jenner, and a scenic two-hour drive north from San Francisco, the Inn awaits you in a setting beyond imagination.

$$ $$$ *TIMBER COVE INN*                      *Champagne Brunch, Sat. & Sun.*
*Continental Cuisine    Private Hot Tubs, Ocean Views, Fireplaces, Balconies*
*Breakfast, Lunch & Dinner              AE, MC, Visa, Diners' Club, Checks.*
*21780 Hwy 1, Jenner, CA. 95450      (707) 847-3231 Res. & Information*

**STILLWATER COVE RANCH**    Set like a gemstone overlooking the moody blue waters of Stillwater Cove is lovely Stillwater Cove Ranch, a splendid playground blessed with crystal clear air and the most reasonable priced accommodations on the Sonoma Coast. Sturdy buildings made of rock and hand-hewn timbers withstand the fiercest of winter storms. Evenings spent around a glowing fire, snug and secure, are the best. Guests can take advantage of seven accommodations with old-fashioned fireplaces, (but the King Room), some with decks and fully equipped kitchens (rates/2 from $45). The Dairy Barn has eight bunks, showers and a kitchen. Stillwater Cove Ranch is the perfect setting for groups or seminars of 25-40 where clear decision-making is easily inspired. Located 16 miles north of Jenner.

*$ STILLWATER COVE RANCH      22555 Coast Hwy 1, Jenner, Ca. 95450*
*Cottages, rooms, barn for groups or couples.    (707) 847-3227 Reservations*

**PLANTATION FARM CAMP**  Plantation is an A.C.A. (American Camping Association) accredited farm camp for children between the ages of 8 and 14. A large barn, several out buildings, corrals and an elegant farmhouse with outdoor decks and patios offers cook-outs, crafts, fort building deep in the redwood forest and hikes to the ocean shores just 1 1/2 miles away.   When kids engage in challenging experiences that allow them to make choices, take responsibility, acquire new skills and work with others; meaningful learning and understanding take place. Living on a farm reinforces the belief in the importance of traditional values and offers a measure of learned stability to fall back on.   You can visit this working farm, a worthwhile place to send your children for an environmentally educational experience.

*$$ PLANTATION FARM CAMP 34285 Kruse Ranch Road, Cazadero, CA 95421*
*A farm camp for boys and girls                    (707) 847-3494 Res. & Info.*

### TIMBER HILL RANCH

Timberhill Ranch is a unique 80 acre Country Inn 1100 feet above the winds and fog of the Sonoma Coast. Twilight is a special time on the ridge, made more so by intimate fireside accommodations, meaningful conversation with other guests from around the world, and masterfully prepared dinners by a chef who knows how to satisfy the demands of the sophisticated traveler.   You'll appreciate the privacy and seclusion with which the cottages have been placed. Aromatic with the scent of warm cedar inside and out, your woodburning fireplace gives off its own special warmth. Tiled private baths and fresh cut flowers are in each cottage.  As you curl up in your homemade quilt, a wonderful sense of well-being envelopes you.  Special guest amenities include a forty foot pool and spa, tennis courts and conference center, all overlooking the majestic southern hills.

*$$$ TIMBERHILL RANCH*
*Luxurious Wilderness Lodging, Mobile 4 Star, Au Relais & Chateaux Property*
*Mailing: 35755 Hauser Bridge Road, Cazadero, CA 95421.   (707) 847-3258*

## OCEAN COVE STORE, CAMPGROUND, BOAT LAUNCH & VACATION RENTAL HOMES

Everyone slows for the 15 MPH hairpin turn at Ocean Cove Store. So picturesque is the century old building (Established 1860) that it has been used in television commercials. Besides a limited line of general merchandise, practical owners Gary and Janet Manaro, operate an oceanside campground where couples and families can enjoy spectacular white water views, clear coastal air and cooking over a fire beneath the stars. Crammed into the tiny store is a good selection of canned goods, meat, poultry, dairy products, sweets, wine, liquor and fresh produce.

In addition, the gas pumps are usually open from 9 am-8 pm (mid week) and 7 am-9 pm (weekends). About 125 secluded sites are scattered over 20 acres with fire pits (firewood is available at the store), hot showers, picnic tables and outdoor toilets. During the spring winds, the creek's freshwater falls are literally blown upstream at the cove. Two beautifully furnished vacation homes with fireplaces, hot tubs, fully equipped kitchens and sweeping views of the Sonoma Coast are available for 2-8 people (sorry no smoking or pets). All in all, the Ocean Cove Store is a good stop, but watch out for that hairpin turn.

*$ OCEAN COVE STORE*　　　　　　*23125 Hwy. 1, Jenner, CA 95450*
*General Merchandise & Campground*　　　*(707) 847-3422 Information*

***SALT POINT STATE PARK***　The 6,000 acre Salt Point State Park is bordered by a rocky shoreline which offers fishing and skin diving and a heavily vegetated forest and grassland which offers camping, picnicking, and trails for horseback riding and hiking. The area is also one of the first underwater parks to be established in California and except for those areas posted as natural preserves is open for fishing. There are 30 campsites at the eerie oceanside Gerstle Campground with tables and fire pits. Running water and toilets are nearby. Upslope and on the inland side of Route 1 is the Woodside Campground with 79 regular campsites (table, firesite and running water), 10 hike and bike sites and 20 walk-in sites where you hike 1/4 to 1/2 mile to a regular campsite.

The Jesse Longacre Nature Trail at Salt Point State Park is a wonderful interactive nature trail that helps children and adults appreciate the unique benefits of this microcosm along the North American coastline. It is important to note that many fragile creatures live in the tide pools, (rocky pockets that retain water when the tides go out). They are fascinating to watch, but please observe the simple rule—Look, But Don't Touch.

*$ SALT POINT STATE PARK*
*Forest & Oceanside Campsites / spectacular setting 20 miles north of Jenner*
*25050 Coast Hwy. 1, Jenner, CA 95450*　　　*(707) 847-3221 Res. Advised*

## SALT POINT BAR & GRILL

We know a great escape 90 miles north of San Francisco at the southern gateway to Salt Point State Park. Not only will you discover cozy oceanview accommodations, some with fireplaces, but also an exceptional restaurant and bar.

The lodge furnishes visitors with 16 modern and comfortable rooms, some with fireplaces, all with private bathrooms and satellite color TV, most with ocean views priced from $50 to $137. All have in-room coffee makers and some have VCRs. Breakfast (from $6.95) is served in the restaurant from 9:00am. The two upstairs rooms have in-room refrigerators and private oceanview decks with hot tubs. The family rooms can accommodate 4 - 6 people. A bonus for all is the secluded community spa/sauna area with the nighttime stars overhead. Salt Point Lodge provides all the comforts of home while allowing the dramatic oceanview setting.

Salmon filet, salmon and chips, oysters, BBQ mesquite smoked chicken and ribs, pasta marinara, Ahi Sashima steak and "the best New York peppercorn steak in the World" are served with homemade clam chowder or garden salad and bread. Vegetarians will enjoy the garden burger, New Mexico polenta pie and a variety of salads. The solarium bar and dining center boasts unobstructed views of the waves rolling into Ocean Cove; sometimes so big they break over the 50-foot headland. The ocean view from the restaurant sundeck stretches over a colorful flower garden providing a relaxed setting for watching whales or winter storms, or just for holding hands with your lover while the ocean serenades.

Proprietors Bill LaFeber, his charming wife Tammarah, and their experienced staff find pleasure in making the north coast accessible for your urban escape. They would like to stress that Salt Point Bar & Grill provides a casual dining experience. Come relax and take your shoes off in this beautiful natural environment where your choices are only limited by your imagination.

*$$ SALT POINT BAR & GRILL    Cozy rooms in a spectacular environment. Breakfast / Lunch / Dinner, Full Bar    23255 Coast Highway 1, Jenner, CA Am Ex, Discover, MC & Visa.    (707) 847-3234 Res. Advised.*

## STEWART'S POINT GENERAL STORE

Since 1881 the Stewart's Point General Store (circa 1868) and surrounding ranch land has been owned and in continuous operation by the Richardson family. The pioneer spirit prevails here (there are enough provisions inside to stock a small army). The store is open everyday from 8 am to 6 pm except for Christmas and Thanksgiving. There are times when the roads are closed and people are isolated for as long as a week. Besides having one of the only diesel pumps on the coast gasoline, oil, propane gas, fishing gear and licenses and camping supplies are sold. On the ground level is fresh produce, canned goods, hardware, car fan belts, rain gear, tanning lotion, coffee pots, premium wine and beer, firewood, ice and tourist information and souvenirs. Stewart's Point General Store is a lifeline for tourists who don't realize how remote this part of northern California can be. Sea Ranch is located just 2 miles north.

*$-$$ STEWART'S POINT GENERAL STORE*    *Chevron, MC & Visa*
*General Merchandise, gas and information  (just past Highway marker 48.00)*
*32000 Highway 1, Stewart's Point, CA 95480*    *(707) 785-2406*

## SEA RANCH LODGE

Set in the haunting beauty of isolation and framed by the dramatic Sonoma Coastline cliffs, meadows and ocean is the Sea Ranch Lodge. Once the site of a coastal sheep ranch, this spectacular stretch of land between Gualala and Stewart's Point on coastal Highway 1 offers you a wealth of natural experiences.

Aged redwood encases the 20 guest rooms, decorated with custom-made furniture in natural woods; all having ocean views and several with fireplaces and hot tubs. Rates for 2 from $150 - $295. Ask about the mid-week and golf packages. A special effort is made to host small unconventional business meetings, conferences, seminars and weddings. A full gourmet restaurant offers an ever-changing menu in the atmosphere of lofty ceilings, mellow cedar walls and oversized picture windows overlooking the Pacific. Breakfast is served daily and there is a Sunday Brunch. Daily specials (including fresh seafood) as well as delectable desserts in large variety top off your dinner experience. There is a full bar and premium wine list. Lunch is more of a salad-sandwich affair; although there is a daily selection of salads, soups, pastas, sandwiches, burgers and other specials.

*$$ THE SEA RANCH LODGE,  CA. 95497. AE, MC & Visa.  Open daily*
*Restaurant & Conference Facilities  Numerous amenities.  Golf packages.*
*Sea Walk Drive, The Sea Ranch,  (707) 785-2371/800-732-7262 Res. Sug.*

## RAMS HEAD REALTY VACATION RENTALS

Some of the most desirable vacation home settings are at Sea Ranch, once a large shoreline sheep ranch located a few miles south of Gualala and 20 miles north of Jenner on Hwy. 1. The largest vacation home service north of San Francisco is Rams Head Realty at the Sea Ranch, with 135 homes to choose from. Besides sheer numbers there is always something that sets the leader apart, and that is the Ram's Head walk-in cabins (WICs). These contemporary redwood homes (approx. 525 sq. ft.) make cozy love nests or ideal settings for script writers, theologians (lots of skylights and windows) or anyone seeking peace and inspiration with the natural forest. Rates are from $180/2 for 2 nights and from $580/week up to 4 persons. A variety of amenities are available at these fully equipped luxurious vacation homes. Please write for a free brochure.

*$$-$$$ RAMS HEAD VACATION RENTALS*
*Simple to Luxurious Oceanview Homes*     *CA 95497 (707) 785-2427*
*Box 123, 1000 Annapolis Rd., Sea Ranch,*     *Toll Free: 1-800-785-3455*

## ANNAPOLIS WINERY

Annapolis Winery and Scalabrini Vineyards is a small family venture nestled on a sunny hilltop in the rural community of Annapolis. The 18 acres of grapes were planted in 1978 and are blessed with an exceptional climate that develops intensely flavored berries. The premium quality fruit is transformed into wonderfully rich, fruity and delightful wines. Sauvignon Blanc, Pinot Noir and Gewurztraminer grapes are grown at the winery; with Cabernet Sauvignon grapes purchased inland from the Anderson Valley. All wines are made in small quantities emphasizing natural methods in both the vineyard and the winery. Less than 3,000 cases are produced annually. Family members handle every phase of production from planting and pruning to bottling and labeling.

I personally found the tasting room a delightful experience with its rich natural decor and local art surrounding vintages of wine invitingly set out on the wine bar set with flowers. Birds were chirping in a meadow of apple trees by the outdoor patio and courtyard. Because the winery is above the coastal wind and fog, it is often warm and sunny and a delightful place to picnic as well as an inspirational location for weddings. This is a rural experience that is close to my heart and was definitely worth the long and beautiful drive from Warm Springs Dam. A shorter 7 mile drive is from Hwy 1 at Sea Ranch.

*$ ANNAPOLIS WINERY 20655 Soda Springs Road, Annapolis, CA. 95412*
*Retail Sales and Tasting Open Thur - Mon noon to 5pm (707) 886-5460*

# SCENIC DRIVES:  ANNAPOLIS ROAD

A must drive is tiny Annapolis Road in northwestern Sonoma County.  This sleepy 14 mile stretch, which is accessible from Healdsburg at Warm Springs Dam by Skaggs Springs Road, or from Highway 1 at Sea Ranch, winds its way along the ridgelines dropping in and out of remote and beautiful coastal valleys.  Along the way you will want to visit the **Annapolis Winery.**  And a detour south down remote Tin Barn Road will reveal the golden Buddhist temple of **Odiyan!**

# SACRED SITES and ENERGY VORTEXES
## Along the Sonoma Coast

### Kashia Pomo Spiritual Roundhouse

North of Odiyan and at the T junction of Tin Barn Road and Skaggs Springs Road is the Kashia Pomo Indian settlement.  Here the Kashaya (the place) and the Kashia (the people) have built the Spiritual Round House for California's Coastal Pomo Nation.  It is open to all who come with Love and Respect.  About 3.6 miles up from Hwy 1 at Stewart's Point Store is a meadow offering a panoramic view to the southwest of ocean and virgin forest.  The Round House is 4.5 miles up from the store and Hwy 1.

The Wehya (or the energy-force-mystery-God) is open to everyone.  If you come upon the path of Love and stay on it, one door after another will open.  It is the time in our sacred world that we connect with each other - there is no separation - between us, Mother Earth, and our path of Love.  It is the time of Light.

The Pomo are a matriarchal society, choosing to honor the wisdom and energy of woman.  "All of our wisdom comes from the woman," strong Pomo Warrior Leaders state.  They know that in honoring the co-creation powers of the female they honor themselves.  This is a sign of great male strength.

*See next page*

# SACRED SITES and ENERGY VORTEXES
## Along the Sonoma Coast

*"The traveling fires in the sky,*
*their name will be SUN.*
*The one who is FIRE,*
*HIS name will be*
*DAYTIME SUN.*
*The one who gives LIGHT*
*in the night,*
*HER name will be*
*NIGHT SUN."*
**Pomo Creation Story**

*Continued from previous page*
From time to time there are sweats and Round House ceremonies. Enter humbly and walk the circle of life. You must first enter the Round House by the backdoor (the south entrance). To show respect and align with the sacred energies, which will empower you, circle the round to your right until you reach the fire pit, which you will

*Fire Pit*

*Bench*

*Circle the Fire Pit Twice*

*Walk*

*South Entrance*

Animal guides "Karma" and "Spirit Wolf" began to howl as we chanted and took turns drumming on the Pomo earthen floor box. Lorin Smith (right) with visiting retreat leaders.

then circle twice before proceeding on to your right to the bench. It is okay to pause here to offer your prayers and personal affirmations. Spread your wings and fly. Then proceed out the front door and into the Light.

Retreat leaders enjoy a spiritual break inside the Round House with Lorin Smith, Weya Pomo healer and medicine man.

Animal guides "Karma" and "Spirit Wolf" began to howl as we all chant and take our turn drumming on the earthen floor box. Feel the strength, listen to Mother's heart beating! Walk away enriched with focused purpose. To receive a treatment from Lorin or visit the Round House write:
*Lorin Smith, P.O. Box 31, Stewarts Point, CA. 95480. (707) 785-9705.*

# SACRED SITES and ENERGY VORTEXES
## Along the Sonoma Coast

Photo by Steve McLaughlin/ I.C.O.

Odiyan, Timber Cove, the Kashia Pomo Round House and the non-denominational Sea Ranch Chapel are a few places to honor your spiritual path.  Pictured is one of the prayer temples at Odiyan where the Nyingma Buddhist fellowship does retreats.

Photo by Tim Dixon

The Sonoma Coast north of Jenner to Gualala is a very popular destination for personal growth and spiritual workshops.  Retreat leaders and participants enjoy pure air, emerald blue waters and fabulous vortex energy centers such as can be found at Timber Cove - either ridgetop or in sacred coves at waters edge.  Pictured above is a group at "Ascension Cove" north of Jenner honoring the Spring Equinox.  The spiritual energy is strong at a vortex when gentle and loving souls gather to honor the spring, summer, fall and winter solstice or equinox.  Both youth and adults become stronger when we honor rites of passage with clear minds and open hearts.

# SACRED SITES and ENERGY VORTEXES
## Along the Sonoma Coast

Photo by Steve McLaughlin/ I.C.O.

Odiyan is the sacred site for the Nyingma Buddhist fellowship. Unfortunately it is closed to the general public and is a long drive up dangerous windy country roads. It can be viewed in its entirety from the air or in small glimpses from Tin Barn Road (see map page 73). Those of us of a spiritual persuasion should be prepared to spend a few moments in prayer in our car parked safely off the road or kneeled on a blanket in meditation. There is no public access to this sacred site and private property rights of residents along the road to the north and south must be respected.

To be in the presence of the kind of love and devotion that created Odiyan is a very moving experience. Inside the temple, prayer wheels spin and millions of prayers dedicated to love and peace go out to the Universe each day. Take this trip to the top of the Sonoma Coast with someone you love and you'll bond in a special way forever.

The Buddhist Lama who presides over Odiyan is Tarthang Tulku. Those who desire to study at the temple may call for information on apprenticeships.

*Odiyan Buddhist Temple*     *33755 Tin Barn Rd., Cazadero, CA 95421*
*Odiyan Coordinating Office,  2425 Hillside Ave., Berkeley, CA. 94704*
*(510) 549-9310,*                    *e-mail: odiyan@nyingma.org,*
*Tibetan Culture House (see page 286)*          *Fax: (707) 485-6286*

---

***For information on Tours of the Sacred Sites of the Sonoma Coast, land or retreat & workshop locations call or write Robert W. Matson at (707) 522-0550, P.O. Box G, Santa Rosa, CA. 95402. Love & Light!***

# SACRED SITES and ENERGY VORTEXES
## Along the Sonoma Coast

### Timber Cove:
### Home of the Dragon King

All around the headlands and towering monolith I noticed Dragon energy in the rocky cliffs embracing Timber Cove. "Dragon King live here", states Dr. Yutang Lin, a Buddhist Priest. I asked Yutang Lin, "Where is the Dragon's Head?" He said "Oh, Dragon Head off Washington." "Really!", I responded. "Well, where is the Dragon's Tail?". "Tail off Mexico", Yutang Lin finished. "Wow!", I exclaimed and quickly continued, "Then the Dragon's Heart must be here!" I anxiously concluded. "No" stated Dr. Lin, "Dragon Palace here - Dragon Spirit Live Here!"

## Sea Ranch Chapel: Non-Denominational Prayer Sanctuary

I am constantly humbled by the spectacular beauty and fantastic creativity of Californians. Just 5 miles north of the Sea Ranch Lodge and General Store at 40033 State Hwy 1 is the non-denominational Sea Ranch Chapel, a splendid prayer sanctuary.

Behold! Art is indeed the bridge between Earth and Heaven. Inside is a composite of ancient wood, stained glass, gemstones, sea shells, "dragon fire and twisted wire that catches the light of moon and sun." *

Bring your camera and spend a brief moment or more in meditation. The chapel is opened daily at 9am and is closed at sunset. Hand carved wooden benches and wrought iron candle holders provide shelter and light from any coastal storm. Bring your own totem, prayer book or journal. You'll want to share your inner thoughts with someone special and the Creator. Abundant blessings upon each of you who takes the time to remember. Brother to Sister - Sister to Brother. Live in Love and Light.

*The Sea Ranch Chapel Foundation, P.O. Box 121, Sea Ranch, CA. 95497*
*Quote from the Hobbit

# MENDOCINO COAST: GUALALA to MANCHESTER

The picturesque
Gualala River
where it flows into
the Pacific Ocean.
The town of
Gualala is in the
upper right just
past the Coast
Highway 1 bridge.

**GUALALA to ANCHOR BAY DINER'S CHOICE: Telephone Area Code is (707)**
**Anchor Bay Store** ($) Hwy 1, Anchor Bay  884-4245;  **Cafe Pacifico** ($-$$) S. Hwy 1  J. Baker
Town  884-1735;  **Fish Rock Cafe** ($$) 35517 Hwy 1  884-1639;  **Food Company** ($$) S. Hwy
1  884-1800;  **Gualala Bakery** ($) Sunstrom Shopping Center  884-9247;  **Gualala Hotel** ($$)
Hwy 1  884-4840;  **Gualala Super Market** ($) Sunstrom Shopping Center  884-1205;  **Java
Point** ($) Hwy 1 Seacliff Center  884-902;  **Oceansong Restaurant** ($$) 39350 S. Hwy 1  884-
1041;  **Old Hotel Smokehouse** ($) 39350 S. Hwy 1  884-9042;  **Old Milano Hotel** ($$$)
38300 Hwy 1  884-3256;  **PB Espresso** ($) 35501 S. Hwy 1  884-1104;  **Saint Orres Inn** ($$)
Hwy 1  884-3303;  **Surf Super Market** ($) 39250 S. Hwy 1  884-4184;  **Top of the Cliff** ($$)
Hwy 1 Seacliff Center  884-1539;  **Upper Crust Pizza** ($$) 39331 S. Hwy 1  884-1324.

**GUALALA to ANCHOR BAY LODGING:**
**Anchor Bay Campground** ($)  Hwy 1, Anchor Bay  884-4222;  **Beach Rentals** ($$$) 39200 S.
Hwy 1  884-4235;  **Breaker's Inn**  ($$$) 3919 Hwy 1, 800-BREAKER;  **Gateway
Accommodations** ($-$$$) Box 100  800-726-9997;  **Gualala Country Inn** ($$)  Hwy 1  800-
564-4466;  **Gualala Hotel** ($$)  Hwy 1  884-3441;  **Gualala Point Park**  ($) 785-2377;  **Gualala
River Redwood Park**  ($)  1 mile east of Hwy 1 on River Rd.  884-3533;  **Mar Vista Cottages**
($$) 35101 S. Hwy 1  884-3522;  **North Coast Country Inn** ($$$) 34591 S. Hwy 1  884-4537;
**Old Milano Hotel** ($$$) 38300 Hwy 1  884-3256;  **Saint Orres Inn** ($$)  Hwy 1  884-3303;
**Seacliff Hotel** ($$$) 39140 S. Hwy 1  884-1213; **Serenisea** ($$) 36100 Hwy 1  884-3836; **Surf
Motel** ($$) S. Hwy 1  888-451-7873;  **Whale Watch** ($$$) 35100 Hwy 1  884-3667.

**TOURIST INFO, BOOKSTORES, GIFTSHOPS and the ARTS**
**Alinder Gallery**  884-4884;  **Artsea Gallery**  884-4809;  **Coldwell Banker Pacific Realestate**
/ Travel Information for Tourists  800-660-3591;  **Cotton Field, The**  884-1836;  **Dolphin Arts**
884-3896;   **Gualala Books** / Travel Information for Tourists  884-4255;  **Gualala Art Center**
884-1138;  **Henley's Gallery**  785-2951;  **Noma** 884-1320;  **The Sea Trader** / Travel
Information for Tourists  884-3248;  **Velvet Rabbit**  884-1501;  **Healing Arts Center** (See Page
256).

**FARMER'S MARKETS and NURSERIES  Gualala Farmer's Market:** ($) Spring thru Fall on
Saturday 3pm-5pm south end of downtown / walts@mcn.org (707) 882-2474;  **Growing Concern
Nursery** ($-$$$) 38520 S. Hwy 1,  (707) 884-3982.

**AERIAL FLIGHTS, FISHING, KAYAKING and WHALE WATCHING:**
**Adventure Rents** ($$)  884-4FUN (4386);  **West of One**  ($$-$$$) Sightseeing Flights over the
coast and wine country  884-4422.

At the Surf Motel you can watch the crashing surf, the whales and breathtaking sunsets, then fall asleep to the sound of the sea.

## SURF MOTEL at Gualala and the GUALALA COUNTRY INN

One of the more reasonably priced oceanview motels on the South Mendocino Coast is the Surf Motel at Gualala. Amenities include a lobby reading library and selection of menus from local restaurants, fresh brewed coffee, teas & chocolates, in-room remote control cable color TV, private bathtub/shower combos, in-room 2 line speaker phones with free local internet access, kitchenettes and king, queen or double beds. Rates are from $79 - $145/2. All major credit cards honored.

The Gualala Country Inn occupies an inspirational setting where you can experience the beauty and serenity of California's North Coast in quiet elegance. Such activities as world famous steelhead fishing in the Gualala River, moments of solitude in the fern canyons and redwood forests, and exploring the beaches and coves makes your stay an enjoyable experience.

Twenty one rooms await. All rooms have ocean and/or river views, private baths, cable color TV and private phones. Three downstairs rooms are the Surf, Sunset and Sea Spray (from $140/2) which boast 2 person whirlpool spas, woodburning fireplaces and are very tastefully decorated. There is a firelit parlor adjacent to the lobby for socializing or gazing at the moody Pacific Ocean.

*$$ GUALALA COUNTRY INN*
*1-800 - 564-4466*
*email: countryinn @ gualala.com*
*www.gualala.com     AAA Approved*

*$$ SURF MOTEL at Gualala*
*1- 888 - 451-SURF (7873)*
*email: surfmotel @ gualala.com*
*S. Hwy 1 in Gualala, CA. 95445*

### BREAKER'S INN

The Breaker's Inn is indeed a "room-with-a-view". Built on a bluff overlooking the mouth of the Gualala River and the Pacific Ocean are twenty four rooms offering spectacular 180 degree ocean views. From their private deck guests can watch flights of birds, seals playing in the river, migrating whales and brilliant hues of an ocean sunset. Evenings reveal the Milky Way, Orion and bright streaks of meteors climaxing their journey with a visit to *our home* - planet earth.

Oceanfront rooms are each elegantly decorated in a regional theme and all feature balconies, fireplaces and double-size whirlpool spas. Rooms include wet bars, coffee-maker, continental breakfast, television, telephone and there are over 2,000 books for your reading pleasure in the Breaker's library. Luxury Spa Rooms have a whirlpool spa in the room where you can soak in the bubble bath, enjoy the crackling fire and ocean views. Many rooms have King poster or sleigh beds, beveled glass windows, European comforters and refrigerators. Rates for two start at $125.00. Limited view rooms with decks, fireplaces, standard baths & king beds start at $95.00. Gift Certificates are available.

From the inn you can walk to charming shops, gourmet restaurants and galleries featuring local artisans and an array of crafts. The ocean and river provide the backdrop for abalone diving, fishing, surfing, horseback riding and bicycle rentals are available. Take advantage of local kayak and canoe rentals. The area boasts miles of secluded beaches for romantic walks or tidepool exploration. Golf and tennis are just minutes away.

The lullaby of the sea, the clear coastal air and the peace and quiet of a small town rejuvenates Breaker's Inn guests for their journey home.

*$$-$$$ BREAKER'S INN*
*Oceanview Bed and Breakfast*
*Box 389, Hwy 1, Gualala, CA. 95445*
*Most credit cards honored.*
*www.breakersinn.com*
*1-800-BREAKER Reservations Suggested*

## OCEANSONG PACIFIC GRILLE

You can begin your adventure on the Mendocino Coast just over the border at the Oceansong Pacific Grille. Lofty dining room views of the untamed Gualala River and Pacific Ocean await.

Dinner means a fabulous sunset view from every seat in the house. Bring the whole family for a ring side seat of the greatest show on earth as pelicans, sea gulls, osprey, sea lions and whales play in the water and sky just outside the restaurant. Weather permitting there is dining al fresco beneath the sun or evening starlit sky. Lovers will find a quiet little nook in the bar or tri-level dining room.

Chef Rene Fueg, who was featured in the internationally acclaimed magazine Culinary Trends, prepares a variety of dinner specials with fresh seasonal produce, herbs, meats and fish. A superb menu features the chef's duck a l'orange with sauce Bigarade, won-ton prawns, smoked salmon polenta with sundried tomato champagne sauce and cornmeal clam chowder. The upper level bar offers beer, wine and mixed drinks. Oceansong is located at the south entrance to Gualala. Advanced reservations are suggested for 5 or more guests.

*$$ OCEANSONG RESTAURANT     39350 S. Hwy 1, Gualala, CA. 95445*
*Seafood and American   www.breakersinn.com/oceansong   (707) 884-1041*

Photo by Ron Bolander

## SURF SUPER MARKET

The largest supermarket on State Highway 1 between Point Reyes and Fort Bragg is the Surf Super Market in Gualala. Here you can stock up on everything for your day hike, camping trip, vacation home rental or romantic evening at a bed and breakfast inn. Isles are well stocked with all the canned and fresh produce and cooking utensils a small town full of tourists would need. In the full service deli/meat department there are fresh filets of fish, homemade salads, country fried chicken and potato Jo-Jo's, and prime cuts of steak, chicken and homemade sausages. The bakery offers fresh baked breads and pastries. The beer and wine selection is extensive. Local newspapers, magazines, toiletries, light hardware and home electrical needs, motor oil and flares are also stocked. Rain or shine you can count on the Surf Super Market and its friendly staff to help you.

*$-$$ SURF SUPER MARKET   39250 Coast Highway 1, Gualala, CA. 95445*
*Full Service Market        (707) 884-4184 Open daily from 7:30am to 8pm*

## GUALALA RIVER REDWOOD PARK

Owners Dan and Donna Brown invite you to "camp in the redwoods, on the river by the sea" at their 120 campsite Gualala River Redwood Park. Each campsite (from $25 and up) has running water and electricity. Open from memorial day to labor day, the campground has a general store, hot showers, flush toilets, RV dump stations, a laundry room, playground and outdoor game area. Accommodations serve a single family to large groups of up to 250.

Guests can sunbathe out of the wind and fog along 3/4 mile river frontage of sandy beaches, as well as swim, canoe and kayak. Hike or bike among the ferns and towering redwoods or fish, dive, golf, whale watch, dine out, shop or tour local art galleries. You can build family traditions around the fire and enjoy nature and starlit skies at their finest. Wake up to singing birds, a rising sun, fresh complimentary coffee and the sound of ocean waves in the distance.

$ GUALALA RIVER REDWOOD PARK     Box 1032, Gualala, CA. 95445
*Riverside Campground with numerous amenities  MC & Visa  (707) 884-3533*

## ADVENTURE RENTS

Adventure Rents outfits self-guided paddling tours on the Gualala River, which forms the border between Sonoma and Mendocino county. Owners Jan and Wayne Harris have 20 years experience exploring the waterways of the redwood coast and welcome singles, couples, families and groups.

Rentals include Grumman canoes for 2-5 persons, single and double Aquaterra, Kiwi, and sit-on-top Ocean kayaks. Watercraft rentals include paddles, life jackets, dry bags and instruction for beginning boaters. All boats and gear are transported to put-in locations, and shuttle service is available. Rates are reasonable. Located in downtown Gualala.

$$ ADVENTURE RENTS     *Kayaks and Canoes*     P.O. Box 489, Gualala, CA
*www.adventurerents.com*               *email: info@adventurerents.com*
*(707) 884-4FUN (4386)*          *or Toll Free 1-888-881-4FUN (4386)*

## GUALALA HOTEL

Home cooking and old fashioned pioneer hospitality abound at the Gualala Hotel, 125 miles north of San Francisco.  Occupying a wind swept bluff in the sleepy town it is named after, the hotel is but a few hundred yards from the crashing Pacific surf.  Here you can take off your shoes and kick up your feet by the parlor woodstove. There are 18 rooms on the 2nd floor; 13 with shared baths and 5 with private baths.  All rooms (from $50 up) are cozily furnished with antique beds and make ideal havens.  Country style breakfasts of biscuits & gravy, egg and meat dishes are served downstairs from $5.00 up.  Lunch and dinner portions are generous and prices moderate. Photographs of fishermen with massive steelheads line the walls of the bar which is often buried with locals and tourists on weekends.  Here you can enjoy the spirit of the early pioneers.

*$$ GUALALA HOTEL  Firelite Parlor & Long Bar  Box 675, Hwy 1, Gualala*
*Rooms, Breakfast, Lunch & Dinner    Parties & Banquets    (707) 884-3441*

## OLD HOTEL SMOKE HOUSE

This cute saltblock style building, located just behind the Gualala Hotel, serves the best fresh fish and chips for the price in this book!  The old adage is find where the locals eat and you'll find the best food at the best price - well the Old Hotel Smokehouse is it.  Owner Leslie Bates and her youthful staff are big on heart and service.  Great fresh local fish & chips with tartar or red sauce, fish burgers, smoked salmon, BBQ pork ribs or beef sandwiches, clam chowder, cole slaw, potato salad, chili fries, pasta and BBQ beans are served daily from 10am - 6pm weekdays / till 8pm weekends. Homemade cheesecake, carrot cake, iced mochas, smoothies and sodas wet your whistle. Leslie has a soft spot in her heart for K-9 friends like local favorite Kyo (pictured here). Seating is indoors or out with orders prepared to go.

*$ OLD HOTEL SMOKE HOUSE      39350 S. Hwy 1, Gualala, CA. 95445*
*Fresh & Smoked Fish & Meats                    (707) 884-9042*

**COLDWELL BANKER** ⑤ **PACIFIC REAL ESTATE**

Coldwell Banker Pacific Real Estate is the largest real estate office serving the Sea Ranch, Gualala, Northern Sonoma and Southern Mendocino coast. Owner/broker Lenny Balter and his wife Colleen Casey have lived on the coast since 1980.  They have two highly visible Gualala locations with over a dozen full time knowledgeable agents and brokers, 2 internet marketing sites, email access and computerized listing & market analysis for their clients - "Making Real Estate Real Easy."  You can surf the website for over 150 coastal homes and then vacation in Gualala or Sea Ranch and take a personal tour with Lenny & Colleen or one of their agents.

*$$$ COLDWELL BANKER PACIFIC REAL ESTATE   http://www.cbpac.com*
*Main Office: Box 700, 39351 S. Hwy 1, Gualala Fax:707-884-9004, 800-944-8941*
*Seacliff Ofc: Box 512, 39140 S. Hwy 1, Gualala Fax:707-884-1933, 800-660-3591*

## FREE LODGING REFERRAL SERVICE

The publisher of Getaway to the North Coast Guest Guide offers a FREE lodging referral service, representing inns, bed & breakfasts, vacation homes, hotels and motels along California's beautiful 200 mile coast highway one. Do you want oceanviews, hot tubs, horseback riding, gourmet dining, king size beds and privacy? There is no charge for your arrangements on the coast. Call ahead for confirmed reservations and mid-week or off-season (November - March) specials. Write for a free guest guide and coast map. ($1.00 postage & handling).

*$$ "GETAWAY" TO THE NORTH COAST      P.O. Box 100, Gualala, CA. 95445*
*Accommodation Referral Service   www.gualalagetaways.com   1-800-726-9997*

## UPPER CRUST PIZZA

Small coastal towns with good pizza parlors make big hits with north coast travelers. The Upper Crust Pizza is one such destination. The menu is divided into Specialties-of-the-House, seafood, chicken and vegetarian pizzas. A delicious sourdough pizza crust topped with a choice of 23 fresh high quality ingredients will put a smile on your face. Fresh garden salads, fruit juice, sodas and mineral water is served. The Upper Crust Pizza is open year-round from 4pm and stays open until 8pm or 9pm, depending on the daily appetite of diners. Indoor/ outdoor oceanview dining or orders to go.

*$$ UPPER CRUST PIZZA            Cash & Approved Checks Accepted*
*39331 S. Hwy 1, Gualala, CA.95445        (707) 884-1324 Orders to go.*

## SUNDSTROM CENTER

Robert and Roberta Sundstrom moved to Gualala in the late 50's to raise a family, work the woods and build homes for a growing coastal community. Robert, a soft spoken go-with-the-flow - kind-of-guy states, "I built the "new" Gualala Post Office in 1970, then the bank, gas station and shopping center a building at a time until we finished in 1986."

Today, residents and travelers enjoy the convenience of the Gualala Market, a sport and tackle shop, pizza and ice cream parlor, bakery, office copy center, craftshop and fabric store, travel agent, florist and video store all under one big roof. Next door is the Dolphin Art Center where visitors can purchase local art and get tourist information.

*$-$$$ SUNDSTROM CENTER         39225 South Hwy 1, Gualala, CA. 95445*
*Gualala Bakery 884-9247, Gualala Market 884-1205, Gualala Pizza and*
*Espresso 884-4055, Gualala Sport & Tackle 884-884-4247, Gualala*
*Union 76 884-1500, Copy Plus Fax: 884-4449 or 884-4448, Dolphin*
*Gallery 884-3896, The Loft Crafts and Fabric 884-4424, Redwood Florist*
*884-4233 and Seaview Travel Agent 884-3505.*

## SEACLIFF SHOPPING CENTER

The Sea Clif Shopping Center offers a variety of art gallerys, craft shops, restaurants, professional offices and oceanview rooms and suites. Top of the Cliff, Java Point, Celebrations, the Velvet Rabbit, the Artsea Gallery & Framing and White Sands offer an array of treats for the senses.

### TOP of the CLIFF

One of the most authentically unique restaurants along Highway 1 is the Top of the Cliff in the Seacliff Shopping Center. The Newfoundland deep dish pot of fresh seafood and assorted shell fish in a mussel broth topped with pastry is itself worth a visit to Gualala. Dinners include homemade soup and garden green salad. Chefs John Ihorn and Shirley Ranieri (who is from Newfoundland) create dishes such as penne pasta with sauteed lobster and scallops, coppa (Italian salami), portobella mushrooms and sundried tomatoes in a Madera cream sauce, stuffed Canadian halibut topped with crab & brie and oven baked with wine sauce, rack of Sonoma lamb served in garlic mustard herb sauce and breast of chicken glazed in wild Mendocino huckleberry chutney. Owners Don Garibaldi and John Ihorn have a wine cellar full of extra-ordinary California vintages. Lunch is from 11:30am-2:30pm and dinner from 5:30 pm and reservations are often necessary.

*$$ TOP of the CLIFF P.O. Box 1068, 39140 S. Hwy 1, Gualala, CA. 95445*
*Seafood & Continental MC & Visa (707) 884-1539 Res. Often Necessary*

**JAVA POINT** A good cup of coffee and a good book have always gone together, but at Java Point you can have a good cup of coffee with a gourmet meal, buy a good book and enjoy the ocean view outside the coffee room's windows, rain or shine. What fun to whale watch, bird watch and listen to the flow of tourists and locals come in and out of the bookstore while sipping an espresso or cappuccino. Chef/owner Carol Sauer serves original meat, vegetarian and vegan dishes plus pastries and chilled juices. Inside are stacks of new and used books for the active and aware mind and an interesting selection of original photographs by local artists. Regulars congregate to share ideas and dreams, gossip and discuss world events.

*$ JAVA POINT P. O. Box 1512, Seacliff Center, Gualala, Ca. 95445*
*Oceanview Coffee House & Bookstore (707) 884-9020 Information*

## CELEBRATIONS

Those who have ever visited the Mendocino Coast giftshops know they are among the most original on the West Coast. At Celebrations you'll discover a truly original line of fine gifts, jewelry, home decorating items and antiques. Such is the case at Celebrations where mother/daughter team Nancy J Anderson and Phyllis T. Pacheco offer an excellent selection of gifts for the home, garden, children and special occasion to commemorate anniversaries or loving moments. Service is very big here, as the extended family of Celebration customers will testify to. "We ship gifts anywhere in America," state Nancy and Phyllis, who have been in business in Gualala for a decade. Stop by and visit between 11am - 5pm daily, during summertime; closed on Wednesdays between September and May.

*$$ CELEBRATIONS  P.O. Box 790, 39140 S. Hwy 1, Gualala, CA 95445*
*Fine Gifts, Jewelry & Antiques     AE, Disc, MC & Visa     (707) 884-1920*

## VELVET RABBIT

One of the most enchanting gift shops and galleries on the Mendocino Coast is the Velvet Rabbit - located in the Seacliff Shopping Center in Gualala.

Proprietress Lois L. Koerber has created a wonderful environment of works of art, Tiffany stained glass lamps, bronze sculptures, water colors and very exclusive gifts and artifacts which light up the eyes of visitors. As opera music plays in the background, whale sculptures, frozen in time, seem to come alive & dance with dolphins. In this fantasyland by the sea you can forget the rest of the world.

*$$-$$$ VELVET RABBIT  Box 676, Hwy 1, Gualala*
*Fine Art and Gifts          Open daily 10am - 5pm*
*MC & Visa               (707) 884-1501 Information*

**The Cotton Field**
A CLOTHING STORE FOR WOMEN

The Cotton Field Coastal Connection is a clothing store for women, located in the Seacliff Center in downtown Gualala. The Cotton Field features relaxed, unstructured clothing in a variety of natural-fiber fabrics. They offer colorful fun clothing, designed for work, play and travel.You will find "one of a kind" or "limited edition" wearable art pieces, hand crafted by well known local artists and others from around the Pacific Northwest, silver from Bali, natural stone jewelry and beautiful vests and jackets from the highlands of Guatemala.

The store is family owned and operated by Peggy Sundstrom, Barbara Boschetti and Lou Anne Fredrickson. They are ready to problem solve your wardrobe dilemmas or assist you with a gift selection. Free gift wrap and fun available! Open Mon-Sat 10am-5pm, Sun 10am-4pm, closed Wed.

*$$ THE COTTON FIELD*
*A Clothing Store for Women  39140 S. Hwy 1, Gualala  (707) 884-1836*
*Bay Area: 3561 Mt. Diablo Blvd., Lafayette, CA. 94549  (925) 284-8401*

## OLD MILANO HOTEL

On a cliff overlooking majestic Castle Rock, one mile north of Gualala, stands the Old Milano Hotel. The decor is an elegant combination of art, antiques, brilliant colors, natural finished woods, iron, crystal and flower bouquets all tucked in a historic hotel (National Register of Historic Landmarks), clinging to the Pacific coast.

The Old Milano Hotel hosts some of the more festive five course dinners served with award winning wines in the warm ambiance of the dining room where service is deluxe and unhurried. Attentive waitpeople insure fires are tended, wines are properly decanted and each course arrives timely.

Smothered by the fragrance of flowers and herbs is the cozy Garden Cottage ($135/2) which is located adjacent the main house. The Master Suite includes a separate bedroom, private bath and sitting room with an incomparable view of the ocean and Castle Rock ($175/2). There are six other lovely rooms in the hotel with ocean or garden views (115/2), and out back is a rip-roaring red caboose. A delicious full breakfast is served either bedside or on the plant filled loggia. Hot tubbers can bake in the summer sun or star gaze on clear nights over a sea of waves illuminated by moonlight. Cobblestones on the waterfall splashed beach below the inn obediently clack back and forth with each ocean wave.

*$$-$$$ OLD MILANO HOTEL      38300 Highway 1, Gualala, CA  95445*
*Bed & Breakfast, Elegant Dinner  www.oldmilanohotel.com (707) 884-3256*

## SAINT ORRES INN

Inspired by Russian architecture, constructed of 100-year-old timbers, Saint Orres weaves an aura of magic and beauty, creating the coast's fantasy spot. On the 50 acres are the Hotel proper, the Meadows area with 4 cabins and the new Creekside accommodations to the north with 8 cottages. Hints of ancient and new age thought are here and there for guests to ponder. Adjacent the Creekside cottages is the spa with showers, sauna, soaking tub and meeting room which doubles as a breakfast nook or recreational lounge. Small crystal balls, set like gemstones, crown the copper domes above the Spa area. Illuminated at night, the imagery is only limited to one's imagination.

Meals in the Hotel are prepared fresh daily from the finest local and imported ingredients. Fresh fish, duckling, beef, chicken, rack of lamb, appetizers, homemade hot or chilled soups, salad courses and desserts are served. Innovative entrees are at prix fixe $30 (3 courses). Hotel rooms with shared baths are from $70-$85/2 and cottages with private baths and fireplaces are from $100-$225/2 with full breakfast.

*$$-$$$  SAINT ORRES INN       P.O. Box 523, Gualala, CA 95445*
*Ocean View Dinner/Lodging/Spa  www.saintorres.com   (707) 884-3303*

## ANCHOR BAY CAMPGROUND

This 5-acre redwood canyon opens onto 3/4-mile long Fish Rock Beach where families have been camping since 1925. The campground snugly occupies the canyon with 26 sites under the trees as well as a few fronting the beach. Each site has a picnic table and fire pit, most with water and some with electric. Facilities include flush toilets, coin-op showers, fish cleaning house, dive gear wash area, and septic dump. Ice, bait, and firewood are for sale, and there are restaurants, markets, gift shops, laundromat, and gas stations in nearby Anchor Bay and Gualala. Activities include fishing, diving, and beachcombing; the beach is safe for kids. Small boats (car tops and inflatables) may be launched by hand across the sand. Anchor Bay's "banana belt" micro-climate means more sun and less fog than surrounding areas. Overnight rate is $25/2, electrical hook-up $2 (1999 rates). Day Use fees are $1 per person and $1 per car. Reservations recommended, phone for a brochure.

*$$ ANCHOR BAY CAMPGROUND  Mailing: Box 1529, Gualala, CA. 95445*
*Campground    www.abcamp.com  4 miles north of Gualala  (707) 884-4222*

## SERENISEA

Hidden on the southern rim of Anchor Bay, and 100 yards seaward, is Serenisea. Proprietor Jim Lotter has found his coastal treasure chest and fortunately for us he wants to share it.

Four comfortable cottages with fireplaces / wood stoves, kitchens, bathtubs, and twin and queen beds await you; $80 - $170 per night for two, which includes access to the bluffside hot tub. The luxury cottage has a stereo, sauna, sundeck and fabulous views. A wintertime creek cascades through beds of watercress into coves abundant in tidepool activity and seaweed forests. There is a trail to the tidepools. Jim's "Serenisea Vacation Homes" offer exceptional ocean views, beachfront or forest locations; some with beach access, kitchens and fireplaces; some with hot tubs ($90 - $180 per night for 2). Guests will soon understand why this special destination is called "Serenisea".

*$$ SERENISEA          www.serenisea.com     4 cottages plus vacation homes*
*Ocean Front Lodging                    fireplaces, tubs, sauna & beach access*
*36100 Highway 1, Gualala, CA. 95445   No Credit Cards.  1-800-331-3836*

## ANCHOR BAY VILLAGE
## MARKETand WINE WORLD

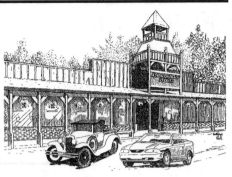

The pioneers of the cliffside community of Anchor Bay parted the trees in 1915 with the construction of the Anchor Bay Store to reveal one of the most pristine sand covered beaches on the Mendocino Coast. For developer Richard McCoy the dream of owning a small town was completed when he finished renovation of the Anchor Bay Store in the summer of 1994. The modernized, yet historic store successfully promotes an old-fashioned general store atmosphere. "Because the community and tourist needs are so diversified, we stock anything from road maps to diapers," states Richard. This is not just another grocery store. It is a very special store with emphasis placed on offering a diversified selection of products including fresh local organic produce, unique deli items, locally baked breads, micro brews, imported beers and premium wines in it's acclaimed wine cellar. Shop here, whether for a simple picnic or a festive banquet. You will also find kerosene lamps, fishing gear, canning equipment, jams, vinegars and oils both local and imported. Much can be "discovered" by browsing the aisles of this modernized and historic coastal shop. *Open daily wintertime from 8am-8pm, summers from 8am-9pm.*

*$-$$ ANCHOR BAY STORE        Highway 1, Anchor Bay, CA. 95445*
*Food, Wines and Provisions   www.anchorbaystore.com   (707) 884-4245*

## FISH ROCK CAFE

A general rule of thumb is, find where the locals eat and you'll find the best food for the best price. In these parts, that would be the Fish Rock Cafe. A row of booths along a dark marble green wall covered with historic photographs of Anchor Bay is occupied by locals and visitors to this upscale diner on Highway 1. Your dedicated hosts to this quaint seaside cafe, Stacy and Chris Aitchison, are well acquainted with this stretch of coastal California. They serve a delicious homemade clam chowder, tasty lightly battered fish and chips and over a dozen sandwiches, plus old fashioned sundaes and fresh baked pies and cakes. Those into health food will enjoy the meatless Mexicana or the Botany veggie burger, with garden salad and fruit smoothie. No Hollywood-by-the-sea, where you leave broke and hungry, you begin the rest of the day satisfied and with money left over at the Fish Rock Cafe.

*$ FISH ROCK CAFE        35517 Hwy 1, Anchor Bay, CA. 95445*
*American and Seafood        MC & Visa          (707) 884-1639*

# POINT ARENA
## Future Gemstone of the Mendocino Coast?

Main Street Point Arena. Point Arena's main street is lined with restaurants & bars, a movie theater, giftshops, a bookstore/coffee house and seasonal farmers market. This picturesque community has been the back drop for several motion pictures including "Forever Young".

**POINT ARENA to MANCHESTER DINER'S CHOICE:** Area Code (707) **Cosmic Pizza** ($$) End of Port Street, Arena Cove 882-1900; **The Galley at Arena Cove** ($$) End of Port Street 882-2189; **Giannini's Fine Food & Bar** ($-$$) 174 Main 882-2146; **Holy Grounds** ($) 245 Main 882-3502; **Pangea** ($$) 250 Main Street 882-3001; **Point Arena Cafe** ($-$$) 210 Main 882-2110; **Point Arena General Store & Deli** ($) 185 Main Street 882-2280; **S&B Market** ($) 19400 Hwy 1, Manchester 882-2805.

**POINT ARENA to MANCHESTER LODGING:**
**Coast Guard House** ($$-$$$) 695 Arena Cove Rd. 882-2442; **Manchester Beach KOA** ($-$$) Box 266 - 1 mile north of Manchester 882-2375; **Manchester State Beach** ($) Box 440, 1 mile north of Manchester 800-444-PARK / 937-5804; **Point Arena Bed & Breakfast** ($$) 300 Main Street 882-3455; **Point Arena Lighthouse & Museum** ($$) Box 11, 4 miles north of Point Arena on Lighthouse Rd. 882-2777; **Rollerville Junction** ($-$$) Box 383, Hwy 1 - 2 miles north of Point Arena; **Sea Shell Inn** ($$) 135 Main 882-2000/2068; **Wharf Master's Inn** ($$-$$$) 785 Port Street 800-932-4031.

**POINT ARENA BOOKSTORES, GIFTSHOPS and the ARTS**
**Du Pont's Mendocino Merchantile** 790 Port Rd. 882-3017, **Everything Under the Sun** 211 Main Street 882-2161.

**MENDOCINO COAST THINGS TO DO:**
**Fishing and Surfing and Whale Watching:**
**Arena Theater** - Concerts, Drama and Motion Pictures 882-2275.
**Arena Cove Fishing Pier** 882-2583 Hot showers, boat launching & fishing.

The 320 foot fishing pier at Arena Cove is the only major public pier between Pacifica and Trinidad.    Fishing, hot showers, whale and bird watcing are all benefits of the pier.

## THE GALLEY Pierside Restaurant at Point Arena Cove

There is an authentic rugged appeal about the Point Arena Cove.  Caught in a time warp and cradled between white cliffs similar to Dover, it could easily pass for a tiny settlement clinging to the sheep dotted edge of the English Coast.

During the Big Surf Year of 1983 the cove got extremely hairy when a log-lifting grandfather wave came through and knocked out the original pier, flooding the packed restaurant with a blast of saltwater up to the bar top.  People inside were knocked around like bowling pins. Heavy rains and the highest tide of the century made the surf so rough it tore the heads off ling cod and popped abalone right out of their shell.   It was a day many locals will never forget, for many lives were spared by sheer luck.

Today the restaurant occupies the 2nd floor of a brand new building and is under the direction of Tim Newman.  A menu of petrale sole, halibut, swordfish, snapper, shark, salmon, Ahi tuna, albacore, oysters, clams, crab and lobster is served.  Some of the fresh catch is unloaded off the boats barely 100 feet away.  Dinners include garden fresh salad, cup of soup or chowder, baked potato, French fried potatoes or mixed wild and white rice as well as fresh vegetables and assorted homemade breads.  There are delicious home cooked daily specials and always a selection of steaks, chops and chicken entrees.  Sushi is served on Friday and Saturday.  Tim and his staff also cater special events creating custom menus and amenities for up to 200 people.

There is a full bar where mixed drinks are blended and imported & domestic beer, wine and soft drinks are served.  San Franciscan's recognize the huge hand carved back bar which came around the horn in 1890.  At 6 p.m. the Arena Cove Bar often fills up with rugged locals tied to the land and sea. Good food and real people in a hearty natural setting often make the best vacation memories.

The Cove has changed since the 1980's —a new concrete and steel fishing pier replaces the old wooden pier destroyed by heavy seas in 1983.  The new Point Arena Pier is 320 feet long and is equipped with heavy duty lifting hoists for small boats and loads of fish and sea urchins.  There is also a harbor master's office, restrooms, showers and public benches on the end of the pier for whale and wave watching. The pier and shoreline is also a good spot for surfing, beach walks and abalone picking at low tide.

*$-$$ GALLEY RESTAURANT  End of Port Street, Box 326,  Point Arena, Seafood and American  Open daily. Dis., MC & Visa  (707) 882-2189  Res.*

### WHARF MASTER'S INN

Prior to telephones in the late 1800's, a panoramic view was important for supervising the busy seaport activities at Point Arena Cove. In Arena Cove the wharfmaster could be in his cliffside home and still literally oversee activities at the port.

Today the century old Wharfmaster's House is registered with the National Historical Society and is complimented by three new two story wings of luxurious and functional accommodations (finished in 1992) boasting unobstructed views of the valley, fishing fleet and pier, reefs, white cliffs and open sea. Twenty three rooms and suites await from $95 - $175/2. Accommodations feature fireplaces, jacuzzi tubs, queen sized four poster feather beds, direct dial telephones, private baths, and open air balconies facing the ocean. All rooms are equipped with coffee makers. The crown jewel is the Wharfmaster's House, with three bedrooms, a whirlpool jacuzzi, fully equipped gourmet kitchen, dining room and parlor with fireplace. Ask about the special facilities for weddings and receptions.

Besides being a surfers headquarters, there are several biking and hiking trails in the area. "Breath-giving" views recharge the lungs with some of the cleanest air in America and offer a cardio-vascular workout the heart will love you for. You can study the coastal geology by day and scan the clear skys at night for heavenly constellations. You can also try your luck at beachcombing, tidepooling or fishing from the pier. To arrive at the Wharfmaster's Inn take the Iverson Avenue exit off State Highway 1 at the south end of town. Bon Voyage!

*$$-$$$WHARFMASTER'S INN Box 674, 785 Port Street, Point Arena, CA. Oceanview Rooms & Suites    Fireplaces & Private Baths    AE, MC & Visa. (707) 932-4031 Info   www.wharfmastersinn.com   1-800-932-4031 Res. Sug.*

## COAST GUARD HOUSE HISTORIC INN

Innkeeper's Mia & Kevin Gallagaher offer landscaped grounds and an excellent vantage point for observing the California Grey whale whose migratory path leads them just off-shore from their historic Coast Guard House. It was built by the Life Saving Service in 1901 and taken over by the U.S. Coast Guard and became officially known as the Life Saving Station at Arena Cove. "Surfmen", launched many daring sea rescues from here. Richey Wasserman and Merita Whatley opened this historic building in 1988.

The furnishings and decor chosen for Coast Guard House reflect the classic lines of the Arts and Crafts Period, 1875 to 1920. Simple lines and natural materials evoke a directness of purpose - - a perfect balance of beauty and function. Among the carefully chosen interior touches are billowy comforters, all-cotton linens and toiletries selected for their pure, natural qualities. The five guest rooms and a separate cottage, from $115, all have private baths. A delicious full breakfast awaits guests each morning. Schooner, the Gallagaher's black & white border collie, will greet you at the door and loves to go on walks with guests.

*$$ COAST GUARD HOUSE*
*Oceanview Bed & Breakfast   P.O. Box 117, 695 Arena Cove, Point Arena,*
*www.coastguardhouse.com  MC & Visa.  1-800-524-9320 / (707) 882-2442*

### DU PONT'S MENDOCINO MERCANTILE at Arena Cove

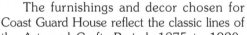

Born and raised in Point Arena, Tracy Du Pont, the towns former mayor, has reason to be proud of the original Mendocino County merchandise she loves to showcase. Visitors will discover a meticulous selection of arts and crafts and gourmet goodies gathered from obscure backwoods studios, wine cellars, herb gardens and the finest gourmet kitchens in Mendocino County. Attractive displays reveal pottery, jewelry, oil & watercolor paintings, toys, dried flower arrangements, antiques and craft items for the home or office. Edibles include jams & jellies, chocolates, coffees, organic herbs & seasonings, beer from county brew pubs and vintages of Mendocino wine.  At Arena Cove small is indeed beautiful.  In another section of the shop there are snack foods,  chilled beverages and gift items including Arena Cove T-shirts. Du Pont's is open daily but Tuesday.

*$-$$ DU PONT'S MENDOCINO MERCANTILE*
*Locally Made Arts,Crafts & Gourmet Goodies   790 Port Rd., Suites 4 & 6,*
*Point Arena, CA. 95468                                    (707) 882-3017*

## ARENA MULTI MEDIA THEATER

One of the last real theaters in northern California, the historic Arena Theater, offers a variety of current and vintage movies, as well as star spangled live musical events. This is no ordinary theater folks, for it has been open since 1929. It is home town theater at its best. The restoration project was generated through the Arena Renaissance Company and community fundraising, and all the labor was donated with great love and heart. With its art deco flair and unique charm, it offers balcony seating, and in the lobby a variety of snacks are served, including homemade double chocolate brownies, organic popcorn with real butter and seasonings, and hot and cold drinks. They even have an antique movie camera on display! The experience alone is worth a stop in Point Arena where you can enjoy dinner followed by a show at the Arena Theater.

*$ ARENA MULTI MEDIA THEATER     214 Main Street, Point Arena, CA.*
*Movies and Special Entertainment Events          Showing # (707) 882-2275*

**COSMIC PIZZA**     Point Arena's Cosmic Pizza offers views of bobbing fishing boats and crashing waves at Arena Cove Pier. The owners create delicious light crusted California fresh pizzas topped with a garden of fresh produce (some locally grown in Point Arena). Each sourdough pizza ($5.00 - $17.50) is beautifully presented with a choice of 2 dozen ingredients. A salad bar and cauldrons of piping hot homemade soup round out your meal. Calzones, vegetarian combo's, light lunches, desserts, ice cream, sodas, beer, wine and cups of piping hot fresh brewed coffee are also served.

*$-$$ COSMIC PIZZA          End of Port Street, Point Arena, CA. 95468*
*Pizza, Calzone, Salad, Beer & Coffee Drinks   (707) 882-1900 Orders to go.*

**SEA SHELL INN**  For years Point Arena has been in a time warp with descendants of pioneer settlers keeping a tight reign on the town's growth and direction. Some visitors find this refreshing. A late bloomer, Point Arena could very well become the gemstone of the north coast; that is if thoughtful and sensitive planning prevails. A good place to observe all this is by hanging your hat at the Sea Shell Inn in Point Arena, which is under new management. There are 32 spacious, clean and economical rooms where tourists and locals put into port, to watch color-cable TV and enjoy time away from home or work. Motel rooms are equipped with kings, queens, doubles, direct dial telephones (local calls free) and coffee makers. Seasonal rates are economical. Behind the units you can hear Point Arena creek cheerfully making its way to nearby Arena Cove and the Pacific. Wildflowers and an occasional deer grace the hillsides above.

*$-$$ SEA SHELL INN  Box 393, 135 Main Street, Point Arena, CA 95468*
*Motel Rooms and Suites                 (707) 882-2000/2068 Res. advised.*

**POINT ARENA GENERAL STORE and DELI**   The Point Arena General Store and Deli is one of the more complete and functional general stores on the Mendocino Coast.   This spacious store fulfills the needs of campers, fishermen and shoppers.   Fresh fish and locally grown produce (in season) are available as well as a variety of health food and gourmet items.   The wine selection represents Mendocino's finest wineries and there is also a selection of locally made and certified organic wine.   From the deli comes an assortment of sandwich meats to T-bone steaks and all the necessities for an afternoon picnic.   The video movie rental section (with VCR) features a wide variety of movie releases.   You will find proprietors Lillian, Tor and Captain Ole Holberg-olsen's seafaring family to be very hospitable and informative on fishing and weather conditions.   The Point Arena General Store and Deli is open everyday of the year from 6 am to 7 pm.
*$ POINT ARENA GENERAL STORE & DELI      185 Main Street, Point Arena,*
*General Store and Deli            CA. 95468      (707) 882-2280 Information*

### EVERYTHING UNDER THE SUN

The simplicity and beauty of Third World living is reflected by the art, crafts and clothing displayed at Everything Under the Sun.   Proprietress Lena Bullamore is proud of the fact that she supports socially conscious gift giving by buying from non-profit organizations who insure that the craftspeople in Vietnam and Africa as well as two dozen other countries get a fair wage for their efforts.   There is a "story" behind each item in the store, making shopping here a unique lesson in creativity and awareness.    It's a treat to meet Lena whose enthusiasm and spirit is everywhere in Everything Under the Sun!  Open 11:30am - 5:00pm Wednesday thru Saturday.
*$$ EVERYTHING UNDER THE SUN       211 Main St., Point Arena, CA.*
*Local and Third World Crafts  Closed Sun, Mon, Tues. (707) 882-2161*

### PANGAEA

Proprietors Shannon Hughes and Mark Pearce offer a winning combination of quality and nutritious food.   Globally influenced recipes feature the cuisine of South America, Africa, Europe, Asia and the Mediterranean.   The word Pangaea is Old Greek and means all the continents were once connected before earth changes and plate tectonics moved them to their current positions.   Bold and innovative, chef/proprietress Shannan Hughes serves hearty country portions which are beautifully presented.   Fresh local in-season organic produce, fresh fish and homemade, yet creative recipes provide a memorable dining experience.   Dinner entrees include fresh fish such as salmon Ahi tuna or crab cakes on Thai curry sauce, roast poultry or game bird, Niman Schell beef and vegetarian creations (from $9.00).   California wines, micro brew beers, fresh brewed coffee drinks and homemade desserts are also served.
*$$ PANGAEA                    250 Main Street,  Point Arena, CA. 95468*
*California Country Cuisine      MC & Visa  Open Wed - Sun from 5:30pm*
*Winter hours may vary.    Call for reservations and info.    (707) 882-3001*

## POINT ARENA CAFE and BED & BREAKFAST

Those of us raised in the city may have dreamed of living in a small town by the sea in a large country home. The Point Arena Bed & Breakfast (built in 1908) offers warm and cozy rooms which join a common area, living room with wood stove, dining room with fireplace and puzzle and game room.

Your innkeepers will prepare breakfast for you or you can dine at the Point Arena Cafe, which is a short walk away. The Point Arena Bed & Breakfast offers European style accommodations. Rates are reasonable; 2 to 3 can rent a room for $50-$75/night or small groups can economically rent the whole inn.

Also available a short drive up Mountainview Road are 2 cottages ($85 each) with private baths, hot tub and one with kitchenette where you can cook a gourmet meal or perhaps a fresh fish you caught at the end of Point Arena's pier.

*$-$$ POINT ARENA BED & BREAKFAST    300 Main Street, Point Arena*
*Bed and Breakfast Rooms and Cottages       (707) 882-3455 Reservations*

## ROLLERVILLE JUNCTION

Just 2 miles north of Point Arena, at the lighthouse access road, is the Rollerville Junction Campground and Giftshop. It is simple shelter at its best. From fire pits the scent of burning logs and evening fare wafts over the grounds. Owners Pat and Sharon Bellew are usually busy in their well-stocked, cupola-roofed giftshop. There are 51 sites scattered over the roomy 1/4mile front (41 full-service RV hook-ups; 10 tent sites with fire pits and water and 5 new camping cabins with room for 2 adults & 2 children in each). A large swimming pool and hot tub add to the amenities of staying at Rollerville Junction. Hot showers, a laundry room, and plenty of firewood add to your convenience. Let the flickering beacon of the historic Point Arena Lighthouse guide you to this special setting.

*$ ROLLERVILLE JUNCTION CAMPGROUND AND GIFTSHOP*
*Box 383, Point Arena, CA 95468    (707) 882-2440. Res & Information*

## POINT ARENA LIGHTHOUSE

Poised on a narrow peninsula and surrounded by white water on three sides, are the accommo- dations of the Point Arena Lighthouse, just north of Point Arena. It's a thrilling stay, especially when flights of rare whistling swans have landed in the Garcia River valley just to the north; their honks occasionally heard over the breaking surf. Ever vigilant, the now automated lighthouse beacon provides early warning for ships at sea of the dangerous reefs. The original French handcut two ton crystal and brass lens was turned off for good in 1977, but can be viewed as part of a living museum under the direction of the Point Arena Lighthouse Keepers, Inc. Three remodeled guest homes await (originally Coast Guard quarters with the helicopter pad nearby and still often used). Modern day creature comforts have been added to this one time military installation. The fabulous views, peace and tranquility is most relaxing.

*$$ POINT ARENA LIGHTHOUSE   P.O. Box 11, Point Arena, CA 95468*
*Historic Oceanview Accommodations        (707) 882-2777 Res. Advised*

## S & B MARKET INC.

Burney Sjolund came home to the Mendocino Coast in 1945 from the San Francisco shipyards with $10,000 and settled in Manchester just 10 miles from where he was raised as a kid in Elk. He and his wife Dorothy and her father A. O. Stornetta purchased the Manchester General Store, which was established way back in the late 1800's. They remodeled and renamed it the S & B Market. Today their son Alan and wife Karen operate this important link to the modern world of conveniences. A true general store, the S & B Market stocks everything for the everyday needs of residents and travelers. Besides a full line of groceries, including fresh produce and choice cuts of beef and poultry, there are premium wines, snack foods, kitchen and camping supplies. A complete hardware store stocks all manner of building supplies as well as automotive needs. A lifeline during inclement weather or challenging coastal conditions, the S & B Market is open daily from 8am - 7pm.

*$-$$$ S & B GENERAL STORE*          *19400 South Hwy 1, Manchester,*
*Full Service Grocery & Hardware*       *CA. 95459*        *MC & Visa*
*Fax (707) 882-3105*         *Phone (707) 882-2805  For Information*

## MANCHESTER BEACH KOA

Cozy Kamping Cabins at Manchester Beach KOA are ideal for families of four.

Secluded by walls of evergreen from the highway and sheltered from brisk ocean wind, guests to the Manchester Beach KOA can truly experience the coast at a first class family resort campground. Soothing barefoot walks across a lush carpet of grass and pine needles as the ocean breezes murmur through the tops of the trees is a treat. Children are delighted to learn that deer and whistling swans are safe here and occasionally visit the edge of the 125 campsites (tent site $28) There are also 18 new log Kamping Kabins ($115 / 4) available and a wonderful flower garden setting to explore with over 140 wild and hybrid varieties of rhododendron. This KOA is for abalone divers, salmon and steelhead fishermen.

There are two large group areas, a hot tub and jacuzzi, swimming pool, a laundry room, giftshop, game room, full RV hook-ups and secluded campsites (seasonal rates are reasonable). Here you can forget your cares by gazing at your campfire or the starlit sky above your base camp, the Manchester Beach KOA.

$ MANCHESTER BEACH KOA     P.O. Box 266, Manchester, CA. 95459
Coastal Campground     5 miles north of Point Arena & just west of Hwy 1
Secluded campsites, log cabins,     AE, Disc, MC & Visa.
fire pits, full RV hook-ups,     http: www.mcn.org/a/mendokoa/
jacuzzi & pool, beaches & trails.     (707) 882-2375 Reservations & Info.

## MANCHESTER STATE PARK:   Located on the San Andreas Fault

Surrounding the western side of Manchester is Manchester State Park. Access can be gained at the south by Stoneboro Road and north by Kinney Road. Forty primitive campsites are located amid grassland with Monterey Cypress and sand dunes for wind breaks. Campsites accommodate tents or RV's up to 30 feet long. Each campsite has a picnic table and fire ring with a grill. Water is available and pit toilets are nearby. Sites are first come, first serve. No reservations are accepted. There also is a group camp that can accommodate up to 12 vehicles and 40 people. The group camp may be reserved May 1st through October 1st.

Two creeks flow year round in the park; Brush Creek located near the center of the park and Alder Creek which is on the north boundary. Alder Creek also marks the location where the San Andreas Fault slips beneath the sea to silently await God's commandment to determine the fate of coastal humankind. On rare occassions campers will feel a tremor while sleeping beneath a night time sky full of stars. Such an experience is both humbling and very inspirational.

$ MANCHESTER STATE PARK     P.O. Box 440, Mendocino, CA. 95460
Oceanview Campground     1-800-444-PARK / (707) 937-5804

# THE INLAND VALLEYS
## Petaluma to Hopland

The Inland Valleys north of San Francisco are full of wonder and discovery. Especially scenic are country lanes such Westside Road (west of Healdsburg) and Highways 116 and 128 in the Russian River Valley and Alexander Valley respectively. Pictured is Highway 101 just north of Geyserville where row upon row of vineyard reach as far as the eye can see.

# MAP INLAND VALLEYS

## FARM TRAILS, THE WINE COUNTRY, LOWER and UPPER RUSSIAN RIVER VALLEYS and THE REDWOOD FORESTS

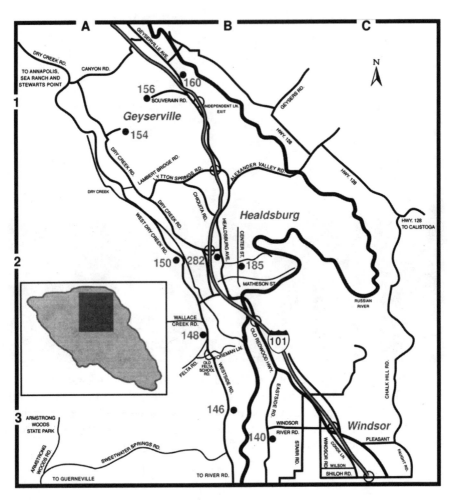

This map is numbered to show Farm Trails destinations.  See Farm Trails Section beginning on page 137.  Other inland valley maps are in the Centerfold - pages 154-157.

## SCENIC DRIVES:
## GETTING THERE THRU PETALUMA
**Exit Highway 101 by way of Washington Avenue to
Bodega Avenue; and take State Highway 1 to Bodega Bay.**

Along the banks
of the Petaluma
River and Petaluma
Boulevard are
quaint cafes, coffee
and dinner houses,
art galleries, antique
shops and night
clubs.  Farms and
ranches surround
the broad river
valley Petaluma
grew up in.

# PETALUMA
# HISTORIC RIVER TOWN
# and former WORLD'S EGG BASKET

Known for its tree lined streets  and elegant victorian mansions, Petaluma
is also the dining capitol of Sonoma County with more restaurants per person
than any other community.  Surrounded by rolling hills, dairy farms and
ranches, Petaluma is also a destination for the bounty northern California
farmers and ranchers produce. Egg production earned Petaluma the title of
"The World's Egg Basket".   At the turn of the century timber and eggs made
there way by barge to an eagerly awaiting populace in the unfolding city to the
south known as San Francisco.  Today, downtown night clubs, theaters, bed &
breakfast inns, cafes and galleries make a stroll down Petaluma Boulevard fun.

If Petaluma's "Anytown, U.S.A." looks familar, its because several motion
pictures including American Graffiti and Peggy Sue Got Married, as well as  TV
commercails were filmed there.   The city is made for strolling, with tree-lined
neighborhoods and a turn-of-the-century downtown.  Pick up free historic
walking tour brochures from the Petaluma Area Chamber of Commerce, the
Museum, or various bookshops.  Petaluma's River Walk includes a pleasant
downtown park, yachts bobbing in the Turning Basin where steamboat races
once took place and a look at the Great Petaluma Mill, a riverfront complex of
galleries, botiques and restaurants.  You"ll find Petalumans warm and friendly
and your stay enjoyable.

**PETALUMA DINER'S CHOICE:  Telephone Area Code is (707).**
**On Petaluma Boulevard: Apple Box** ($),  Petaluma Blvd. N. at 224 B St.  762-5222;
**Cafe Passport** ($), 160 Petaluma Blvd. N. 778-6470;  **Deaf Dog Coffee** ($), 134 Petaluma
Blvd. N. 762-3656;  **Graziano's Ristorante** ($$$) 170 Petaluma Blvd. N. 762-5997;  **Le
Bistro** ($$), 312 Petaluma Blvd. S. 762-8292; **McNear's Saloon & Restaurant** ($$), 23
Petaluma Blvd. N. 765-2121;  **Old Chicago Pizza** ($$), 41 Petaluma Blvd. N. 763-3897;
**Original Marvin's** ($$), Petaluma Blvd. S. 765-2808;  **Thai Cuisine** ($$), 610 Petaluma
Blvd. N. 769-8802;  **Thai Issan** ($$), 208 Petaluma Blvd. N. 762-5966.

**Western Avenue: La Famiglia Deli Cafe**  ($) 220 Western Ave. 778-8211;  **Pedroni's
Delicatessen**  ($), 16 Western Ave.  762-7000;

**Kentucky Street: Aram's Cafe** ($), 131 Kentucky 765-9775;  **Buona Sera** ($$), 148
Kentucky St. 763-3333;  **Petaluma Natural Foods**  ($-$$), 137 Kentucky St.  762-8522.

**Washington Street: Dempsey's Ale House** ($$), 50 E. Washington 765-9694;  **Food For
Thought** ($-$$), 621 E. Washington 762-9352;  **Kwei Bien Chinese** ($$), 613 E.
Washington  778-6939;  **JM Rosen's Bakery & Waterfront Grill**  ($$), 54 E. Washington
773-3200;  **Mary's Pizza**  ($$), 359 E. Washington 778-7200;  **Volpi's Deli & Speakeasy**
($), 124 Washington St. 762-2371.

**McDowell Boulevard: Hunan Village** ($$), 295 N. McDowell  763-7156;
**Jerome's** ($), 1394 N. McDowell 795-2114; **Johnson's Oyster & Seafood Co.** ($$), 253
N. McDowell 763-4161;  **Lakeville Garden Chinese Cuisine** ($$), 1410 S. McDowell 778-
1872;  **Romeo's Sourdough Pizza** ($$), 239 S. McDowell
762-6668.

**Various Other Dining Locations:  De Schmire** ($$$), 304 Bodega Ave. 762-1901;
**Giacomo's Ristorante & Pizzeria** ($$), 2000 Lakeville Hwy 765-1700;  **River House** ($$$)
222 Weller 769-0123;  **Petaluma Coffee Company** ($), 189 H Street at First & H Sts. in the
Foundry Wharf  763-272;  **Tivioli II Saloon & Restaurant** ($), 219 Lakeview St.  762-9927;
**Two Niner Diner** ($), 561 Sky Ranch Dr. 765-2900;  **Sonoma Joe's Casino** ($$), 5151
Montero Way 795-6121;  **Sonoma Taco Shop** ($), 953 Lakeville Hwy  778-1050;  and the
famous **Washoe House** ($$), at Stony Point & Roblar Rds. take Petaluma Blvd. north to stop
light and Denny's Restaurant;  turn left on Stony Point Rd. and go 7 miles  795-4544.

**ATTRACTIONS:  Great Petaluma Mill,** a collection of over 20 specialty shops and
restaurants in downtown Petaluma.

**GREAT OUTDOORS: Moreda's Sporting Goods** ($-$$$),  114 Petaluma Blvd. North
762-8082.

**HEALTH & FITNESS: Redwood Club** ($) 719 Southpoint Blvd. 778-8788.
**24 Hour Fitness** ($) #6 Petaluma Blvd N.  789-9050.

**PETALUMA LIVE MUSIC & DANCING**
**Kodiac Jacks**($) Petaluma Blvd. N.  765-5760;  **McNear's Saloon & Restaurant** ($$), 23
Petaluma Blvd. N. 765-2121.

# MAP of PETALUMA

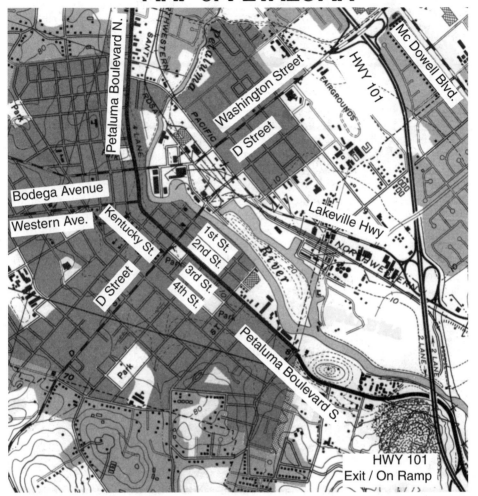

**PETALUMA THEATERS & CINEMA**
**Cinnabar Theater** ($-$$), 763-8920; **Mystic Theater & Music Hall** ($$), 21
Petaluma Blvd. N. 765-6665; **Copperfield's Bookstore Special Author Events**
($), 153 Kentucky 762-0563; **Pacific Petaluma Cinema's** ($), 1363 N. McDowell
Blvd. 769-0700 **Washington Square Cinemas 5** ($), 219 S. McDowell Blvd.
762-0006.

**PETALUMA LODGING**
**Best Western Petaluma Inn** ($$), 200 S. McDowell 763-0994; **Cavanagh Inn
Bed & Breakfast** ($$), 10 Keller St. 765-4657; **KOA San Francisco North /
Petaluma Campground** ($), 20 Rainsville Rd. 763-1492; **Motel 6** ($), 1368
Mc Dowell Blvd. N. 664-9090; **Quality Inn** ($$), 5100 Montero Way 664-1155.

## CENTER CITY DINER - An American Bistro

Located right in the heart of Petaluma with upscale decor and California cuisine is Center City - An American Bistro. When chef/owners Michael and Diane Valmassoi moved to Petaluma to raise their family and open Center City Diner, they brought a wonderful originality.   Large plate glass windows, an old fashioned soda fountain bar with cozy booths in the back for you and your sweetie make dining comfortable at this upscale American Bistro.   But don't expect the normal fries and burgers from Michael.  Large three egg omelettes loaded with seasonal vegetables, eggs benedict with homemade English muffin and hollandaise sauce, French toast and cereals are great ways to start the day.

A basket of homemade Foccacia bread is served with your lunch special. Mixed green salad, the soup of the day sprinkled with a "fresh breeze" of herbs, gourmet veggie burgers, Center City burgers piled high with fresh vegetables and cheeses and delicious vegetarian or smoked salmon pizzetta's are served.   There are homemade milk shakes, ice cream sundaes with homemade chocolate or caramel sauce and banana splits from the fountain.

Dinner specials include the finest and freshest selections of seafood, beef, poultry and game - grilled, roasted, braised and poached with fresh organic herbs and served with the most delicious of sauces.  Homemade desserts include baked apple tart and creme brulee.   Center City Diner is open Mon - Fri 10am - 9pm, Saturday 8am - 9:30pm and Sunday Brunch served from 8am to 8pm.

*$-$$ CENTER CITY       107 Petaluma Blvd. N., Petaluma, CA  94952*
*An American Bistro / California Cuisine     MC & Visa   (707) 766-9232*

## DEAF DOG COFFEE

Located just up the boulevard from Petaluma's "Barmuda Triangle" of dance bars is Deaf Dog Coffee. This pleasant alternative, with rich red brick interior, is operated by Ron Salisbury,  a ambitious coffee entreprenuer who grew up 50 miles from the rocky Atlantic coastline of Maine.  Now he lives and works 30 miles from the Pacific.  "Post", the Deaf Dog mascot, is an Australian Heeler who was born deaf but is an extremely talented best friend who lives with the Salisbury family.

Ron also owns the popular Deaf Dog Coffee House located on the east side of Highway 101 in Petaluma's Washington Square shopping center.  Both locations serve the finest coffee beans from around the world as well as fresh baked goods and desserts and a light daily menu.    The coolers overflow with chilled juices, mineral waters, root beer and sodas.  Open 6:30am - 9:30pm Mon - Thur / 6:30am - 10:00pm Fri & Sat and 7am - 7pm Sun.  Ron also operates drive-thru espresso stops and the Deaf Dog is on the move to other locations as well.

*$ DEAF DOG COFFEE                Coffee House Sit down or to go*
*134 Petaluma Blvd. North, Petaluma, CA. 94952      (707) 762-3656*
*351 S. McDowell Blvd., Petaluma, CA. 94954          (707) 763-8111*

Located in the very heart of Petaluma is the historic two story brick Mc Near's building.  It was built by entrepeneur John McNear in 1886, who also constructed the Mc Near Mill and helped with the dredging of the Petaluma River which became the major avenue of commerce for Sonoma County's farm, ranch & timber products.

## Mc NEAR'S SALOON & RESTAURANT
At the long bar of McNear's Saloon mixed drinks, beer and wine is served while patrons enjoy a variety of sporting events on the big TV screen.  Fresh fish, poultry, steaks and prime rib, garden fresh salads, and homemade soups are served in the dining room.  A late night menu is served until 1am nightly.  Upstairs are pool tables, another bar and live music is played on the weekends.  On warm summer evenings there is side walk dining al fresco with the chef grilling BBQ'd oysters on the weekends.  It's a pleasant setting, especially during full moons.
*$-$$ American Cuisine     23 Petaluma Blvd. N., MC, Visa,   (707) 765-2121*

## Mc NEAR'S MYSTIC THEATER & MUSIC HALL
Next door to the saloon and restaurant is the Mystic Theater & Music Hall where big named musicians and entertainers perform all year round.  A bar and dance floor add to the entertainment.  Call (707) 765-6665 for monthly showtimes and dates.  Formerly a motion picture theater, the Mystic can be rented for private parties, banquets and special events such as film festivals.
*$ McNear's Mystic Theater  21 Petaluma Blvd. N., Petaluma  (707) 765-6665*

### DEMPSEY'S RESTAURANT & BREWERY

Peter and Bernadette Burrell have created one of the most popular restaurant/brew pubs in northern California.  The cuisine and beer is excellent and Dempsey's Brew Pub is often packed.  Brews include Ugly Dog Stout, Golden Eagle Ale, Red Rooster Ale and Bad Bear Brown Ale and are sold on tap.
Bernadette serves winter soups, summertime gaspacho, spinach and gourmet mixed salad greens, mashed potatoes & gravy, vegetarian and cheese burgers with house cut fries, crab cakes, New Orleans gumbo with rice, roast chicken and homemade desserts.  Dining is indoors or outside along the promenade on the riverfront. Find the wooden bridge in downtown Petaluma and find the beer at Dempsey's Brew Pub and a lot more.
*$-$$ DEMPSEY'S BREW PUB and the SONOMA BREWING COMPANY*
*Continental Cuisine        50 E. Washington St., Petaluma, CA. 94952*
*Beer and Wine,  MC & Visa  (707) 765-9694 Reservations & Information*

## Le BISTRO

This charming dinner house is an ideal hideaway for that special someone in your life. The flower known as intimacy blossoms amid the cozy decor and exceptional French-Mediterranean cuisine served at Le Bistro.  Chef/owner Corey Basso has made a commitment to serve only the freshest seasonings, garden produce, seafood, meats and poultry. Dinners can begin with a Caesar salad or roma tomato and mozzarella salad (seasonal) with virgin olive oil and raspberry vinegar, the homemade soup of the day or the Chef's appetizer special.  Entrees include the fresh fish special from king salmon to swordfish, pasta fettuccini with prawns (vodka, cream and crushed chili flake sauce), grilled lamb tenderloin served with cabernet red current sauce or grilled fillet mignon with Stilton cheese and red wine.  The homemade desserts are divine.  There is a selection of premium wines which go well with the amorous candlelight and stained glass. As your relationship grows why not affirm all that is wonderful about your special friend or soulmate at Le Bistro.

*$$ Le BISTRO        312 Petaluma Boulevard S., Petaluma, CA. 94952*
*French Mediterranean Cuisine                    MC & Visa*
*Open Wednesday - Sunday  from 5pm        (707) 762-8292 Reservations*

## ORIGINAL MARVINS RESTAURANT

The Original Marvins restaurant has healthfully and heartily served breakfast and lunch to Petalumans in an old creamery building since 1979.  The recipes are freshly prepared daily using fresh local Sonoma County farm and ranch products.  Omelettes, the specialty of the house, come right from Petaluma, the egg capital of the world. Awesome omelettes are loaded with sauteed vegetables and sausages handmade locally.  Meat eaters wolf down New York steaks and eggs, Italian or country sausage and English bangers.  The sides of bacon were voted Best in Petaluma by their discriminating clientele.

The high fiber oriented enjoy nutritious fresh squeezed sunshine (orange juice), a serving of fresh fruit & granola, pancakes, waffles, oatmeal with raisins or grilled maple walnut muffins.   Lunch is a soup - salad - sandwich affair featuring two dozen sandwiches, garden fresh salads and homemade soup.

The Original Marvins is located on the same boulevard where the movie "American Graffiti" was filmed.

*$-$$ ORIGINAL MARVINS   317 Petaluma Boulevard S., Petaluma, CA.*
*American  Cuisine                MC & Visa        (707) 765-2808*

## PETALUMA COFFEE COMPANY

The Petaluma Coffee Company has quickly caught fire as a popular gathering place for up-beat and original thinkers who live and work in Petaluma. Many begin their day here over a piping hot cup of espresso, cappuccino, cafe latte', cafe mocha, selection of teas, fresh juices, mineral water and freshly delivered pastries. Only God knows what creative endeavors they will accomplish by days end.

The scent of fresh roasted hot coffee beans from around the world wafts out of the French door entrance like a seductive cloud to waft down the street, enticing passerbys inside. Proprietress Sheila Bride and her dedicated staff serve light luncheons such as pasta salads, sandwiches and tortas. The comraderia and spirit of this riverside cafe insures it's continued success.

*$ PETALUMA COFFEE COMPANY  2nd & H Streets in the Foundry Wharf*
*Fresh Roasted Coffee, Pastries & "Lite" Luncheons   Petaluma, CA. 94952*
*Open Mon. - Fri. 6:30am - 6:30pm,  Sat. 7:30am-5pm and  Sun. 8am-2pm*
*MC & Visa.        1-800-929-JAVA    (707) 763-2727  Sit down or to go.*

## J.M.  ROSEN'S Bakery and Waterfront Grill

"Local sister's become famous" is a phrase that describes well the Rosen sisters - Jan and Michele. Born and raised in Petaluma, Jan and Michele opened their award winning cheesecake bakery in 1976, the year America celebrated its 200th birthday.

*J.M.Rosen's*
**WATERFRONT GRILL**

Rich, creamy - sensational - the crowning achievement of dairy country is the J.M. Rosen cheesecake.

Today you'll find Jan and Michele at the J.M. Rosen's Waterfront Grill, located on the Petaluma River in the Golden Eagle Shopping Center. Indoor / Outdoor dining on fresh seasonal produce, seafood, poultry, meats and pasta is why the dining room is often packed. Tables are set with cobalt blue goblets, silverware, beige rattan chairs and of all things overhead Martian orange lights There is also a list of premium California wines, espresso and mineral water to quench the thirst. Call for hours and reservations.

*$$ J.M. ROSEN'S        54 East Washington Street, Petaluma, CA. 94952*
*Cheesecake Wholesale: (707) 773-4655  Cheesecake Retail: (707) 763-9644*
*Continental Cuisine  MC & Visa          (707) 773-3200 Reservations Sug.*

## GRAZIANO'S RISTORANTE

One of the finest Italian restaurants in Sonoma County is located on Petaluma Boulevard, the main drag in George Lucas's film "American Graffiti". You can leave the hustle of the boulevard by walking under the big green canopies of Graziano's Ristorante. Inside is a charming Italian restaurant where family is important. The aquamarine interior is complimented by white table linens and true grapevine decor surrounded by wines from all over the country. At the handcrafted oak bar you can enjoy a fine drink from a wide selection ranging from micro beer on tap, to well drinks. The wine list which is awarded yearly by "The Wine Spectator", includes champagnes, dessert wines, ports and rare vintages from California, France and Italy. Special samplings by the glass are just part of the daily offerings. Upstairs is Club Notte, a night club where you can dance into the wee hours of the evening. Club Notte can also be rented for special events.

Possessing a gentle boyish face and unusual culinary abilities, chef/owner Graziano Perozzi, magically blends herbs and spices with traditional and imported Italian delicacies into "New Italian Cuisine." The aromas that waft over the counter from the kitchen are delectable. In the exhibition kitchen the dedicated chef tries never to forget how important it is to have fun with the guests and entrees. "Have a little sample of the Panzotti," he says to a curious guest. A delightful smile takes shape and Graziano has won over another patron. Dinner entrees are served with soup or salad and French bread, vegetables, pasta and rice. All entrees are prepared individually using certified organic fresh local produce, whenever possible. Over a dozen varieties are served daily ranging from Panzotti to Gnocchi al Pesto. A very exciting selection of seafood, garden and farm fresh entrees as well as house specialties await you for dinner. If you like fine food prepared to please, you'll truly appreciate Graziano's Ristorante.

*$$ GRAZIANO'S RISTORANTE     Dinners Tues - Sun, 5:30pm - 10:00pm*
*New Italian Cuisine          170 N. Petaluma Blvd., Petaluma, CA 94952*
*Full Bar & Night Club        MC & Visa   (707) 762-5997 Reservations*

## THAI ISSAN

Thai Issan is a royal dining experience located in a landmark Petaluma building at the busy corner of Petaluma Blvd. and Washington Street. The spacious dining room is big enough for a herd of trumpeting elephants. The Xiong family, from the Thai Issan region in Thailand, have captured the appetites of Sonoma County residents with an extensive array of authentic Thai delicacies. "Issan" denotes prosperity and vastness in the Thai language.

An extensive menu, which is changed seasonally, consists of appetizers, salads, soups, curries, vegetarian, seafood, beef, poultry, pork and "Chef Suggestions". Tasty Thai dishes include Pla Lard Prik (deep fried salmon with spicy garlic chili sauce), Choo Chee lobster, huge BBQ'd oysters, sauteed assorted vegetables with bean curd, pumpkin curry and sour & spicy prawn soup with lemon grass. Wine, beer, espresso and hot or cold Thai beverages compliment your meal. Dining is indoors, on the garden patio or you can order to go. By the Millennium you can enjoy a romantic evening in Thailand at Thai Issan seated on pillows inside one of ten private huts for two with exotic Thai dancers entertaining you during a luscious five course dinner. Dinners from 5pm every night, lunch 11:30am-2pm M-Sat..

*$$ THAI ISSAN*
*Authentic Thai Cuisine and Entertainment*
*208 Petaluma Blvd. N., Petaluma, CA. 94952*
*AX, MC & Visa    (707) 762-5966*

# VOLPI'S RISTORANTE, Old World Bar, Deli and Market

It is rare to find a destination where the dynamics of a European market, historic tavern and excellent restaurant work to satisfy so many desires.

Photo by Murray Rockowitz

Second and third generations of the Volpi family carry on a proud tradition at Volpi's Ristorante. From left to right: John W., Sylvia, Gina, Deanna and seated John Sr. and Mary Lee Volpi.

At the Volpi's Ristorante, Old World bar and deli, Petaluma's past and present are big as life. In Volpi's historic bar the cocktails and conversation often flows around memories of a guarded past when European immigrants settled these rich coastal valleys. They carved out ranches and farms and raised their families amid the dignity of the soil and water.

When Silvio and Mary Volpi opened the now famous Volpi's Fine Italian Market, Deli and Bar in 1925, they provided a familiar market for Italians to shop Italian and a haven in the back bar for ranchers, who traveled for miles to sip homemade wine, relax and enjoy a quiet respite from the happy but hard-edged world of the roaring 20's. The Old World bar dates back to prohibition. Today Mary Lee and husband John honor the original tradition plus the contemporary addition of great upscale cuisine served next door in their family style Italian Ristorante. In the original Volpi's deli you can enjoy a special array of Italian sandwiches while rubbing shoulders with the people of Petaluma.

Italian cuisine is served in a delightfully relaxed non-smoking atmosphere. Appetizers include calamari Fritti or steamed clams. Authentic and delicious Italian specials are created daily from fresh herbs, olive oil, vegetables, fish, veal, chicken, beef and pasta. Delicious homemade minestrone soup, Caesar salad, veal saltimbocca, gnocchi al pesto, chicken Toscana, rib eye steak and the fresh fish of the day are featured. Family style dinners include soup and salad, homemade pasta, entree, coffee and ice cream.

As you can tell Volpi's is quite a find for those who love the romantic foods and Italian way of life.

*$$$ VOLPI'S RISTORANTE, OLD WORLD BAR, DELI and MARKET*
*Italian Cuisine          122 Washington Street, Petaluma, CA. 94952*
*Full Bar and Wine    MC & Visa          Live accordion & piano music*
*Bar & Deli: (707) 762-2371  Restaurant: (707) 765-0695 Res. accepted*

### THAI CUISINE

Jiraporn and Phith Somphanith had a dream . . . . they would come to America to share the cuisine of their native countries of Thailand and Laos. Their destination became Petaluma where they now fulfill their dream at the Thai Cuisine Restaurant, which is located in a large Victorian mansion at 610 Main Street on Petaluma Boulevard.

Once inside the ornate high ceiling dining room, guests will be introduced to the gentle charm and the fragrant cuisine of the centuries old Thai civilization. A favorite is seafood noodles soup - a large bowl of spicy broth overflowing with prawns, scallops, and calamari with rice noodles, bean sprouts, lemon grass, chilies, mint, sweet basil and coconut milk. Fresh produce and herbs, local Petaluma chicken, beef, pork and seafood is prepared in a variety of authentic Thai ways. Soup, salad & yum, fried and barbequed plates, Thai curry and peanut dishes, vegetarian with rice entrees and exotic desserts are yours for the choosing.

Thai daily specials include entrees like Salmon Shoo-Shee (pan fried fresh salmon with red curry, coconut milk, citrus leaf lemon grass, rhizome root and Thai sweet basil) and Duck Curry (roasted with garlic & herbs, simmered in red curry with pineapple and sweet basil), which are priced from $8.95 to $12.95. Most entrees come with a salad and rice - all other dishes are served a la carte. Jiraporn and Phith explain that "Pon Pon" means make a wish from God and receive a blessing. Well . . . . make a wish!

*$$ THAI CUISINE*          610 Petaluma Blvd. N., Petaluma, CA. 94952
*Authentic Thailand Cuisine  Lunch: 11:30am - 3pm, Dinner 5 - 9:30pm Sat*
                          *and Sunday till 10-pm.   Beer and Wine,*
                          *MC& Visa. (707) 769-8802 Res.*

### KODIAK JACK'S Honky Tonk & Saloon

This popular Country Western nightclub and saloon is a great destination to learn the Two Step, Line Dances or West Coast Swing, followed by a night on the town with new found dance partners. Kodiak Jacks was opened by Wayne Vieler in 1994. The voluminous interior (8,500 sq. ft.) is designed around the Old West. A historic 1870 ore wagon hangs above the elevated bar and antique stuffed animals gaze down upon the spacious dance floor. Dance lessons are taught 7pm - 9pm nightly for a modest cover charge (weekends free). Light food is served on weekends including pizza, buffalo chicken wings and bar snacks and there are pool tables at the Petaluma Boulevard entrance. Cowboys and cowgirls take turns riding Kodiak, a one of a kind computerized bull who pitches and bucks like his famous namesake who was the National Finals Rodeo Champion. With as much room as a indoor gymnasium, Wayne points out he is eager to host special events during the daytime - so give him a call or stop by Tuesday through Sunday in the evening to celebrate.

*$ KODIAK JACK'S*        256 Petaluma Blvd. N., Petaluma,CA. 94952
*Dance Floor, Bar & Live Music*     *Full Bar, Pool Tables & Bull Rides*

## De SCHMIRE RESTAURANT

De Schmire is a very cozy hideaway located in west Petaluma. Some Petalumans discreetly show DeSchmire off to their guests while at the same time guarding the location of this popular eatery from those outside their clique of friends. The environment is eclectic with bright splashes of art hanging on the walls, rivulets of premium wine streaming into glasses and enthusiastic diners devouring plates of sumptuous cuisine. The setting is very Bohemian to say the least.

Chef proprietors Robert Steiner and Matthew Roche are open to experiment with the cornucopia of foods harvested within the borders of Sonoma County. The rest they import from select purveyors and prepare in the exhibition kitchen much to the enjoyment of their dinner guests. All entrees begin at $13.00. A few of the 16 to 20 entrees served include king salmon filet; poached or grilled with herb salsa or hollandaise sauce, prawns pernod (a favorite) with lemon, white wine and cream, chicken "Zanzibar" in a curry sauce with bananas, apricots and almonds, "rack of lamb" baked with mustard and herbs de Provence crust with red wine reduction plus other nightly specials. De Schmire is open from 5:30pm every night.

*$$ DE SCHMIRE RESTAURANT   304 Bodega Ave., Petaluma, CA. 94952*
*International Cuisine      AE, Disc, MC & Visa    (707) 762-1901 Res. Sug.*

## O'MALLEY'S TIVOLI II Saloon & Restaurant

This popular gathering place for Petaluma's business and ranching community is under the direction of Dennee O'Malley and her dedicated staff. Tivoli II is located across from Petaluma's historic railroad depot. This festive and at times noisy bar is often packed to the gills with guests who enjoy excellent meals at fair prices in a setting they have come to trust. Mid West filets, aged New York steaks, chicken, pork, seafood, Harris Ranch beef burgers and daily specials leave you with the desire to return for more. Almost any thirst can be satisfied at the long bar which is flanked by television sets playing the sports channel; and if the mood arises the juke box and dance floor is a few steps away. Weekly luncheon specials (from $8.25) include southern fried chicken with mashed potatoes, homemade gravy and fresh vegetables, stew and polenta, corned beef & cabbage and stuffed portabello mushrooms. Dinners from $9.75 include homemade soup and garden fresh salad. Scrumptious homemade desserts include Tiramisu which are lady fingers, espresso caffe, mascarpone cheese with whipped cream & chocolate. With seating for 75, Tivoli II is a good pick for parties and special events. Luncheons are served from 11:30am - 2:30pm, dinners from 5pm-9pm and drinks till 1:30am. AE, MC Visa and ATM Cards are honored.

*$-$$ O'MALLEY'S TIVOLI II      219 Lakeview St., Petaluma, CA 94952*
*Italian & American Cuisine      Full Bar,            (707) 781-3121*

## WARREN PERCELL
## STUDIO GALLERY

American artists such as Warren Percell bless us with truly inspirational works, bringing us to tears or perhaps to anger over the relationship man has with the family of mammals that live around us.

Warren also creates portraits, wooden toy soldiers and many of the more creative business signs and logos you see at prominent Sonoma County locations as well as custom paint jobs on motor homes and cars. A friend has suggested that Warren "bends light". See for yourself by visiting his studio where works in progress as well as finished pieces hang on the walls for viewing.

Many of his works inspire philosophical meanings and our profound connection with nature. Careful prepping and disciplined brush strokes finish each work. His original paintings vividly portray a series of events which often touch us deeply. Portraits of ocean mammals, wolves, coyotes and birds of prey capture once in a lifetime moments. Scenes of the Southwest may portray a Shaman Indian woman performing out of body travel; a mural might depict diver and shark both after the same fish. I wonder who wins?

Warren Percell's murals have a style that brings on a spontaneous laugh or perhaps captures the hope for a better tomorrow portraying some of nature's and human kinds splendid moments.

*$$-$$$ WARREN PERCELL STUDIO GALLERY*
*Original Wildlife Art, Custom logos    Painting - Studio and Gallery*
*1514 Bodega Ave., Petaluma, CA. 94952    (707) 765-6512*

Photo by Reed Baldwin

The Marin French Cheese Factory is located  9 miles west of Petaluma and 10 miles east of Point Reyes Station. The lawns and duck pond make a wonderful destination to picnic as well as taste excellent California cheeses and premium wines.

## MARIN FRENCH CHEESE FACTORY

Located mid-way between Coast Highway 1 and the wine country's Redwood Highway 101, and set amidst a broad expanse of rolling coastal hills and farmland is the Marin French Cheese Company, makers of the world famous Rouge et Noir Brand Cheeses.

Often called the "queen of cheeses" Camembert cheese was named by Napolean after the tiny hamlet of Camembert in Orne, France where it originated. It is mild in flavor, soft creamy to buttery in texture, with a "nutty" tanginess unlike any other soft ripened cheese.  Rouge et Noir Camembert along with the other excellent cheeses created at the Marin Cheese Factory can be purchased here or can be mail  ordered to your home all year around.

The Marin French Cheese Factory is a wonderful stop for a picnic.  Along with the fine cheeses and cheese tasting, there is a complete deli, selection of premium California wines, refreshing beverages and over 5 acres of lawn area set aside  to walk, exercise in or simply soak up the warm California sunshine.  There are picnic tables and small groups can use the BBQ area or feed the birds on the large and picturesque duck pond.

*$-$$ MARIN FRENCH CHEESE FACTORY*
*Rouge et Noir Cheese & Picnic Grounds*
*Open:  9am - 5pm/Tours 10am - 4pm.*
*Point Reyes - Petaluma Rd., 10 miles*
*east of Point Reyes Station, 7500 Red Hill Rd.*
*Petaluma, CA. 94952.  (707) 762-6001 / 800-292-6001*
*E-Mail: Cheesefactory@SFNet.Net  or*
*www.SFNet.Net/cheesefactory/*

## STORMY'S SPIRITS & SUPPER
### Established in 1854,

Stormy's Spirits & Supper is the oldest roadhouse in California, and has become an important destination dining establishment. The rural coastal setting of sheep and cattle dotted hillsides, wind breaks of giant eucalyptse, large ranches and hearty family style meals set in the traditional roadhouse style appeals to many urban residents.

Wintertime you can toast around the fieldstone hearth or sit at the long bar with friends. Suppers include Cramer's clam chowder, garden salad with house dressing, vegetable and sourdough bread. A tureen of thick, rich clam chowder, served with sourdough bread is delicious. A diverse selection of entrees include prime rib, lamb chops, Porter House steak, New York steak, chicken (saute' or golden fried), jumbo prawns and fresh in-season fish. Desserts vary but include cheesecake and fresh strawberries with whipped cream. Your hosts are Roger and Carolyn Cramer, daughter Taylor Marie and grandmother Ellen "Stormy" Cramer. Open Thur- - Sun / Thur - Sat serving from 5pm, Sun from 3pm.

*$-$$ STORMY'S SPIRITS & SUPPER    6650 Bloomfield Rd., Bloomfield,*
*Prime Rib, Steaks, Seafood & Spirits     CA. 94952   (707) 795-0127 Res.*

## LITTLE AMSTERDAM House of Oysters

At the end of a highway that changes names three times between Petaluma and the coast junction of State Highway 1 is Little Amsterdam House of Oysters. Native to Holland, Evert Winkelman, his wife Debbie and their family provide a unique setting to stop at.

Custom smoked albacore, salmon, ham (no preservatives or DES), and several varieties of homemade sausage are prepared for home, BBQ or outings to the beach. In the Dutch delicatessen guests will find a wonderful variety of imported chocolates, spice cookies, fruit cakes and Indonesian delicacies and spices indigenous to the Dutch Indies.

There are pool tables and occasionally films are shown in the bar where premium beer and wine is served. Dining is Family style on fish and chips, seafood combo, smoked sausage, garlic bread, homemade soup, deep fried zucchini, mushrooms & onion rings, French dip, burgers, BBQ'd sandwiches, chicken, beef, pork ribs and homemade desserts. Weekend feeds of award winning BBQ'd oysters and occasional live entertainment is very popular.

*$-$$ LITTLE AMSTERDAM House of Oysters*
*Bar, Restaurant & Delicatessen featuring smoked fish & custom meats*
*12830 Valley Ford Rd., Petaluma, CA. 94952  (707) 795-3420 or 876-3169*

## ROMEO'S PIZZA & PASTA

Warm and cozy, Romeo's is a very popular Petaluma destination for those seeking a filling meal of pizza or pasta; or a lighter entree of soup and salad or perhaps a sandwich. Owner Abdollah Mohebali and his energetic staff prepare each order from fresh local produce and high quality Sonoma County meats and cheeses. Abdollah likes to treat his patrons as if they were personal guests in his home. All pizzas are made the old fashioned way in the big brick oven, the pizza dough and sandwich bread is made on the premises and the parmesan cheese is freshly grated daily. It is no wonder that the front dining room with elevated booths is often full of happy diners.

Choose from over 24 toppings to create your own Romeo's pizza or enjoy the combination pizza with a dozen meat & vegetable toppings, Romeo's vegetarian combo or vegi pesto pizza, as well as the seafood combo or smoked chicken pizza (the 10" small is $8.95 / the 14" large is $15.95). Pastas served with fresh hot garlic bread include seafood fettuccini, veggie linguini, spaghetti, lasagna and beef ravioli. Beer, vino, mineral water, coffee and soft drinks are served. Light eaters will enjoy the house salad of crispy greens or spinach, the Caesar or Mediterranean salad ($4.45 - $5.50)

*$$ ROMEO'S PIZZA & PASTA      239 S. McDowell Ave., Petaluma, CA.*
*Pizza, Pasta, Soup & Salad   MC, Visa, Disc.  Open daily 10am to 10pm*
*(707) 762-6668 Sit down, to go or delivered within Petaluma's city limits.*

## TWO NINER DINER

Dining at a small community airport always adds to the travel spirit. Pilots shoot "touch and goes" and aircraft leave and arrive from all over America. Two Niner Diner is located at the eastern edge of Petaluma where a broad expanse of rural Americana stretches from one end of runway Two Niner to the other; as far as the eye can see.

The spotless interior with 1950's style soda bar, black and white checker tile floor and cushy booths by the windows takes one back to a less hurried time. Family owned and operated by Dan and Jone Kelly, their chef/son Nathan and daughter Melissa, this out-of-way destination boasts casual dining "with the eagles". Dan, a lithographer, designed the colorful menu and has amassed a large collection of historic aviation photographs which line the walls. Breakfast recommendations are bisquits and gravy, omelettes, waffles, Flying Aces, Country Pilots and Two Niner Specials. Lunch features appetizers, sandwiches, soup and salad combinations, grilled chicken, prawns, steaks and hamburgers. Desserts include cake, pie or blueberry coffeecake and there is a tempting array of fountain sundaes, banana splits, malts and shakes. Two Niner Diner is open Tuesday through Friday from 8am to 3pm and weekends from 7am to 3pm.

*$-$$ TWO NINER DINER     561 Sky Ranch Drive, Petaluma, CA. 94952*
*American / Breakfast & Lunch          (707) 765-2900  Sit down or to go.*

## PETER'S EXXON

One of the most inspirational service stations on the West Coast is Peter's Exxon, which is located just four blocks west of Highway 101 at the East Washington Street Exit in Petaluma. Proprietor Peter Foster and his dedicated staff are known

The Guarding Angel at Peter's Exxon in Petaluma reminds us that we are never without divine guidance - whether a city, family or individual.

for prompt courteous service whether you need gasoline, diesel fuel, propane, a quart of

oil, tire repair, hot cappuccino or chilled drink. The 1960's decor and original art makes a stop here fun and inspirational. The crew at Peter's Exxon are fuel injection, tune-up, carburetor, brake, electrical, clutch, transmission and air conditioning specialists. The beautiful two story mural was painted in 1994 by John Mitchner to commemorate Polly Class, a youthful Angel who became an inspiration for all of America.

*$-$$ PETER'S EXXON       532 East Washington, Petaluma, CA. 94952*
*Full Service Gas Station & Mini Store  Major Credit Cards   (707) 769-0769*

## STEEL BEAR DELI

The Petaluma Steel Bear Deli is Captain Ahab's dream come true - a "Moby Dick with a wine cellar inside." Both Steel Bear Deli locations offer travelers a convenient roadstop with provisions and beverages within walking distance of motel rooms. The

Petaluma Steel Bear Deli is located near Petaluma Cinema's, a major motion picture chain. A variety of homemade salads, deli sandwiches, fresh ground and brewed coffee, premium wines, imported and domestic beers are available. Double rainbow is featured in the ice cream parlor. Health food, fruit & veggie drinks, mineral water, salsa & chips, desserts, bread, pet food, canned goods, motor oil and sundries are also stocked.

Where are you headed? Steel Bear Deli is an excellent destination to receive information and plot a meaningful course full of discovery in this spectacular region. There is a great mural on the outside of the Petaluma location and inside are guide books, road maps and a helpful staff. Open daily from 7am to 10pm.

*$ STEEL BEAR DELI      Full Service Store, Delicatessen & Wine Cellar.*
*5155 Old Redwood Hwy, Petaluma    1750 Santa Rosa Ave., Santa Rosa*

## SCENIC DRIVES:
## GETTING THERE THRU COTATI/ROHNERT PARK

Exit Highway 101 at the Cotati exit and take Highway 116 west to Sebastopol.  Once in Sebastopol you can take Bodega Highway (at the stop light in the heart of town) to Freestone, Occidental or Valley Ford and State Highway 1.  You can also proceed through Sebastopol on the Gravenstein Highway (Hwy 116) to Graton, Forestville and River Road at Mirabel Park.

Along the way you can stop at several farms and ranches to pick up Sonoma Select products for an enriched stay at the coast or for use in the your kitchen at home.

Cotati is named after the Coastal Miwok Village of Kotata. The interesting six sided plaza is flanked by coffee houses, restaurants and night clubs. Nearby Sonoma State University makes Cotati a college town where health food and fun rules.

# COTATI
## The Hub of Sonoma County

**COTATI DINER'S CHOICE:  Telephone Area Code is (707).**
**Inn of the Beginning** ($) 8201 Old Redwood Hwy  794-9453;  **Johnny's Java** ($) 8429 A Gravenstein Hwy  (707) 794-0168;  **Redwood Cafe** ($) 8240 Old Redwood Hwy  795-7868;  **Washoe House** ($$), at Stony Point & Roblar Rds. take Petaluma Blvd. north to stop light and Denny's Restaurant;  turn left on Stony Point Rd. and go 7 miles  795-4544.

**GENERAL STORES, GIFTSHOPS and the ARTS:  My Market and Delicatessen** ($)  7180 Gravenstein Hwy  792-2180;  **Oliver's Market** ($-$$) 7180 Gravenstein Hwy  792-2180.

**ATTRACTIONS:  Buffalo Billiards** ($-$$)  8492 Gravenstein Hwy  794-7338 or 800-400-4CUE

**HEALTH & FITNESS:**
**24 Hour Health Club** ($) 682 East Cotati Ave.  795-0400.

## JOHNNY'S JAVA

One of the most convenient espresso, breakfast, lunch and snack stops along Highway 101 is located on the west side of Cotati at the Cotati/Sebastopol Exit. "Johnny's Java is a commuters dream come true," states owner Johnny Drake. There is plenty of parking for cars, RV's and big rigs. In this coffee shop the upbeat and relaxed, casual dining atmosphere is very conducive to trip planning, sales meetings or good olde fashioned relaxation with a friend. Johnny's Java is easy on/easy off access if you are headed southbound. If you are headed north bound then go under the overpass and west on Gravenstein Hwy and into the small and sheltered Apple Valley Shopping Center.

Muffins, pastries, breads and desserts go well with the coffee and espresso drinks. Heat and serve meals include garden burgers, breakfast burritos, enchilada pie, pizza, veggie pot pies, quiche, garden salads and homemade chicken or tuna salad sandwiches. Popular reggae and jazz bands play on the weekends till 11pm. Johnny, the "Java King" with the "freeway far side sense of humor" has several locations to serve you. Open 5am to 8pm daily.

*$ JOHNNY'S JAVA            8492 A Gravenstein Hwy, Cotati, CA. 94931*
*Coffee House & Live Entertainment              (707) 794-0168*
*ALSO: 3080 Marlow Rd., Santa Rosa  (707) 528-0168;  2700 Yulupa Ave.,*
*Santa Rosa  (707) 570-0168;  201 West Napa,  Suite #9, Sonoma,*
*933-3881;  8944 Brooks Road South, Windsor  95492  838-9739.*

## GOUVEIA'S GALLERY

Those visiting the wine country also love to tour Sonoma County's art galleries. On your way to the redwoods or coast why not stop at Gouveia's Gallery and have your creative side stimulated. Proprietor Helen Gouveia specializes in custom framing, fine art &

Siberian Husky Puppies by Scott Kennedy

jewelry, limited edition prints and office art. The spacious showroom / gallery overflows with the works of Bev Doolittle, Frank C. Mc Carthy, Braldt Bralds, Brent Townsend, Bonnie Morris, Stephen Lymann and artists from the Greenich Workshop Collective. Of special interest to many are the gorgeous prints of North American wildlife and scenic American landmarks of the West and Pacific Northwest.   Sonoma County's fertile valleys, coastline and wine country are an inspiration to view in your home or office, especially after having been framed and matted by Helen.

*$$ GOUVEIA'S GALLERY     8492 Gravenstein Hwy, Suite D, Cotati, CA.*
*Fine Art, Prints, Jewelry, Framing & Matted   MC & Visa   (707) 792-4433*

## WASHOE HOUSE

There is a California great escape waiting for you scarcely two miles off Highway 101 in the heart of rolling hills and eucalyptus. Washoe House was founded in 1859 when patrons used to pay for their spirits and meals with gold dust. Today the menu is limited, yet very adequate. Daily entrees are written on a chalk board at the end of the bar. They include a 16 oz. New York Steak ($15.00), Jumbo Prawns ($10.75), Chicken in the basket ($7.25), Fish and Chips ($7.25), and Prime Rib: served Tuesday thru Sunday ($11.00). Dinners include French bread, tossed green salad or soup, vegetables, hand cut French fries, and delicious home made biscuits. Special cut steaks are tender and juicy and always cooked to perfection. You may also want to try the popular Washoe House Buffalo Burger which is made from real American Buffalo. For dessert you have a choice between sherbert or vanilla ice cream or homemade pies. Washoe House hosts a large selection of local wines and imported and domestic beers.

Dining at the Washoe House means a historical education as well as a pleasure. Old photographs, oil paintings, original old-fashioned advertisements, lithographs, and a wide variety of rare antiques cover the walls. There is an old-fashioned nickelodeon piano should you fancy good time music. There is a large "country" parking lot and the dress is casual.

*$-$$ WASHOE HOUSE*            *Stony Point & Roblar Rd., Cotati, CA.*
*Western American*      *Box 750217, Petaluma, CA. 94975. (707) 795-4544*

## BUFFALO BILLIARDS

Buffalo Billiards is the largest and most famous billiard and pool hall in northern California. Every aspect of this fun sport can be enjoyed here. There are professional instructors to teach you all the tricks to this game and a complete showroom stocked with all the accessories you will need. Throughout the week you can watch the champions and amateur pool sharks square off for the grand prize - perhaps a purse of loot or a kiss from an admirer.

Beer and wine, coffee, mineral water, light meals, hot dogs and salads are served at the snack bar. Mozart to the latest hits play on the juke box. A buffalo head silently stares at the front entrance and portraits of White Buffalos and the American West hang here and there. Extremely valuable antique pool and billiard tables provide a flair extraordinaire. Buffalo Billiards is open daily from 10am to midnight.

*$ BUFFALO BILLIARDS*       *8492 Gravenstein Hwy, Cotati, CA 94931*
*Billiards, Pool, Snacks & Retail Sales*    *(707) 794-7338    800-400-4CUE*

Once Waldo Rohnert's seed farm and home to magnificent draft horse teams, Rohnert Park today is a sprawling bedroom community. The Sonoma County Wine and Visitors Center is a highly educational stop with demonstration winery, vineyards and duck pond. Movies, displays, a well stocked information center and a tasting room where wine from over 100 wineries is poured makes a visit here interesting. A stroll in the park makes a nice break. Motels, restaurants and coffee houses are nearby.

# ROHNERT PARK
## From Seed Farm to Booming Bedroom Community

**ROHNERT PARK DINER'S CHOICE: Telephone Area Code is (707).**
**All Star Pizza** ($$) 1451 Southwest Blvd. #118 795-9000; **Double Tree Hotel Restaurant** ($$) 1 Double Tree Dr. 584-5466; **Fresh Choice** ($) 5080 Redwood Dr. 585-1007; **Thai House** ($$) 227 Southwest Blvd. 795-4013.

**ROHNERT PARK LODGING:**
**Best Western** ($$$) 6500 Redwood Drive 584-7435; **Good Nite Inn** ($) 5040 Redwood Drive 584-8180 / 800-648-3466; **Motel 6** ($) 6145 Commerce Blvd. 585-8888; **Double Tree Hotel** ($$$) 1 Double Tree Drive 584-5466 / 800-547-8010.

**ATTRACTIONS: The California Welcome Center** ($-$$) 500 Roberts Lake Road 586-3795, Fax: 586-1383. Open daily from 9am to 5pm.

**HEALTH & FITNESS: The Bike Hut** ($$) 917 Golf Course Dr. 585-8594.

### THE SONOMA COUNTY WINE and VISITORS CENTER
One of the most educational information centers in northern California is located just off Highway 101 in Rohnert Park at the entrance to the Sonoma County Wine Country. Take the Golf Course Drive exit at the Spanish style towers of the Good Nite Inn. The information center is on the east or mountain side of the freeway. A large giftshop full of lodging, dining and wine tasting information, a wine tasting room, demonstration vineyards and winery, multi-lingual audio visual displays, movies and special events await.
*$-$$ SONOMA COUNTY WINE & VISITORS CENTER*
*5000 Roberts Lake Rd., Rohnert Park, CA. 94928  (707) 586-3795*
*e-mail: info@sonomawine.com      website: www.sonomawine.com*

# SONOMA STATE UNIVERSITY

The beautiful gardens and pond near the student commons, restaurant, pub and activities center.

A walk around the campus at Sonoma State University and you will think you are in a floral paradise. It is hard to imagine that, just forty years ago, this campus was as stark as a prison courtyard. In fact, in its early days, the campus was jokingly tagged "San Quentin North." But the concrete facades have softened, trees have grown tall, and rose gardens have blossomed. And today, as they celebrate SSU's 40th year, it truly is one of the gems of the state university system.

Things are on the move at Sonoma State. While the campus has changed in the last quarter century, more changes are afoot for the next four or five years. Consider this construction is already underway for a new Information Center and ground has also been broken for new student apartments to accommodate the growing number of students who choose to live on campus. Plans are moving forward for a new concert hall facility, expected to be completed by 2002.

SSU continues to earn marks as an innovative campus and as an educational destination of innovation. On one front, SSU was recently cited as a great bargain for undergraduate education. The source: Kiplinger's Personal Finance Magazine, a national publication. In the March 1997 issue, an article compared the value of a state school education versus that of more prestigious private and public schools. The author recommends that parents and students look at a handful of small public schools that are functioning in many ways like small private schools, such as Saint Mary's in Maryland and

# SONOMA STATE UNIVERSITY

Sonoma State in California, before they lay down their big bucks on the larger institutions.

A stroll around the campus will reveal an excellent academic bookstore, brew pub, cafe/cafeteria, library, outdoor decks and secluded study areas.

SSU could not boast of new facilities and programs if it was not for the generous gifts they have received from several supporters, including the late actor Raymond Burr, a longtime friend of the university, who at one time taught drama in the School of Arts and Humanities. Burr began raising orchids on his Sonoma County ranch in the 1980s, and by 1993, had a collection numbering over 11,000. After his death, the collection was sold and the proceeds were used to establish two endowed funds at SSU in Burr's name: the Raymond Burr Lecture Fund and the Orchid Preservation Fund.

Another well-known supporter of the university is Snoopy, or his creator, Charles Schulz. The cartoonist and his wife, Jean, an SSU alumna, donated $5 million to the university and another $5 million matching gift. Their generosity will help fund the new concert hall. Besides being known in Sonoma County as the father of the telecommunications industry, Don Green, an avid choral music performer, was a longtime member of SSU's own Sonoma Bach Choir.

And so beginning with the new millennium, Sonoma State University will leap into the 21st century with the opening of the Jean and Charles Schulz Information Center. It will be the largest addition to the campus in their forty year history, but will change the face of how they educate their students and ourselves.

Students enjoy a spacious landscaped campus for outdoor exercise between classes, sunning themselves, or visiting snack and special event booths set up year around.

The Good Nite Inn in Rohnert Park offers 123 rooms, a convenient location to everything and lots of in-room amenities.

## GOOD NITE INN

The lights of the big three story Spanish style Good Nite Inn in Rohnert Park is a welcome sight for travelers seeking convenience, economy and numerous amenities in a overnight stay. The Good Nite Inn offers 123 rooms with stairwell and elevator access and is located 50 miles north of San Francisco and right alongside Highway 101 at the Golf Course Drive exit.  King, queen, single and hide-a-beds await with rates for 2 from $44.95.  The family suite with 2 queens, hide-a-bed and king sleeps 8 and costs $79.95.  Cash, travelers checks, ATM or credit cards are ok.

The heated swimming pool and jacuzzi is open from 8am - 10pm.  There is free morning coffee and snack machines.  In room local direct dial telephone calls are free.    There are also free showtime movies or in-room pay movies,   air conditioning, a laundry room and small and well behaved pets are ok.  Senior discounts are honored or you can pay for 10 nites and get the 11th night free. The Spanish style building offers landscaped grounds, stairwells and a elevator and is a short walk to numerous restaurants and stores. A rapid transit bus stop is just out front and there is plenty of private parking with security patrol.

*$-$$ GOOD NITE INN*
*Motel Rooms and Suites*
*5040 Redwood Drive, Rohnert Park, CA. 94928*
*Numerous Amenities, Economical Rates,*
*All Major Credit Cards, Swimming pool & Jacuzzi,*
*In room direct dial telephones.*
*Fax: (707) 584-1725   Res: (707) 584-8180*

Sebastopol was named by Russian settlers who established an agricultural community here in the early 1800's. They brought with them the Gravenstein apple. Sebastopol is grounded in the apple and farming industry. The annual Apple Blossom and Harvest Festivals are in Spring and Fall and are wonderful times to enjoy the bounty of the west county gardens and Farm Trails. Sebastopol also has a spiritual, healing arts and "Green" community. Many paths mean diversity and that healthy diversity is reflected in the many innovative businesses Sebastopol is known for.

# SEBASTOPOL
## Home of the Gravenstein Apple

**SEBASTOPOL DINER'S CHOICE: Telephone Area Code is (707).**
**Andy's Produce** ($-$$$) 1691 Gravenstein Hwy N.  823-8661; **Apple Creek Cafe** ($) 9890 Bodega Hwy (3.5 mi W. of Seb.) 829-3065;  **Cafe Da Vero** ($$) 7531 Healdsburg Ave.  823-4418; **Chez Peyo** ($$) 2295 Gravenstein Hwy S. 823-1262; **DeMarco's Pizzeria & Pasta House** ($$) 6811 Laguna Parkway  824-8808;  **East West Cafe** ($) 128 North Main St. 829-2822; **Fiesta Market** ($-$$$) 550 Gravenstein Hwy  823-1418;  **Fircrest Market** ($$) 900 Grsavenstein Hwy S.  823-9171; **Food For Thought** ($) 6910 McKinley St.  829-9801;  **Giovanni's Italian Delicatessen & Wine Shop** ($) 173 Pleasant Hill Rd. 823-1331; **Greek Bistro** ($$) 305 North Main  823-4458; **Intermission Cafe & Fountain** ($) 6811 Laguna Parkway  823-5045; **Jaspar O'Farrells** ($$) 6957 Sebastopol Ave. 823-1389; **Katz Coffee Roastery** ($) 6761 Sebastopol Hwy 829-6600; **Lucy's Cafe & Brick Oven Bakery** ($$) 110 N. Main  829-9713; **Papas & Pollo** ($) 915 Gravenstein Hwy S.  829-9037; **Pasta Bella** ($$) 796 Gravenstein Hwy S. 824-8191; **Sebastopol Grille** ($$) 1015 Gravenstein Hwy S. 829-9537;  **Screamin' Mimi's** ($) 6902 Sebastopol Ave.  823-5902; **Slice of Life** ($$) 6970 McKinley St. 829-6627; **Sushi Hana** ($$) 6930 Burnett 823-3778; **Taqueria Sebastopol** ($$) 250 S. Main  829-8025; **Thai / Lao** ($$) 969 Gravenstein Hwy. S.  829-2679; **Thai Pot** ($-$$) 6961 Sebastopol Ave.  829-8889; **Village Bakery** ($) 7225 Healdsburg Ave. 829-8101; **Viva Mexico** ($) 841 Gravenstein Hwy S.  823-5555.

**BOOKS, GIFTS and the ARTS: Copperfield's** ($) 138 N. Main 829-1286; **Incredible Records - Rock n' Roll Museum** ($-$$) 112 N. Main St.  824-8099. **Milk & Honey** ($-$$$) 137 N. Main  824-1155; **Millenium Arts** ($$) 132 S. Main 829-5541 **Rosemary's Garden** ($) 132 N. Main 829-2539; **Sensuality Shop** ($-$$) 2489 Gravenstein Hwy S. 829-3999; **Tribal Beginnings** ($$-$$$) 6914 Sebastopol Ave, 829-2174; **Wild Things** ($-$$) 130 S. Main  829-3371.

# SEBASTOPOL and VICINITY

MAP Courtesy Sebastopol Chamber of Commerce
265 South Main, Sebastopol, CA 95472 (707) 823-3032

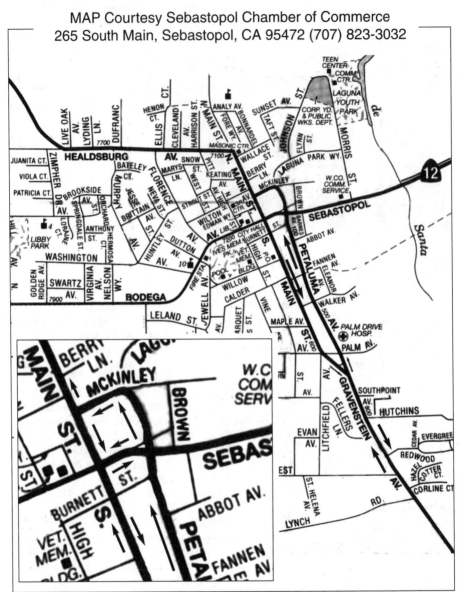

**HEALING & TRANSFORMATION**  See Pgs 257, 258, 269, 271, 283, 286, 303.

**LODGING:  Fountain Bleu Estate** ($$$) 10017 Cherry Ridge Rd., 823-7755;
**Holiday Inn Express & Suites** ($$) 1101 Gravenstein Hwy S.  829-6677;
**Sebastopol Inn** ($$) 6761 Sebastopol Ave. 829-2500.

## COPPERFIELD'S BOOKSTORE & CAFE

One of the most successful community oriented northern California bookstore chains exists within the borders of Sonoma County. Avid readers are abundant in this part of the world and Copperfield's Bookstores and Cafes are extremely successful at providing for their needs. Great selections of new and used titles purchased by founders Paul Jaffe, Dan Jaffe, Barney Brown and their staff, plus a monthy showcase of autograph parties have provided encouragement to the spirited thinkers in the Redwood Empire. Pleasant and spacious bookstores include reading areas, music centers and magazine sections.

Those seeking physical nourishment can indulge in a wonderful smoothie with fresh fruit and protein powder, shakes, hot apple cider, homemade soup or garden fresh salads. Coffee drinks, a large variety of sandwiches, baked goods and specialty teas for the discriminating tea drinker are also served.

*$-$$ COPPERFIELD'S BOOKSTORE & CAFE     Open 7 days a week.*
*650 - 4th Street,    Downtown Santa Rosa, CA. 95404   (707) 576-7681*
*138 N. Main Street,    Sebastopol, CA. 95472        (707) 823-2618*
*2316 Montgomery Dr.,  Santa Rosa, CA.95405          (707) 578-8938*
*140 Kentucky Ave.,    Petaluma, CA. 94952           (707) 762-0563*

### JASPAR O'FARRELLS

Above all else Jaspar O'Farrells is a watering hole and social gathering place for Sebastopol and west county residents. It is a great place to tune your ears to up and coming musicians as well as old time favorites who play Blues, Zydego, Cajun, Reggae, and Rock & Roll. Celtic and Irish music is often played on Sundays. American, British, Irish and Scottish beer is served on draught or by the bottle as well as California wines and coffee drinks. The pub food is always good. Appetizers, homemade soups, salads, locally renowned fish & chips and burgers compliment the brew.

The large and historic long bar (circa 1890), high ceilings, hung with European flags, trophys, original art, beer mirrors and beer steins provides a bullseye setting for a game of darts and good conversation.

*$$ JASPAR O'FARRELLS       6957 Sebastopol Ave., Sebastopol 95472*
*Pub Faire & Live Music    Open Tues-Sun from 11am    (707) 823-1389*

## FIRCREST MARKET

Located at the south entrance of Sebastopol on the Gravenstein Highway is Fircrest Market. An exceptional grocery store is the heartbeat of any community. Shoppers find isles full of California fresh produce (traditional and organic), vineyard and garden grown goodies, premium wines, domestic and imported beers, including local micro brews and apple ciders and block ice for the beach or wine country picnic. Daily necessities for every lifestyle need and every room in the home or RV are also stocked from diapers to road flares.

Garden fresh vegetables and fruits from hot inland valleys and other products are stocked. Inside is also a full service meat market and delicatessen with salads, cheeses, fresh fish from Bodega Bay and locally grown beef, lamb and poultry. The meat department features a large assortment of traditional and chemical free meats. In the fish market at least a dozen varieties of ocean and fresh water fish are showcased daily. The attendant will point out which were caught locally by the Bodega Bay fleet and whether they are fresh or fresh frozen. Fircrest Market is open daily from 9am -9pm.

*$-$$ FIRCREST MARKET      900 Gravenstein Hwy. S., Sebastopol, CA.*
*Full Service Grocery Store        Meat Market & Deli (707) 823-9172*
*Open daily from 9am to 9pm   ATM, AE, MC & Visa  (707) 823-9171 Info*

## PAPAS and POLLO

Celeste White used to run a tiny cafe on the fringe of the deep forests of the Lost Coast at Hales Grove and became locally famous for surf fish fries on Friday night. Today she basks in the summer sun at Papas and Pollo serving Southwest mesquite BBQ entrees to residents and visitors of Sebastopol. Great tasting, low in fat meals of mesquite grilled fish, chicken and vegetables, washed down with premium micro brewed beer or mineral water really hit the spot. You can dress your tofu, fish, beef or chicken tacos up at the salsa bar or munch a enchilada, quesadilla, stuffed baked potato or one of 15 varieties of burrito grande. The "guilt free burrito" is a McDougall style burrito made with delicious artichoke hearts, diced baked potatoes and served with organic salad mix - what a concept! For under $5.00 you can leave full or splurge on a mesquite grilled feast of chicken (after 4:30 pm), side dishes (rice, beans etc) and tortillas for 2 to 6 people from $11.50 to $23.00. Open daily from 11am to 9pm. Inside / Outside Patio Dining or to go.

*$-$$ PAPAS and POLLO       915 Gravenstein Hwy. S., Sebastopol, CA*
*Southwest Mesquite BBQ  Beer, Wine & Patio Dining   (707) 829-9037*

## PASTA BELLA

Ryn Wood's culinary career has been brilliantly and divinely guided to her Pasta Bella restaurant on the south side of Sebastopol. Ryn trained at the famous Tassajara Zen Center and Green's Restaurants in San Francisco and was actor Don Johnson's personal chef. Her enthusiasm bubbles over onto the sumptuous Italiafornia dishes she has named after her friends. Try Lorelei for a salad, wild greens, fuji apples, carmalized walnuts and gorgonzola with champagne citrus vinaigrette; Lisa Shiffman, a delicious grilled chicken with prosciutto-sage cream sauce and fresh roma tomatoes over linguine or Susie Murray, a gorgonzola cream sauce with spinach, fresh tomatoes and toasted walnuts over gemelli with sauteed prawns. Beer, wine, fresh made desserts & coffee drinks are served. The quality shines and prices are moderate.

*$-$$ PASTA BELLA*                                796 Gravenstein Hwy S., Sebastopol
*Italiafornia Cuisine*          ATM, MC & Visa      (707) 824-8191 Res or to go.

## SEBASTOPOL GRILLE

One could write a book about Irishman Jack Webb, who came to Sebastopol to open his Sebastopol Grille. Jack also manages the famous Ireland 32 Bar & Grill in San Francisco. Dinners include relish tray, salad with choice of dressing, fresh vegetables, potatoes (mashed, baked or fries) or rice pilaf with bread & butter. Chef Roger Boileau, who is from the Pyrennes Mountains of southern Europe, is locally famous for his rack of lamb, cannelloni crepes and prime rib of beef au jus (served Fri & Sat). Warm and authentic paintings of Ireland line the dining room walls. Homemade desserts, coffee, lemonade, cider, champagne, micro brewed beers and California wines are also served.

*$$ SEBASTOPOL GRILLE*                  *$ IRELAND 32 BAR & GRILL*
*Irish, American & Italian*                    *3920 Geary Blvd., S.F.*
*1015 Gravenstein Hwy S.  (707) 829-9537*          *(415) 386-6173*

**VILLAGE BAKERY**  The award winning Village Bakery offers three locations in Sebastopol, Santa Rosa and Windsor where you can enjoy fresh brewed coffee drinks with fresh baked fruit tarts, raspberry swirls, cheese cakes, wild berry pies, cream puffs, macarones, tea cake, binzer cookies, chocolate angel food cafe, scones, swirls, bear claws, muffins and croissants.  Brigitta  Schofield, who is from Sweden, creates the hand-crafted European hearth breads and array of bakery treats.  She blends science, art and tradition to create bread that has nourished civilization for centuries utilizing organic grains and supporting sustainable agriculture.  Artful presentations make get-togethers special and memorable.  Open M-Sat 7am - 5:30pm and Sun 8am - 2pm.  Dine indoors or out or take your order to go.

*$ VILLAGE BAKERY*              *Cafe / Bakery  Catering & Special Events*
    *7225 Healdsburg Ave. Sebastopol, CA. 95472.*        (707) 829-8101
    *8782 Lakewood Dr., Windsor, CA. 95492*              (707) 837-9551
    *1445 Town & Country Drive, Santa Rosa, CA. 95404*   (707) 527-7654

**TAQUERIA SEBASTOPOL**    This festive taqueria is often packed with locals who treasure the delicious portions that the Familia Coronel are known for.  An extensive selection of breakfast items, side orders, Mc Dougall style entrees, salads, appetizers, tacos, Marisco (seafood), burritos, especialidades Mexicanas, combinaciones grandes, beer & wine, Mexican beverages and desserts are served.  Try the Seafood Parrillada which is grilled prawns, scallops and grilled filet of fresh fish with chunks of carne asada carnitas & grilled

chicken served with rice, beans, salsa, guacamole, sour cream and tortillas.  There is dancing in the Mareache Bar.  Be sure to look for the big red apple on the side of the Taqueria Sebastopol catering truck for delicious Mexican food to go.

*$ TAQUERIA SEBASTOPOL      250 South Main St., Sebastopol 95472*
*  Mexican Cuisine and Mariachi Bar  MC & Visa  (707) 829-8025*

**THAI POT**    It's easy to see why the Thai Pot is western Sonoma County's most popular Thai restaurant.  For one the Thai cuisine is delicious, the servings are generous and the prices are very fair.  Kuang, Hsiu and David Yang have been putting smiles on the faces of Sebastopol residents and visitors for almost a decade.

The menu is divided up into appetizers, soups, salads, entrees, curries, seafood, vegetables & tofu, fried rice, noodles, side orders, desserts and beverages. Delicious luncheons include appetizer, steamed rice and choice of soup of the day or salad with peanut dressing ($6.00). Two or more can have a royal feast  with 6-10 gourmet courses (from $13.00 per person). All orders can be prepared to go. Open 11:30am - 9:30pm Mon-Sat; Sun 12 - 9pm.

*  $-$$ THAI POT          6961 Sebastopol Ave., Sebastopol 95472*
*  Thai Cuisine   AX, Dis, MC & Visa   (707) 829-8889 Sit down or to Go*

### The POWERHOUSE BREWING COMPANY

The Powerhouse is a handsomely restored fieldstone building with brewery, wine and beer bar, restaurant and night club.  The innovative decor created by proprietors Bill Bradt and Kathy Weir include beautiful art from the American South and Caribbean.  Fresh handcrafted ales-on-tap such as blonde ale India pale ale, porter, and seasonal brews are created in the microbrewery.  A selection of premium Sonoma County wines are also served by the glass or bottle.

Exceedingly capable chefs present artful servings of California - International cuisine at fair prices.  Dinner specials change weekly and feature selections like Chicken Carnival at $9.95 (grilled boneless chicken breast rubbed with a special Caribbean spice blend, served with grapefruit salsa, white bean salad and sauteed fresh vegetables. Other entrees include portobello mushroom pasta, rib eye steak, New Orleans red beans & rice and the Powerhouse's fresh fish of the day.  Starters such as "High Voltage" garlic and hot pepper French fries and sinfully delicious desserts are also served. The Powerhouse presents the best in local and national live music and is a great place to meet new friends and shed your cloak of formality.

*$$ POWERHOUSE BREWING COMPANY 268 Petaluma Ave., Sebastopol*
*  Microbrewery & California - International Cuisine    (707) 829-9171 Info.*

## SEBASTOPOL FINE WINE CO.

Tony Marti is quite the wine country scholar who has a large selection of wines from small Sonoma County wineries as well as a great import section. With his 20 years of experience, Tony is glad to personally help with a selection. Most days of the week from 10am - 7pm he pours 25 - 35 choices of whites, reds, blends, ports and sherrys. Refreshing gourmet presentations are served for lunch including smoked salmon and red bell peppers, asparagus ginger soup, prosciutto with fresh mozzarella & pesto sandwich and the cheese plate. There are special tastings and guest events. Why not join the Sebastopol Fine Wine Company Sparklers Club?

*$ SEBASTOPOL FINE WINE CO.  6932 Sebastopol Ave., Suite A, 95472*
*Wine Shop and Gourmet Foods    Fax: (707) 829-7873    (707) 829-9378*

## TRIBAL BEGINNINGS

Tribal Beginnings in Sebastopol is an important portal into antique and contemporary Native American art. California and Southwestern baskets and jewelry, Navaho classic blankets and rugs, Zuni fetishes and a new discovery; pottery from the village of Mata Ortiz are displayed throughout the store. Proprietors Michael and Diana Holloway have over 20 years experience as collectors of the fine arts and crafts that have come from the multitude of sophisticated Native American cultures of the North and South American Continentents. The intricate basketwork of Sonoma County Pomo people is also featured. Collectors take note that acquisition, liquidation and appraisals are available. Open 11am - 5:30pm Tues - Saturday or by appointment. All major credit card accepted.

*$$ TRIBAL BEGINNINGS       6914 Sebastopol Ave., Sebastopol, 95472*
   *Native American Art Gallery            (707) 829-2174 Information*

## INTERMISSION CAFE & FOUNTAIN

The Intermission Cafe & Fountain offers a upbeat decor with dining in-doors or outdoors on the back patio beside trees, flowers and a mini-garden. Its a pleasant off the beaten path cafe with American Cuisine - burgers (beef or veggie), shakes, French fries, fish & chips, green salads with radish, celery & pickles, homemade soups and a variety of sandwiches. Choices are abundant at this cafe, coffee house, ice cream parlor where you can watch a little TV, down a beer or enjoy a glass of wine. Sebastopol's cinema is across the parking lot and the art center is next door making it easy for a quick espresso, "Alaskan coffee" or a sit-down meal. The owner, Mike Ketchum is a hard working "far side" kind of guy who came to Sebastopol in 1987 to raise his family.

*$ INTERMISSION CAFE & FOUNTAIN 6811 Laguna Parkway, Sebastopol*
   *American Cuisine     MC & Visa        (707) 823-5045 Sit down or to go*

## CAFE DA VERO

There is a sparkle in the eyes of Sue Friske as she seats guests to her Sebastopol Trattoria. Her husband Bryan is in the kitchen preparing each entree from fresh seasonal ingredients. Sue and Bryan's desire is to provide elegant and sophisticated Italian Cuisine for their guests.

Generous servings of pasta, seafood, poultry, beef and vegetarian entrees are served a la carte with an array of appetizers, soups and salads. You might begin with a classic coastal favorite - Vongole al Bordelaise (steamed clams in garlic, white wine and butter), Zuppa di Verdura (the soup of the day) or salad of assorted baby mixed greens with shaved asiago cheese and house dressing followed by fresh Salmon Funghetto. Premium wine, domestic & imported beer, mineral water, cappuccino, espresso and an array of tantalizing homemade desserts compliment your meal. The upstairs dining room (for 45) is ideal for private parties. Lunch Tuesday-Friday / 11:30am - 2pm; dinner Tuesday-Sunday from 5pm.

*$$ CAFE DA VERO        7531 Healdsburg Ave., Sebastopol, CA. 95472*
*Italian Cuisine     Beer & Wine     AE, MC & Visa     (707) 823-1531 Res.*

SEBASTOPOL'S GROCERY STORE

## FIESTA MARKET & PACIFIC MARKET

Located at the north entrance of Sebastopol on the Gravenstein Highway is Fiesta Market. Take the word harvest in its literal sense here - for a harvest of California fresh produce, Sonoma Select farm, vineyard and garden products, premium wines & beers fill the isles. Daily necessities for the individual, home or car plus gifts and cards from A-Z are also stocked.

Locally grown certified organic fresh herbs, garden fresh vegetables and fruits and other products are stocked. Inside is also a full service meat market and delicatessen with salads, cheeses, fresh fish from Bodega Bay and locally grown California beef, lamb and poultry. The meat department features a large assortment of traditional and chemical free meats. In addition there is a sushi bar where dozens of delicacies can be purchased and bakery where fresh baked breads and rolls are displayed. There are dozens of beverages from spirulina smoothies, fresh squeezed carrot and orange juice and ice for the beach or wine country picnic. Open daily from 9am to 9pm ATM, AE, MC & Visa

*$-$$ FIESTA MARKET    550 Gravenstein Hwy. N., Sebastopol, CA. 95472*
*Full Service Grocery Store     Deli: (707) 823-4916   Store: (707) 823-9735*
*PACIFIC MARKET 1465 Town & Country Dr., Santa Rosa (707) 546-3663*

## TAFT STREET WINERY

When John Tierney started making "amazing wines" on Taft Street in Oakland in the 1970's, his family and friends decided to create Taft Street Winery in Forestville. During the 1980's Taft Street created fine Chardonnays and a blend of a Cabernet/Merlot/Cabernet Franc. Today Taft Street has relocated their winery and tasting room to a secluded setting with picnic area where they make and offer tastings of Chardonnay, Sauvignon Blanc, Merlot, Pinot Noir, Cabernet Sauvignon, Zinfandel and Lambrusco from vineyards in Sonoma County's Russian River, Dry Creek and Alexander Valleys. The taste and price of Taft Street vintages make you smile.  Open 11am-4pm Mon-Sun.

*$-$$ TAFT STREET WINERY  2030 Barlow Lane, Sebastopol, CA. 95472*
*    Tasting Room and Picnic Area     MC & Visa     (707) 823-2049 Info.*

## MARY'S APPLE CREEK CAFE

A charming little cafe thats big on heart and convenience is Mary's Apple Creek Cafe located between the Sonoma Coast and Sebastopol's apple and farm dotted countryside.  Owner Mary Rushworth and friend William Wright worked hard and smart to create this roadside cafe, small farm with pet pigs and goats and courtyard with craft persons and healers.  Light breakfast and lunch is served Tuesday - Sunday. Breakfast bagels, burritos, fresh fruit, assorted muffins & pastries, gourmet sandwiches, homemade soup, garden fresh salads, combos, homemade desserts, lemonade, tea, coffee drinks and beer & wine are served.  Dining is outdoors on the charming garden patio or inside the kitchen dining room with oak long bar.  Call for hours, live music events and to see what Mary is "country cookin" up for dinner.

*$-$$ MARY'S APPLE CREEK CAFE   9890 Bodega Hwy., Sebastopol, CA.*
*    Information: (707) 823-3915             Restaurant: (707) 829-3065*

## FOUNTAIN BLEU

Retreat leaders and meeting planners will love this luxurious country estate, which reminds one of a star ship that has landed in the Sonoma County apple country.  Surrounded by a moat and fountains, with beautiful landscaped gardens and inspirational views of the valley and mountains, the tri level, 9,000 sq foot Fountain Bleu is ideal for retreats or workshops designed to heal the physical, mental, emotional and spiritual bodies. Fountain Bleu offers five bedrooms, 9 bathrooms, fireplaces, a conference/banquet area for 120 (weddings to 200), gallery and observation room with wrap around decks.

*$$ FOUNTAIN BLEU   MC & Visa (707) 823-7755 Reservations a must*
*Bed & Breakfast Retreat / Healing Center          http:www.fbleu.com*

Old Town Graton has experienced a renaissance in the 90's leaving the heart of town with fresh new store fronts and innovative cafes set in the palm of Green Valley. Apple orchards, swaying willow trees and vegetable gardens are in great abundance.

# GRATON
## A Watershed Valley of Orchards and Rolling Hills
**GRATON DINER'S CHOICE: Telephone Area Code is (707). Zip 95444**
**Berry's Market** ($) 3195 Gravenstein Hwy 824-8041; **Cafe Sunflower** ($) 9050 Graton Rd 824-1326; **Cape Fear** ($$) 8989 Graton Rd. 824-8284; **Mexico Lindo** ($-$$) 9030 Graton Rd. 823-4154; **Passionfish** ($$) 9113 Graton Rd 823-9003; **Willow Wood Market** ($) 69030 Graton Rd. 829-2700;
**WINE TASTING: Blackstone Winery** ($) 9060 Graton Rd. 824-2401.
**GRATON LODGING: Gravenstein Inn** ($$-$$$) 3160 Hicks Rd. 829-0493;
**Vine Hill Bed & Breakfast** ($$-$$$) 3949 Vine Hill Rd. 823-8832.
**AUTO REPAIR: Turner's Automotive** Foreign/Domestic 9001 Graton Rd. 823-6966

### CALIFORNIA CIDER COMPANY
### and the ACE in the HOLE PUB

Thanks to Jeffrey House, a flamboyant entrepreneur from England, the good ole' U.S.A. can enjoy a delicious liquid gold hard cider called Ace Honey Cider. When Jeffrey started the California Cider Company in 1994 he teamed up with cider maker David Cordtz. Together they searched the apiaries of Sonoma County like busy little bees to find the perfect apple-honey taste. They combined Russia's gift to America, the Gravenstein Apple, with Sonoma County wildflower honey to make one of the most delicious hard ciders in the world. Award winning Ace Pear Cider and Ace Apple Cider followed. The fourth Ace is in the works.

At their new cider tasting room and pub, the Ace in the Hole, you can enjoy these award winning/heart warming juices of the Gods plus an original selection of experimental hard cider and ACE beverages.

*$-$$ CALIFORNIA CIDER COMPANY* Ordering & Info:  *(707) 829-1101*
*and the ACE in the HOLE PUB*     3100 Gravenstein Hwy N., Sebastopol,
*Cider Tasting & Nibbles*          CA. 95444   (707) 829-1ACE

## COLD MOUNTAIN BOOKS

Cold Mountain Bookstore is named after Cold Mountain poems that were written in China. Han Shan who lived in the wilderness on the slope of Cold Mountain wrote the philosophical poems around 900 AD. Nancy Blanchard and Charles Collum have quite a selection of quality literary works spanning two century's for you to investigate. They specialize in used and rare books and do out of print book searches as well as host frequent events including readings and benefits. Open Tues - Thur 10:30am - 5:30pm and Fri & Sat 1:30pm - 8:30pm.

*$-$$ COLD MOUNTAIN BOOKS        9050 Graton Rd.,*
*Used and Rare Books        Graton, CA.    (707) 823-2881*

## CAFE SUNFLOWER

This cozy colorful cafe/bakery shares space with Cold Mountain Books and is owned by Meg Cain who prepares a variety of treats to enjoy there or to take out. Fresh baked breads including French, whole wheat

or rye, Gingerbread, muffins, biscotti, cookies, Danish pastries, croissants, to name a few. For lunch homemade soup accompanied by homemade piroshkis, Lavosh (Greek wraps), calzone or hot sandwiches or in summer cold soups and salads. Herbal and regular teas, fresh squeezed juices, espresso drinks, mochas made with real chocolate, locally roasted Taylor Maid organic coffees make Cafe Sunflower a real hit. Open: 7am Mon - Fri, closed Tues, 9am weekends Sat and Sun.

*$ CAFE SUNFLOWER                    9050 'B' Graton Rd., CA. 95444*
*Coffee House & Baked Goods                    (707) 824-1326*

## PASSIONFISH

Named after a Hollywood movie, the Passionfish serves an eclectic combination of Cajun-California cuisine with fresh fish, gumbo and pizza at the top of the menu. Formerly the location of the notorious "Skip's Bar", the Passionfish is a delicious ripple replacing what was once shark infested waters.

The cheerful dining area lines the length of the longbar where boutique California wines are poured along with local micro brewed beer, cider and espresso beverages. Skylights let the sunshine or moonlight in and during summers the outdoor dining area is a delight. Breakfast, lunch and dinner is very popular with more than generous servings and reasonable prices. The produce is local and fresh, the chef very capable and meals are tasty to say the least.

Vegan, vegetarian, seafood and meat pizzas are handmade from scratch (from $13.95/feed 2-4). For breakfast try the Mongo's morning meal - 3 eggs, sausage, bacon and pancakes ($8.95), or the grits, biscuits and Andouille gravy ($4.95) Locals drive for miles just for the oven fried catfish served with cornbread, slaw, red beans and rice.

*$$ PASSIONFISH                    113 Graton Rd., Graton CA. 95444*
*Cajun - American   Beer and Wine   ATM & Major Credit Cards  (707) 823-9003*

## VINE HILL BED & BREAKFAST

Kathy Deichmann knew a good thing when she saw it - especially the grand old 1897 farm house surrounded by organic gardens, vineyards and forested ridgelines with songbirds and quail, which she remodeled and named the Vine Hill Bed & Breakfast. Guests will adore the architecturally perfect rooms with private baths, big comforters and jacuzzi whirlpool tubs. Vine Hill B & B is a perfect place for a romantic getaway or honeymoon with swimming pool and decks to enjoy the panoramic vineyard views. You'll enjoy a full breakfast of French toast, pancakes or egg entree served with fresh baked muffins and pastries, fresh fruit compote with sorbet and juice, tea and coffee.

*$$-$$$ VINE HILL B&B*
*Bed and Breakfast*
*3949 Vine Hill Rd., Sebastopol. CA. 95472*
*Private Baths, Jacuzzi, Swim Pool  WEB: vine-hill-inn.com  (707) 823-8832.*

## MEXICO LINDO

Mario Ramo's Mexico Lindo is a breath of fresh air as Mexican restaurants go in Western Sonoma County. No stranger to providing a festive dining environment, Mario invites you to enjoy the South of the Border cuisine he and his daughter Gabriela, son Benjamin and authentic team of Mexican chefs serve.

Shortly after sunrise at 9am the coffee is brewing and guests are feasting on platters of huevos a la Mexicana (scrambled eggs with Mexican sauce and bell or serrano pepper), huevos rancheros, machaca (scrambled eggs with shredded "machaca" beef), and the popular breakfast burrito. Tortilla chips are made fresh daily and served with fresh made salsa and guacamole. For lunch or dinner try the chile relleno which is made with the delicious Pasilla chile and filled with cheese, coated with light batter and served with rice, beans and tortillas. Also served are flautas, enchiladas, tamales, burritos, chimichanga, quesadillas with or without chicken, tostadas and tortilla soup. Combination plates are from $5.95. Mexican and America beers, sangria, wine margaritas, lemonade, penafiel, soda, coffee and tea satisfy your thirst. Mariachi bands play every Tuesday. Mexico Lindo is open daily from 9am to 9pm.

*$ MEXICO LINDO              9030 Graton Road, Graton, CA. 95444*
*Continental Mexican Cuisine  MC & Visa  (707) 823-4154 Sit down or to go*

# Farms, Gardens & Ranches

## *A City Slickers Guide to the Country*

Buying direct from our small family farms keeps one healthy, weathly and wise. It's fun and it's an adventure as you discover the wonders of Sonoma County's **"Garden of Eatin".**

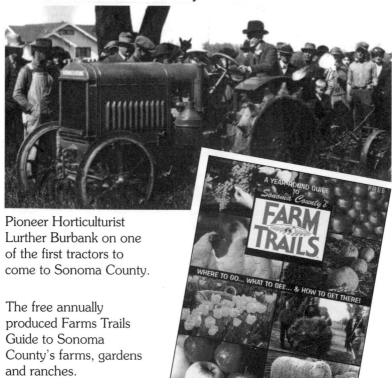

Pioneer Horticulturist Lurther Burbank on one of the first tractors to come to Sonoma County.

The free annually produced Farms Trails Guide to Sonoma County's farms, gardens and ranches.

Each year more and more residents of San Francisco, Berkeley, Oakland and Marin realize the tremendous benefits of touring and purchasing farm fresh products from Sonoma County's Gardeners, Sonoma Select and Farm Trails members. Whether by car or by tour bus you can explore "shopping isles" full of in-season and super nutritious fruits, vegetables and products grown in rich river valleys and along coastal plateaus and ridgelines where the air is crystal clear and the views are spectacular. Smart shoppers are now organizing into groups and touring the Sonoma County Farm Trails mid-week, as well as on weekends.

**Seasonal Produce Hotlines:**
**Select Sonoma County (707) 571-8894**
**FARM TRAILS INFO    (707) 571-8288**
**www.farmtrails.org    800-207-9464**

The
FARM TRAILS
# GUIDE

## FARM TRAILS LISTINGS

Look for the listing number and location of participating Farm Trails and Sonoma Select Members in the Centerfold Map Section of this book.  See page 156.

### PARTIAL LIST of Past & Present SONOMA FARM TRAIL'S MEMBERS

| | |
|---|---|
| Adams & Friend Farm 775 | Korbel Champagne Cellars 116 |
| Angelo's Meats 515 | Kozlowski Farms 304 |
| California Carnivores  301 | Martinelli Vineyards & Orchards 780 |
| Cray Croft Gardens 172 | Pet-a-Llama Ranch 385 |
| Dot's Pots-Orchids-Apples-Aprons 334 | Starcross Trees & Wreaths 170 |
| Dutton Ranch 425 | Timber Crest Farms 154 |
| Foxglove Farm 305 | Topolos @ Russian River Vineyards 302 |
| Green Valley Blueberry Farm 310 | Twin Hill Ranch 352 |
| Grossi Farms 715 | Westside Farms 144 |
| Hallberg's Apple Farm 327 | Willie Bird Turkey No. 1  745 |
| Imwalle Gardens  800 | Ya-ka-ama Native Plant Nursery 300 |

### PROVIDERS of FLOWERS, VEGETABLES, FRUIT, HERBS  and SEAFOOD

1.  Balletto Farms                Seasonal Garden Fresh Produce, Salad Mix & Herbs
2.  Bloomfield Farms                  Seasonal Garden Fresh Produce & Herbs
3.  Bodega Bay Sport Fishing Center     Salmon, Rock Fish & Whale Watching
4.  California Flora Nursery                        California Native Plants
5.  California School of Herbal Studies        Herbs, Medicinal Plants & Classes
6.  Cottage Garden Growers    Perennials, Roses and Clematis Vines    778-8025
7.  Crab Pot                   Smoked Salmon, Ling Cid and Cooked Crab
8.  Dragonfly Farm Floral Design     Flowers, Foilage & Vines for Special Events
9.  Foggy Bottom Farm CCOF    Culinary Herbs and Gourds for Art  829-2781
10.  Forever Green Farms       Green Leaf Sprouts by the Case plus Wheatgrass
11.  Freestone House       Nursery, Plants, Landscaping, Fruit Trees and Herbs
12.  Garden Valley Ranch         8,000 Rosebushes, Nursery, Tours & Weddings
13.  Harmony Iris Gardens    Tall & Medians Irises, Brilliant Colors of the Rainbow
14.  Imwalle Gardens                 Seasonal Garden Fresh Produce & Herbs
15.  Laguna Farms        CCOF Produce, Herbs, Salad Mix and Apprenticeships
16.  Lucas Wharf            Fresh Seafood, Oysters, Mussels & Smoked Salmon
17.  Marin French Cheese Factory                        French Cheese
18.  Mom's Head Gardens                   Medicinal and Culinary Herbs
19.  99th Monkey Gardens                     Organic Vegetables & Herbs
20.  Tides Wharf          Fresh Seafood, Oysters, Mussels & Smoked Salmon

## DESCRIPTION of GROWING METHODS

The fruits and vegetables at Community Market are identified according to growing methods, and the signs are color coded to help with your selection.  There are 3 main groups.

**ORGANICALLY GROWN:**  Produce grown in accordance with the California Organic Foods Act of 1990.  Farming methods are used that renew and sustain soil fertility, without using synthetically compounded petroleum based fertilizers, pesticides and other materials.

**DOCUMENTED ORGANIC:**  Growing methods are documented and submitted by growers to the California Department of Food and Agricultural.  There is an enforcement division for misrepresentation, but no requirement for independent verification.

**CERTIFIED ORGANIC:**  Grown according to strict standards with third-party verification by an independent organization or state government agency.

**CCOF (California Certified Organic Foods):**  Grown or processed in California according to strict standards with third-party verification by an independent organization or state government agency.

**UNSPRAYED PESTICIDE FREE:**  A farmer's personal statement that no pesticides were sprayed on the crop, though synthetically compounded chemical fertilizers may have been used.  There is no record keeping or certification currently required for this label.

**CONVENTIONALLY GROWN:**  Produce grown with farming methods that may have included the use of synthetically compounded materials.  Community market will purchase conventionally grown produce of the freshest, highest quality, only when Organic and Unsprayed products are unavailable.

**IPM (Integrated Pest Management):**  IPM farmers use non-chemical methods as their first line of defense against pests and diseases.  IPM methods do not exclude the use of synthetic fertilizers and pesticides, but aim to reduce their use.

*Chart Info Courtesy  Community Market of Santa Rosa*

## WHERE TO BUY SONOMA COUNTY FARM FRESH PRODUCE

Andy's Produce / Sebastopol CCOF
Communtiy Market / Santa Rosa CCOF
Fiesta Market / Sebastopol
Food For Humans / Guerneville  CCOF
Food For Thought / Santa Rosa,
        Sebastopol &  Petaluma  CCOF

Oliver's Market / Cotati  CCOF
Organic Groceries / Santa Rosa CCOF
Petrini's Market / Santa Rosa
Santa Rosa Farmers Market /
        Downtown Santa Rosa  CCOF
Speer's Market / Forestville

# The
# FARM TRAILS
# GUIDE    FARM TRAILS LISTINGS

## FARM TRAILS MEMBERS

**775 ADAMS & FRIEND FARM**
Goose down and feather pillows cleaned.
Comforters renovated. Custom designed &
woven pillows. Spinning wool, Navajo-
Romney sheep, lambs, chicken, eggs, figs.
3022 Trenton Rd., Santa Rosa 546-9598

**301 CALIFORNIA CARNIVORES**
Peter & Marilee     838-1630
7020 Trenton-Healdsburg Rd., Forestville.
Specializing in insect eating plants, 500
varieties on display, many for sale "Arresting
assemblage" - SF Examiner "A botanical
museum" NY Times. Mail order. Picnic spot.
All year 10-4. Please call ahead in winter.
www: californiacarnivores.com

**428 CHERRY RIDGE RANCH**   823-8365
9845 Cherry Ridge Rd., Sebastopol.
Reg Angora goats, Lincoln sheep, breeding
stock, butcher lambs, fleece, yarn, carding
service, gifts. Mail order. All year by appt.

**172 CRAY CROFT GARDENS**   785-2962
40755 Annapolis Rd,., (PO Box 82),
Stewarts Point. Award winning Cymbidium
Orchid plants. Catalog, Will ship. By
appointment all year.

**439 DE VOTO FARMS**     823-6650
Stan & Susan Devoto 655 Golf Ridge Rd.
Sebastopol 95472. Twenty acres field-grown
flowers, salad greens, apples, dry flower
bouquets. Self guided garden tour. Groups
by appt 12-4pm Mon-Sat Spring - Fall.

**334 DOT'S POTS - ORCHIDS - APPLES
& APRONS**     823-0645
Fred & Dorthy Schleth, 9275 Ferguson
Court, Sebastopol. Cymbidums, apples:
Gravs & Goldens, Exclusive garden aprons,
bread bags & towel sets. All year, call ahead
daily 9-5 by appt.

## FARM TRAILS MEMBERS

**180 DRAGONFLY FARM**     433-3739
Bonnie & Malcolm Yuill-Thornton 425
Westside Rd, Healdsburg 95448.
1500 Roses. Certified organic heirloom &
European varieties. Decorative materials,
arrangements, bouquets. Sunflowers, starts.
Apr-May Mon-Fri 1-5, Sat-Sun 10-5. Call for
opening dates. By appointment only.

**425 DUTTON RANCH**     823-6864
10717 Graton Rd Sebastopol 95472.
Apples: Grav, Jonathan, Red & Golden Del,
Rome   Aug 1-Sept 1 by appt only.

**305 FOXGLOVE FARM**     887-2759
5280 Gravenstein Hwy N, Sebastopol
Organically grown vegetables & fruits
including grn. beans, corn, tomatoes, basil,
squash, Gravenstein & other apples, figs,
pumpkins, Victorian gifts & courtesy crafts.
Jun-Oct daily 10-6. Rest of year by appt.

**310 GREEN VALLEY BLUEBERRY FARM**
    887-7496
Bruce Goetz 9345 Ross Station Rd.
Sebastopol 95472. Blueberries,
Boysenberries, jam, pies, muffins, tarts, (ice
cream & Plants) June 15 - July 31 Farm
Store Daily 9-6 or at Farmers Markets.

**715 GROSSI FARMS**     664-1602
Ed Grossi 6652 Petaluma Hill Rd, Santa
Rosa 95404   Organically grown-picked fresh
corn, mellons, tomatoes, squash, lettuce,
garlic, peppers, pumpkins and Halloween
activities & more. Also and U-PICK
strawberries. May-Oct Tues-Sun 9-6.

**331 HALLBERG BUTTERFLY GARDENS**
8687 Oak Grove Rd., Sebastopol 823-3420
Gorgeous parade of butterflies warm sunny
days from 10am - 4pm. An old fashioned
butterfly garden: Sanctuary for the Pipevine
Swallowtail Butterfly. Butterfly plants, trees
& schrubs, native plants & perennials.
Classes and tours by reservation only.

## FARM TRAILS MEMBERS

**706 HARMONY IRIS GARDENS 585-1800**
1610 Crane Canyon Rd., Santa Rosa
Newer tall & median irises. Redbloomers,
Pacific Coast & Spuria irises. Gardens bloom
April/May tours and lectures by arrangement.
Mail order. Email: lynnw@harmonyiris.com

**800 IMWALLE GARDENS 546-0279**
685 W 3rd St., Santa Rosa 95401.
Fresh vegetables, nursery bedding, plants,
tomatoes, corn, beans, pickling cukes, red
onions, pumpkins, dill, eggs, mushrooms.
Since 1886. Retail sales all year. Mon-Sat
8:30am-5:30pm, Sun 11am-4pm.

**116 KORBEL CHAMPAGNE CELLARS**
13250 River Rd., Guerneville 824-7216
Wine, champagne, ale and brandy. Tours of
the cellars daily. Garden tours in summer.
Wine tasting, gourmet deli, picnic and party
area, Tours and Bus access.
Email: sschlabach@korbel,com

**304 KOZLOWSKI FARMS 887-1587**
5566 Gravenstein Hwy N, Forestville 95436.
Fresh berries, organic apples in season,
homemade jams, mustards, no-sugar products
& more. Bakery open daily. Fresh cider &
jam tasting. Mail order. Picnic spot. Open
daily 9-5, except major holidays.

**780 MARTINELLI RANCH**
1-800-346-1627 / 525-0570
Lee & Carolyn Martinelli. 3360 River Rd.,
Windsor 95492. Wines & gift packs. Apple
butter, mustards, sauces, vinegars, coffees,
honey, dried fruits, pumpkins, nuts. Mail
order. Art gallery, picnic spot. Daily 10-5.

**385 PET-A-LLAMA RANCH 823-9395**
Chuck & Pat Warner 5505 Lone Pine Rd.
Sebastopol 95472. Llamas for sale.
Handspun llama garments. Carded llama
fleece. Knitting yarn. Tours by appt. small fee.
Jan-Mar, open Sat only 10-4. Apr-Dec open
Sat-Sun 10-4 Free.

**589 PETERSON'S FARM 765-4582**
Ray & Ettamarie 636 Gossage Ave.,
Petaluma 94952. Pumpkins, dried flowers,
honey. Oct 1-31 from 10-6. Call ahead rest
of year. School groups by appt. Animals to
feed. Classes on flower wreath making avail.

## FARM TRAILS MEMBERS

**304 SEBASTOPOL VINYRDS 829-WINE**
8757 Green Valley Rd., Sebastopol, 95472
Wine Tasting Room, Giftshop, Gourmet foods
and snacks. Award winning Pinot Noir and
Chardonnay. Grav, Jonathan, Red & Golden
Del, Rome Aug 1-Sept 1. Tasting Room open
year around and by appointment.

**170 STARCROSS TREES & WREATHS**
526-0108 / 886-5446
P.O. Box 14279, Santa Rosa 95402.
Christmas trees: Scotch pine, hand crafted
wreaths. Both shipped UPS on phone or
mail order. Brochure available.

**705 STONECROFT FARM 584-1414**
Marcus & Lynda Garcia 1610 Crane Canyon
Rd., Santa Rosa 95404 Honey and award-
winning honey products including BBQ sauce,
honey-lemon nectar, honey jellies, beeswax
candles, herbs, herbal cosmetics and more.
Open Thur-Sun 11-5. Call ahead.

**302 TOPOLOS @ RUSSIAN RIVER VINYRD**
Restaurant: 887-1562 Winery: 887-1575
Michael Topolos 5700 Gravenstein Hwy N.
Forestville, 95436 100% Sonoma County
gold medal, dry farmed, organically grown
wines. Tasting room (Restaurant, indoors &
outdoors) Mail order. Open daily 11-5:30.

**352 TWIN HILL RANCH 823-2815**
1689 Pleasant Hill Rd, Sebastopol 95472
Apples, almonds, walnuts, persimmons, dried
fruits, firewood. Apple products: juice, pies &
bread. Tours, picnic area. 8:30-5 daily but Sun

**437 WAYWARD GARDENS 829-8225**
Leana Beeman-Sims 1296 Tilton Rd.
Sebastopol 95472. Delightful flower gardens
surround this hilltop nursery that specializes in
plants that attract birds & butterflies. Also,
fragrant plants, cottage garden favorites & cut
flowers. Mar-Nov Fri-Sun 11-5 Fax: 829-3277

**144 WESTSIDE FARMS 431-1432 /**
Pam & Ron Kaiser 7079 Westside Rd.,
Healdsburg 95446. Put a little farm in your
life! Fresh/dried flowers, produce, yarn,
wreaths, popcorn & more. Farm animals.
June - self serve U Pick berries. October - daily
for the Pumpkin Festival.

## The
## FARM TRAILS
# GUIDE

# FARM TRAILS LISTINGS
## and
# INDEPENDENT GROWERS

### FARM TRAILS MEMBERS

745 WILLIE BIRD TURKEY   545-2832
5150 Hwy 12, Santa Rosa 95407. Deli:
Turkey, fresh ground, sausage, steaks, eggs,
smoked turkey & chicken. Open all year Mon-
Fri 9-6, Sat 9-5.

300  YA-KA-AMA INDIAN ED. CNTR.
    887-1541
6215 Eastside Rd. Forestville. Native plants &
grasses, specialty seeds, demonstration
gardens, U-Pick organic vegetables & herbs,
gourds. Contract growing. Indian arts & crafts,
Indian publications and bookstore. All year
Mon-Fri 9-5, Sat-Sun 10-3.

### INDEPENDENT GROWERS / SUPPLIERS

COTTAGE GARDEN GROWERS  778-8025
4049 Petaluma Blvd. N. up Pine Tree Lane),
Petaluma. Daria Morrill & Bruce Shanks.
Grower direct variety, quality and savings on
unique perennials, roses and clematis vines.
Educational & self guided tour. Open daily 9-5

FULTON CREEK NURSERY FARM
Box 558, Fulton, CA. 95439   578-6010
Live plants. Herb garden window boxes,
culinary and medicinal plants, vegetables,
flowers and fruit trees. See at Sonoma and
Marin County farmer's markets.

GARDEN VALLEY RANCH ROSES
WEB: www.gardenvalley.com   792-0377
Rayford Reddell  498 Pepper Rd., Petaluma,
CA. 94952  8,000 Rosebushes, one acre
fragrance garden, self guided tour & guided
tours, wedding & event site, nursery. Finest
garden roses in America. Wholesale only

GRASS ROOTS FARM email:devin@sonic.net
Small permaculture farm. Starts and plants
for your home or office garden. 100's of
vegetables, salad greens, edible and medicinal
herbs lovingly grown with organic soil, well
water & Sonoma sunshine.
Mary @ 829-4733 or Carrie @ 824-0257

### INDEPENDENT GROWERS / SUPPLIERS

LAGUNA FARMS   823-0823
1764 Cooper Rd., Sebastopol, 95472
Certified organic farm on the Laguna de Santa
Rosa. 100's of healthy - chemical free fruits,
vegetables & herbs. Model of sustainable
agriculture. Wildlife, growers and nature are in
friendly balance. Workstudy & internships.

LANDMADE COMPANY, The   829-6337
Box 1543, 2701 Gravenstein Hwy S.,
Sebastopol 95472  www.thelandmadeco.com
Aroma-therapeutic herbal soaps with pure
essential oils and organically grown or wild
crafted herbs. Medicinal soaps, bath oils, bath
salts & scrubs. Consciously created from
ingredients gathered from Sonoma forests,
meadows and coastline by Donna & family.
Gifts your angel would adore.

LEFT FIELD FARM   829-8102
Lawrence  4220 Walker Ave., Santa Rosa
95471. CCOF Vegetables, fruits, culinary &
medicinal herbs and flowers.

MOM'S APPLE PIES   823-8330
4550 Gravenstein Hwy S., Sebastopol 95472
Fresh baked fruit pies (whole or by the slice),
coffee and beverages. Eat indoors or to go.

MOMS HEAD GARDENS   585-8575
4153 Langner Ave., Santa Rosa, CA. 95407
e mail: momshead@ap.net  Fax:585-1264
Whimsical organic garden where 100's of rare
medicinal and culinary herbs from around the
world are carefully grown. Classes and special
events  The brain child of two motion picture
film editors - Vivien Hillgrove and Karen
Brocco. Write for a newsletter (for $5 per
year) that has information about herbs and
zany anecdotes about the garden.

ORTIZ BROTHERS   542-5238
766 Bellew Ave., Santa Rosa  Vegetables,
fruits, culinary & medicinal herbs and flowers.
MOM'S HEAD GARDENS

### INDEPENDENT GROWERS / SUPPLIERS

**OCCIDENTAL ART & ECOLOGY CENTER**
15290 Coleman Vly Rd, Occidental 874-1557
Fax: 874-1558 Email: oaec@igc.org   A must
see educational/intentional community,
seasonal plant sales, tours, visionary classes in
sustainability and creating innovative &
practical solutions. Brochure & curriculum.

**RAINBOW'S END FARM**          874-2315
13140 Frati Lane, Sebastopol 95472  Over
20 years growing organic produce without
pesticides or poisons. Vegetables, fruits &
herbs. Also: www.counterculture.com

**SUNSHINE FARMS**          894-3984
Egmont Tripp, 26653 River Rd., Cloverdale,
95425 Organically grown vegetables.
Gourmet garlic from around the world, 40 +
varieties, food & seed stock.  Avail by mail
order or on the farm Fri 10-5 or call in your
order 24 hrs ahead May - Nov.

**SUNDANCE FARMS**      525-0779
3015 Petaluma Hill Rd., Santa Rosa, CA.
95404  Vini or Sandy  17th Century Bio-
Organic Gardeners.  CCOF Vegetables, fruits,
culinary & medicinal herbs, flowers and
saffron.  Inquire about the 17th Century
Organics Newsletter with tasty recipes, news
items and tips revealing the truth of small
verses corporate organic farming.  Whats

really safe for your family, children or loved
ones? Call or write.

**TAYLOR MAID FARMS**          824-9110
6793 McKinley, Sebastopol 95472  Premium
organic coffees,organic herbal teas, jams &
jellies, herb, seed & vegetable farm/retreat
center.  Feel good coffee/good seed company.

**WILD ABOUT MUSHROOMS**     887-1888
Box 1088, Forestville, CA. 95436
email: charmoon@trr.metro.net
www.wildmushrooms.qpg.com/  Charmoon
Richardson studied the Web of Life with Jesse
Longacre (see page 52).  Learn how to forage
for edible and medicinal mushrooms in
northern California.  Forays for boletes,
matsuke & chantrelles as well as many other
fine edibles, great feasting parties, specimen
study tables and much more at beautiful
locations.  Group mushrooms camps,
identification classes & evening presentations.
Call or email for a free brochure.

### FARMER'S MARKETS
**SANTA ROSA**  Veterans Memorial Bldg
parking lot.  Saturdays all year 9am-noon.
**SEBASTOPOL**  McKinley St. & Petaluma Ave
(Weeks Way parking lot) May-Oct Sunday 10-1
**PETALUMA**
A Street parking lot.  May-Oct 2pm - 5pm
**GUALALA**  Community Center May 15-Oct 31
Saturday 3pm-5pm. Walter Stillman  882-2474

## THE GROWING CONCERN

   Giants in the garden are not only redwood trees.
There is a giant in each of us that needs to be let out and
The Growing Concern is the destination to do just that.
Thousands of plants in pots kissed by the clear coastal
breeze, golden sunlight, butterfly's and hummingbirds are
ready to come home to your garden.  Since 1987 Kathy
Massara has cultivated a relationship with plants and
people.  Walk behind the white picket fence and enter
her spectacular garden setting overflowing with flowers,
herbs, vegetables, fruit trees, ferns, succulents, vines,
cactus and ground cover.  Inside the Garden Shop are
seeds, organic fertilizer, garden tools, irrigation systems,
books, cards, ornate pots and outside are fountains, statuary, garden tables and
chairs.  The seasonal Christmas store gets rave reviews and be sure to ask about
special classes, events and discounts.  "We are here to promote successful
gardening and fun." states Kathy.
*$-$$ THE GROWING CONCERN*      *Hwy 1@ Pacific Woods, Gualala, CA*
*Plants, Gifts and Advice*      ATM, MC & Visa      *(707) 884-3982*

Harmony Farm Supply's demonstration orchard's gardens and nursery (left). The huge retail store located just 3 miles north of Sebastopol, California (below). "Little green friends" enhance our home and office life enormously.

### HARMONY FARM SUPPLY

A visit to Harmony Farm Supply is an important first step to take to secure the future for yourself and your loved ones.  Plan on making Harmony Farm Supply's 5 acre demonstration orchard, gardens and nursery; as well as their retail store a destination the next time you are in Western Sonoma County.

Since 1980 Harmony Farm Supply has grown to become one of the most complete garden and farm suppliers north of San Francisco. Harmony Farm Supply's resident experts work everyday to make your garden the best on the block and your farm the most productive.  They offer friendly and expert advice, pointing out a splendid library of books and special reports, as well as certified organic seeds, plants and soils, organic fertilizers, natural pest controls, irrigation equipment, the proper hand and power tools, light to heavy garden and farm equipment, landscaping and nursery stock.  A special treat is to stroll amid thousands of baby plants, shrubs and trees in the nursery with one of Harmony's expert horticulturists or gardeners.  Free workshops are offered throughout the year on various topics, including organic gardening and drip irrigation.

Whether you are a vintner, innkeeper, chef, or want the very best for your family, friends, pets and clients, an edible or medicinal landscape around the home or work place is a sure way to enhance your life.  Watch the stress level go down after a break with your loved ones or co-workers in the office or home garden.  Conference calls or data basing on the computer go much better if you are surrounded by lots of little green friends who love you.  You can also shop the aisles of the Harmony Farm Supply retail store and warehouse through their mail order catalog which showcases all their products and then some. The highest quality seeds, books, and supplies can be shipped to your garden gate. Harmony Farm Supply also has E Mail and an Internet Site http://harmonyfarm.com

*$-$$$ HARMONY FARM SUPPLY   3244 Gravenstein Hwy N., Sebastopol, Farm and Garden Supplies  Mail Order, Major Credit Cards (707) 823-9125*

## GREEN VALLEY FARM

In 1940 Elizabeth Goetz brought the first blueberries to California; ignoring all the horticultural rules that blueberries won't grow here - not cold enough people warned. "Worth a try." Elizabeth said. Fifty years later her grandson, Bruce Goetz and his family continue to cultivate her original plantings and have added a few of their own.

The snare drum of patriotism and duty called Bruce to be the first Sonoma County Farm Trails president in the early 1970's. I remember the early meetings when farmers would come in from the fields with weeds and soil still on their clothes to speak their thoughts at loosely organized meetings which would lay the foundation for the yet to come thriving growth of the Sonoma County Farm Trails. Today a tour map and full showcasing of Sonoma Select Products are in place. "Our very survival as farmers as opposed to being bulldozed into housing developments

was tied to those early meetings", states Bruce. Today's farmer is unique compared to the past, but the simple dignity of tilling the soil till harvest remains the same.

Today's visitors who come to purchase quarts and lugs of blueberries will also enjoy the farm store where *blueberry* milk shakes, muffins, tarts, pies, cookies and fresh brewed coffee is served. Attractively labeled jars of jam line the walls including blueberry, red raspberry, boysenberry, strawberry, wild blackberry, loganberry, huckleberry, black raspberry, kiwi, apricot, apricot / pineapple, sweet pepper marmalade and apple butter. A thriving mail order business showcases Green Valley Farm products. The mail order country catalog features attractive gift packs with jars of jams & jellies in rich redwood boxes and wicker baskets overflowing with fancy fruits, nuts, conserves, chutney, marmalade, mustard, spices, salsas, popcorn and wine. All the wonderful touches from the farm to put that special old fashioned spark and glitter in the holidays, birthdays, anniversaries and special events are available by stopping by Green Valley Farms, calling toll free 1-800-827-9590 or writing for a free mail order catalog at the address below. A visit to the farm enriches my body and soul with the memories of a rich childhood of living and working on the farm. Plop a ripe blueberry into the mouth - gently squeeze - and it goes off in a luscious explosion of unforgettable flavors!

*$ GREEN VALLEY FARM 9345 Ross Station Road, Sebastopol, CA. 95472*
*Fresh berries, Soda fountain, & Mail Order Catalog.*
*Farm Store open daily during the harvest / otherwise 9am - 5pm Mon - Fri.*
*(707) 887-7496 or          Fax: (707) 887-7499 Orders and Information*
*http://www.metro.net/greenvalley/          Toll Free: 1-800 - 827-9590*

The Kozlowski Family enjoying each other on the farm's picnic grounds overlooking their berry field and apple orchard.

***"We don't claim to make the most . . . only the best."***

## KOZLOWSKI FARMS

Established in 1947, Kozlowski Farms is one of the oldest established family farms in Sonoma County. Tony and Carmen Kozlowski began farming the rich, sandy loam soils of West Sonoma County;   growing cherries, apples and berries of unrivaled quality by utilizing innovative farming techniques during the 50's & 60's. Sensing the demand for the delectable, luscious red raspberries among Sonoma County residents, and farming an over production of apples, Tony planted 15 acres of red raspberries in 1968 and soon became known as the "Berry King" of Sonoma County.

Today the 3rd generation of Kozlowski Farms, Carol, Perry & Cindy, please people just like you with their delicious jams, jellies, fresh baked pies, and fresh squeezed fruit juices at their farm store located just outside Forestville.  Due to the pioneering efforts of the entire Kozlowski Farms family,  Sonoma County farm fresh fruits "are spread coast to coast" on bagels, muffins and bread at sunrise each morning.   Increased demand for the style of specialty foods produced by the Kozlowski Farms has compelled the family to expand their product line to well over 65 items.  Included are the original, old fashioned jams and jellies, 100% fruit added spreads, wine jellies, gourmet mustards, 100% fruit added fruit butters, marmalades, 100% fruit added chutneys, berry vinegars, fat free and no oil salad dressings, pasta sauces and a delicious country style BBQ sauce enhanced by the flavor and richness of cabernet sauvignon wine.

The farm and picnic area overlooking beautiful Green Valley is located 70 miles north of San Francisco on Highway 116 near Forestville.  Be sure to stop by and sample and taste the farm fresh products that helped make the Sonoma County farm country famous.  You can also write for a free mail order catalog showcasing the wonderful array of Kozlowski farm fresh products.

*$ KOZLOWSKI FARMS 5566 Gravenstein Hwy (116), Forestville, CA. 95436*
*MC & Visa    Open daily from 9am to 5pm.          Fax: (707) 887-9650*
*Tele: (707) 887-1587        Mail Orders: 800-473-2767 or 800 4 R FARMS*

## WESTSIDE FARMS

Located along the Russian River in the beautiful Sonoma County wine country is Westside Farms. We all hear the call. It is in our genetic memory to grow and harvest crops. Yet fewer than 1/2 % of Americans become real farmers. "You are brave," stated one guest who was on a tractor drawn hay wagon ride through the vineyards and farm crops of Westside Farms. Pam and

Ron Kaiser are locally famous for their farm tours and store which entertains and educates thousands of children and adults between May and October.

In the cozy Westside Farms Store, fresh seasonal produce grown just outside the windows is eagerly purchased by visitors. Beautiful hand-made wreaths, wedding flower bouquets and a large assortment of country gifts are attractively displayed. Classes in ornamental flower arranging and wreath making fill up. Seasonal crops include 2 dozen varieties of fresh flowers, herbs, peppers, tomatoes, garlic, sweet onions, sweet corn, Indian corn and the ever popular pumpkin harvest. Children and adults love the pumpkin painting, carving and pie baking contest. The hay rides through the Westside Farms U-pick pumpkin fields and vineyards are followed by a lecture and sampling of grapes picked right off the vine. The farm animals are a delight to children who have never seen a baby donkey or full grown pig let alone pet one.

The original farmhouse at the top of the hill still stands thanks to its sturdy foundation of first-cut redwood beams and rocks (yes, the floors and doorways are all a little crooked, but it certainly has charm!). Pam and Ron Kaiser purchased the farm and large hop kilns in 1988 and named it Westside Farms. Now consisting of 62 acres, the Kaisers have revived and restored this traditional family farm and are pleased to be able to share the beauty and serenity of life at a slower pace with you today. When you visit Westside Farms you *"Put a little farm in your life!"*.

Be sure to ask about or write for the Westside Farms Home Catalog. It is full of marvelous gifts that will bring warmth and light to your life. Candles, one item in the mail order catalog includes the following description by Pam and Ron. "Here at the farm our family dinner hour is about the most important part of the day. We gather ourselves together - to share a meal, yes - but mostly to share the events of the day. We turn down the kitchen light, take a long relaxing breath, and light a candle to soothe our day-weary minds. The candle calms us down and slows our pace. And we all look so pretty in candle light! We've done it this way for years."

Westside Farms is open from May 25 - November 26. The Farm Store is usually open from 10am to 5pm, however hours change monthly with the seasons.

*$-$$ WESTSIDE FARMS      7079 Westside Road, Healdsburg, CA 95448*
*Working Farm and Store MC & Visa.   Mail Order Catalog: (707) 431-1432*
*Credit Card orders by Fax: (707) 431-9433.    Information: 800-431-9434*

## SEBASTOPOL VINEYARDS

Joe and Tracy Dutton had a dream. That they would one day raise a family and own their own vineyards and winery. Today, at Sebastopol Vineyards, Joe and Tracy's toddler children are being raised  on an emerald green hilltop of vineyards and forested slopes of apple orchards. Tracy and Joe knew that their dream would begin with a thought, then the spoken word and finally a plan of action. They both came from pioneer Sonoma County farming families. Joe was raised on Dutton Ranch, where he learned his father, techniques to grow apples and high quality wine grapes. Tracy is a 3rd generation Kozlowski of Kozlowski Farms. Their legacy and farming empire is known from shore to shore and from the White House to Europe.

They invite you to visit their tasting room located between Sebastopol and Forestville in the Green Valley of the Russian River grape growing appellations. Besides Sebastopol Vineyards vintages of Chardonnay and Pinot Noir, you can taste the award winning releases from other wineries, specially created with 100% Dutton Ranch grapes. The tasting room is most attractive and show cases a variety of Dutton Ranch fresh apples, Sonoma County goodies and gifts.

*$ SEBASTOPOL VINEYARDS     8757 Green Valley Rd., Sebastopol, CA.*
*Wine Tasting Room, Apples & Gourmet Gifts  MC & Visa  (707) 829-WINE*

## STONECROFT FARM and SONOMA MOUNTAIN HONEY

140 years ago, stone sections on mule driven wagons were brought to the Sonoma Valley Property which is Stonecroft Farm. These sections were cut into thick square blocks and fashioned into a two-story house by master stone masons. Marcus and Lynda Gracia own and manage the farm, which is located at the foot of majestic Sonoma Mountain. From the top of this mountain you can see the Golden Gate Bridge.

It is here that honeybees collect their nectar and pollen, which the bees make into the wonderful honey used by Marcus and Lynda for all their marvelous honey products, Honey Lemon Nectar, Honey BBQ Sauces, Honey Jellies, Beeswax candles, herbal cosmetics, and much more. Marcus and Lynda are dedicated to educating everyone on the fantastic life of the honeybee. Children and adults have a lot of fun on their first safe adventure visiting a honeybee hive. Come and visit the organic farm and purchase the wonderful honey and honey products all year around. Call for information and special events.

*$ SONOMA MOUNTAIN HONEY 1610 Crane Canyon Rd., Santa Rosa,*
*Award Winning Honey and Products  CA. 95404   Open Thur-Sun 11-5*
*Email: sonomamountainhoney   Internet: wwwsonomamountainhoney.com*
*Fax:  707) 585-9433              (707) 584-1414 Directions & Info*

## WILLIE BIRDS

Photo by Harvey Henneson

"It was 1963 when I started raising and selling fresh free range turkeys and chickens during a Future Farmers of America project," states Willie Benedetti. "I was thirteen. Grandpa had been raising turkeys since 1924 during prohibition. Then in 1939 my father started raising turkeys, and now myself," continued Willie - "hence the name Willie Bird Turkeys."

"My turkeys are special," Willie continues. "They are all free range birds, raised on all natural grains and vegetable protein; never frozen - and delivered fresh from the farm to insure superior quality. My poultry goes to the smoke house where they absorb depth and character from alder wood smoke."

" In 1975 we opened our retail sales outlet making turkey a one item meal. In 1980 we went into the restaurant business to show consumers the many ways turkey could be served. Now we have our own "Willie Bird" restaurant in south Santa Rosa on Santa Rosa Avenue which opened in 1980," concludes Willie.

In the comfortable restaurant and bar in Santa Rosa it can be Thanksgiving and Christmas all year around. Delicious variations of turkey are served for breakfast, lunch and dinner along with fresh fish, beef and vegetarian entries. You can start the day with the Willie Bird Special - 2 eggs, Mama Bird's homemade turkey sausage, home fries and toast or choose from a variety of omelettes, side orders, orange juice, milk, coffee and tea. The lunch menu lists a variety of hot and cold sandwiches, salads, homemade soup, special Diet I,II & III dishes or the child's plate.   Both the lunch and dinner menu also offer oysters, prawns, scallops and extra large steaks. Don't forget the full bar with private and comfortable booths and there is a private dining room with seating for up to 60.

Just before Thanksgiving the retail farm store parking lot resembles the Golden Gate bridge at rush hour. So many cars line up that the highway patrol has to direct traffic. It's best to order and pick up your turkey a week in advance. The store is open all year around and is stocked with smoked turkey, smoked chicken, smoked Muscovy duck, roasted & smoked turkey breast, turkey sausages, smoked pheasant, smoked quail, smoked squab and smoked partridge. Snacks, excellent sandwiches, salads, coffee, soft drinks and mineral water are also served daily.

Willie Birds is the last independent turkey producer in the San Francisco Bay Area.  Their turkeys are raised at the Estero Americana in a pristine location of clear coastal air and pure water with lots of personal attention for the flock.

*$-$$WILLIE BIRD'S STORE & DELI*
*Smoked Poultry and Sandwiches*
*5350 Sebastopol Rd., Santa Rosa*
*Open daily 9am - 5pm / Sat till 4pm*
*MC & Visa  Fax: (707) 575-9036*
*(707) 545-2832     www.williebird.com*

*$-$$ WILLIE BIRD'S RESTAURANT*
*American Cuisine*
*1150 Santa Rosa Ave., Santa Rosa*
*Breakfast: 6am - 11am,  Lunch:*
*11am - 3pm,  Dinner: 5pm - 9pm*
*AE, MC & Visa  (707) 542-0861*

# FORESTVILLE
## Orchards, Vineyards and Rolling Hills

**FORESTVILLE DINER'S CHOICE:  Telephone Area Code is (707).**
**Chez Marie** ($$) 6675 Front St. 887-7503;  **Forestville Inn Mexican Restaurant** ($) 6625 Front Street 887-1242. **Green Valley Farm** ($) 9345 Ross Station Rd.  887-7496;  **Journey's End Coffee House** ($) 6544 Front Street  887-9647;  **Kozlowski's Farms** ($) 5566 Gravenstein Hwy N. 887-1587;  **Mom's Apple Pie** ($) 4550 Gravenstein Hwy N. 823-8330;  **Spanky's Pizza** ($$) Westside Shopping Center  887-9574; **Topolos @ Russian River Vineyards** ($$) 5700 Gravenstein Hwy N. 887-1562;  **Willowside Cafe ($$)** 3535 Guerneville Rd.  523-4814.

**FORESTVILLE LODGING:**
**Farmhouse Inn ($$)**  7871 River Rd. 887-3300;  **Raford House ($$)** 10630 River Rd.  887-9503.

**FORESTVILLE WINERIES:**
**See Winery Tasting Room Listings on Page 183**
**Davis Bynum Winery, Mark West Vineyards, Martinellis Winery, Martini & Prati, Sebastopol Vineyards, Topolos @ Russian River Vineyards and Villa Pompei Vineyards.**

## TOPOLOS @ RUSSIAN RIVER VINEYARDS

An Orthodox Russian steeple rises from the vineyards in a lush valley bordering the sleepy town of Forestville, California. This castle fashioned from redwood timbers is the home of Topolos at Russian River Vineyards, wine and cuisine. With a do-it-yourself pioneer spirit, Michael, Jerry and Christine, "hand make everything" to maintain the high standards of quality they feel their guests deserve.

The grounds and buildings are enchanting. Rows of vineyards, lush hillsides and meadows flow to infinity. Michael and his crew of experienced vineyard workers prune many of the vines to improve the grape. "You can't make great wine from bad grapes," Michael explains, "We prune for quality, not quantity." Throughout the entire life cycle of the grape meticulous attention to quality is maintained. Chardonnay, Zinfandel, Cabernet Sauvignon, Petite Sirah and Alicante Bouschet are produced and bottled at the winery. To gather a hint of the pleasures in store you can visit the tasting room or better yet have dinner with the Topolos's in their charming restaurant.

Jerry and Christine expertly guide their dinner guests through the evening's offerings. Spirited dining is at its best here. Christine and chef Robert Engel, create exceptional variations of Greek and continental dishes. Your entree is accompanied with tzatziki (a garlic, cucumber yogurt dip) sweet butter and French bread. Wonderful soups & salads are served a la carte. The catch of the day, New York Steak with green peppercorn sauce, Souvlaki (marinated lamb en brochette) Spanakopita and Breast of Chicken and daily specials, appetizers and desserts are served. Seating is indoors in one of three dining rooms, one of which is a brick patio with fireplace. Weather permitting, the outdoor patio is the best way to appreciate the fragrance of the gardens, singing birds, and the melody of the splashing fountain. Sunday brunch is a festive affair from the Quiche Lorraine to Eggs Benedict. Light country lunches attract guests to savor the Greek salad, Vineyard sandwich, Tiropitas, or Quiche.

*$-$$ TOPOLOS AT RUSSIAN RIVER VINEYARDS*
*Continental/Greek Cuisine      Tasting Room open year round Wed. - Sun.*
*5700 Gravenstein Hwy. N    from 11am-5:30pm. Sun. Br. from 10:30am,*
*Forestville, CA. 95436    Dinners frm 5:30pm, AE, Dis, Diners, MC, Visa.*
*Restaurant: (707) 887-1562           Winery: (707) 887-1575*

## JOURNEY'S END COFFEE HOUSE

This upbeat coffee house hosts poetry readings, live music from acoustical to blues and serves hot food at prices that don't burn. Needless to say its a popular stop for local artists and surfers who want to relax or catch up on some reading at a table or on the comfortable couch, play chess or catch up on surfing news. The burnt orange brushed interior tends to pick up your energy while you are perusing the selections of pastries, light snacks, and wafting in the smell of high powered coffee drinks. Proprietors Lana Marra, and surfer Dale Williams serve delicious breakfast & lunch burritos, sumptuous desserts, smoothies and hot and cold beverages. *Open 6am-6pm weekdays, 8am-8pm weekends*

*$ JOURNEY'S END COFFEE HOUSE      6544 Front Street, Forestville,*
*Coffee House                            CA. 95472    (707) 887-9647*

## SPANKY'S PASTA & PIZZA

Smart restaurateurs know the secret to success is to serve a quantity of quality of food at a fair price. At Spanky's Pizza in Forestville you can feed a family of four for under $20. Located atop the hill in the Westside Shopping Center, Spanky's offers great parking, a spacious dining room and tree top views of Forestville. Generous servings of spaghetti and ravioli, sandwiches, hamburgers and homemade pizza are served daily from 11:30am to 9pm (till 10pm on friday & saturday). Light eaters will enjoy Spanky's salad bar (sm $2.50 / large $3.50). Proprietor Don Auch, his son Dan and his wife Michelle create each pizza from scratch out of homemade dough, herbs and sauce topped with a choice of over a dozen ingredients. Meat eaters will enjoy the Spanky's Combo with mozzarella, provolone, cheddar, pepperoni, mushrooms, olives, sausage, linguica, green peppers and onions. The Vegetable Supreme is topped with mushrooms, olives, green peppers, onions and garlic. In addition, Mc Dougal style fat free pizzas can be made.

Don also teaches aviation at Santa Rosa Junior College. Be sure to ask him about a spectacular flight over the Sonoma Coast for some whale and wave watching topped off with a flyover above the fabled golden Buddhist Temple of Odiyan.

*$ SPANKY'S PIZZA    P.O. Box 580, Westside Shopping Center,  Forestville,*
*   Pizza, Pasta & Salads    CA. 95436   MC & Visa      (707) 887-9574 to go*

## MARTINI & PRATI WINERY

Few wineries can boast a century of winemaking with five generations of family. Such is the case at Martini & Prati. The story of family commitment, service, fun, ingenuity and vision is revealed through a visit and tour of this historic winery.

History lines the walls of the Italian Country Store and tasting room, with historic tours offered daily at 11am. The proud Italian heritage is exemplified by exceptional vintages of Sangiovese, Barbera, Moscato Bianco and Meritage as well as more traditional releases of Chardonnay, Sauvignon Blanc, Cabernet Sauvignon, Merlot, and Zinfandel. You'll enjoy tasting these award winning vintages and picnicking by the vineyards. The Italian Country Store is stocked with gifts and Italian food specialties to compliement your picnic or special home event.

Look for the giant silver water tank towering above the vineyards at the winery's entrance on Laguna Road, which is 5 miles west of Santa Rosa. The tasting room is open June-Oct from 10am - 5pm and Nov-May from 11am - 4pm.

*$$ MARTINI & PRATI        2191 Laguna Road, Santa Rosa, CA. 95401*
*Tasting, Tours, Retail Sales & Giftshop    MC & Visa Fax: (707) 829-6151*
*Web: martiniprati.com                        Information: (707) 823-2404*

## MARK WEST
## ESTATE WINERY

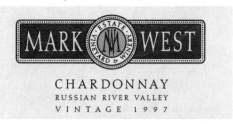

Mark West Vineyards is located a short drive up picturesque Trenton-Healdsburg Road where it conjuncts River Road making it a convenient wine country stop between Highway 101 and the coastline at Jenner. The views are spectacular and there is a lovely picnic area where you can enjoy the premium wines of Mark West Vineyards as well as cheese and crackers from the tasting room giftshop.

Mark West winemaker Kerry Damskey takes advantage of the soil conditions, rainfall and daily temperatures, to produce grapes for full flavored, perfectly balanced award winning wines. Releases of Chardonnay, Gewurztraminer, Sauvignon Blanc, Merlot and Pinot Noir are a few of the wines Mark West is famous for. You can savor the wines inside the tasting room, which is also stocked with culinary goodies and country gifts, or outside on the picnic tables under the shade of redwood and fir. The tasting room is open from 10am - 4:30pm June thru October and 11am - 4pm November thru May.

*$$ MARK WEST ESTATE VINEYARDS   7010 Trenton - Healdsburg Road,*
*Tasting and Retail Sales  MC & Visa                Forestville, CA. 95436*
*Web: markwestwinery.com    Fax: (707) 836-0147    Info: (707) 836-9647*

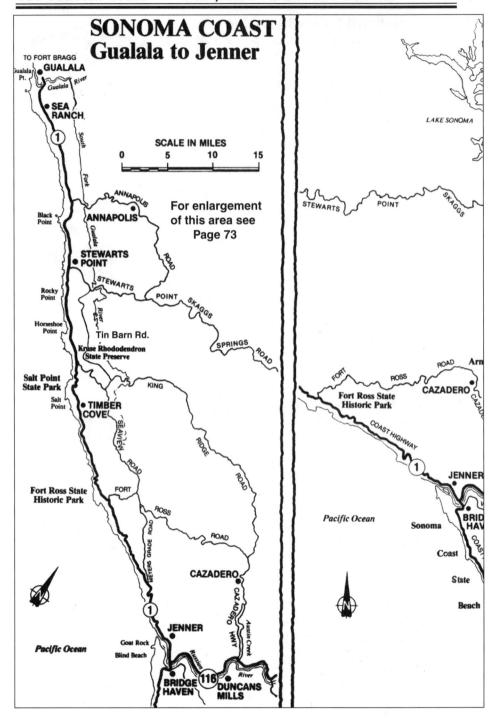

# SONOMA COAST
# Gualala to Jenner

TO FORT BRAGG

GUALALA

Gualala Pt.

Gualala River

SEA RANCH

1

South Fork

**SCALE IN MILES**

0    5    10    15

Black Point

ANNAPOLIS

For enlargement
of this area see
Page 73

ANNAPOLIS

Gualala

STEWARTS POINT

Rocky Point

STEWARTS

POINT

SKAGGS

River

Horseshoe Point

Tin Barn Rd.

SPRINGS ROAD

Kruse Rhododendron
State Preserve

Salt Point State Park

KING

Salt Point

TIMBER COVE

SEAVIEW ROAD

RIDGE

ROAD

Fort Ross State
Historic Park

FORT

ROSS

ROAD

MEYERS GRADE ROAD

CAZADERO

1

Goat Rock

JENNER

CAZADERO HWY

Austin Creek

Blind Beach

Pacific Ocean

Russian River

116

River

BRIDGE HAVEN

DUNCANS MILLS

N

LAKE SONOMA

STEWARTS     POINT     SKAGGS

FORT     ROSS     ROAD     Arn

CAZADERO     CAZAD

Fort Ross State
Historic Park

COAST HIGHWAY

1

JENNER

Pacific Ocean

Sonoma

BRID
HAV

Coast

State

Beach

COAST

N

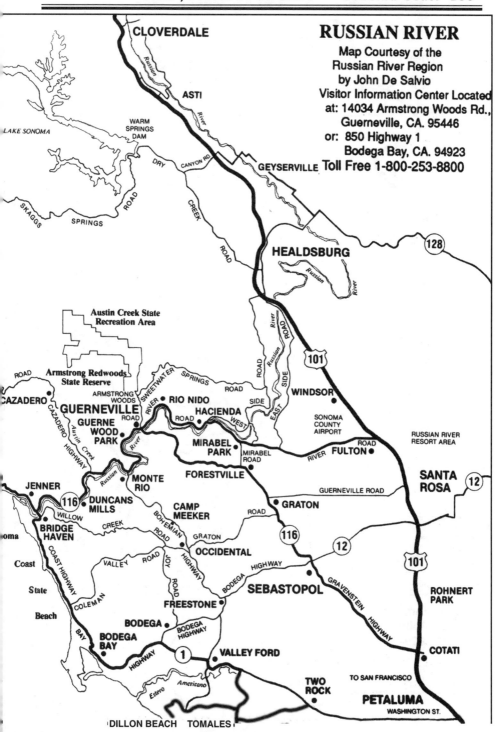

# RUSSIAN RIVER

Map Courtesy of the
Russian River Region
by John De Salvio
Visitor Information Center Located
at: 14034 Armstrong Woods Rd.,
Guerneville, CA. 95446
or: 850 Highway 1
Bodega Bay, CA. 94923
Toll Free 1-800-253-8800

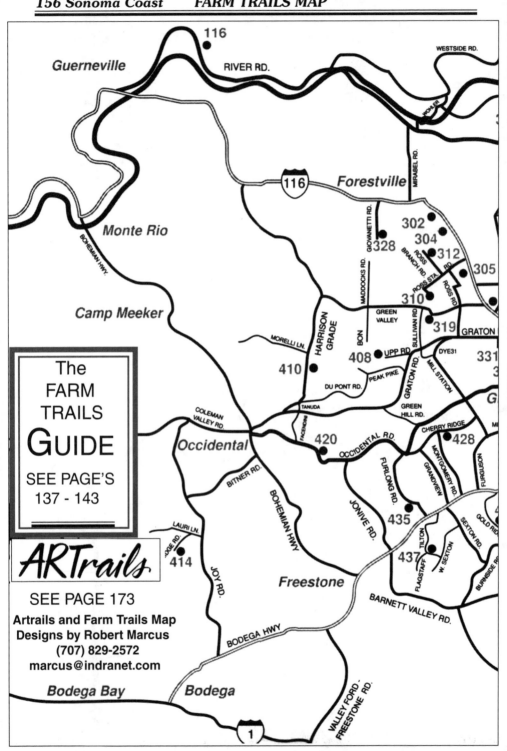

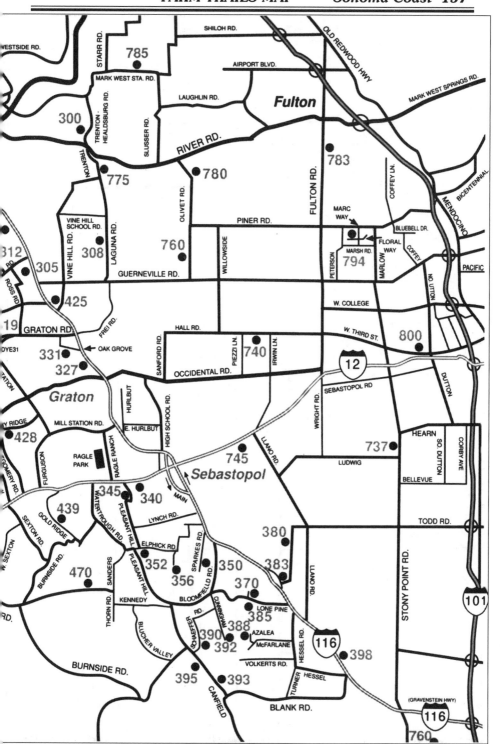

# SANTA ROSA and VICINITY

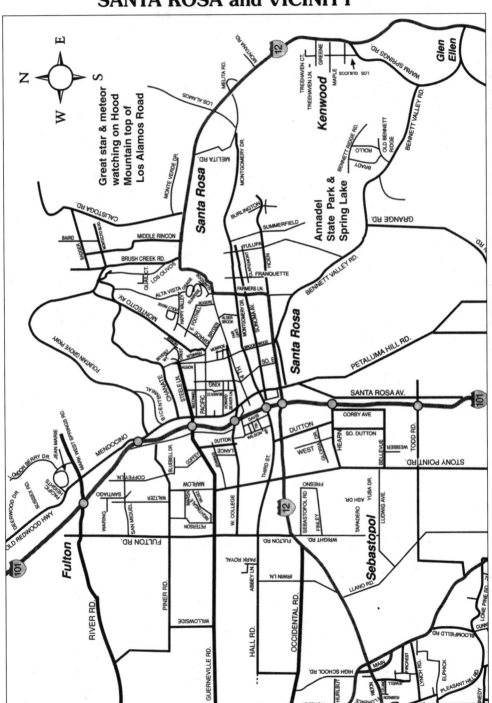

Great star & meteor watching on Hood Mountain top of Los Alamos Road

# DOWNTOWN SANTA ROSA MAP

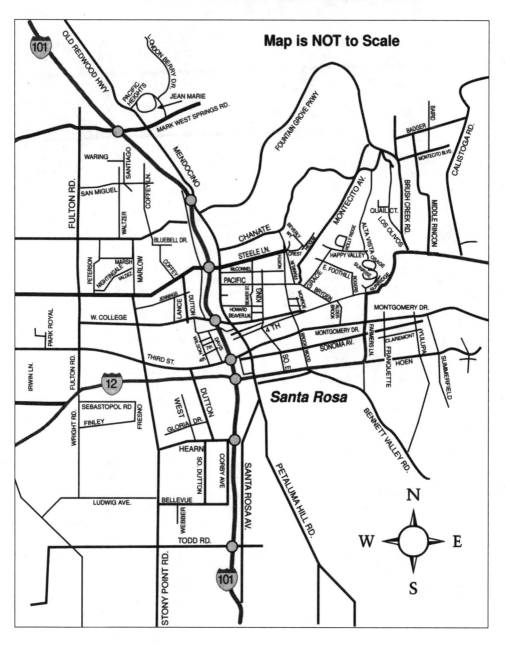

Map is NOT to Scale

Santa Rosa

N
W E
S

Courthouse Square in downtown Santa Rosa is the host of numerous cafes, bookstores, art galleries, shops, cinemas, theatres, and a summertime farmer's market. It is the business hub of northern California.

## SANTA ROSA

Santa Rosa, at first glance, appears to be a typical California city which grew from a Spanish Rancho to an expanding American metropolis. In this fabled scenic valley a unique historical identity was carved out by names like the Fort Ross Russians, General Mariano Vallejo, the Bear Flaggers, Luther Burbank, Jack London, the Fountain Grove Utopians, pianist Paderewski, to the contemporary comic strip artist of "Peanuts" fame, Charles Schulz.

Santa Rosa developed in the center of a broad valley that stretches from San Francisco Bay to the Russian River. With the Russians settling on the north coast in 1812 this valley became the crossroads of a strategic frontier. To prevent the threat of further Russian expansion the Spanish extended their chain of missions northward, and in 1833 the Mexican Government sent General Mariano Vallejo to Sonoma County for purposes of colonization. Senora Carillo, his mother-in-law, founded Rancho Cabeza de Santa Rosa, the first permanent settlement in the area. The arrival of American settlers, and the ensuing Bear Flag Revolt in 1846, turned Santa Rosa into an American trading post which became a surveyed village seven years later. The town fathers maneuvered a special election in 1854 which moved the county seat from Sonoma. Legend tells of a midnight ride with a galloping team that successfully stole court records from Sonoma and delivered them to Santa Rosa, a move intended to block any legal objections from Sonoma. Santa Rosans celebrated with a two day barbecue and fiesta.

In his experimental gardens "Plant Wizard" Luther Burbank produced major variations on some three hundred and eighty-five plants, including the Shasta Daisy.  Visionary's like Henry Ford, Helen Keller, the King of Belgium, pianist Paderewski and Thomas Alva Edison came to Santa Rosa to meet Burbank.  By 1900 he was Sonoma County's most celebrated citizen.  The local school children staged annual pageants honoring Burbank.  The Rose parades brought tourists to see the land of flowers and sunshine!  Charles Schulz, the cartoonist, is today the most famous Santa Rosa resident.  He also walks the path of humor and philanthropy, having created the beloved "Snoopy" cartoon dog as well as donating millions to K-9 companions, Sonoma State University and the arts.

Santa Rosa suffered severely from the great earthquake of 1906.  Nevertheless, the town rebuilt and flourished as an agriculturally oriented town and county seat.  A repeat performance from nearby Roger's Creek fault could devastate downtown Santa Rosa, but with love motivated community leadership, the spirit and the drive of Santa Rosan's could be directed to rebuild the city, making it a true "Partnership Model".

With the opening of the Golden Gate Bridge in 1937 modern transportation linked the area more closely to San Francisco.  During World War II the entire area underwent another population boom, doubling in size between 1940 and 1960.  Today, with a population near 120,000, Santa Rosa is the largest California city north of San Francisco.  It is the gateway to the Redwood Empire, and the economic center of the North Bay Region.  A famous wine country is adjacent, and the surrounding gardens, farms and orchards show that agriculture is still a mainstay of the communities.  Suburban dwellers and retirement settlers show much enthusiasm for the Santa Rosa Valley.

Many sites of historical interest can be explored.  The old Carillo adobe is a crumbling, unmarked remnant.  The Sonoma County Museum, Luther Burbank Gardens and the Church Built From One Tree, which now houses the Robert "Believe it or Not" Ripley Museum, are situated close to the downtown area.  The chief historical attractions, however, are the beautiful old homes.  MacDonald Avenue suggests an unparalleled example of nineteenth century architectural design.  So beautiful is this avenue with its splendid homes that it has been used as a filming location in several motion pictures.

Just to the north of town is the site of Santa Rosa's utopian "love" colony, 1875-1934, on Fountain Grove Ranch, . . . now shared with Hewlett Packard's modern electronics plant.  Local parks like Spring Lake, Annadel State Park, mystical Hood Mountain Regional Park and Sugar Loaf State Park showcase the spectacular beauty of the Santa Rosa area.

Santa Rosa, then, is a vest pocket history of the forces that have shaped the land called California.  The City of Roses, today, is at a crossroads.  Santa Rosa faces a different problem - population growth.  Sonoma County has been described as one of the fastest growing areas in the San Francisco Bay Region.  The demand to live here creates traffic conjestion, high property prices and high rents, which creates homelessness and separation.  Though this crucial problem has not yet been resolved, more and more area residents are concerning themselves in the effort to retain the beauty and unique identity which belongs to Santa Rosa.  The partnership model brought about by those who motivate out of love, not fear, holds the answer.

# FARMER'S MARKETS

By far the most popular is the Santa Rosa Farmer's Market. It can be romantic to stroll the rows of booths and tents overflowing with personality, fresh produce, herbs and flowers as well as arts and crafts and entertainment ranging from rock n' roll, blues, Haiko drummers to guitar strumming street musicians. A bevy of 4th Street coffee shops, bistros, pubs and bookstores compliment the experience. The market is open from 4pm to 9pm one night a week from June through September. Check with the Santa Rosa Chamber of Commerce for which day by stopping by 639 First Street. or calling (707) 545-1414.

Santa Rosa's 4th Street during the evening Farmer's Market is alive with people looking for love as well as the ultimate flower boquet, herb garden or queen of the garden veggies. For a list of other Farmer's Markets see the Farm and Garden Section on page 137.

*Photos Courtesy of Lenny Siegel Photographic (707) 433-5011*

# OLD TOWN, DOWNTOWN, FEEL ALL RIGHT. . . .
## On A Starlit Santa Rosa Night.

A stroll through Historic Railroad Square will reveal antique shops, art galleries, cafes, dinner houses, night clubs and overnight accommodations.

## DINER'S CHOICE in HISTORIC RAILROAD SQUARE:
**A'Roma Roasters** ($), 95 5th 576-7765; **Chevy's Mexican** ($$), 24 4th 571-1082; **Josef's** ($$), 308 Wilson 571-8664; **La Gare** ($$), 208 Wilson 528-4355; **Mixx** ($$), 135 4th 573-1344; **Omelette Express** ($), 112 4th 525-1690; **Ristorante Capri** ($$) 115 Fourth St. 525-0815.

## LODGING in HISTORIC RAILROAD SQUARE:
**Day's Inn** ($$-$$$) 175 Railroad Square 573-9000 / (800) 325-2525; **Hotel La Rose** ($$-$$$) 308 Wilson 579-3200; **Pygmalion House** ($$-$$$) 331 Orange 526-3407.

## JOSEF'S
### Restaurant & Bar

Born in Switzerland and trained at classy hotels in Geneva, Zurich and Verbier winter resort, Josef Keller has "come home" to the stimulating countryside of northern California to serve Sonoma County farm fresh products, the fresh Pacific Coast catch of the day and premium vintages from our many award winning winerys. His beaming face and contented smile

portrays a citizen who knows how to serve and enjoy the richness of life. The proud tradition he lives can now be enjoyed at Josef's Restaurant and Bar, located in the historic Hotel La Rose in Santa Rosa's Historic Railroad Square. Above the restaurant are the tastefully decorated rooms and suites of the hotel.

Josef elegantly caters to his loyal Santa Rosa clients and world travelers who appreciate the ambience created by class and respect. The menu focuses on Sonoma County's seasonal heritage as well as delicacies imported from near and far. Evening hors d' oeuvres include baked Dungeness crab cakes served with remoulade sauce or artichoke bottoms filled with mushroom duxell. A wonderful lobster bisque or French onion soup might be your next choice. Homemade desserts are not to be missed. A cordial relationship with Sonoma County's vintners since the 1970's has helped with the acquisition of a cellar full of rare and special vintages. Josef's historic long bar is also a good place to close that million dollar deal or engage number one in a memorable evening of romance.

*$$-$$$ JOSEF'S RESTAURANT and BAR    308 Wilson Street, Santa Rosa,*
*Classic French Cuisine       CA. 95401        (707) 571-8664 Res. advised*

## LA GARE

La Gare, one of the finest Classic French restaurants in northern California, is located in Old Town Santa Rosa. Seasoned professionals such as Roger Praplan and Jacqueline Bazeley created this

setting of simple French elegance with a charm and grace all to its own. From the menu you may choose variations of beef, lamb, poultry, seafood and vegetarian courses. All produce is as fresh as possible. Dinners include soup, salad and fresh vegetable (from $11.95 to $17.95). There is an excellent wine list featuring premium Sonoma County wines as well as smooth dessert wines. To begin, you might choose Le Pate' en Gelee' a la francaise aux Truffles followed by a salad of South American hearts of palm. Your entree might be Filet of Boeuf Wellington, Demi Canard a l' orange, or Carre' d' Agneau persille. Each night exciting seasonal specials are also available. Strawberry or raspberry flambe" for two and chocolate decadence are but a few of the desserts which are made on the premises. The pleasure will be all yours with dinner at La Gare followed by a stroll through Historic Railroad Square.

*$$ LA GARE                 Dinners: Wed - Thurs. 5:30pm - 10pm*
*Classic French Cuisine      Fri & Sat 5pm - 10pm, Sun 5pm - 9pm.*
*208 Wilson Street, Santa Rosa      (707) 528-4355 Reservations advised*

## OMELETTE EXPRESS

In Historic Railroad Square where Main Street (4th Street) empties into Old Town Santa Rosa you'll find a cozy restaurant called the Omelette Express. Santa Rosan's and visitors constantly file in and out from 6:30am to 3pm for (you guessed it) some of the greatest omelettes in Sonoma County and certainly the largest variety (over 100 combinations are possible).

The railroad theme menu is divided into Mainline omelettes (from $5.35), Switchman's combination omelettes, Switchman's vegetarian and seafood omelettes, and eggs with Baggage and Side Tracks. A few omelette ingredients include artichoke hearts, avocado, bacon, bell pepper, chili, ham, green chilies, linguisa, lox, mushrooms, rarebit sauce, shrimp, turkey and zucchini - plus seven kinds of cheese! Side Tracks include piping hot oatmeal with raisins & walnuts, cottage fries, ranch chili, guacamole and fresh fruit cups topped with yogurt. The Bread Car is loaded with carrot cake, coffee cake, cinnamon French toast, blueberry and bran muffins. The luncheon menu is served from 11am and includes Fireman's charbroil burgers, Pullman Car sandwiches, Brakeman's salads, Little People's choices, Porter's beverages and the Caboose dessert of the day. The interior of the restaurant was carefully renovated. A must see are the vintage front ends of restored Jaguar sport cars mounted on the brick walls in the dining room. "All aboard" the Omelette Express where the food and prices are just right!

$-$$ OMELETTE EXPRESS    112 Fourth Street, Santa Rosa, CA. 95401
Omelettes & Specialties    MC & Visa    (707) 525-1690 Sit down or to go

**AROMA ROASTERS**    Located in the cheery red brick railroad depot in Santa Rosa is Aroma Roasters, an exceedingly popular coffee house and night club. You can charge yourself up at "Aroma's" with a caffe latte, espresso or cappucino made from fresh roasted Aroma Roaster beans and topped with whipped cream, a shot of one of 20 syrup flavors, plus cinnamon, chocolate and honey. A la carte snacks include homemade soup, garden fresh salads, breakfast burritos, green chili burritos, foccocia, croissants and pastries. On weekends there is live entertainment with local jazz, blues, folk and reggae entertainers. Special events and the daily parade of life in and out this historic building is most fun to watch.

$ AROMA ROASTERS    95 Fifth St., corner of Wilson, Santa Rosa, 95404
Coffe House  Open 7am till 11pm , Midnight on wk ends  (707) 576-7765

## RISTORANTE CAPRI

As a youngster Luigi Di Ruocco used to dive off the cliffs into the warm aquamarine sea water off the Isle of Capri.  The Isle of Capri, where he was raised, is a paradise off the coast of Southern Italy.  Here, Luigi learned the fine art of becoming a restaurateur and launched an international adventure preparing the cuisine of the Isle of Capri at famous restaurants and hotels in  Italy,  Switzerland,  England, Bermuda, New York and San Francisco,  Today he pours the great wines of California and serves the cuisine of his native island in historic Railroad Square in downtown Santa Rosa.

The Ristorante Capri is a work of art with rare Venetian plaster walls and decor that reflects the light, creating a colorful luminescent glow that is very appealing. Old Roman tile floors, genuine European hospitality and romantic cuisine make the Capri a must-dine-at restaurant when in Santa Rosa.  "You must come to my restaurant to see how beautiful it is!,"  states Luigi with his rich Italian voice.  The bounty of the Sonoma County farms and coastline creates the Isle of Capri cuisine - rich and full of promise.  Seafood, vegetarian, pasta, poultry, beef and lamb dishes are served with an array of mouth watering appetizers, soups, salads and desserts.  At the wine bar you can taste award winning Sonoma County wines. The artistic Italian banquet room upstairs seats 20-25.  So come and visit this magical setting for a truly romantic evening out on the town or a stress free business lunch away from work.  Open daily, but Sunday from 11:30am to 2:30pm and 5pm to 10pm.

*$$ RISTORANTE CAPRI       115 Fourth Street, Santa Rosa, CA. 95401 Isle of Capri Cuisine   Trans Media, AE, MC & Visa   (707) 525-0815 Res.*

## BERRY'S MARKET

This locally owned Sonoma County community oriented convenient store chain has its fingers on the pulse of the neighborhoods they serve.  Travelers can count on good service, fresh brewed coffee - hazelnut & Irish cream etc., and homemade deli sandwiches topped with salami, turkey, roast beef, 5 types of cheese, mustard, mayonnaise, lettuce, sprouts and tomatoes.  Supplies for the baby, pet or car and picnic goodies for the wine country are all inclusive.  Each Berry's Market is located along main wine country or coastal highways.  Most are open from 6am to 10pm and have ATM's and Lotto.

**Santa Rosa Locations:** *3690 Moorland Ave., 584-0879;  1020 Hopper Ave., 526-9440;  5290 Aero Drive  575-5018.* **Rohnert Park:** *6475 Redwood Drive  586-0722.* **Forestville:**  *10651 River Rd. 887-2362.* **Sebastopol:** *3195 Gravenstein Hwy 824-8041.* **Windsor:** *8197 Old Redwood Hwy.  838-6614.* **Admin Office:** *5290 Aero Dr. 571-7887.*

# A Downtown Santa Rosa Walkabout Where Beauty and Spirit Manifest Before Your Eyes

There is a term called geomancy which translates to divination by means of lines and figures. It comes from geomagnetism which is the study of geomagnetic fields. There are subtle and invisible reasons why communities are built at certain locations other than being beside creeks, rivers and animal migration paths. There are meridian lines of energy in the earth. Dowsers are familiar with these energy fields and occasionally insightful shop owners whose purpose is to promote beauty, spirit and awareness set up shop above them. Such is the case in the heart of Santa Rosa, setting the stage for a fabulous walk-about in color, smell, taste and sound. Your guides are waiting.

If the gap between heaven and earth can be bridged by the arts, then the stairway of memories between the two worlds would most surely be at destinations like the interior decorator showroom at **Randolph Johnson Design Studio**. We need places to go to remind us of our inner greatness where we can purchase totems to embrace and take home. A stroll through the **Mailer Galleria** on Fourth Street will reveal the **Tibetan Culture Center, Hampton Court,** and **Timothy Patrick Jewelers**. Next door is the **Opened Heart Bookstore** where you can browse by angelic murals, touch gemstones and crystals, taste and smell herbs, read books and listen to music to learn how to heal, meditate and increase your frequency. **Treehorn Books** and **Hemp Solutions** are just to the north. Across the street is **Positively Fourth Street** and **Copperfield's Bookstore** and a block away is **Chelsea,** which is a buy, sell, trade store that specializes in women's career and casual wear, as well as new and recycled gifts for the home or office. The **Fine Art and Frame Gallery** offers visitors a peek at Sonoma County art which is displayed on beamed and red brick walls. There are scads of prints, posters and frames which can be mounted to your request by proprietors Maureen and Kevin.

A real treat can be enjoyed at the **Sonoma Sound Masters** or the **Soundscape Gallery of Audio-Video Art.** At Sonoma Sound Masters there are exhibits of rare motion picture memorabilia from Star Wars. Ed, who manages Soundscape, has bridged the awareness gap between understanding the natural environment of our hunter forager ancestors versus the high tech environment of today's modern human. Physically we haven't changed that much, however   mentally we are able to handle a lot more than our ancestors ever could have then. Lifetimes and worlds are condensed in minutes - even seconds. No primitive Cromagnon could ever stay in his body if set in front of such futuristic information and stimulus. Think about it and you'll begin to see why so many of *us* feel overwhelmed sometimes. On the plus side, color-sound therapy of inspiring images and uplifting music helps to open the heart and mind, helping us to evolve and heal. The demonstration screen at Soundscape shows awe inspiring beauty as waves of images, vibrant colors and soothing music surround your being.

" . . . I firmly believe from all that I have seen that this is the chosen spot of all the Earth as far as nature is concerned. The climate is perfect . . . the air is so sweet that it is a pleasure to drink it in . . . the sunshine is pure and soft; the mountains which gird the

# Luther Burbank Home and Gardens

Valley are lovely. The Valley is covered with majestic oaks placed as no human hand could arrange them for beauty . . . the great rose trees climb over the houses, loaded with every color of blossoms . . . I almost have to cry for joy when I look at the lovely panorama from the hillside . . ."

*Luther Burbank, 1875*

**Luther Burbank 1849-1926**

In the above quote Luther Burbank was talking about the Santa Rosa Valley he viewed shortly after his arrival in 1875. It is no longer the "Chosen Spot" it was then due to mass development and population growth. Though quoted in the mast head of the Press Democrat Newspaper and exploited by the chamber of commerce, the city government and realestate speculators for tax revenue and profit, the only thing left of Burbank's idyllic image is the gardens he loved and tended at his home in downtown Santa Rosa and the farm in Sebastopol. However, there is good news. A vibrant and growing Sonoma County garden and farm movement is supported by area chefs and smart health conscious consumers. This blesses all of us with countless vegetable and flower gardens growing along the tree lined streets of Santa Rosa.

Luther Burbank Gardens is a Registered National, State and City Historic Landmark and is open to the public daily. The Burbank home, Carriage house and Greenhouse is open to tour from April through October. The property was given to the city of Santa Rosa by Elizabeth Burbank upon her death in 1977. The city staffs it with volunteers who accept donations, run a giftshop and conduct tours and community outreach programs for schools and organizations.

$ *LUTHER BURBANK HOME & GARDENS   Santa Rosa & Sonoma Aves.*
*Gardens, Greenhouse and Historic Home  Box 1678, Santa Rosa  524-5445*

## The SONOMA COUNTY MUSEUM - SONOMA COUNTY'S TIME MACHINE

Sonoma Countie's time machine doesn't whir and light up like the one Rod Taylor used in H.G. Wells classic film "The Time Machine". As a matter of fact it doesn't go anywhere! This solid as a rock concrete vault is designed to protect displays and relics highlighting the geological and historical past millennium of Sonoma County. Saved from the wrecking ball in 1979, by the Sonoma County Bicentennial Commission, this 1,800 ton historic building was moved two blocks to its current location and opened in 1985. The museum has gone from zero holdings to over 25,000 relics of meaning, worth millions.

Ongoing displays showcase Native America tools and baskets, antiques from the gold rush, agriculture and wine country booms of the 1800's through 1900's to the modern day high-tech computer industry. Visitors are guided by historians through rooms full of murals, displays, paintings, fine art, hand crafted furniture, antiques and memorabilia. "Is there a future living in the past?", I asked Harry Lapham, past trustee Emeritus of the Sonoma County Museum. "Each of our exhibits are frozen in time, but the mind can travel forward or backward at will.", he said with a wink. Open daily from 9am to 6pm. There is a museum giftshop and annual memberships are available.

*$ SONOMA COUNTY MUSEUM 425 Seventh St., Santa Rosa, CA. 95401*
*Ongoing Show, Permanent Exhibits & Special Events (707) 579-1500 Info.*

## LUTHER BURBANK CENTER for the PERFORMING ARTS

Sonoma County's headquarters for entertainment from A-Z is at the Luther Burbank Center for the Performing Arts. Concerts, theatre arts performances, ballet, speakers on every subject, theologians, indoor and outdoor special events, classes and seminars are held every month. Charity functions to help homeless people and animals are *also sponsored. For a calendar of events you can call or write: L.B.C.,*
*50 Mark West Springs Rd., Santa Rosa, CA. 95404.   (707) 546-3600 Info.*

Busy Fourth Street in the City of Roses is a great place to buy new or used books, catch a movie or savor the best mochas in northern California.

**DOWNTOWN SANTA ROSA** Area Code **(707)** 4th Street: **Arrigoni's Delicatessen** ($), 701 4th 545-1297; **Caffe Portofino** ($$), 535 4th 523-1171; **Cantina** ($$), 500 4th 523-3663; **Checkers** ($$), 523 4th 578-4000; **Copperfield's Bookstore Cafe** ($), 650 4th 576-7681; **4th Street Bistro** ($$-$$$) 645 Fourth St.526-2225; **Fresh Choice** ($), 1018 Santa Rosa Plaza 525-0912; **La Bufa** ($), 703 4th 576-9729; **La Vera Pizza** ($$), 629 4th 575-1113; **Ma Stokeld's Old Vic** ($), 731 4th 571-7555; **Mac's Kosher Style Delicatessen** ($), 630 4th 545-3785; **Moonlight Cafe** ($), 515 4th 526-2662; **Ristorante Capri** ($$) 115 Fourth St. 525-0815; **Sonoma Coffee Co.** ($), 521 4th 573-8022; **Thai House** ($$), 525 4th 526-3939; **Wolf Coffee Co. & Caffe'** ($), 614 4th 524-8036.

**CLOSE PROXMITY to DOWNTOWN SANTA ROSA**
**Ca'Bianca Italian Restaurant** ($$) 835 - 2nd St. 542-5800; **Cafe Lolo** ($$), 620 5th 576-7822; **Gary Chu's Chinese** ($$), 611 5th 526-5840; **Musashi Japanese Cuisine** ($$), 518 7th 575-0631; **Starbuck's Coffee** ($), 200 D St. 577-0665; **Taj Mahal** ($$), 535 Ross 579-8471; **Teppan Mana** ($$), 416 B 544-6262; **3rd Street Ale Works** ($), 610 3rd 523-3060; **Traverso's Gourmet Foods & Wines** ($-$$), 3rd & B Streets 542-2530; **Viva Mexico** ($-$$), 630 Third St. 546-7777.

**Mendocino Avenue: Acapulco Mexican** ($$), 505 Mendocino Ave. 544-8400; **Belvedere** ($$), 727 Mendocino Ave. 542-1890; **Silver Moon Chinese** ($$), 1880 Mendocino 576-7878; **Sizzling Tandoor** ($$), 409 Mendocino 579-5999; **Sonoma Valley Bagel Co.** ($), 2310 Mendocino 542-2435; **Taqueria Santa Rosa** ($), 1950 Mendocino Ave. 528-7956; **Wolf Coffee Co.** ($), 1810 Mendocino 546-9653.

**Outskirts of Downtown Santa Rosa Dining Locations: Barleycorns Saloon** ($$), 2700 Yulupa Ave. 526-3511; **Borolo's Gourmet Pizza** ($$) 500 Mission Boulevard 539-3937; **East West Cafe** ($-$$), 2323 Sonoma Ave. 546-6142; **Equus** ($$), 101 Fountgrove Pkwy 578-0149; **Italian Affair** ($$) 1055 Fourth Street 528-3336; **Lisa Hemenway's Bistro & Take-Out** ($$), 710 Village Ct. 526-5111;

*Continued on Next Page*

**Mark West Lodge** ($$),  2520 Mark West Springs Rd.  546-2592;  **Mary's Pizza Shack** ($), 549 Summerfield Rd.  538-1888;  **Mistral (formerly Ristorante Sienna)** ($$-$$$), 1229 N. Dutton Ave.  578-4511;  **Rose, The** ($-$$) 2074 Armory Dr.  546-ROSE;  **Sweetriver Saloon** ($), 248 Coddingtown Cntr.  526-0400;  **Villa, The** ($$-$$$), 3901 Montgomery Dr.  528-7755;  **Willie Bird's** ($), 1150 Santa Rosa Ave.  542-0861.

**LODGING:  Best Western Garden Inn** ($$),  1500 Santa Rosa Ave.  546-4031;  **Days Inn** ($$),  175 Railroad Square  573-9000;  **Doubletree Hotel** ($$),  3555 Round Barn Rd.  523-7555;  **Flamingo Resort Hotel** ($$),  4th & Farmers 545-8530;  **Fountain Grove Inn**   ($$),  101 Fountain Grove Parkway  578-6101;  **Hotel La Rose** ($$) 308 Wilson  579-3200.

**LIVE MUSIC & DANCING:  Doubletree Hotel** ($$),  3555 Round Barn Rd.  523-7555;  **Flamingo Resort Hotel** ($),  4th & Farmers  545-8530;  **Ma Stokeld's Old Vic** ($), 731 4th  571-7555;  **Moonlight Cafe** ($), 515 4th  526-2662;  **Rose, The** ($-$$) 2074 Armory Dr.  546-ROSE;  **Villa, The** ($$), 3901 Montgomery Dr.  528-7755.

**ATTRACTIONS:  Farmer's Market** ($) located on Fourth St. June - Sept.  **Health & Harmony Fair**  (June $-$$$), 525-9355;   **Lincoln Arts Center** ($-$$), 709 Davis  579-8618;  **Luther Burbank Center for the Arts / LBC** ($-$$) Hwy 101 @ River Rd.  546-3600;  **Luther Burbank Home & Gardens** ($), Corner Mendocino & Sonoma Ave. 524-5445;  **Santa Rosa Junior College Theatre Arts** ($-$$), 1501 Mendocino Ave.  527-4696;  **Santa Rosa Junior College Planetarium** ($), Main Entrance/1501 Mendocino Ave. @ Elliot Ave Parking Lot  527-4371 Info;  **Sonoma County Fairgrounds** ($-$$$),1350 Bennett Valley Rd.  545-4200;  **Sonoma County Library**, 3rd & E  545-0831;  **Sonoma County Museum** ($), 425  7th  579-1500.

**HEALTH & FITNESS:  Monthly memberships or $5 to $10 daily drop-in rates:  Body Central** (ladies only) ($) 545 Ross St.  525-8663;  **Gold's Gym** ($) 515 Fifth St.  545-5100;   **Parkpoint Club**   ($) 1200 North Dutton  578-1640;   **Shape Makers Spa**  ($) 3345 Santa Rosa Ave.. 579-9500.

**GREAT OUTDOORS:**  Annadel State Park,  Bennett Valley Municipal Golf Course & Park,  Doyle Park,  Hood Mountain State Park,  Howarth Park,  Julliard Park,  Spring Lake County Park.  See Section on Starwatching on page 286.  **Bicycle, Hiking, Rock Climbing, Boating and Surfing Shops see Marin Outdoors** ($-$$$), 2770 Santa Rosa Ave.  544-4400;  **Sonoma Outfitters** ($-$$$), 145 3rd  528-1920.

**TOURIST INFORMATION:**
**Santa Rosa Chamber of Commerce** ($-$$)  637 First St.  545-1414;  **Santa Rosa Conference and Visitors Bureau**  ($-$$) 637 First St.  545-1414.

# CHECKERS

Checkers pizza and pasta began in 1986 in the heart of the famous health resort town of Calistoga on main street (Calistoga Ave.). Locals and wine country visitors love Checkers' fresh baked pizzas, pasta dishes, homemade soups and garden fresh salads.

Proprietors Ron Goldin and Mark Young opened the Santa Rosa Checkers in 1990 and true to tradition located it on main street (4th Street) in the heart of Santa Rosa. They have local produce delivered daily and serve a nice selection of beer and wine from both Sonoma and Napa Counties. Of special note is the museum quality art that hangs in the dining room and pieces of eccentric sculpture and lighting created by Sonoma County artists. Entrees include Linguini Carbonara, Ravioli Aurora, sauteed prawns and firecracker chicken. Pizzas include the Garden, Thai, Spinach and Combination, as well as other designer pizzas. Calzones include pepperoni, vegetarian, sausage & mushroom and fajitas. Dining is indoors or on the sidewalk al fresco, or at their beautiful wine and espresso bar. All orders can be prepared to go. Open weekdays from 11:00am / Sat & Sun from 12:00 noon.

*$$ CHECKERS PIZZA & PASTA  523 Fourth Street, Santa Rosa, CA. 95402*
 *Pizza & International Cuisine  AE, MC & Visa  (707) 578-4000 Orders to go*
 *Also in Calistoga at 1434 Lincoln Ave.        (707) 942-9300 Orders to go*

**TREEHORN BOOKS**    The retail bookstore scholars and archives of some of the finest minds in Sonoma County reside at Treehorn Books, where row upon row of rare and out of print books await the intellectual conniseur. Michael Stephens and Keith Hotaling founded Treehorn Books in 1978, and take great pride in performing searches for rare or out of print books as well as appraising single titles to entire collections. There is also an excellent selection of discounted new books from regional authors and national best sellers. Treehorn Books is open from 10am to 9:30pm Mon - Sat, 12 - 6pm Sunday and is a great stop for those visiting or new to Sonoma County.

 *$-$$$ TREEHORN BOOKS        625 Fourth St.,  Santa Rosa, CA. 95404*
 *Rare, Out of Print and New Books   AE, Disc, MC & Visa   (707) 525-1782*

**SAWYER'S NEWS**    Age old companions, coffee and the morning newspaper wait side by side at Sawyer's News, the largest newsstand north of San Francisco. This historic information center was founded in 1936, first in San Rafael, then in Santa Rosa in 1945 by Doctor Fred E. Sawyer. Today great grandson John Sawyer runs this spacious news center with over 2,000 magazines and newspapers displayed along well lit shelves. The picture window gallery displays the spectacular to the bizarre. Centro Espresso owners Susan and Andy serve their rich lattes, cappuccino, macchiatos and mochas with muffins, croissants, sticky buns and bagels. Many locals say Sawyers is the best magazine read and coffee in Sonoma County. Open daily from 7am to 9pm (Fri & Sat till 10pm).

 *$-$$ SAWYER'S NEWS        733 Fourth St., Santa Rosa, CA. 95404*
 *Largest Newsstand north of San Francisco   MC & Visa   (707) 542-1311*

**ARTrails**

*What fun!*
*What Inspiration!*
*Touring up and*
*down windy country*
*roads lined with apple orchards, vineyards and towering redwood trees to secret little studios tucked in hollows and nooks where artists and their creations bridge the gap between Heaven and Earth. Artrails was created in 1985 when it became apparent that so many artists were inspired by the gentle and pure nature of rural Sonoma County. The cities of Santa Rosa,*

Ceramic by Sarah Voorhles

*Petaluma, Healdsburg and Sebastopol also have neighborhood and urban studios you can tour. And yes - you can meet and buy direct from the artist - even commission them to do custom or special works just for you, your loved ones, working associates or clients.*

Sculpture by Faith Morgan

*Sponsored by the Cultural Arts Council of Sonoma County, the Artrails Open Studio Tour has become an autumn tradition in October of each year. You can receive a free copy of the Artrails Catalog with the works of over 100 artists showcased in it.*

*$-$$$ ARTRAILS    C.A.C. of S.C., P.O. Box 7400, Santa Rosa, CA. 95407*

*Ongoing Shows & Tours    (707) 579-ARTS (2787) log onto www.artrails.org.*

**ARRIGONI'S**    Since 1960 Arrigoni's Delicatessen has been an exceedingly popular destination for an early morning cup of coffee, lunchtime date or mid-afternoon break.  Proprietors Jacob and Raja Naber know how to keep their guests happy with a sparkling cafe interior and deli cases lined with a sensational selection of International entrees, festive soups and salads and sumptuous desserts. Arrigoni's puts you in the mood to complete any task or adventure before days end.  The large picture window views of Santa Rosa's street life hints at the simple to complex of this city as you dine on the bounty of Arrigoni's.

*$ ARRIGONI'S DELICATESSEN  701 Fourth Street, Santa Rosa, CA. 95402*
*International Cuisine / Sit down or to go  Dis., MC & Visa  (707) 545-1297*

## LA BUFA

Located in the center of Santa Rosa's commerce district at 4th & D Streets is La Bufa Mexican restaurant. This old fashioned Mexican diner is a popular lunch break for Santa Rosa merchants. Service is usually fast and friendly, prices reasonable and portions generous. La Bufa is the name of a mountain in Mexico. Delia, the owner, is as genuine as a mountain and as beautiful as a rose. Her daughter Anna carries on the tradition she started. Appetizers, combination plates, and La Cocina Specialties are served all day long for both lunch and dinner (from $7.00). The popular lunch plate is served with salsa & chips, rice & beans and choice of taco, enchilada, chile relleno, tomale, tostada, burrito or quesadilla. Coffee, iced tea, sodas and domestic and Mexican beers are also served. Open Monday thru Saturday from 11am to 8:30pm.

*$ LA BUFA            703 Fourth Street, Santa Rosa, CA. 95404*
*Mexican        MC & Visa,  Beer & Wine,  (707) 573-8915 Sit down or to go*

## Ma STOKELD'S The OLD VIC

The Old Vic is a popular gathering place for spirited libations, good food and a range of live entertainment. The energy begins to build at lunch time and usually peaks after dinner with the pub social atmosphere at its best during live performances, spontaneous sing-alongs and dance band music. Presiding over it all are proprietors Chris & Maud Stokeld along with son Nicholas. Tribal gatherings full of male & female bonding make especially lively evenings. A selection of micro brews, ales, bitters and lagers are served on tap.

The afternoon tea served from 12 to 4pm in the main dining room (Wed-Sat) is a very civilized affair with a selection of finger sandwiches, scones & butter with preserves and a choice of cake or trifle served with a pot of tea. Ma Stokeld is famous for the meat pies, English pasties (puff pastry turnovers with a variety of fillings), bangers (Yorkshire - style pork sausages), homemade soups, French bread, chips (real potatoes), mushy peas, cole slaw and garlic mashed potatoes with gravy. On cold winter evenings the warm interior of the Old Vic, plus a hearty meal and brew will make you feel right at home. Desserts include English trifles, lemon cake, cheesecake and mince meat pies (holidays).

One local patron put it well "Cool little bands that come from nowhere and make you want to dance, good food and good company make the Old Vic the place to be."

*$-$$ MA STOKELD'S The OLD VIC  731 Fourth St, Santa Rosa, CA. 95402*
*British Pub Faire & Live Entertainment        (707) 571-7555 Information*

## CAFE LOLO

Experienced gourmands who have traveled frequently and dined at the finest restaurants are in for a pleasant surprise at Cafe Lolo in downtown Santa Rosa.  Chef/owners Michael Quigley and Lori Darling have innovative creations in store for you.  They are fiercely dedicated to supporting a Sonoma County buying ethic and purchase local organic produce at farmer's markets.  Seating is limited so be sure to call for reservations.

A half dozen "Starters" (from $3.75). include house-cured salmon with frisee and arugula salad, horseradish vinaigrette and crispy bagel chips or fresh crab cake with a watercress salad and spicy remoulade.  Lunch ($6.95 to $12.95). includes salads such as the smoked chicken with spinach, red onions, roquefort, roasted peppers and crispy coppa or soup, sandwich and entrees.  Dinners ($9.95 to $18.50) include oven roasted lamb top sirloin with green garlic mashed potatoes, wild mushrooms, pan juices and olive tapenade or seared day boat sea scallops over a ragout of spring vegetables, potato chive fritters, lobster aioli and fried basil.  Homemade desserts, espresso, premium wines and beers are also served.

Open for lunch from 11:30am to 2pm and dinner is served from 5:30pm to 9:30pm - closed on Sundays.

$$ CAFE LOLO                620 5th Street, Santa Rosa, CA. 95404
California Cuisine   AE, Diners, MC & Visa    (707) 576-7822  Res. advised

## THIRD STREET ALE WORKS

The Ale Works features all house brewed beers, "pub food with a bow tie" and offers a great beer garden.   At the long bar you can sample 6 - 8 Alework's brews.  Hearty Aleworks meals such as the 1/2 lb ground beef burger, beer battered fish & chips and pasta of the day put you back into your body.  Menu items include Roadhouse Chili, Aleworks onion rings, caesar salad, pub greens and Chinese chicken salads (from $3.75).  Half a dozen sandwiches come with Parmesan garlic fries, mashed potatoes or cole slaw, one or two person meat or vegetarian pizzas, and Pub specialties round out the faire.  Root beer, coke, iced tea, mineral water, apple juice and Third Street Aleworks micro brews are poured.

The interior of the Aleworks could be out of the movie set "Under Siege", earthquake proof with battleship gray steel stairwells leading to pool tables and TV sets.  Surf boards - some in tact, some broken in half (no shark bites) are mounted to the walls along with snow boards and from the ceiling hangs vintage bicycles.  The Third Street Aleworks is a fun place to hang out, down a brewski or two, ground out on a full meal and then hit the road (drive safely).

$-$$ THIRD STREET ALEWORKS     610 Third Street, Santa Rosa, CA.
   Brewery, Pub and Dinner House        Res. & Events: (707) 523-3060

## HAMPTON COURT

You can purchase wonderful heart warming gifts that will baby the Angel in your life at Hampton Court. Located in the heart of downtown Santa Rosa since 1988, this shop has a special resonance for those who find romance, warmth, compassion, unconditional love and spirit-in-action important themes in gift giving. Proprietress Pam Atchison, a highly spirited red head of Irish - German and Cherokee descent will help you find the perfect gift. She offers a selection of skin, hair and body care products from Kiehl's, aromatherapy potions, vintage jewelry, ladies clothing and adorable stuffed animals. You do have a dream teddy bear don't you? Luscious fragrances fill the air - check out the hand cut Tahitian vanilla natural glycerine soaps and other flavors. Hampton Court is open Monday through Saturday from 10am to 6pm.

*$-$$ HAMPTON COURT   Major Credit Cards   631 Fourth St., Santa Rosa*
*     Skin, Hair, Bodycare and Romantic Gifts             (707) 578-9416*

### TIMOTHY PATRICK JEWELERS

There are many schools of thought in the jewelry business. Timothy Patrick uses modern tools and old fashioned craftsmanship to create original and inspiring designs. He has also recreated ancient Celtic designs with his own interpretation fashioning truly remarkable pieces in gold, silver and precious stones. Timothy states, "Some like the stones touching their fingers - some don't - everyone has their own path and for a moment we walk it together as I create a lasting totem of self love for them or someone special in their life to cherish." Designs around spirit are a special pleasure for me to create.

*$$$ TIMOTHY PATRICK JEWELERS*
*Contemporary & Ancient Jewelry Designs    Open Tues - Sun 10am - 6pm*
*Box 12275, 631 Fourth St. #2, Santa Rosa, 95406          (707) 544-4713*

## SIMPLY SHEEK

Simply Sheek specializes in womens career and casual wear and buys top of the line clothing for a discriminating clientele. Shopping at Simply Sheek is a contemporary escapade that is enhanced by the atmosphere of the establishment. There is a charming neighborhood feel with wrought iron balconies and works by local artists on the wall. To ice the cake, most things in the store are affordable to expensive.

*SIMPLY SHEEK                    730 Third Street, Santa Rosa,*
*Casual to Upscale Clothing    CA. 95402  (707) 578-8044*

## CHELSEA

Chelsea is a mixture of the new and homey. There is a woodsy, down home feel to this small establishment which brings to mind picket fences and flower boxes.    There is a tasteful mixture of the all American and the exotic in proprietress Patricia Zanger's store. Furnishings, cabinets and quilted pillows all are moderately priced and is watched over by a woman that obviously loves what has been created here by local artists and collectors.

The shopper is made to feel at home by Tyler: a beautiful golden retriever who greets customers with his gentle nature and trusting eyes. One can't help but think of an old fashioned general store in Patricia's tastefully designed establishment..

*$$ CHELSEA  720 Third Street, Downtown Santa Rosa, CA. 95402*
*Women's Clothing and Home Furnishings    MC & Visa    (707) 573-0327*

## POSITIVELY FOURTH STREET

Randy and Melissa Harris have their hearts and minds on the pulse beat of downtown Santa Rosa.    Voted the best gift store in Sonoma County, at Positively Fourth Street you can peruse an array of heart warming hand made gifts from local and international artists. A few of the treasures displayed here are velvet dresses,    printed sox, purses, hats, scarves, leggings, jewelry and ear ring organizers.    In addition there are musical thumb pianos, wind chimes, candles galore, incense, journals, address books, cards and stationary.    Beautiful hand crafted wooden boxes, wrought iron and glass candle holders, sculpture, garden benches and statuary round out the attractive selection of gifts at Positively Fourth Street.

*$$ POSITIVELY FOURTH STREET  628 Fourth St., Santa Rosa, CA. 95404*
*    Gifts, Clothing and Accessories    AX, Disc, MC & Visa    (707) 526-3588*

**GARY CHU'S**
**Gourmet Chinese Cuisine**

The award winning Gary Chu's restaurant, located in downtown Santa Rosa is a winner for those seeking exceptional gourmet Chinese cuisine and a elegant dining environment. Upon entering the front door you leave the busy-ness of downtown Santa Rosa as you are greeted enthusiastically by Gary or more cordially by one of his staff. Subdued lighting gives one a feeling of privacy and relaxation. Along one wall is a glowing emerald green dragon, a symbol of the ancient wisdom and courage of the Asian culture. Gary has reason to be proud for he is a 4th generation restaurateur who understands the business, science and art of running a very successful Chinese restaurant. The entire Chu family creates the magic here with wife Janice, mother Chin Yeh and brother Christopher all working in the kitchen or in the dining room. Father Wei Chu, who retired in 1989, grows a few special herbs and vegetables which he occasionally brings in for their personally trained chef to prepare.

Over 75 entrees are on the menu (sit down or to go) as well as nutritious executive luncheons, Dr. John Mc Dougall approved entrees, Gary's personal recommendations and the special family style dinners.

The nutritious executive luncheons (from $5.50) include sauteed fresh garden vegetables, Imperial or California prawns, Szechwan sesame chicken, Mongolian beef and sauteed Happy Family. Mc Dougall entrees (from $5.95) can be prepared upon request from a melody of vegetables, tofu and oriental herbs and spices. Gary's personal recommendations (from $7.50 to $24.00) include the Imperial salad ($19.95) which are lightly sauteed Chinese vegetables, surrounded with colorful fresh Sonoma County vegetables, ham and prawns in Gary's own mustard and garlic dressing, champagne scallops, dragon prawns (an exciting presentation), and Peking Duck (24 hour notice required), sizzling lobster (sauteed lobster meat & vegetables in light oyster flavor sauce) and fresh crab Hong Kong style (sauteed crab in the shell with ginger and black bean sauce). Groups of 2 to 6 can enjoy festive 5 to 9 course family style dinners which are the closest you can get to China without leaving Santa Rosa.

Dress is casual and parking is just outside the door. One visit is not enough to enjoy the complexity of this Santa Rosa culinary retreat. Those checking into a motel or bed and breakfast can enjoy everything on the menu to go.

*$-$$ GARY CHU'S                    611 5th Street, Santa Rosa, CA. 95404*
*Gourmet Chinese Cuisine    Lunch: 11:30am - 3pm  Dinner: 3pm - 9:30pm*
*Disc., MC & Visa      Fax: (707) 526-3102    (707) 526-5840 Res. or to go.*

## MISTRAL

For some people being a restaurateur seems to be the natural thing to do. Michael Hirschberg started his long culinary career in 1974 at a small vegetarian restaurant in downtown Santa Rosa called the Mandala. Today Michael and Darlene along with their children operate Mistral on the westside of Santa Rosa where they serve northern Italian cuisine. In 1992 they opened the Mezzaluna Bakery where they bake fresh breads and desserts, which are served at Minstrel and sold to local Sonoma County markets.

Mistral is a first class restaurant for business luncheons or that special person in your life. Dining takes on a romantic hew in the evening with sumptuous entrees prepared by chefs Maria de Corpo and Alan Villemaire and served with candlelight by an attentive staff. Homemade pasta and tasty pizza with homemade dough, sauce, local cheeses and fresh herbs and toppings are served along with Italian main courses of fresh seafood, beef, poultry, game and vegetarian entrees. Insalata dishes feature 1/2 a dozen garden fresh salads including the Mista, Caesar, Spinaci, Sottaceti and Giardino - from $3.50. Open from 11:30am to 2pm Mon - Fri and 11::30am - 9pm daily but Monday.

*$$ MISTRAL*          *1229 N. Dutton Ave., Santa Rosa, CA. 95404*
*Northern Italian Cuisine*     *AE, MC & Visa   (707) 578-4511 Reservations*

## CALIFORNIA THAI

The gentle charm and fragrant cuisine of Thailand is served with California's fresh bounty by gracious hosts at California Thai. Fresh produce and herbs, local chicken, beef, pork and north coast seafood is prepared in a variety of authentic Thai ways creating a memorable lunch or dinner. Prices are fair, servings filling. Homemade desserts, beer, wine and coffee compliment your meal.

*$$ CALIFORNIA THAI*          *522 Seventh Street, Santa Rosa, CA 95401*
*Authentic Thai - California Fresh   Beer & Wine, MC & Visa  (707) 573-1441*

## MUSASHI

A dozen roses and sushi can put one in the mood for love. The Musashi Sushi Bar greets you with the 2,000 year old culture where food was once consumed as the art of survival and now as civilized artful dining. The feel of wood between the fingers and raw tasty morsels on the tongue excites and humbles. Seasoned rice wrapped with toasted seaweed topped with choices of octopus, squid, sea eel, salmon, sea urchin, prawn, crab or abalone (Sushi Nigiri) are delicious.

*$$-$$$ MUSASHI*          *518 Seventh Street, Santa Rosa, CA. 95401*
*Sushi and Japanese Cuisine   Beer & Wine   MC & Visa   (707) 575-0631*

Karin and Marco with son Nico

## CA' BIANCA

Built in 1876, this large Victorian white house has been a gathering place for prominent Santa Rosans and their guests for over a century. Today it is Ca' Bianca (Italian for the white house), and is home of a elegant Italian restaurant under the proprietorship of Karin Hoehne and Marco Diana. Karin, who is from Munich, Germany and Marco, who is from Lago Maggiore, Italy, met in San Francisco and began a wine country love affair that manifested Ca' Bianca in spring of 1996.

A smartly dressed staff of veteran restaurateurs seats and attentively fulfills your culinary desires. Dining begins with an extensive list of Sonoma County and Italian wines. A selection of Starters (from $3.95) include Terrina Insalata Di Campo (organic mixed green salad) and Antipasto Di Mare, all'olio e limone (fresh mixed seafood on a bed of greens). Of the 1/2 dozen pasta dishes (from $7.00) I suggest the Tagliolini al Pomodoro e Basilico (tagliolini with tomatoes and fresh basil). Main courses (from $10.50) include vegetarian, chicken, pork, veal, rack of lamb and fresh fish of the day prepared with original Italian recipes, herbs and ingredients. Desserts (from $5.00) are divine - try the Crema al Croccante di Mandorie (Italian almond custard) or the Tiramisu (lady fingers, espresso, rum & mascarpone cheese).

Seating is indoors in one of three dining rooms amid stained glass windows, ceramic fireplaces, chandeliers and original art. Ca' Bianca is perfect for intimate banquets for 20 - 35. Dining al fresco is on the front porch or in the secluded garden area behind the Victorian with humming birds and flowers. This idyllic island, which lies

but 3 blocks from the heart of Santa Rosa's business district, is a very pleasant lunch, dinner or wine tasting destination. Lunch hours are Mon - Fri 11am - 2:30pm / Dinner nightly 5pm - 10pm.

$$ CA' BIANCA                     835 Second St., Santa Rosa, CA. 95404
   Northern Italian Cuisine    AX, MC & Visa  Full Bar & Wine Tasting
   Fax: (707) 542-2129          (707) 542-5800 Reservations Suggested

One of the most romantic dinner views in Santa Rosa is from the dining room of the Villa restaurant. The moonrise over Sonoma Mountain outside large 20 foot high dining room picture windows is fabulous.

## THE VILLA

One of the most romantic dinner views in Santa Rosa is from the dining room of the Villa restaurant. The Villa rests atop a knoll and boasts tree top views of Bennett Valley and the moonrise over Sonoma Mountain from outside large 20 foot high dining room picture windows. Seating is in luxurious wrap around "spaceship" booths. On the canopied outdoor patio with overhead heaters you can dream your dreams in comfort winter or summer. The restaurant is a virtual showplace and the breath taking view is sure to capture your heart. Although the building is impressive it maintains a warmth rarely attained by restaurants of its size (seating and banquet facilities for 160 in 3 banquet rooms). Guests are expertly served in the European style of dining.

The food is excellent! The menu features crab cioppino, calamari saute, pepper steak, the fresh catch of the day and homemade pasta dishes such as gnocchi, linguini, fettuccini and lasagna. For the health conscious, delicious fat free McDougal style entrees are served. From the Il Forno oven (wood fired) come fresh baked gourmet pizzas with imported Italian tomatoes, fresh vegetables, herbs, meats and cheeses. Fresh baked foccaca, chibata and potato chibata breads are served with homemade olive oil. Lunch is served from 11:30am till 4pm with early bird dinners (from 4pm - 6pm) and daily specials are something to always look forward to. Dinners are from $11.95 and the daily specials are from $9.50.

The Villa offers a wide selection of premium California wines as well as imported wines from the owner's native country of Italy. There is also a complete bar. Music and dancing is on the weekends. The dance floor offers lofty views of the tree lined slope with the lights of Santa Rosa spread out beneath you. It is an enchanting setting to meet someone new or sweep your sweetheart off their feet.

*$$ THE VILLA        3901 Montgomery Drive, Santa Rosa, CA.  95402*
*Family Style Italian and Seafood Dining    Open daily from 4pm for dinner*
*Full Bar, Dancing,   Major credit cards honored    (707) 528-7755 Res. Sug.*

## HANK'S CREEKSIDE CAFE

The tree lined watershed of Santa Rosa creek is a pleasant alternative to the cities busy streets at Hank's Creekside Cafe. You can't miss Hank. As soon as you walk in the door you'll spot the tall chef tossing omelettes in his exhibition kitchen. His artist/wife Linda, proud mother of their six children (twins, triplets and solo John) runs the dining room of this exceedingly popular breakfast, lunch cafe. Hot off the griddle hot cakes, French toast, biscuits & gravy, sausages, omelettes, sandwiches, sirloin burgers and garden fresh salads are served from 6am to 2pm.

## CREEKSIDE BISTRO

Evenings at Creekside are under the guidance of Chef Emile Waldteufel, who is also a former olympic bicycle contender. Emile has created a romantic setting with extra ordinary cuisine and reasonable prices. Local fresh in-season produce, seafood, meats and poultry are served. First courses include warm seafood salad with balsamic vinaigrette, soup of the day and field greens with dijon mustard vinaigrette. Entree's served with cup of soup or petite salad include pan seared halibut with risotto, garlic tomatoes & bay shrimp and vegetarian penne pasta with sundried tomatoes & basil. Wonderful desserts are mango ice cream with warm French chocolate & caramelized bananas. Creekside also offers an extensive wine list, mineral water, herbal tea and fresh ground and brewed coffee.

*$-$$ HANKS CREEKSIDE CAFE and  CREEKSIDE BISTRO*
*American Breakfast & Lunch / French Cuisine Dinner Wed-Sun from 5:30*
*2800 Fourth St., Santa Rosa, CA. 95405        (707) 575-8839 Res. Sug.*

## LISA HEMENWAY'S BISTRO and TAKE OUT

Located in Santa Rosa's Montgomery Village on the east side of town is Lisa Hemenway's. Lisa and her well trained staff create the cuisine of the world from Sonoma County's eclectic range of fresh herbs. vegetables, fruits, seafood and meats. Favorite signature dishes include chicken & lemon grass hash, Hanoi spring rolls, Lisa's legendary Sonoma Caesar and numerous daily specials. The  deli hosts a delicious array of finger foods, salads, pastas, torte milanese, smoked fish and poultry and sumptuous homemade desserts. Why not pick up a gourmet box lunch and be off on a urban adventure? The wine bar hosts an extensive selection of Sonoma County wines by the taste, glass or bottle. The summertime outdoor patio is the perfect setting for conversation. All reasonable requests for catered events are accepted. Your charming host is Lisa Hemenway, a local legend who serves the abundance of Sonoma County's Gardens of Eden.

*$-$$ LISA HEMENWAY'S BISTRO and TAKE OUT*
*California/French Cuisine        710 Village Court, Santa Rosa, CA. 95405*
*AE, MC & Visa,              Wine Bar, Tote Cuisine Deli & Catered Events*
*Fax: (707) 578-5736            (707) 526-5111 Sit down or Orders to go*

Historic round barn and swimming pool at the lux - urious Fountain Grove Inn just north of Santa Rosa.

## FOUNTAIN GROVE INN

Since the beginning of recorded time men and women saw in the first horse a power, speed and grace to be wished for. Equus (the horse) is enshrined in the Inn's main lobby - Equus III, a spirited redwood sculpture bathed from natural light above; behind it water cascades over stone in the summer and fire soars above the reflective pool in the winter gently balancing the indoor temperature.

The custom made furnishings and decor were designed to please. Rounded oak detailing, polished brass, private baths (some with spas) and choice of king, queen or double beds with special in-room touches including stereo TV, double closets, separate dressing alcoves and built-in work space for traveling executives make very homey accommodations.  Rates are $119/2.

Next door is the Equus restaurant where dishes are served that surprise with their originality and satisfy with their simple taste.  The wine list reflects a selection from over 200 wineries to choose from - many are silver and gold medal winners.  The Equus restaurant's selection of wines is so substantial that it won the Sweepstakes Award at the Sonoma County Harvest Fair.

The Fountain Grove Inn is a special tribute to the horse and an exceptional wine country retreat for any individual, couple or group seeking a stay with a difference.

_$$ FOUNTAIN GROVE INN   101 Fountain Grove Parkway, Santa Rosa,_
_Lodging and Meals     CA.  95403  (707) 578-6101 / 800-222-6101 Res._

## THE ROSE Restaurant & Pub

Santa Rosa's first authentic pub was the English Rose Pub, founded in 1978. Renamed "The Rose," it is located on Armory Drive just off Hwy 101 and 3 blocks south of the intersection of Armory and Steel Lane (take the Hwy 101 Steel Lane / Coddingtown Exit).

Dark wood paneling, multi-level dining with wooden chairs  overlooking the colorful pub/bar and dart boards creates a casual, yet festive dining experience. The Rose stocks up to 50 varieties of beers, ales, lagers, porters, malt liquor, micro-brews, classics and ciders with 9 imported beers from around the world on tap.  Publicans Pamela and Carl Augusto oversee the preparation of delicious pub fare including Cornish pasty, vegetable pasty, Shepherd's pie, fish & chips, roast beef & Yorkshire pudding, turkey pasty with cranberry sauce and beer battered Icelandic cod, homemade soups and garden salads.  Pamela and Carl have a large following of locals who find great value in the environment, drinks and hearty fare.  The Celtic and Irish atmosphere is "fearrde 'tu' " so come by for the "craic".

Wonderful desserts such as  Sherry Trifle (pound cake, vanilla, custard, strawberries, sherry, toasted almonds and whipped cream - yum!).  Live entertainment is offered on weekends.   M - Thur food 11:30am to 9pm / pub 11:30pm - midnight; Friday food 11:30am to 11pm / pub 11:30pm - 2am;  Sat food 3pm - 11pm / pub 3pm - 2am.

$$ THE ROSE Restaurant & Pub   2074 Armory Dr., Santa Rosa, CA 95401
Celtic / Irish Cuisine     AE, MC & Visa      (707) 546-ROSE Information

# SANTA ROSA JUNIOR COLLEGE

Enter the gates to Santa Rosa Junior College and spend " A Day Under the Oaks". Here dedicated visionaries including plant horticulturist Luther Burbank helped create a garden of eden setting for higher learning.

## From the acorn springs the mighty oak!

Imagine Heaven on Earth. You have spent considerable time on earth contemplating what heaven might be like. You discover a place where busy souls are completing planned tasks assigned by guardian angels in a garden of eden setting. Look no further than the Santa Rosa Junior College Campus.

When Santa Rosa Junior College was officially established in 1918, the city of Santa Rosa had a population of 13,000 and was the hub of a county almost entirely rural in nature and agricultural in economy. Work weeks then in Sonoma County, were six days long and wages $1.50 per day. Today Sonoma County's population is 425,000 strong and growing.

The original campus of Santa Rosa Junior College was scattered about town and at Santa Rosa High School. It wasn't until August of 1980 that the SRJC trustees accepted the deed to 40 acres of parklike setting covered with majestic oak trees and a great variety of wild flowers that horticulturist Luther Burbank had planted. One stipulation to accepting the deed was that no campus buildings would be erected closer than 350 feet from Mendocino Avenue, permanently protecting a magnificent stand of Valley Oaks as well as Burbank's original gardens which are affectionately called "the jungle".

The first campus building, Pioneer Hall, was completed on May 29, 1931. Doyle Student Center (the Bear's Den and Coop Cafeteria) was completed in May 1953. The red brick buildings and landscaping create a special ambience. An aviation program began in the fall of 1939. The government paid for flight training students and the college conducted ground school for future pilots at Santa Rosa Municipal Airport. From 1950 to 1959 the college owned its own aircraft culminating with a completely remolded Cessna 172. The aviation club issued gold wings to students who earned their pilot license in the school airplane.

Today the campus boasts a broad curriculum for 36,00 students. The Registrar (527-4685) can provide you with a catalog full of classes, schedules, scholarships and information. The large Campus Bookstore (527-4321) overflows with text books and classroom amenities and is open daily when school is in session. The Campus Library (527-4391) has tons of books and internet access. The Theater Arts Department provides a platform for talent and inspiration (tickets 527-4342). The SRJC Repertory Theater performances are sensational. The track at Baily Field is popular among students and the community alike who like to walk or run for health and recreation.

## A Day Under the Oaks and the SRJC Native American Museum

A Day Under the Oaks at SRJC is held each spring semester on the 1st weekend in May.

In 1940 the Jesse Peter Native American Museum opened. Assisted by his wife Mabel Crone, Jesse served as director until his death in 1944. The Native American Museum (527-4479) is located in Bussman Hall. During the annual "Day Under the Oaks" the museum co-ordinates and sponsors the annual Spring Gathering, featuring Native American singers and dancers, a traditional crafts fair, and children activities.

Upon entering the front door of the Museum the outside world vanishes into a realm of Native American Art, baskets (large to minute), artifacts and photographs of Native Americans. The Great Spirits presence is strong here. I found the interior of the museum sacred. I heard the voices of my past, felt the energy of my heart renewed and uplifted - tears came to my eyes and I suppressed the urge to chant aloud an Indian song I had never known before. These words came to my mind . . . .

The museum showcases the works of North American Indian tribes with emphasis on northern California. There is a life size model of a Pomo Roundhouse that contains many examples of the basketry treasures of the Pomo including some of the smallest miniature baskets known to exist in the world, one the size of a pinhead. The Museum is open from noon to 4:00pm Monday thru Friday beginning in the Fall Semester on August 15 thru the Spring Semester till May 25th. Closed on all school campus holidays.

> "Proud strong faces, Beautiful Souls Suppressed Anger Healed by Our Love and Respect."

### The Oak Leaf Newspaper

In 1924 the first junior college newspaper made its debut with the title of "Bear Facts". In 1927 the "Bear Facts" was renamed the "Oak Leaf" and the college year book became "The Patrin" - dedicated to the memory of Luther Burbank. On March 25, 1927 the election made possible the formation of a junior college district. Of this election it was said in the Patrin, "The acorn was then planted. Roots have even now sprouted which shall bury themselves deeply in the heart of a community, for this acorn was quick with the vision of the people."

### Santa Rosa Junior College Planetarium

The gemstone of the campus is the Planetarium. Visitors get a education, inspiration and a sense of their place in the Universe. The Planetarium (527-4465) is under the direction of Ron Oriti. The projector reproduces the appearance of the sky onto the dome overhead, giving an exact representation of the sun, moon, planets and stars. An added feature is its ability to move forward or back in time so that millennia of celestial movement can be shown in minutes, and configurations from the distant past or far-off future can be viewed. Shows are Fri - Sat 7pm & 8:30pm and Sun 1:30pm & 3pm. See Star watching Story on page 286.

## Student Housing ($$$): Overcoming Fear With Love.

To some the high rents students have to pay while attending Santa Rosa Junior College is a real burn. The vast majority of students have to rent a tiny room in a older home within Santa Rosa's city limits. Isn't there enough pressure on our students without excessive rents created by greed, speculation and government regulation?

The Associated Student Body Card allows for a variety of student discounts. A well organized Student Housing Union could encourage landlords to give SRJC students a break on the rent in exchange for discounts and benefits from the college and community. In the mean time students should ask for and receive reasonable rents from enlightened landlords and accordingly love and respect the home they are renting.

## Places to Eat, Drink and be Merry adjacent the SRJC Campus.

There are a variety of coffee houses, restaurants and markets in close proximity to SRJC. At the **SRJC Cafeteria** (527-4355) breakfast, lunch, dinner, snacks, pizza and an espresso bar awaits. You don't need to be a student to eat there and you'll enjoy quality food at fair prices. Across from the SRJC main entrance on McConnell is the **L&L Used Book Store** where you can buy text and regular books at great prices. The **Community Market** ($) at 1899 Mendocino Ave. is a popular stop for health foods. Next door is **Higher Grounds Cafe** for breakfast, lunch, pastries, coffee drinks, pool and computer & internet time. **Wolf Coffee Company** ($) and the **Juice Shack** ($) are located at 1810 Mendocino Avenue. The **Juice Shack** does a good job educating the public about the merits of fresh squeezed fruits and vegetables. **The Rose** ($$) is a popular British Pub on Armory Drive between Highway 101 and the campus. Convenience stores include **Fast & Easy Market** ($) **and Merv's Little Super.** At the **Fast & Easy Market** located at 1880 Mendocino Ave. are "people you can trust, prices you can afford and service with a smile." I like that!

## Epilog: Keeping the High Watch.

The true wealth of a nation can be judged by the thoughtful resourcefulness of its youth and by the unselfish guidance of its adults. A real investment in our future is to treat students like gold. They should not be exploited, but rather nourished by the community they live and study in. New growth, if nourished, will eventually bear a lush harvest - graduates will bless us and hopefully never forget the fertile soil where they felt free and unrestricted to learn and eventually receive their diploma. As a graduate of Santa Rosa Junior College I have many fond memories of being a student there. The aura of youthful enthusiasm is a refreshing oasis I personally treasure. I take great pride as I stroll across this campus, for I know that from many of these acorns will spring mighty oaks.

# RIVER ROAD
# LOWER RUSSIAN RIVER WINE and REDWOOD
# COUNTRY:  FULTON to GUERNEVILLE

The fabled Russian River Valley has been a haven for year around vacationers for decades. Hot summers and mystical winters with cryptic wisps of fog swirling in the tops of redwoods has provided the setting for many a romantic dreamer to create in love.

**FULTON to GUERNEVILLE DINER'S CHOICE:  Tele. Area Code is (707).**
**Chez Marie** ($$) 6675 Front St.  887-7503;  **Cricklewood** ($-$$) 4618 Old Redwood Hwy 527-7768;  **Farmhouse Inn** ($$-$$$) 7871 River Rd.  887-3300; **John Ash and Company** ($$-$$$) 4330 Barnes Rd.  527-7687;  **Russian River Pub** ($-$$) 11829 River Rd.  887-7932.

**FULTON to GUERNEVILLE LODGING:**
**Farmhouse Inn** ($$) 7871 River Rd.  887-3300;  **Hilton Park Campground** ($-$$) 10750 River Rd.  887-9206;  **Raford House** ($$-$$$)  10630 Wohler Rd. 887-9573;  **Ridenhour Ranch House Inn** ($$-$$$) 12850 River Rd.  887-1033; **Santa Nella House** ($$)  12130 Hwy 116  869-9488;  **School House Campgrond** ($-$$) 12600 River Rd.  869-2311;  **Vintner's Inn** ($$-$$$)  4350 Barnes Rd.  575-7350.

**GROCERY STORES & SERVICE STATIONS:**
**Berry's Market @ Hacienda Bridge** ($) 10651 River Road  887-2362;  **Egg Basket** ($)  1150 River Rd.  546-6091;  **Molsberry Market** ($-$$)  522 Old Redwood Hwy-Larkfield Shopping Center  546-0307;  **Speer's Market**  ($-$$$) 7891 Mirabel Rd.  887-2024;

**THE GREAT OUTDOORS and ATTRACTIONS:**
**Burke's Canoe Trips** ($$)  Junction Mirable Rd. & River Rd.  887-1222; **California School of Herbal Studies** ($$-$$$) 9309 Hwy 116  887-7457; **Luther Burbank Center for the Performing Arts** ($-$$)  Hwy 101 @ River Rd. 527-7006;  **Select Sonoma County Products** ($) Mail: 1055 West College Ave. #194  or stop by 875 River Rd., Fulton 571-8894;  **Westside Farms** ($) 7079 Westside Rd.  431-1432.

## LOWER RUSSIAN RIVER VALLEY WINERYS *With Tasting Rooms*

Tasting Room and Giftshop Hours are often seasonal especially if located outside a city. All of these tasting rooms are open weekends and many daily. Call for current hours just to be sure. Remember to drive safely being aware of children, pets, wildlife and other vehicles.

 1. **Armida Winery**              2201 Westside Rd., Healdsburg    433-2222
 2. **Belvedere Winery**           4035 Westside Rd., Healdsburg    433-8237
 3. **Davis Bynum Winery**         8075 Westside Rd., Healdsburg    433-5852
 4. **De Loach Vineyards**              1719 Olivet Rd., Santa Rosa    526-9111
 5. **Hanna Winery**           5353 Occidental Rd., Santa Rosa    575-3371
 6. **Hop Kiln Winery**             6050 Westside Rd., Healdsburg    433-6491
 7. **Iron Horse Vineyard**         9786 Ross Station, Sebastopol    887-1507
 8. **Joseph Swan Vineyards**       2916 Laguna Road, Forestville    573-3747
 9. **Kendall - Jackson Wine Center**      5007 Fulton Rd.., Fulton    571-7500
10. **Korbel Champagne Cellars**     13250 River Rd., Guerneville    887-2294
11. **Mark West Vineyards** 7010 Trenton-Healdsburg Rd., Forestville    544-4813
12. **Martinelli's Winery**              3360 River Rd., Windsor    525-0570
13  **Martini & Prati**          2191 Laguna Rd., Santa Rosa    575-8064
14  **Paradise Ridge Winery** 4545 Thomas Lake Harris Dr., Santa Rosa 528-9463
15. **Porter Creek Vineyards**      8735 Westside Rd., Healdsburg    433-6321
16. **Rabbit Ridge**               3291 Westside Rd., Healdsburg    431-7128
17. **Rochioli Vineyards**         6192 Westside Rd., Healdsburg    433-2305
18. **Sebastopol Vineyards**     8757 Green Valley Rd., Sebastopol    829-WINE
19. **Taft Street Winery**         2030 Barlow Lane, Sebastopol    823-2049
20. **Topolos @ Russian River** 5700 Gravenstein Hwy N., Forestville    887-1575
21. **Villa Pompei Vineyards**         5700 River Rd., Santa Rosa    545-5800

## JOHN ASH & COMPANY, VINTNER'S INN and KENDALL JACKSON Wine Center

Located at the entrance to the lower Russian River wine country in Fulton is a small neighborhood of superb facilities. John Ash is a legendary chef who has educated millions as to the merits of combining food and wine. Today he hosts a food and garden radio show on KSRO (AM 1350) with Steve Garner on Saturday mornings. John has moved on, but the restaurant he founded in the 1980's is under the direction of an extremely capable staff. It is located at the Vintner's Inn which offers superb wine country, corporate and wedding accommodations. Fabulous receptions and special events can be hosted at the nearby Kendall Jackson wine center (pictured above) with its grand piano, heirloom gardens, gift shop and tasting room. Year around you can watch the seasons change the landscape while enjoying great food, wine and lodging.

*$$ JOHN ASH & COMPANY  (707) 527-7687, $$ VINTNER'S INN  (707) 575-7350  $$KENDALL JACKSON WINE CENTER  (707) 571-7500. Res. & Info.*

## RUSSIAN RIVER VALLEY WINEGROWERS

The Russian River Valley Winegrowers are a friendly lot who are engaged in the noble lifestyle of co-creation with nature. To the larger degree they preserve Sonoma County's agricultural lands with muscle, sweat, love and compassion.

Look around you while driving through the Russian River Valley as it rolls westward to the sea, through row upon row of well tended grapevines. Behind each vineyard, well intended human hands nurture the plants to fruition - protecting the vines on chilly winter nights. Vineyard owners and managers are encouraged to protect their ripening crop from wild birds, rabbits and deer with non lethal, but effective agents and ensure water quality for all living things by using natural biological deterrents.

The Russian River Valley is viewed largely as a Region I climate, with strong maritime intrusions of early morning fog and afternoon winds sweeping in through the Petaluma Gap. Such early ripening varieties as pinot noir and chardonnay thrive in this region, and in the more northerly, warmer end of the appelation, zinfandel and cabernet sauvignon also flourish. The majority of this grape acreage is planted on bench or bottom land with good drainage assured by the high percentage of degraded sandstone and shale in the soil, along with alluvial gravels deposited by the Russian River and its tributaries during their wandering across this region.

You can get involved in the winegrowing magic of the Russian River Valley by joining the Russian River Valley Winegrowers with a private or corporate membership. For the general public there are special maps, tours and the annual "Grape to Glass" wine tastings and tours.

Whatever you decide to do, be sure to look for the Russian River Valley Winegrowers' signs at the entrance to each vineyard or winery and / or stop by the administrative office and information center at 875 River Road. Normal hours are Monday through Friday from 8am to 5pm.

$ RUSSIAN RIVER VALLEY WINEGROWERS  Insiders Look at Vineyards Tours, Special Events & Memberships  875 River Road, Fulton, CA.95439
FAX: (707) 546-3277                    Info:  (707) 546-3276

## MARTINELLI VINEYARDS

Situated in a large red Hop barn on River Road two miles west of Highway 101 is a historic and colorful stop where tourists can browse the cavernous turn of the century redwood barn of the Martinelli Ranch.  The smell of fresh produce and inviting picnic tables beneath the arbor greet guests at the front entrance.  Tourists can sample farm fresh apples and premium apple cider, Martinelli wine and a variety of delicious sun ripened apples neatly displayed with gourmet foods, dried fruits and nuts, local jams and jellies, cheese, gift packs and estate bottled wines.  Complimentary hot apple cider (wintertime) or chilled apple juice (summertime) is always available by the taste.    The delicious apples and grapes are all grown by the Martinelli family on land surrounding the tasting room.  Under the Martinelli label, premium vintages of Zinfandel, Chardonnay, Gewurztraminer, Sauvignon Blanc and Muscat are available by the taste at the handsome oak & redwood bar or by the fifth or case.

*$-$$ MARTINELLI RANCH*
*Premium Wines/fresh apples*
*and fresh pressed cider.*
*3360 River Rd., 2 miles west*
*of Hwy 101, Guerneville exit.*

*Wine tasting & retail sales, giftshop,*
*farm fresh produce, gourmet & picnic*
*packs. Open 10am-6pm, Off-season:*
*10am - 5pm.        (707) 525-0570*
*Or call Toll Free:  1-800-346-1627*

## VILLA POMPEI

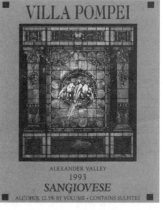

Prominently situated atop a knoll overlooking miles of the fabled Russian River Winegrowing Valley, with views of hill covered vineyards and orchards is Villa Pompei.  In the tasting room wine country explorers can taste premium vintages of Sauvignon Blanc, Chardonnay, Cabernet Sauvignon, Sangiovese, Pinot Noir and Zinfandel while enjoying views befitting royalty.  In the giftshop are creamy truffles, picnic baskets and snacks, fashionable clothing, tour guides and maps.    In addition the works of local artists are featured in the gallery entrance.  Proprietors Penny and Carl Pompei also host fabulous weddings and receptions at the Villa Pompei estate. There is also a thriving mail order business so be sure to pick up a newsletter or catalog.  Villa Pompei is located on River Road just five miles from Highway 101, making it a nice break in your north coast trip.  Be sure to bring your camera - the year round views are fabulous.

*$$ VILLA POMPEI    5700 River Rd., Santa Rosa, CA. 95401  MC & Visa*
*Tasting, Giftshop, Picnics, Weddings  Fax: (707) 545-5801  (707) 545-5899*

## ARMIDA WINERY

With it's hillside location, Armida Winery has spectacular views of the surrounding Russian River and Dry Creek Valleys, with the Alexander Valley, Geyser Peak and Mount St. Helena to the east and north.  Three geodesic domes majestically preside atop the naturally landscaped hillside housing the tasting room, fermentation cellar and aging cellar filled with French and American oak barrels.  The lofty outdoor deck surrounded by flower gardens with a bocce ball court below, catches the morning light creating a perfect invitation to enjoy Armida wines with gourmet goodies.  Butterflys and hummingbirds dance about while waterbirds splash in the large pond with fountain and cat tails.

Armida Winery was founded by Bob Frugoli who changed his corporate pace between Chicago and San Francisco by farming vineyards in the Russian River Valley.  In 1989 he purchased land above Westside road and began to restore an older winery into a practical well-balanced destination that transformed premium Russian River Valley grapes into award wining wines.  A changing of the guard occurred in 1994 when Bob entered into partnership with brothers Steve and Bruce Cousins who further refined the facilities into the inviting presence it is today.  Winemaker Mike Loykasek's creativity and enthusiasm has earned Armida Winery numerous awards for the complexity of hand-crafted releases of chardonnay, merlot, zinfandel and pinot noir.  Today, Bruce, Sandra, Steve and Cyndi invite you to visit them at the tasting room to enjoy their premium wines, fabulous view, splendid hospitality, unique gifts and picnic facilities.

Of special note is "Wino", the sweetest most heart centered dog I've met at a winery tasting room.

The majority of Armida's wines are produced from fruit grown in the Russian River Valley, an area ideally suited to the growing of Chardonnay, Merlot and Pinot Noir. Not only does Armida harvest their own grapes, but they are privy to purchasing grapes from outstanding growers producing extraordinary fruit. Of course this makes winemaker Mike Loykasek very happy. With this premium quality fruit from one of America's greatest wine valleys he can then reward the tastebuds of Armida wine consumers.

Of special note is "Wino", the sweetest most heart centered dog I've met at a winery tasting room. He lovingly greets each visitor with a wagging tail and big welcome smile. "Sport" is also very sweet and occasionally greets cat lovers. In the Armida tasting room you can taste wines and become a member of "Wino's Pack" which entitles you to receive premium releases four times a year delivered to your home or office. In the tasting room giftshop you can purchase crystal or hand blown wine glasses, picnic baskets, T-shirts, candles, note cards and books. A portion of your purchase is donated to help homeless cats and dogs at a nearby animal shelter. You can also preview the wines and Wino on the Armida website. A toast to the pack means one for all and all for one!

So there you have it. Armida Winery is a splendid partnership between romance, humor, grapes, dogs, cats and people. At Armida you'll discover a winery family that is on line with life, going places with their wines and expanding their "pack" of wine connoisseurs daily. Whether you howl by the light of the full moon, meow by a fireplace or honor your loved one in the perfect setting, know that the heart and soul of Armida wines will add warmth to your special event.

*$$ ARMIDA WINERY*        *2201 Westside Road, Healdsburg, CA. 95448*
*Tours, Tastings and Retail Sales     MC & Visa   Open 11am to 5pm daily*
*Web: armidawine@aol.com    Fax: (707) 433-2202    Info: (707) 433-2222*

# WINE COUNTRY TOUR
## WESTSIDE ROAD: One of the Most Beautiful Country Drives in the Sonoma County Wine Country

During a drive along Westside Road from Healdsburg to Forestville you can visit Mill Creek Vineyards, Armida Winery, Rabbit Ridge, Belvedere Wine Company, Hop Kiln Winery, J. Rochioli Vineyards, Westside Farms, Davis Bynum Winery and Porter Creek Vineyards. Anytime of the year this beautiful river valley wine country offers inspirational views of some of the most productive and famous vineyards in California.

### HOP KILN WINERY

The Hop Kiln Winery is one of the most charming places you can visit in Sonoma County. This winery, which is owned by Dr. L. Martin Griffin, Jr., is housed in a 1905 stone and redwood hop kiln overlooking the Russian River and has been declared both a county and state historic landmark. The Griffin's premium wines, produced from their surrounding vineyards, are of excellent quality. You should definitely include a stop and tasting of Marty's Big Red, Zinfandel and Johannisberg Riesling and purchase a few bottles or a case for special gatherings, $7.50 to $18.00 per bottle - case discounts available. The winery is open daily from 10am - 5pm for tastings. A visit to the Hop Kiln Winery is truly a delightful experience.

*$$ HOP KILN WINERY      6050 Westside Rd., Healdsburg, CA 95448*
*Tasting, Picnics, Generic & Varietals, Amex., MC & Visa. (707) 433-6491*

### DAVIS BYNUM WINERY

Distinguished as the first winery on Westside Road in Healdsburg, Davis Bynum was the initial producer of a vineyard designated Pinot Noir with a Russian River Valley appellation. That was in 1973, and the grapes came from neighbor Joe Rochioli's now famous vineyard. More than a quarter of a century later, guided by the original winemaking team, the heritage of Davis Bynum continues in the creation of small lots of handmade wine from the finest vineyards. Award winning winemaker Gary Farrell limits production so that the wines reflect the individuality of each vineyard. Located about 8 miles down the Russian River from Healdsburg, the wineries Region 1 growing district is ideal for Pinot Noir and Chardonnay grapes.

*$$ DAVIS BYNUM      8075 Westside Rd., Healdsburg, CA 95448*
*Tasting & Retail Sales daily from 10am - 5pm. MC & Visa (707) 433-5852*

## RUSSIAN RIVER PUB

The Russian River Pub, a cozy cedar log bar and restaurant with indoor-outdoor dining (weather permitting), is a convenient stop for fine brew  and hearty faire if you are on your way back from the Sonoma Coastline or inbound for the wine country.  This popular air conditioned locals destination, with long bar, pool table and wide screen TV, is famous for their buffalo style chicken wings.

Lunch and dinner (from $5.00) are served year around from 11am.  Cajun eggs, chili & eggs, veggie eggs and steak'n eggs are served for Sunday Breakfast (from 10am - 2pm) at a modest price.  The menu includes a variety of burgers (including a veggie "garden burger"), chicken wings (by the pound or bucket), stuffed baked potato, chili, mixed fish basket, calamari, Caesar salad, chicken Caesar salad and the Cajun sausage sandwich.  Other sandwiches include the veggie grilled cheese, BLT, BBQ chicken breast, and steak sandwiches.  Russian River beaches are a stones throw away.  Korbel Champagne Cellars, campgrounds and bed & breakfast inns are within a few miles.  Of special note is the pool table, warm log cabin bar decor of the Russian River Pub and juke box with hot tunes spanning the last four decades.

*$-$$ RUSSIAN RIVER PUB    11829 River Road, Forestville, CA.  95436*
*American & Mexican   Bar Open from 11am,  MC & Visa. (707) 887-7932*

## BURKE'S CANOE TRIPS Inc.

For several decades Burke's Canoe Trips Inc. have provided thousands of vacationers to the lower Russian River canoe trips from spring thru fall between Forestville and Guerneville.  Along this stretch the river meanders at a slow pace revealing forest settings and wildlife as well as bridges, vineyards and swimming holes in which to play Tarzan and Jane.   Tent campers, RVers, bicyclists and cars full of families and friends can rent canoes, paddles and camping equipment as well as stock up on picnic supplies at Burke's convenience store or nearby Speer's Market - a full service grocery store featuring traditional and health food, charcoal, meats and deli supplies plus beer and wine.  Burkes offers a "blue school bus" shuttle service for canoeists.  Camping is also available at nearby Schoolhouse Canyon Campground (707) 869-2311 or Hillton Park Campgound (707) 887-9206.

*$$ BURKE'S CANOE TRIPS   Box 602, 8600 River Road, Forestville, CA.*
*Canoe Trips, Picnic & Camping Supplies     (707) 887-1222 Reservations*

## KORBEL CHAMPAGNE CELLARS, GOURMET DELI & BREW PUB

Korbel Champagne Cellars, Brew Pub and Gourmet Delicatessen are located in a beautiful valley just south of Guerneville on River Road.

## RIDENHOUR RANCH HOUSE INN

One of the few country style bed & breakfast inns in the lower Russian River Valley lies 5 miles east of Guerneville on River Road. The Ridenhour family farmed the 900 acre ranch consisting of land on both sides of the Russian River and adjacent to historic Korbel Winery. Today the ancient Gravenstein apple trees, hollowed by time, still yield an abundant crop as well as persimmon, plum, pear and fig trees. Travelers will note that here rambling orchards become redwoods.

The 11 room country house has 8 bedrooms (5 with private baths), a large country kitchen and dining room. The proprietors prepare a creative breakfast for guests each morning. Dinners are also available by reservation.

Secluded river beaches are a short walk away and a hot tub is available to guests. Each room is decorated intimately and individually with antiques, quilts, flowers and plants. Guests are invited to sip wines from nearby wineries in front of the comfortable living room fireplace. Landscaped grounds with meandering paths under redwoods and oak trees invite all to stroll. Long time or new guests to the inn enjoy a stay at Ridenhour Ranch House Inn.

*$$-$$$ RIDENHOUR RANCH HOUSE INN*

*Bed & Breakfast          Open year around.  Numerous Restaurants*
*12850 River Road        Hot Tub and Recreational Facilities Nearby*
*Guerneville, CA 95446          (707) 887-1033 Res. Advised*

# GUERNEVILLE
## Nestled in a Valley of Redwoods on the Russian River

Guerneville has been a summertime vacationland for people escaping San Francisco for decades. Once the location of the most voluminous stand of redwoods on earth - since logged - a remnant still stands in protected Armstrong Redwoods State Park. The old and the new bridge stand side by side. The old of steel and wood and the new of concrete with amethyst crystals secretly imbedded in each pillar by a Native American bridge builder who wanted to promote safety and goodwill.

### GUERNEVILLE to MONTE RIO DINER'S CHOICE: Area Code (707).

**Applewood** ($$-$$$) 13555 Hwy 116 869-9093; **Brew Moon** ($) 16248 River Rd. 869-0201; **Buck's** ($$) 4th & Mill Sts. 869-0101; **Burdon's** ($$) 15405 River Rd.  869-2615;  **Coffee Bizaar** ($)  14045 Armstrong Woods Rd. 869-9706; **Garden Grille** ($) 17132 Hwy 116  869-2878;  **The Hubcap** ($) 16337 Main St.  869-2393; **Ina Bee's**  ($-$$)  17121 River Rd.  869-2INA; **Korbel Deli** ($-$$) 13250 River Rd.  824-7313;   **Last Great Hiding Place** ($-$$)  15025 River Rd.  887-9506; **Main Street Station Pizza** ($$-$$$) 15045 River Rd.  869-0501; **Midway Deli & Cafe** ($-$$)  20108 Main St. 869-0501; **Molly's Country Club** ($$)  14120 Old Cazadero Rd.  869-0511; **Northwood Restaurant** ($$)  19400 Hwy 116  865-2454;  **Pat's Restaurant & Bar**  ($)  16236 River Rd.  869-9904;   **Rainbow Cattle Company (Gay Bar)** ($)  16200 Main St.  869-0206; **Rio Inn**  ($-$$)  4444 Wood Rd.  869-4444;  **Rio Nido Bar, Cafe & Pool**  ($-$$)  14540 Canyon #2  869-0821; **River Inn** ($-$$)  16377 Main St.  869-0481;  **Sweets River Grill**  ($$-$$$) 16251 River Rd.  869-3383; **Taqueria La Tapatia** ($-$$) 16632 River Rd. 869-1821.

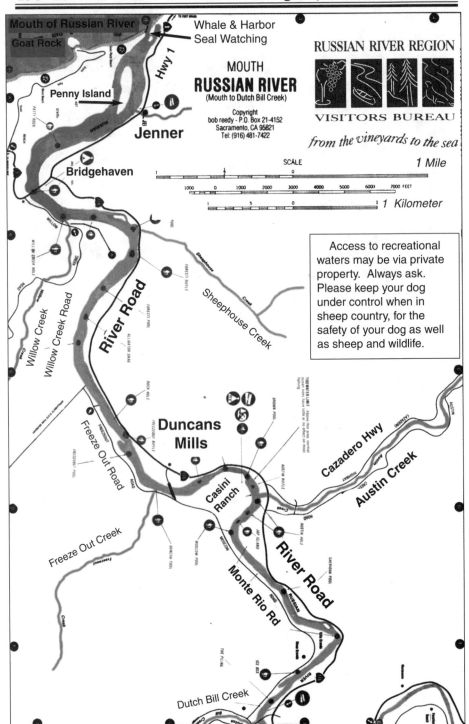

Mouth of Russian River

Goat Rock

Penny Island

Whale & Harbor
Seal Watching

Hwy 1

**MOUTH**
**RUSSIAN RIVER**
(Mouth to Dutch Bill Creek)

Copyright
bob reedy - P.O. Box 21-4152
Sacramento, CA 95821
Tel: (916) 481-7422

**Jenner**

Bridgehaven

**RUSSIAN RIVER REGION**

**VISITORS BUREAU**

*from the vineyards to the sea*

SCALE
0
1 Mile

1000   0   1000   2000   3000   4000   5000   6000   7000 FEET

1          5          0          1 Kilometer

Access to recreational
waters may be via private
property.  Always ask.
Please keep your dog
under control when in
sheep country, for the
safety of your dog as well
as sheep and wildlife.

Willow Creek

Willow Creek Road

River Road

Sheephouse Creek

Duncans
Mills

Casini
Ranch

Freeze Out Road

Freeze Out Creek

Monte Rio Rd

River Road

Cazadero Hwy

Austin Creek

Dutch Bill Creek

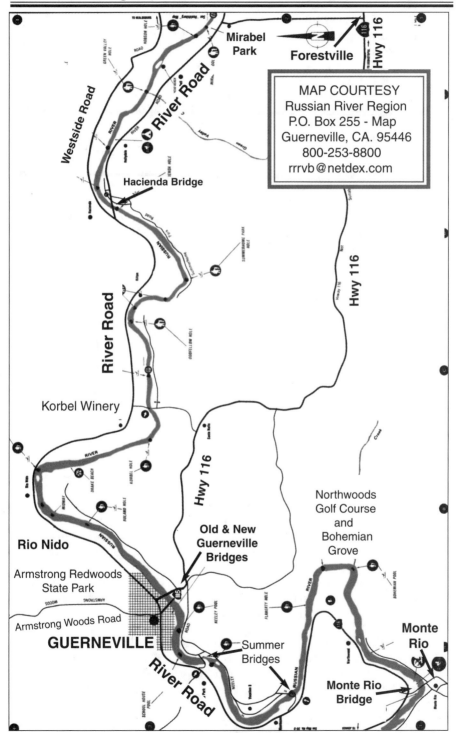

Mirabel Park

Forestville

Hwy 116

MAP COURTESY
Russian River Region
P.O. Box 255 - Map
Guerneville, CA. 95446
800-253-8800
rrrvb@netdex.com

Westside Road

River Road

Hacienda Bridge

River Road

Hwy 116

Hwy 116

Korbel Winery

Hwy 116

Northwoods
Golf Course
and
Bohemian
Grove

Rio Nido

Old & New
Guerneville
Bridges

Armstrong Redwoods
State Park

Armstrong Woods Road

GUERNEVILLE

River Road

Summer
Bridges

Monte
Rio

Monte Rio
Bridge

**GUERNEVILLE WINERIES:**
**Korbel Champagne Cellars** ($-$$) 13250 River Rd. 824-7000.

**GUERNEVILLE to MONTE RIO LODGING:**
**Applewood** ($-$$) 13555 Hwy 116 869-9093;  **Avalon** ($-$$) 4th & Mill
Sts. 869-9566; **Creekside Resort** ($-$$) 16180 Neeley Rd 869-3623;
**Fern Grove Cottages** ($-$$) 16650 River Rd. 869-9083;  **Fifes Resort**
($-$$) 16467 River Rd. 869-0656; **Highlands Resort** ($-$$) Box 346 869-
0333;  **Huckleberry Springs Country Inn** ($-$$) 8105 Beedle Rd. 865-
2683;   **New Dynamic Inn** ($-$$) Mill St. 869-9400; **Northwoods Lodge**
**& Resort** ($-$$) 19455 Hwy 116, 865-1655; **Ridenhour Ranchouse Inn**
($-$$) 12850 River Road 887-1033;  **Rio Inn** ($-$$) 4444 Wood Rd. 869-
4444; **Rio Villa Beach Resort** ($-$$) 20292 Hwy 116, 865-1143;
**Riverlane Resort** ($-$$) Box 313 869-2323;  **Russian River Resort** ($-
$$) 4th & Mill Sts. 869-0691; **Santa Nella House B&B** ($-$$) 12130
Hwy 116 869-9488;  **Willows, The** ($-$$) 15905 River Rd. 869-3279;
**Village Inn** ($-$$) Box 850, River Blvd. Monte Rio. 865-2304.

**BOOKSTORES, GIFTSHOPS and the ARTS:**
**Crone's Corner** ($-$$) 16626 Hwy 116  869-0588;  **River Reader**
**Bookstore** ($-$$) 16355 Main Street  869-2240;  **Twice Sold Books** ($-$$)
14045 Armstrong Woods Rd., 869-1479.

**GROCERY STORES & SERVICE STATIONS:**  **Country Tire** ($-$$$)
15290 River Rd. 869-2929;  **Food For Humans** ($-$$) 16385 First St. 869-
3612;  **Noonan's Garage & 24 Hour Towing Service** ($-$$$) 16312 Fifth
St. 869-2781 / 887-7359; **Hubcap Delicatessen**  ($-$$) 16337 Main St.
869-2393;   **Safeway** ($-$$$) 16405 River Rd. 869-9433;
**River Road Shell 24 Hour Quickstop** ($) 15190 River Rd. 896-0809.

**ATTRACTIONS and the GREAT OUTDOORS: Armstrong Woods Pack**
**Trips** ($-$$) 579-1520;  **Armstrong Woods State Park** ($) 17000
Armstrong Woods Rd. 869-2015 / 869-2391 Visitor Center 869-2958;
**Burke's Canoe Trips** ($$) 8600 River Rd., Box 602, Forestville 887-1222;
**California School of Herbal Studies** ($-$$) Box 39, Forestville, 887-7457;
**King's Sport & Tackle** ($-$$$) 16337 Main St. 869-2156;  **Northwoods**
**Golf Course** ($-$$) 19400 Hwy 116 Rd. 865-1116; **Rio Theater ($)**
20396 Bohemian Hwy. 865-0913; **Rosemaries Russian River Day Spa &**
**Massage** ($$) 16370 First St. 869-3322;  **W. C. "Bob" Trowbridge Canoe**
**Trips** ($$) 20 Healdsburg Ave., Healdsburg 433-7247 / 1-800-640-1386.

**TOURIST INFORMATION: Armstrong Redwoods Visitor Center**
17000 Armstrong Woods Rd. 869-2958; **Guerneville Chamber of**
**Commerce** 16200 First Street 869-9000; **Russian River Region Inc. -**
**Visitors Information Center** 14034 Armstrong Woods Rd. 869-9212.

## COUNTRY TIRE

Occasionally our trips are delayed by unexpected tire damage.   We all know the feeling of being in a strange town and asking ourselves:  Who can I turn to?  Who can I trust?

Folks who live here or regularly visit the Russian River Resort Region know Country Tire has the largest selection and best prices on quality used or brand new tires.  For over 30 years, through flood and earthquake, the olde fashioned country ethics utilized by owner Stan Buck and his hard working staff have kept consumers coming back tire after tire.  Whether you need a brand new set of radials, off-the-road 4X4 high traction treads, highway truck tires (regular or split rim) for your big rig or RV, recaps and used are all stocked in the Country Tire warehouse.  "The reason for our low prices," state Stan and his son Mark, "We buy direct from the manufacture and eliminate the middleman."   There is a waiting room with fresh brewed coffee and quality magazines such as National Geographic.  Stop by and compare Country Tire prices with where you regularly shop.

*$-$$ COUNTRY TIRE        Open Mon - Fri 8am - 6pm, Sat 8am - 3pm,*
*New and Used Tires  15290 River Rd., Guerneville, CA    (707) 869-2929*

## NOONAN'S GARAGE and 24 HOUR TOWING

The folks at Noonan's Garage and Towing are locally famous for saving lives and vehicles since 1961.  Be prepared for the worst, but expect the best are wise words for any vacationer driving   the

rugged coastal ridgelines above the crashing surf.

Sean Loundagin and his experienced staff have seen the worst and the best.  Not only do they have four heavy duty tow trucks to pull your RV, let alone your car up the steep coastal cliffs, but most importantly - *the experience!*   The Noonan's staff serve Forestville to Sea Ranch and know the roads well - they grew up here!   Their service doesn't stop once your vehicle is back on the road or towed in.  They can also complete all necessary minor or major repairs right in their high-tech shop in Guerneville, while you are enjoying the local sites or spending the night or few days at one of the areas modestly priced accommodations.

The shop is ASA and ASC certified and approved and the body shop is I-CAR approved to standards of quality and excellence.   Remember - breakdowns lead to break throughs!  A hot cup of coffee and a thorough briefing by Sean or one of the crew and you'll soon be back on the road enjoying the spectacular scenery.

*$$ NOONAN'S GARAGE and AUTO BODY  16312 Fifth St, Guerneville, CA*
*24 HOUR TOWING  Fax: (707) 869-1057   Tele: (707) 869-2781 / 887-7359*

## RIO INN

"Conferences of new thought and new play for a new world" is the higher confluence vision Dawson Church has for his Rio Inn located just east of Guerneville. Finally we have a retreat center, bed & breakfast inn and restaurant where the mind and body can soar with the angels amid the redwood forest.

The Rio Inn (formerly the Rio Nido Lodge) is a historic landmark (circa 1896). Big bands played at the lodge in the 30's and 40's as greats like Tom Dorsey and Harry James came to sing and play. Majestic redwood corridors came alive as music drifted through them to the 150 vacation cabins surrounding the lodge. Now, just as then great creative minds come to play and create under the boughs of the towering monarchs outside the Rio Inn's rooms and conference center. Guests will find 10 rooms. There are also five conference meeting/gathering spaces for 65 to 450 people - the Parlor, Tudor Rose Restaurant, St Andrew's Terrace and Druid's Circle. Nice spiritual energy and a hard work ethic hold the lodge firmly in the physical plane. This allows our more ungrounded and etheric visitors to feel safe and very blessed. The Rio Inn has the intent to provide a supportive and nurturing destination for you to contribute to your life's work and soar with the angels.

*$$ RIO INN*                    *4444 Wood Rd., Guerneville, CA. 95446*
*Bed & Breakfast Retreat Center*          *Group and Personal Retreats*
*dawsonic@wco.com  www.rioinn.com  (707) 869-4444  / 1-800-344-7018*

## COFFEE BAZAAR

A Dream Catcher catches bad thoughts and lets the good ones pass through. Every writer or thinker needs a coffee house to sit in and sort out their thoughts. Life is a river and coffee a stimulus. It can get us off our butts and out into the river of life. Coffee Bazaar is the main island for java heads cruising through the redwood corridors and into Guerneville. The burnt orange walls behind the counter of Coffee Bazaar draw attention to the menus and energizes the inside of this java room. Original art and photos line the other wall. Picture windows and canopies shield insiders from the street life, winter storms or late afternoon sun. Soups, salads, sandwiches, pastries, Italian sodas and ice cream sundaes satisfy cold or hot day appetites on the river. Coffee Bazaar is open daily from Sunday thru Thursday 6am-8pm and Friday and Saturday 6am to 11pm. Cash and travelers checks accepted.

*$ COFFEE BAZAAR  14045 Armstrong Woods Rd., Guerneville, CA 95446*
*Coffee House, Gallery & Used Bookstore*        *(707) 869-9706 Orders to go.*

## BURDON'S RESTAURANT

Small and intimate, with a quiet air of relaxation, Burdon's is where many on the Russian River go when they want excellent Continental dining.

The Prime Rib, served Friday and Saturday, is the finest. Other popular dinner items include seafood such as crab and shrimp cakes and the fresh catch of the day. Filet mignon, rack of lamb, rosemary chicken and baked lasagna come with fresh baked breads, soup du jour, and salad. Soft music, fresh flowers and friendly service mix well with the fine cuisine. To compliment your dining pleasure, a full service bar and an extensive list of local wines are available.

Whether on a wine tour or a Sunday drive to the redwoods, be sure to stop for fine dining at Burdons. Al fresco dining available weather permitting. Closed the month of January. When you come to ponder the beauty of the region don't forget about people like John who thoughtfully provides civilized amenities to the Russian River traveler. Open Wednesday thru Sunday 5:00pm - 9:00pm.

*$$ BURDON'S*            *15405 River Rd., Guerneville, CA. 95446*
*American and French Cuisine*    *MC & Visa. (707) 869-2615 Res. Sug.*

## MAIN STREET STATION PIZZA & JAZZ CLUB

A fun place to dine on gourmet pizza, taste premium California wine, drink great beer, laugh yourself dizzy to the antics of a stand-up comedian or swoon to the music of a Russian River Jazz ensemble is Main Street Station.

Proprietress Suzi Feehery is no stranger to introducing quality to several community oriented stores in the Russian River Region. Suzi's latest enterprise is her Pizza Cafe and Jazz Club which she and her family operate. The pizza sauces and dough are created daily from scratch using famous local recipes.

The pizza crust is delightful - light and crunchy - very nutritious, while the herbed red sauce is thick and juicy like a fresh picked tomato. Suzi's son Pavi states, "Being a visual artist in the kitchen pays off in the dining room." Also featured are "generous" deli style sandwiches, salads and a selection of international items. Ten beers are on draft, mineral water, sodas, herb teas, fruit smoothies and nutritious fresh squeezed fruit and vegetable juices are also served. During the winter rains a hot bowl of soup & slice of pizza can really hit the spot.

Beach picnics to go can be put together at Main Street Station. For pizza, music and fun "have a slice of Guerneville" at Suzie's Main Street Station.

*$-$$ MAIN STREET STATION*        *16280 Main Street, Guerneville, CA*
*Gourmet Pizza, Jazz Club, Beer & Wine. MC & Visa (707) 869-0501 To Go*

## The HUBCAP CAFE & DELI

In Guerneville the Hubcap Cafe & Deli is where the locals eat - and bring hubcaps! While you check out the decor of vintage hubcaps, license plates, etc. you can browse over the full deli menu. The choices of sandwiches, homemade salads and soups are further expanded by owner/chef Brenda Weddle's daily hot  platters. Brenda's beer and garlic roasted pot roast is a Russian River staple. If you need a break from the sun there is plenty of indoor seating. If a picnic is your style, the Hubcap will pack you one with all the trimmings. Where to picnic is never a problem on the river. From the Hubcap you can leave your car parked and walk one block to Johnson's Beach or to the new Plaza Park adjacent to Guerneville's famous steel girder bridge. Don't forget to bring your camera to photograph some of the tallest trees in the world, the crashing Sonoma Coast breakers or hidden wineries. A Hubcap picnic is a stop you will remember and Guerneville a town you will want to return to. Your hosts are Brenda Weddle and Shaughn Hanes

*$ The HUBCAP CAFE & DELI    16337 Main Street, Guerneville, 95446*
*Indoor deli dining and picnics to go  Open 8am 7pm      (707) 869-2393*

## RIVER READER BOOKSTORE

The River Reader provides a gallery of books, magazines, maps, posters, cards and special author events for the resident and visitor to Guerneville. Frances Werner, a former public interest lawyer, runs a clean and elegant bookstore that is well stocked and interesting. Tourists can find good books or magazines to take to the public beach, two blocks away, and guides to where to hike, bike, wine and dine your way through Sonoma County. The store carries a large selection of gay and lesbian books, spiritual literature, children's books and has a strong fiction section. Regular author readings, children's storytelling hour and book club meetings are hosted. You can call or write for a calendar of events. Open daily Wintertime: 10am-6pm, Summers: Sun-Thur 10-6, Fri & Sat 10-8.

*$-$$ RIVER  READER     16355 Main Street, Guerneville, CA. 95446*
*General, Gay / Lesbian, Spirituality, Children's Books*
*Fax: (707) 869-2242        Information and Events 707) 869-2240*

## RIVERLANE  RESORT
### On the Russian River

Wallie and Alby Kass's Riverlane Resort is designed for Russian River family holidays with housekeeping cabins fully equipped to accommodate 1 to 8 persons. The oldest house in Guerneville sits beside the swimming pool (heated Apr - Oct) and Spa (available throughout the year till midnight). Cozy cabin amenities include private bathrooms, kitchens, color TV's and BBQ's. All cabins have fireplaces or woodburning stoves, sleeper sofas and private decks with river views (rates from $50/2 to $170/8; weekly rates at $300/2 to $790/8). Ask about the special off season.

Riverlane has its own beach at the river with a well known fishing hole. Active in the community and theatre arts for 20 years, the Kass family provide valuable recommendations to their guests regarding cultural events and excellent restaurants. Riverlane Resort regrets that it cannot accept pets.

$$ *RIVERLANE RESORT*     Box 313, 1st &  Church St., Guerneville, CA
*Family Resort*           (707) 869-2323 or **800-201-2324**   Res. advised

## KING'S SPORT and TACKLE SHOP

The keys to a fishermans paradise is also known as King's Sports and Tackle Shop in Guerneville. Located on Main Street and open 7 days a week (special early morning hours during steelhead and salmon season), King's is the essential stopping off point before exploring the Russian River and its exciting and challenging fishing spots. In fact, owner Steve Jackson is so committed to the sportsman's pleasure he issues an informational sheet about the river, its seasonal catches and the best bait and lures to use to bring home the catch. King's also can book any sportfishing trips or hook you up with local river guide services. Up-to-date river and ocean conditions are found at Kings along with a friendly and knowledgeable fishing staff ready and willing to tell you everything but tales about the one that got away.

$$ *KING'S SPORT & TACKLE SHOP* 16258 Main St., Box 347, Guerneville
*Fishing & Outdoor Recreation Store*   CA. 95446. (707) 869-2156 Fish Info

## FERN GROVE COTTAGES

This lover's hideaway is neatly tucked in a pocket of 100 foot high redwoods only 1/4 mile from downtown Guerneville. New proprietors Anne and Simon Lowings welcome families and well behaved pets. The lodging on these 8 acres includes 20 romantic antique pine cottages which come with a continental breakfast. The cottages and large pool are beautifully maintained. Fern Grove is ideal for honeymooners and couples who are looking for unique lodging facilities from which to take walks in the redwoods, wine taste, swim or canoe in the Russian River, or explore the nearby Pacific coastline.

The cottages are equipped with 1 or 2 bedrooms, cable TV, private decks and porches and 11 include fireplaces. Fern Grove Cottages will also host small groups. A delicious breakfast of coffee, orange juice, fruit, cheese, homemade breads and pastries comes with your room. Rates vary from $69 - $159. Mid-week rates are available.

*$-$$ FERN GROVE COTTAGES   16650 River Rd., Guerneville, CA. 95446*
    *AE, MC & Visa, Discover             (707) 869-8105 Reservations*

## TAQUERIA LA TAPATIA

Located on the north end of Guerneville in a redwood hexagon dining room is Taqueria La Tapatia. Owner Porfirio Vazuez opened the restaurant in the winter of 1997 just before the floods. Porfirio became locally famous because of the Mexican cuisine he served from his taco truck along a wine country route between Healdsburg and Guerneville. Very likeable, Porfirio can be quite the comedian.

Taqueria La Tapatia is a traditional taqueria for sit down or to go. Many days the taqueria is packed with locals and tourists. The menu is divided into appetizers, tacos, burritos, salads, dinner (from $7.95), Mexican specialties and seafood specialties. Vegetarian and McDougal entrees are featured. Favorites include #48 which is Camarones Rancheros - sauteed prawns with tomatoes, onions and garlic in a ranchero sauce (regular or spicy - $8.95). Mexican breakfasts are served all day long - huevos Mexicanos, beef machoca and chorizo con papas. All food is prepared to order only with the freshest ingredients - cooked in cholesterol free oil. The salsa and chips are made fresh daily. The cooler is full of Mexican and American beer, fruit juices and non-alcoholic beverages.

*$-$$ TAQUERIA LA TAPATIA   16632 Hwy 116, Guerneville, CA. 95446*
*Mexican Cuisine             ATM, AE, MC & Visa    (707) 869-3023*

## NEW DYNAMIC INN

No matter how powerful, successful and strong you are, there is always a time when you need help.   At the New Dynamic Inn, Nick Mehta and his family will not only provide you with a restful sleep, but also give you renewed insight. Rooms and suites have double, queen and king beds, private baths and cable color TV. Workshops and retreats can be

hosted.  Nick uses Vedic Astrology to bring great clarity & direction to your life.

## BROOKSIDE LODGE

At Brookside Lodge guests can enjoy the lush landscaped garden setting with swimming pool.  Motel rooms (from $78/1-2) include king, queen or double beds, color cable TV, fireplaces and tub/shower.  Some cottages have fully equipped kitchens, wet bars, microwave ovens, patios and private decks with hot tubs (from $98).  Special weekly and corporate extended stay rates are available.

| | |
|---|---|
| *$$ NEW DYNAMIC INN* | *$$ BROOKSIDE LODGE* |
| *Rooms and Vedic Astrology Readings* | *Rooms and Cottages* |
| *14030 Mill St., Guerneville CA.* | *Box 382, Guerneville, CA. 95446* |
| *Renewed Vision (707) 869-5082* | *Major Credit Cards. (707) 869-2470* |

## INABEE

For years Wolfgang and Sybille Gramatski and their daughter Ina Barbara lived by the sea in tiny Jenner where the Russian River meets the sea.  As "Ina B"grew up she learned restaurateur skills from her parents whose River's End restaurant  became famous.  Today Ina B serves a grille and bar style menu

in her tri-level restaurant that her father had built just before he transitioned in 1998.  InaBee's sits in the redwoods overlooking Hulbert creek just north of Guerneville.

This friendly upscale neighborhood grill with full bar offers a nice selection of micro-brew beers, California wine, mixed drinks and espresso.   From three redwood outdoor decks you can toast your lover north-south-east and west. Entrees include the fresh catch, lobster, fabulous coconut shrimp, pasta with vegetables, rack of lamb, Bar Bee Q chicken, prime rib or New York steak served with seasoned veggies or potato and choice of homemade soup or house Caesar salad.  Desserts include lemony cheesecake or honey, crunchy apple strudel.

*$$ INABEE BAR & GRILL        17121 Hwy 116, Guerneville, CA. 95446*
*California Continental  MC & Visa  (707) 869-2INA  Res. party of 6 or more*

The lights of big Northwood Lodge are a welcome sight for many weary travelers seeking safe and warm accommodations in this region of the Redwood Empire. The obviousness of the lodge disguises the almost secret settings that lie within the expansive grounds. Twenty antique and period decorated rooms, six cottages, and a swimming pool await. The room and cabin rates vary in price from $50 to $160 per night depending on the number of people per unit, time of year and the chosen accommodation. All rooms and cabins have private baths, non smoking rooms are available, sorry no pets allowed.

This vacation spot has numerous amenities including in-room coffee, refrigerator, micro wave oven and small and large screen cable color TV. Cabins have skylights and fireplaces. There is even room for you to park your RV. An inner sanctuary canopied by a large stand of redwoods and walled off by rough wooden slabs conceals the bubbling waters of the hot tub spa. A few hundred yards away is the famous Bohemian Grove and next door the popular Northwood Golf Course and adjoining restaurant. Your friendly hosts are Vino and Meena Rayani.

*$-$$ NORTHWOOD RESORT LODGE   19455 Hwy 116, Monte Rio, CA.*
*Motel Rooms and Cabins    Redwood grove on the Russian River, hot tub,*
*swimming pool, fireplaces, private baths, wet bars.   Major credit cards ok.*
*Fax: (707) 865-1657          For Reservations call (707) 865-1655.*

## NORTHWOOD GOLF COURSE

Redwood ambassadors of the past tower over golfers at the Northwoods Golf Course. The Russian River carves a swath through these giants just to the south.

In the proshop, Gaylord Schaap provides profes-sional service golfers from around the world look forward to. This 9 hole 36 par golf course was designed by famed golf architect Allistair MacKenzie.

Quiet Northwood is definitely a course you should walk to take in all the re-creational beauty the redwood forest and greens have to offer. The sound of woodpeckers hammering out a meal amid the reassuring "thwack" of the driver is delightful. Just outside the sun deck of Northwood restaurant is the first hole, a par 4 at 296 yards. Crafty locals pull out a fairway wood or long iron and aim left of a big dead center redwood to drive the ball a little over 200 yards and just short of the green. At 509 yards, number 9 is a par 5 and the longest hole on the course. The 18 holes are rated a 67.5 for men and 71.5 for the ladies. At the course is the Northwoods Bar and Restaurant serving fresh seafood, poultry, steaks and vegetarian entrees; plus premium California wines and micro-brewed beers. Group lodging and tours of this spectacular region can be arranged by Gaylord.

*$$ NORTHWOOD Restaurant & Pub*     *$$  NORTHWOOD GOLF COURSE*
*Seafood & Steaks / Full Bar Box 52     9 Hole Par 36  Set amid a spectacular*
*19400 Hwy 116, Monte Rio, CA. 95462     redwood forest.   Open seasonally;*
*MC & Visa  (707) 865-2454 Res.                call for hours.  (707) 865-1116*

## RIO VILLA BEACH RESORT

Adjacent the banks of the Russian River and Monte Rio bridge is Rio Villa. A variety of accommodations for couples, families and individuals include rooms with fully equipped kitchens, private baths, couches, king and queen beds, cable color TV, dining rooms, outdoor BBQ's, and sundecks for dining and reading beneath the sun or stars. A spacious cabin overlooking the river with fully equipped kitchen with refrigerator, private bathroom with tub/shower, and fireplace is $179. Rio Villa rates for 2 are from $79-$179 wk ends and $69-$139 mid week. A stroll through the colorful olde fashioned herb and flower gardens leaves one refreshed and grateful. On weekends (only) a buffet breakfast of homemade coffee cakes, breads, muffins, fresh fruit, juices and fresh brewed coffee is served on the redwood patio (weather permitting). Grocery stores and restaurants are close by.

*$$ RIO VILLA BEACH RESORT   20292 Hwy 116, Monte Rio, CA. 95462*
*Cabin, Rooms & Suites    http:www.riovilla.com   (707) 865-1143 Res. Sug.*

## VILLAGE INN

The rustic old English architecture of this 1906 three story inn was known in the forties as the "Holiday Inn" and scenes from the Bing Crosby movie of the same name were filmed here. Today one may sleep under towering redwoods, dine on fresh Sonoma County cuisine and sip world-renowned wines at the Village Inn. The newly remodeled restaurant and bar are now located on the second floor and enjoy spectacular river views. All rooms have private baths (from $85/2). Five are located in the Inn on the top floor with river views and private balconies. The Lodge's five rooms have garden views and outside entrances. A gradual ramp joins the two buildings adding to the already ample view decks for everyone.

*$-$$ VILLAGE INN & RESTAURANT     Box 850, River Blvd., Monte Rio,*
*Riverview Rooms and Suites          CA. 95462     Fax: (707) 865-2332*
*www.village-inn.com                                   (707) 865-2304 Res.*

## CAZADERO
## GENERAL STORE

Once a logging boom town, Cazadero is now a sleepy little stop along the way hosting a well equipped general store as well as some of the heaviest winter rains in California. Cazadero Road is a narrow corridor lined with magnificent redwoods and runs parallel to Austin Creek. Proprietors Dale and Heidi Bohan are Sonoma County pioneer family descendants. Their Cazadero General Store is well equipped with traditional and health foods, premium wine and imported and domestic beer, canned and bulk foods, bulk herbs & vitamins, picnic supplies, fishing & rain gear, hardware, batteries and charcoal. Fresh brewed coffee, hot pizza, popcorn and hot dogs are also served. In the retail store next door are video rentals, a video arcade, books, magazines and local crafts.

Austin Creek has many small emerald green swimming holes in the summertime. The music from a nearby music camp mysteriously drifts through the ancient redwood groves. To the west of "Caz" is wilderness, sheep and cattle ranches so note and heed posted land and private property signs. It's a beautiful drive to the coast.

*$ CAZADERO GENERAL STORE*
*Food and Provisions*
*6125 Cazadero Hwy, Cazadero, CA 95421*
*(707) 632-5287 Information*

## CAZANOMA LODGE

Where else on the rugged north coast can you catch your own fresh trout from the pond and have it expertly prepared for your dining pleasure? Four upstairs suites in the lodge furnished with queen beds overlook the waterfall and 2 cozy cabins lie hidden in the woods. Family style dinners ($12 - $16) include relishes, salads, homemade soup, fresh vegetables, potato pancakes with applesauce.        Overnight accommodations are $70 - $135 for 2 and include a continental breakfast.

Sunday brunch is served on the creekside redwood deck beneath towering redwood trees.  Your hosts, Randy and Gretchen Neuman, promise Cazanoma Lodge will be a rare retreat for culinary and environmental pleasures.

*$$ -$$$ CAZANOMA LODGE      Box 37, 1000 Kidd Creek Rd., Cazadero,*
*B&B, Full Bar, German-American Cuisine   CA. 95421   (707) 632-5255 Res.*

## ELIM GROVE RESTAURANT

Deep in the redwood forest of Western Sonoma County and bordering picturesque Austin Creek is Elim Grove Restaurant. Completely remodeled, this upbeat destination offers gourmet country cuisine for visitors as well as

more traditional meals for locals.  For lunch, appetizers, salads (try the chilled wedge or chicken Caesar) soups (oyster stew), sandwiches (from $5.95) such as black angus burgers, garden burger (vegetarian) or fresh fish.  Homemade pizzas are topped with fresh herbs, vegetables and meats (sit down or to go).  Dinner entrees (from $9.95) are served with soup or salad and include filet mignon, bistro steak, lamb stew, fresh fish (salmon or sea bass) and marinated chicken - pan roasted in herbs.  Evenings a panorama of stars twinkle above the tips of 200 foot - 1,000 year old redwood trees.  Hours for lunch are 11 am to 2 pm, dinner 5:30pm - 10pm and sunday brunch 10am - 2pm.

*$-$$ ELIM GROVE RESTAURANT  5400 Cazadero Hwy, Cazadero, CA.*
*Country American Cuisine      95421   (707) 632-6099 Sit down or to go.*

## CAPE FEAR RESTAURANTS and FEARLESS ICE CREAM

Cape Fear restaurant is named after a famous resort area in North Carolina, where the Outer Banks are formed by the Atlantic Ocean and the Cape Fear River. Ambitious owners Joel Wiygul and Jim Harkey have opened Cape Fear restaurants in Duncans Mills and Graton and the Fearless Ice Cream Parlor in Duncans Mills. Delicious gourmet entrees are served for breakfast, lunch, dinner and weekend brunch. Entrees include the Cape Fear Hot Pot ($15.95) with salmon, prawns, mussels in vermouth with garlic over linguini; Carolina chicken, "Company's Comming" prime rib with au jus and horseradish and golden Portabella mushroom salad with sweet corn & black beans in balsamic vinaigrette. Appetizers include spicy Thai mussels, garlic ginger oysters or crab & salmon cakes with assertive aioli. For breakfast there are frittatas, egg entrees, pancakes and waffles. Try the Southport Ham steak & eggs or Savannah banana pancakes. Brunch entrees include sweet potato pancakes and the Charlestone benedict - shrimp, prosciutto and lemon hollandaise over poached eggs on black pepper grits. Garden fresh salads, pastas and sandwiches are served for lunch. Try the Skipjack tuna remoulade salad or Cape Fear burger. Both restaurants are open from 9am-3pm and 5pm-9pm daily.
*$-$$ CAPE FEAR     E-mail:acre@monitor.net     Fax: (707) 869-2659*
*8989 Graton Rd, Graton, CA   95444     (707) 824-8284     MC & Visa*
*25191 Main St., Duncans Mills, CA 95430     (707) 865-9246 Reservations*

## CASINI RANCH FAMILY CAMPGROUND

One of the largest campgrounds on the north coast is the Casini Ranch Family Campground. This 120 acre sanctuary sits on a broad peninsula surrounded on 3 sides by a mile of the Russian River. The large recreation hall, built in 1862, was originally a horse barn used by Ulysses S. Grant. There is a old-fashioned general store, laundry and arcade. The clean, well-planned campground includes pull-through trailer hookups, a trailer rally area, TV hookups, bathrooms with shower facilities and a club house. Trailer sites have picnic tables and BBQ pits; and many are shaded with river views. Steelhead, shad, black or striped bass, catfish, crappie, trout, and silver salmon fishing  is very popular. "One year the Monarch of North America paid us a visit we'll never forget," states George Casini,  "I guess the Bald Eagle liked the fishing, because he stayed 4 months!"
*$$ CASINI RANCH FAMILY CAMPGROUND        22855 Moscow Road,*
*Campground & Store   Box 22, Duncans  Mills, CA 95430  1-800-451-8400*

# DUNCANS MILLS

In the spring of 1886, Sam and Alexander Duncan had lost their logging camp to high water for the 14th time since moving down to the Russian River from Salt Point. They barged their sawmill five miles upstream to a fine sunlit flat in a curve of the Russian River. They floated their United States Post Office, built in 1862, upriver, as a mark of stability. A permanent address made a river bank a Place, a legal part of the United States. Duncans Mills! Population 20, elevation 36 feet; Duncans Mills became an awakening "Sleeping Beauty." Today there is the **Duncans Mills General Store**, a campground, three restaurants including **Gold Coast Coffee Company, Cape Fear and the Blue Heron Tavern,** plus two bed & breakfast inns, the **Wine and Cheese Tasting Center** and richly landscaped courtyards and gardens. And yes, you can still mail your cards and letters home from the post office that originally anchored Duncans Mills to the United States of America.

## BLUE HERON RESTAURANT & TAVERN

The Blue Heron is one of those special little restaurants where a lot of people with a lot of love got together to create a gourmet experience in a rustic setting. The dinner menu is highly imaginative with emphasis on fresh and local.

It's a delightful place with a turn of the century remodeled tavern, a handcrafted redwood dining room, and a large kitchen. The staff makes it a top priority to utilize the freshest produce whenever possible. An after meal stroll through Duncans Mills or along the banks of the Russian River may reveal the gentle, yet deliberate Blue Heron patiently stalking the shallows, her six foot wings tucked gracefully at her sides. Later in the evening before retiring to your favorite B & B Inn you can enjoy a wide selection of imported wines, beers and cocktails in the tavern by candlelight.

*$$ BLUE HERON Restaurant & Tavern*
*Restaurant & Country Tavern  1 Steelhead Blvd., Duncans Mills, CA.*
*95430                MC & Visa.        (707) 865-9135 Res. accepted*

## SUPERINTENDENT'S HOUSE

Set on a hillside overlooking the historic railroad town of Duncans Mills (established in 1877) is the "caboose red" Superintendent's House. This stately Victorian ranch house basks in a wonderful climate of mixed inland and ocean air warmed by the sun and fertile earth of the Russian River valley. Guests enjoy the victorian country charm of days gone by with a bonus of pure well water, clean air, the daily presence of wildlife, a heavenly view of stars at night and a one of a kind innkeeper - Phil Dattola. With down to earth sincerity Phil does his best to insure his guests enjoyment, whether sharing a fresh caught salmon, leading an expedition to discover little known corners of Sonoma County or cheerfully providing a bowl of popcorn and a good movie for the VCR. Guests can choose from five 1st or 2nd floor bedrooms with country breakfast (from $65/2). Winter storms and crackling fires make for romantic memories at the Superintendent's House. A stroll down the hillside places you in the heart of tiny Duncans Mills with its artistic shops & boutiques, cafes, olde fashioned barber, general store, horse stables and railroad museum. There are still a few places where they "make em like they used to" and one is in Duncans Mills at the Superintendent's House.

*$$ SUPERINTENDENT'S HOUSE   24951 Hwy 116, Box 17,  Duncans*
*Bed and Breakfast         Mills, CA. 95430.   (707) 865-1572 Res. Sug.*

## QUERCIA BALCONY GALLERY

**Quercia**
**Balcony**
**Gallery**

Fine Art
Quality Framing
Frame Restoration
Exhibiting Antique &
Contemporary Works
of Reginal Artists

In a small artist framing shop in Duncans Mills, Ron Quercia has been thoughtfully remounting and framing masterpieces and contemporary works for a long list of regular and new clients inspired by the artisans who have lived and painted this spectacular region of America. Rebuilding antique frames is another time honored art Ron and Bobbi Jeanne have mastered due to years of experience in northern California. You'll find Ron to be thoughtful and inspired to match original or print to frame as well as to client and environment they will be hanging in. The frame shop also doubles as a gallery where the works of local artists are displayed. So here we have the artist surrounded by artists in this beautiful river valley near the sea. Hours are seasonal but Quercia Gallery is usually open Thur - Mon from 11am to 5pm.

*$-$$$ QUERCIA BALCONY GALLERY     Box 246, 25193 State Hwy 116,*
*Fine Art and Framing         Duncans Mills, CA. 95430   (707) 865-0243*

ISLAND SHORES - SNOWY EGRET by Carl Brenders.  This is a sample of the many fine prints available at Christopher Queen Galleries in Duncans Mills.

## CHRISTOPHER QUEEN GALLERIES

The rich interior of Christopher Queen Galleries is full of original art treasures depicting scenes of early California as well as the creations of more contemporary artists.  The gallery was founded in 1976, the year America celebrated its 200th birthday, by Alfhild Wallen and her daughter Nancy Ferreira.  In 1985 this dynamic mother / daughter team added a large collection of Early California art 1860 to 1940 with a sizeable collection provided by Arnold (Swede) Wallen, Alfhild's husband.

Today the gallery continues on a dedicated journey of showcasing originals and prints of exquisite landscapes, florals, wildlife, nautical and genre paintings.  A visit to Christopher Queen Galleries is more like visiting a museum than a gallery.  Paintings, prints, original oils and sculpture truly uplift the spirit of the visitor and remind us of what an incredible world we live in.

The gallery is located in the historic town of Duncans Mills and is open daily from 11:00am to 5:00pm.  Major credit cards are honored and Alfhild and Nancy will arrange to ship art anywhere in the world.  Write or call for a free brochure on current shows and releases by your favorite artists.

*$$-$$$  CHRISTOPHER QUEEN GALLERIES*
*Originals and Prints of Landscapes, Florals, Wildlife, Nautical and Genre as well as a large collection of Early California Art 1860 to 1940.*
*Box 28, Duncans Mills, CA 95430   Newsletter & Info  (707) 865-1628*

# HWY 101, HWY 128 and Dry Creek Road
## UPPER RUSSIAN RIVER WINE COUNTRY
### Windsor to Cloverdale

The Healdsburg Bridge and Memorial Beach is popular for swimming, canoeing and sun bathing.

You can take in the splendor of the Russian River Wine Country by airplane, helicopter or hot air baloon. The Sonoma County Air Museum (pictured below) at the Sonoma County Airport is a must.

**WINDSOR to HEALDSBURG DINER'S CHOICE: Tele Area Code is (707).**
**Cricklewood** ($$) 4618 Old Redwood Hwy.  527-7768 ;  **Diana's Market Y Taqueria** ($) 10351 Old Redwood Hwy.  838-1733;  **Guanajuato** ($$) 275 Windsor River Rd.  838-8845;  **Hot Tamales Taqueria** ($) 8465 Old Redwood Hwy.  838-9511;  **Mary's Pizza Shack** ($$) 9010 Brooks Rd.  836-0900;  **Playa Azul Marisco** ($$) 8832 Lakewood Dr.  838-0977;  The **Road House** ($$) 8430 Old Redwood Hwy.  837-0598;  **Sellini Grille & Cafen'eo Bar** ($$) 2250 Airport Blvd.  573-6900;  **Star's Restaurant** ($$) 8499 Old Redwood Hwy  838-2944 ;  **Yinkeng Restaurant** ($$) 8840 Lakewood Dr.  838-2101.

**WINDSOR to HEALDSBURG LODGING:**
**Country Meadow Inn** ($$-$$$) 11360 Old Redwood Hwy.  431-1276;

**ATTRACTIONS: Pacific Coast Air Museum** ($) 2330 Airport Blvd.  575-7900

**HEALTH & FITNESS: Airport Fitness Club** ($) 432 Aviation Blvd.  528-2582.

**GREAT OUTDOORS: Aerial & Photo Flights Above Sonoma County**
American Aviation ($$) 2238 Airport Blvd.  526-0708; ($$) Dragon Fly Aviation 2222 Airport Blvd.  575-8750;  Unique Travel ($$) 2238 Airport Blvd.  542-8687;

**Hot Air Baloon Flights** ($$) Aerostat Adventures  579-0183; ($$) Air Flambuoyant 838-8500;  ($$) Sonoma Thunder  829-9850.

## UPPER RUSSIAN RIVER VALLEY WINERYS *With Tasting Rooms*

Tasting Room and Giftshop Hours are often seasonal especially if located outside a city. All of these tasting rooms are open weekends and many daily. Call for current hours just to be sure. Remember to drive safely being aware of children, pets, wildlife and other vehicles.

20. **Alderbrook Winery**            2306 Magnolia, Healdsburg   433-9154;
22. **Alexander Valley Vineyards**      8644 Hwy 128, Healdsburg   433-7209;
24. **Canyon Rd. Cellars / Nervo** 19550 Old Redwood Hwy, S., Gey.  857-3417;
25. **Chateau Sourverain**      400 Souverain Road, Geyserville   433-8281;
26. **Christopher Creek**        641 Limerick Ln., Healdsburg   433-2001;
27. **Clos Du Bois**        19410 Geyserville Ave., Geyserville   857-3100;
28. **de Lorimier Vineyards & Winery**  2001 Hwy 128, Healdsburg   857-2000;
26. **De Natale Vineyards**        11020 Eastside Rd., Healdsburg   431-8460
29. **Dry Creek Vineyards**   3770 Lambert Bridge Rd., Healdsburg   433-1000;
23. **Everette Ridge Vineyards**  435 W. Dry Creek Rd., Healdsburg   433-1637;
30. **Ferrari - Carano Winery**     8761 Dry Creek Rd., Healdsburg   433-6700;
31. **Field Stone Winery**          10075 Hwy 128, Healdsburg   433-7266;
32. **Foppiano Vineyards**    12707 Old Redwood Hwy, Healdsburg   433-7272;
33. **Geyser Peak Winery**        22281 Chianti Rd., Geyserville   857-WINE;
34. **J. Fritz Winery**       24691 Dutcher Creek Rd., Cloverdale   894-3389;
35. **Hanna Winery**             9280 Hwy 128, Healdsburg   431-4310;
36. **Hop Kiln Winery**         6050 Westside Rd., Healdsburg   433-6491;
37. **Johnson's Alexander Winery**   8333 Hwy 128, Healdsburg   433-2319;
38. **Kendall - Jackson**        337 Healdsburg Ave., Healdsburg   571-7500;
40. **Lake Sonoma Winery**       9990 Dry Creek Rd., Geyserville   431-1550;
41. **Lambert Bridge Winery**  4085 West Dry Creek Rd., Healdsburg   431-9600;
42. **Mazzocco Vineyards**    1400 Lytton Springs Rd., Healdsburg   433-9035;
43. **Mill Creek Vineyards**        1401 Westside Rd., Healdsburg   433-5098;
44. **Murphy - Goode Winery**      4001 Hwy 128, Geyserville   431-7644;
45. **J. Pedroncelli Vineyards**      1220 Canyon Rd., Geyserville   857-3531;
46. **Pezzi King Vineyards**   3805 Lambert Bridge Rd., Healdsburg   433-3305;
48. **Preston Vineyards**        9282 W. Dry Creek Rd., Healdsburg   433-3372;
49. **Quivira Vineyards**        4900 W. Dry Creek Rd., Healdsburg   431-8333;
50. **Ridge / Lytton Springs Winery** 650 Lytton Springs Rd., Hldbrg.  433-7721;
51. **Rodney Strong Vineyards**   11455 Old Redwood Hwy., Hldbrg.  433-6511;
52. **Sausal Winery**             7370 Hwy 128, Healdsburg   433-2285;
53. **Simi Winery**        16275 Healdsburg Ave., Healdsburg   433-6981;
21. **Sommers Vineyard**         5110 Hwy 128,  Hldbrg.   433-1944;
54. **J Stonestreet**          337 Healdsburg Ave., Healdsburg   571-7500;
55. **Trentadue Vineyards**   19170 Geyserville Ave., Geyserville   857-3104;
56. **White Oak Vineyards**        7505 Hwy 128, Healdsburg   433-8429;
57. **Windsor Vineyards**     239 A Center Street, Healdsburg   433-2822.

**SCENIC DRIVES:**
**GETTING THERE THRU HEALDSBURG**
Take the Highway 101 exit north of Healdsburg and proceed thru the wine
country of the Dry Creek Valley. Turn left at Warm Springs Dam and climb
over the mountains on Skaggs Springs Road to Stewarts Point. Or take the
Highway 101 exit at the south of end of Healdsburg and proceed west on
Westside Road into the wine country and River Road.

The historic
Healdsburg Plaza is a
delightful setting for
a stroll or picnic.
Cafes, bookstores,
bed & breakfast inns,
bistro's, and art
galleries surround the
Plaza.

# HEALDSBURG
## The Upper Russian River Wine Country

**HEALDSBURG DINER'S CHOICE: Telephone Area Code is (707).**
**Acre Restaurant & Lounge** 420 Center St. 431-1302; **Bear Republic
Brewing Co.** ($$) 345 Healdsburg Ave. 433-BEER; **Bistro Ralph** ($$) 109
Plaza St. 433-1380; **Catelli's The Rex** ($$$) 241 Healdsburg Ave 433-6000;
**Center Street Deli & Cafe** ($) 304 Center St. 433-7224; **China
Restaurant** ($$) 336 Healdsburg Ave. 433-4122; **Costeaux French Bakery**
($) 417 Healdsburg Ave. 433-1913; **Dry Creek General Store Deli** ($)
3495 Dry Creek Rd 433-4171; **El Farolito Mexican R.** ($$) 128 Plaza St.
433-2807; **Fitch Mountain Eddie's** ($$) 1301 Healdsburg Ave. 433-7414;
**Giorgio's** ($$) 25 Grant Ave. 433-1106; **Healdsburg Charcuterie &
Delicatessen** ($) 335 Healdsburg Ave. 431-7213; **Healdsburg Coffee
Company Cafe** ($) 312 Center 431-7941; **Healdsburg Natural Foods** ($)
325 Center 433-1060; **Madrona Manor** ($$$) 1001 Westside Rd. 433-
6831; **Malone's Tamale Restaurant** ($$) 245 Healdsburg Ave. 431-1856;
**Matuszeks** ($$) 345 Healdsburg Ave. 433-3427; **Ravenous Cafe** ($) 117
North St. 431-1770; **Sellini Grille & Cafen'eo Bar** ($$) 2250 Airport Blvd.
573-6900; **Singletree Inn** ($) 149 Healdsburg Ave. 433-9893; **Western
Boot Steak House** ($$) 9 Mitchell Lane 433-6362.

**GREAT OUTDOORS: W. C. "Bob" Trowbridge Canoe Trips** ($$) 20
Healdsburg Ave. 433-7247 / 1-800-640-1386.

## HEALDSBURG LODGING:
**Belle de Jour Inn** ($$) 16276 Healdsburg Ave. 431-9777; **Calderwood Inn** ($$) 25 West Grant 431-1110; **Camellia Inn** ($$) 211 North St. 433-8182; **Dry Creek Inn** ($$) 198 Dry Creek Rd. 433-0300; **Frampton House** ($$) 489 Powell Ave. 433-5084; **George Alexander House** ($$) 423 Matheson St. 433-1358; **Grape Leaf Inn** ($$) 539 Johnson St. 433-8140; **Haydon Street Inn** ($$) 321 Haydon St. 433-5228; **Healdsburg Inn on the Plaza** ($$) 110 Matheson St. 433-6991; **Honor Mansion** ($$) 14891 Grove St. 433-4277; **L & M Motel** ($$) 70 Healdsburg Ave. 433-6528; **Madrona Manor** ($$) 1001 Westside Rd. 433-4231; **Vineyard Valley Inn** ($$) 178 Dry Creek Rd. 433-0101.

**ATTRACTIONS: Healdsburg Museum** ($) 221 Matheson St. 431-3325; **Raven Theater** ($) 115 North St. 433-5448; **Wine Library of Sonoma County** ($) Healdsburg Library at Piper & Center Sts. 433-3772.

**HEALTH & FITNESS: A Simple Touch Spa & Massage** ($$) 239 #C Center St. 433-6856; **Healdsburg Health & Fitness** ($$) 1500 Healdsburg Ave. 433-9500; **Healdsburg Municipal Pool** ($) 360 Monte Vista 433-1109; **Russian River, Veteran's Memorial Beach Park** ($) Healdsburg Ave. south of town at the bridge. 433-1625; **Spa Off the Plaza** ($$) 706 Healdsburg Ave. 431-7938; **Spoke Folk Cyclery** ($$) Bicycle Rentals & Accessories 249 Center St. 433-7171.

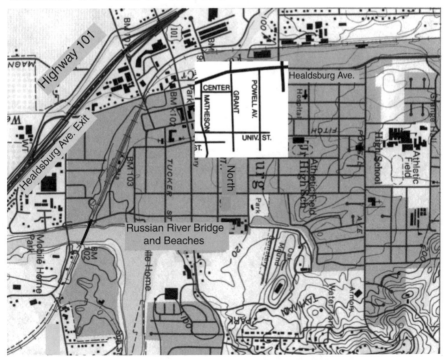

Downtown Healdsburg and Vicinity

## FOPPIANO VINEYARDS

The Foppiano family has been welcoming guests and wine lovers to its Healdsburg estate for over 100 years. Founded in 1896, Foppiano Vineyards is the oldest continually-owned family winery n Sonoma County. Today, under the Foppiano Vineyards label, the Foppiano family produces a select line of award-winning red wines.

Much has changed at the winery since its beginnings. Back at the turn of the century, immigrant family's came from far and wide to fill their jugs and barrels at the winery. The Foppiano distribution network consisted of horse-drawn wagons and boats which traversed San Francisco Bay loaded with wine headed for the Italian North Beach district in San Francisco.

Today, under the direction of 4th generation Louis M. Foppiano, the wines are found in fine restaurants and wine shops across America, Europe, Asia and Canada.

Foppiano continues to meet and greet its long time friends at the winery, but is also passing on its tradition of high quality and high value red wines to a new generation. Today visitors can enjoy complimentary tastings in the historic tasting room, with the wines probably being poured by a member of the family. In addition, a picnic area overlooking the vineyards is available, along with a self-guided vineyard tour explaining the grape growing process.

Foppiano Vineyards is located just south of Healdsburg on Old Redwood Highway. Take the south Healdsburg exit off Highway 101 and go 1/2 mile south. The tasting room and winery is open daily, 10:00am to 4:30pm.

*$-$$ FOPPIANO VINEYARDS*
*Tours, Tastings & Retail Sales*
*12707 Old Redwood Hwy,*
*P.O. Box 606, Healdsburg,*
*California   95448*
*Self Guided Vineyard Tour*
*AE, MC & Visa  (707) 433-7272*

## MADRONA MANOR

Surrounded by eight acres of wooded and landscaped grounds, Madrona Manor has been a prominent Sonoma County landmark since 1881. A stay at the mansion places you close to numerous recreational facilities such as golf, tennis, hiking, canoeing, swimming and fishing. The proprietors are William and Trudi Konrad and the innkeepers are Joseph and Maria Hadley.

Madrona Manor provides its guests a tranquil ambiance and elegant country lifestyle with its 18 rooms and 3 suites. All are exquisitely detailed with king or queen beds, private baths and fireplaces in all but three rooms. Many of the rooms in the mansion contain magnificent antique furniture. The Carriage House is a Victorian jewel furnished and decorated throughout with handcarved rosewood and architectural amenities from Kathmandu, Nepal and China. Rates for two are from $175 - $380 and include a sumptuous full breakfast. The ambiance of Madrona Manor, absent of artificial distractions, is very conducive to high intellectual output, making it ideal for conferences and seminars (up to 30).

Dining at Madrona Manor is a memorable experience. The chefs compose menus that elevate to prominence the finest fresh produce and seafood available each day. The kitchen utilizes a brick oven, mesquite grille, smokehouse, orchard and herb/vegetable garden to create a refreshingly unique cuisine that harmonizes foods of outstanding quality, freshness, aroma and flavor. The always exciting a la carte menu is served sunday through thursday with entrees from $17 to $26. Carefully selected premium domestic and imported wines are cellared to complement the varied menu.

To arrive at the Madrona Manor take the Healdsburg exit off Hwy 101 and drive about 1/2 mile west down Westside Road to the arch over the entrance.

*$$-$$$ MADRONA MANOR*
*Bed & Breakfast Dinner Lodging  Elegant Wine Country Rooms & Suites*
*New California Cuisine                    Dinner: Sun-Thur. 6pm-9pm*
*1001 Westside Road, Box 818, Healdsburg, CA. 95448*
*www.madronamanor.com    800-258-4003    (707) 433-4231 Rec. Nec.*

W.C. "Bob Trowbridge Canoe and Kayak trips can be enjoyed along the Russian River and Sonoma Coast estero and open ocean waterways. Picnics and camping add to the memories of a visit to the Redwood Empire.

# W.C. "BOB" TROWBRIDGE RUSSIAN RIVER CANOE TRIPS

Floating past gently rolling blue hills and vineyards; soaking up some warm sun in a wilderness setting is "just right" as the Russian River sets the pace for a lazy day of canoeing in Sonoma County. The Russian River has become the most popular canoe river in the world due to 60 miles of safe but exciting waterway, and the efforts of the late W.C. "Bob" Trowbridge, whose specially built Grumman canoes have delighted thousands since 1959.

Nine one day canoe ($29 - $34 / 5 to 11 miles) and kayak trips ($22) are available,  two-two day trips ($49 / 22 miles) and three to five day canoe trips ($70 / 45 - 50 miles) are available.  Campgrounds, ingress and egress points, transportation, and special wildlife viewing points are all highlighted on tour maps provided by W.C. "Bob" Trowbridge Canoe Trips.  April through October the Russian River between Asti and Monte Rio drops slowly with only a few sections of swift flowing current for variety.  Some overhanging and submerged branches along the bank of the river can be difficult to negotiate - especially at low tide (check tide table books) - but most places are shallow enough for wading should you capsize.

If the group is large and lively, some will probably end up in the river; so dress accordingly and bring a dry change of clothing.  Be sure to bring cold drinks and a picnic lunch: bottles, cans and food should be secured in plastic bags and tied to the canoe.  Keep all refuse tied in another bag for easy disposal at the end of the trip.  Tennis shoes or those that tie on won't get lost overboard.  Bring life preservers (or rent them) and protection from the sun.  For those lucky enough to end up at Healdsburg Beach saturday or sunday between 4pm and 7 pm a hearty BBQ steak, chicken or vegetarian entree served with hot buttered French bread, delicious salad and hot baked beans made from Bob's "out of this world" recipe may be enjoyed for $7-$8.

*$$ W.C. "BOB" TROWBRIDGE CANOE TRIPS Box 942,  20 Healdsburg Ave.,*
*Canoe and Kayak Rentals and Trips              Healdsburg, CA 95448*
*AE, MC & Visa    Open 1 April - Oct 31  (707) 433-7247 / 1-800-640-1386*

## L & M MOTEL

The cozy L & M Motel with garden courtyard and indoor swimming pool, spa and sauna is located at the south end of Healdsburg just off Hwy 101 and four blocks from downtown plaza and 3 blocks from beautiful Russian River parks and beaches. Louis and Marie pursued their dreams in the wine country when they bought land in the 40's and built the L & M Motel in the 50's before the freeway was expanded north to Healdsburg. This quaint and charming wine country destination has been proudly owned and operated by the same family since it was built. Family pride means clean rooms, reasonable rates (from $60/2) and your children and pets are welcome! The owners point out that dogs are allowed only in a few of the 19 units. The L & M is a pleasant alternative for those who tire of high prices and petty pretentiousness at other nearby wine country accommodations. "We have the only indoor swimming pool at a motel in Healdsburg," proudly states Wanda. The family keep the L & M remodeled and ship-shape. All rooms have cable color TV's, in-room direct dial telephones (local calls are free), private baths and a few have kitchenettes. Excellent restaurants, art galleries, antique shops, canoeing and dozens of wineries are a short drive away.

*$$ L & M MOTEL*          *70 Healdsburg Ave., Healdsburg, CA. 95448*
*Motel Rooms*                *AE, MC & Visa.*          *(707) 433-6528*

## GIORGIO'S PIZZERIA

In the late 1970's many Bay Area restaurant critics endorsed Giorgio's Restaurant on Clement Street as the best pizza in San Francisco. George Anastasio sold his pioneering pizzeria to the Contini family in 1978. Giorgio's is still one of the most popular pizza destinations in San Francisco.

The same year he sold, George moved north to the wine country, trading the bobbing heads walking the streets of San Francisco for the waving grapevines marching up the hillsides around Healdsburg. The view out the kitchen windows is much like his former home on the island of Ischia in his native Italy. At Giorgio's, daily entrees, of pasta, poultry and beef are laboriously prepared and served. Dinner includes soup, salad, pasta and beverage. Be sure to try Giorgio's original mouth watering calzone (pizza dough stuffed and rolled with fresh vegetables and meats and baked with herbs and olive oil). The ever popular pizza's are superb and can be enjoyed with premium wines or mixed drinks from the full bar. Today Loni and Bill carry on the fine tradition Giorgio's is known for. Lunch/Dinner served 11:00am - 10:00pm / Weekends from 4pm-10pm.

*$$ GIORGIO'S   Amex, Dis, MC & Visa*      *25 Grant Ave., Healdsburg, CA.*
*Italian Cuisine and Pizza  Banquets to 60  (707) 433-1106 Sit down or to go*

## EVERETT RIDGE VINEYARDS & WINERY

Venture up the wooded drive to Everett Ridge, one of Dry Creek Valley's earliest wineries, and you will be greeted by a grand old redwood barn, circa 1880, home in the past to draft horses, mules, and stage coach teams. Named after founder E. Everett Wise, this family owned-and-operated winery is under the direction of Jack and Anne Air who developed the surrounding vineyards organically, and augment this time honored approach with the finest winery equipment and technology available. The tasting room offers magnificent valley views. You'll be offered barrel samples of future vintages, award winning releases of Chardonnay, Pinot Noir, Cabernet Sauvignon, Syrah, Sauvignon Blanc, and popular Workhorse blends. *EVERETT RIDGE VINEYARDS and WINERY    435 West Dry Creek Rd., Picnic tables, Wine Country gifts & retail wine sales  Healdsburg, CA. Open daily 11-4,  Web: www.everettridge.com   Fax: (707) 433-7024  Info: 433-1637*

## BEAR REPUBLIC BREWING CO.

Big and bold like the Bear Flag Revolt of 1846 is the Bear Republic Brewing Company, located on Healdsburg's Historic Plaza. It was founded in 1994 by 3rd and 4th generation Sonoma County residents Richard and Sandy Norgrove and their brew master son Richard and his wife Tami.   You can taste Bear Republic's gold medel winning hand crafted lagers and ales including Wine Country WheatTM, Extra Special Bitter and Rocket Ale along with special brews like their Racer 5 IPA and one-of-a-kind Hard Apple Cider.    Tea toddlers can enjoy the non-alcoholic Root Beer and Cream Soda which are delicious.

A spicy selection of appetizers, homemade soups and chili, salads, sandwiches and delicious seafood, vegetarian and meat entrees (from $7.95) are served. The mountain bike museum exhibits and original art decor make dining at the Bear Republic Brewing Co. a real pleasure.

*$$ BEAR REPUBLIC BREWING CO. 345 Healdsburg Ave., Healdsburg, CA Brew Pub, Tavern & Restaurant  Fax: (707) 433- 2205  / 433-BEER (2337)*

## WESTERN BOOT STEAK HOUSE

At the Western Boot Steak House you can enjoy over a dozen aged and hand cut steak dinners including sirloin 8oz - 22oz, filet mignon, New York, T-bone, terriyake, ground beef, platter of ribs as well as ravioli, spaghetti, prawns and 1/2 chicken.   Appetizers, teriyake burgers, soup & salad, homemade desserts, fresh brewed coffee and a super extensive list of premium Sonoma County wines and micro brewed beers are available. Proprietors Ken and Cheryl Rochioli also offer complete catering services for weddings, banquets and picnics. Open for lunch 11:30am-4pm Mon-Fri, dinners from 4pm-9pm.

*$$ WESTERN BOOT STEAK HOUSE  #9 Mitchell Lane, Healdsburg, CA. 95448 American Cuisine, Beer & Wine   Complete Catering Services   (707) 433-6362*

## TOYON BOOKS

The best and most established bookstore in the wine country between Santa Rosa and Ukiah is Toyon Books which is located on Healdsburg's historic plaza. Toyon is named after a native chaparral shrub, commonly known as California Holly. Proprietress Martha Dwyer first opened the doors to Toyon Books in 1986 and has since grown the store to over 20,000 titles on every imaginable subject

**Toyon Books -** *Do you see Dorothy the cat?*

for the casual to avid reader.   New releases, mysteries, best sellers, religion, psychology, biographies, cookbooks, travel, history, nature, bargain books and used books are all carried.   There is a children's reading area, a section of books on tape to rent or buy, calendars, music tapes & CD's and notecards to match the wine country's far-sided sense of humor.   Of special interest is the traveler information section with plenty of tips on Northern California destinations as well as in depth guides for the international traveler.   Stop by before or after dinner. Toyon is open every night till 10:00pm / Sunday till 6:00pm.

*$-$$ TOYON BOOKS          104 Matheson St., Healdsburg, CA 95448*
*General Interest Bookstore  AE, Discover MC & Visa  (707) 433-9270 Info*

## SUSAN GRAF, LTD.

Susan Graf has opened an exceptional upbeat clothing store on the plaza in Healdsburg.   One of her priorities in life is to make people look terrific, which she is a natural at.   A world traveler, Susan hand selects the finest men's and ladies

clothing while on trips; especially to New York and Europe.  "Tassels," here store in Bern, Switzerland is still thriving.  When Susan moved from Bern to Healdsburg she was delighted to find the same provincial charm.

She showcases well known labels like Bogner of Germany, Hanro, Paul & Shark and Wolford.  Besides terrific clothing lines, Susan carries hanro lingerie for men and women and fabulous accessories including Kate Spade handbags, Eric Javits hats and fun giftware.  Susan also loves horses and is an accomplished equestrian.  Susan and her savvy staff have pin-pointed the perfect Northern California look, which they help you create and have lots of fun doing it!  Open Mon - Sat 10am-6pm, Sun 15 - 5pm.

*$-$$$ SUSAN GRAF, LTD.  AX, MC & Visa    100 Matheson St., Healdsburg*
*Mens & Womens Clothing  Fax: 433-6496  www.sgraf.com  (707) 433-6495*

## COSTEAUX FRENCH BAKERY

Located on Healdsburg's main street and just 1 1/2 blocks from the picturesque Healdsburg Plaza is this award winning wine country bakery. Nancy and Karl Seppi have also created a truly upscale wine country bistro/cafe featuring a daily array of fabulous international dishes, homemade soups and salads, gourmet sandwiches, panini, focaccia, irresistible desserts and espressos. Karl learned the sacred art of baking sourdough from former owner Jean Costeaux. Guests can sit down in the cafe or pack a picnic for the wine country or beach. No catering job is too big or too small. Family owned and operated since 1923, Karl, Nancy and family invite you to rejuvenate at their famous bakery/cafe. "Our food is as good as our award winning bread, so come join us!"

*$-$$ COSTEAUX FRENCH BAKERY*
*Award Winning Bakery / Cafe    417 Healdsburg Ave., Healdsburg, CA 95448*
*MC & Visa     cfbake@aol.com      Fax: (707) 433-1955         (707) 433-1913*

## OUT of HAND and OUTLANDER

Chris and Bill Bryant have been at the forefront of important trends for decades - whether it be precious metals & jewelry, computer technology or promoting self esteem and imaging through fine clothing. Chris is the proprietress of Out of Hand which is located just off the plaza in Healdsburg where she showcases exquisite wine country ladies fashions and leather ware. Bill has created a mens clothing and gadget store out of an old bank building where he showcases items reflecting the famous northern California look of laid-back-success. Rich yet casual silk, cotton, wool, leather, denim, canvas and hemp shirts, pants, jackets, ties and scarfs set off the male image. Ladies become show stoppers after a visit to Chris's Out of Hand where isles of clothing and accessories, leather skirts and jackets, scarves, belts, jewelry, purses and silk party dresses are displayed. Both stores are open from 10am daily.

*$$-$$$ OUT of HAND*              *$$-$$$ OUTLANDER*
*Ladies Clothing and Accessories*   *Mens Clothing and Gadgets*
*333 Healdsburg Ave., Healdsburg*   *101 Plaza Street, Healdsburg*
*(707) 431-8178 / 888-431-8178*     *(707) 433-7800 / 888-433-7800*

## WINDSOR VINEYARDS TASTING ROOM

One of the friendliest and most hospitable staffs in the Sonoma Wine Country can be enjoyed at Windsor Vineyards tasting room located right on the Plaza in charming downtown Healdsburg. When you visit, you'll enjoy complimentary wine tasting any time from 10am - 5pm, seven days a week. Wines from Windsor Vineyards won more medals in 1998 and 1999 than any other winery n America, and the friendly staff will help you taste and choose your favorites from this award-winning selection. Bring your copy of this book to the tasting room, show the hospitality staff and save 20% off the price of your purchase!

*$$ WINDSOR VINEYARDS Tasting Room   308-B Center Street, Healdsburg*
*Open Mon-Fri 10-5, Sat-Sun10-6, (707) 433-7302 www.windsorvineyards.com*

**NOBLE DESIGNS**    Tucked between coffee houses and wine tasting rooms is a jeweler with extra ordinary intuitive abilities at matching gemstones and precious metals into personalized designs. For the past 25 years Jo Anna Noble, a native Californian, has inspired many with her custom made creations. Her shop/gallery boasts the largest selection of earrings in the County as well as the whimsical to sublime in handcrafted jewelry and gifts from around the world. Open 10am-6pm.

*$-$$$ NOBLE DESIGNS        310 Center Street on the Plaza, Healdsburg*
*Jewelry and International Gifts      Major Credit Cards      1-800-351-4303*

## GRAPE LEAF INN

A magnificently restored turn-of-the-century Queen Anne Victorian home, best describes the delightful Grape Leaf Inn. Seven guest rooms named after grape varietals and decorated with old-world grace have all modern conveniences. Each has a private bathroom (five with whirlpool / tub showers for two and four with sky light roof windows) and all are air conditioned with king/queen size beds. A full country breakfast with home baked breads, fresh coffee, egg specialty dishes, country potatoes, fresh fruit and juices is served by your innkeeper every morning.

After breakfast a myriad of activities await. Innkeepers Richard and Kae Rosenberg take special care to promote the many fine northern Sonoma County wineries, and are happy to help their guests plan tours of the wineries and other activities. Later, you may return to your home away from home and enjoy the whirlpool/tub showers for two, complimentary premier wines and cheeses each evening, or just relax in the parlor and living room or outside on the veranda and in the garden. The Grape Leaf Inn is indeed a victorian wine country experience.

*$$-$$$ GRAPE LEAF INN   539 Johnson Street, Healdsburg, CA. 95448*
*Bed and Breakfast         MC & Visa   (707) 433-8140  Reservations*
*email: grapeleaf.inn@cwix.com              www.grapeleafinn.com*

### TRENTADUE WINERY

"Par Excellence" is the only term applicable to describe the quality of the wines produced at the Trentadue Winery.  Trentadue, meaning "thirty two" in its native Italian, is a small, yet influential winery founded in 1969.  The Trentadue family own and operate the winery as well as the vineyards, and are responsible for the precise attention paid to the production of quality wines.  The goal of the Trentadue family is to produce wines which reflect the mellow warmth and flavor of the beautiful Sonoma County in which they are grown.  Located 65 miles north of San Francisco, the Trentadue Winery and Vineyards are presented in the midst of rich farmland and vineyards, framed by an idyllic setting of rolling hills and clear sea-blue skies.  This is the setting in which the superb Trentadue wines are produced.

Leo Trentadue is renowned throughout Sonoma County as one of the first innovative growers in the area to plant Vitis Vinifera Varietals in any significant amount.  Aged in 58 gallon American and French oak barrels, the Trentadue red wines are thus allowed to reach their full distinct flavor.  The remaining wines produced at Trentadue are all well vintaged and carefully Estate bottled.  Keeping in the tradition of producing wines retaining the fullest natural flavors, the wines of Trentadue have relatively little or no filtering and remarkable few chemicals.

So come to Trentadue, browse among the treasures of the gift shop which include imported crystal, wine glasses, original art, books, maps, posters and wine related gifts.  Sip and savor the wide variety of superb wines before making your purchase.  Weather permitting you can enjoy the outdoor picnic area by the growing vines and fountain.  A special treat are the gondola rides through the vineyards.  Trentadue wine, created in an environment of rolling hills and carefully cared for vineyards is an experience you will treasure.

*$$ TRENTADUE WINERY*
  *Tasting, Picnic Area & Giftshop*
  *19170 Geyserville Ave., Geyserville, CA. 95441*
  *100% Varietal Wines.    MC & Visa*
  *Open 10am - 5pm daily   (707) 433-3104 Info.*

# HWY 128 ALEXANDER VALLEY

The world famous Alexander Valley is the home of half a dozen wineries with tasting rooms open daily to the public. Lodging is available in Healdsburg and Geyserville, There is canoeing and rafting on the Russian River and romantic carriage and gondola rides through the vineyards..

**FUN and PROVISIONS:  Area Code (707)**
**Alexander Valley Store and Bar**  ($) 6487 Hwy 128   433-1214;
**Jimtown Store** ($$)  6706 Hwy 128  433-1212.

**WINE TASTING:  See Winery Map Page 150 and Listings Page 209.**
**Alexander Valley Vineyards**, 8644 Hwy 128  433-7209;   **De Lorimier Winery**  2001 Hwy 128  857-2000;  **Field Stone Winery**  10075 Hwy 128  433-7266;  **Johnson's Alexander Valley Wines**,  8333 Hwy 128  433-2319;  **Murphy - Goode Winery**  4001 Hwy 128  431-7644;  **Sausal Winery**, 7370 Hwy 128  433-2285;  **Sommer Vineyards**, 5110 Hwy 128  433-1944.

### ALEXANDER VALLEY STORE & BAR

Located in the heart of the vineyard covered Alexander Valley and just a mile from the Russian River is the bustling Alexander Valley Store and Bar.   From 5:30 am travelers are welcomed by proprietress Jan Gustine and her friendly staff, as they serve up fresh brewed coffee, pastries and a wide assortment of sandwiches, salads and picnic fare from the deli.   The store also offers a full line of groceries, beverages, paper goods, snacks, local vintages, directions and travel tips.   The air conditioned bar welcomes you beginning at noon.  Be sure to stop in and sample the local hospitality, and soak up this historic locations' ambiance while stocking up for your day in the wine country.  Open daily 5:30am - 7:00pm.

*$ ALEXANDER VALLEY STORE & BAR*      *6487 Hwy 128, Healdsburg,*
*General Store and Bar*                *CA.95448     (707) 433-1214*

## SAUSAL WINERY

Named after the willows that hug a tiny creek that flows from the eastern foothills of the Alexander Valley to the Russian River, Sausal Winery is a pleasant destination in the heart of the northern Sonoma County Wine Country. On the way in you'll pass under the boughs of one of the largest oak trees I've ever seen.

The Demostene family purchased this 125 acre ranch in 1956. Leo and Rose raised four children, grew prunes, apples and grapes and planned for the future. Unfortunately Leo died in 1973 before he could realize his dream of creating a winery. Today the children: Peachie, Cindy, Dave and Ed offer half a dozen estate bottled wines under the Sausal label and together with Rose share the title of the oldest wine making family in the Alexander Valley. The new tasting room opened in 1986. The grapes for these award winning wines all come from the Sausal Ranch. The Century Vine Zinfandel is made from vines over 100 years old. After several years in oak barrels and adequate bottle aging, this deep, rich wine has intense raspberry, oak and ample tannins reflecting the heritage of the century old vines. Under the attentive care of winemaker David Demostene, the two other Zins, the Cabernet Sauvignon, Sausal Blanc and Sangiovese have become excellent wines for that special occasion or dinner party.

Ed Demostene, the vineyard manager, can still remember the days when he worked behind horses, cultivating the hillside vines and watching the changes in vineyard spacing and plantings as tractors and trucks came on the scene. Peachie and Cindy love to fill people in on the history and story of Sausal Winery. The tasting room is truly a destination you should add to your list of Sonoma County wineries. The roots have grown deeper, the estate vintages complex and the future looks secure for the 3rd generation of Demostenes as Sausal Winery continues to grow in the direction Leo would have wished.

*$-$$ SAUSAL WINERY*
*Tasting, Retail Sales,*                          *Open daily from 10am - 4pm*
*7370 Hwy 128, Healdsburg, Ca. 95448*              *(707) 433-2285*

## SCENIC DRIVES:
## GETTING THERE THRU GEYSERVILLE

Take either Highway 101 exit into Geyserville and proceed west up Canyon Road into the wine country to Dry Creek Road. Turn right on Dry Creek Road and proceed to Warms Springs Dam. Take the rugged but spectacular Skaggs Springs Road to State Highway 1 at Stewart's Point or to Annapolis Road; thru Annapolis and into Sea Ranch. It is a spectacular drive through the country.

The Redwood Highway (Highway 101) climbs a hillside at Geyserville giving travelers a panoramic view of vineyards and orchards growing on the floor of the Russian River Valley. Pictured here is downtown Geyserville. Inns, restaurants, grocery stores and a old fashioned general store line main street.

# GEYSERVILLE
# Upper Russian River Wine Country and Rural Ranchland

**GEYSERVILLE DINER'S CHOICE: Telephone Area Code is (707).**
**Chateau Souverain Winery** ($$$) 400 Souverain Rd. 433-3141; **Jarro Cafe** ($$$) 21021 Geyserville Ave. 857-3829; **Main Street Bar & Cafe** ($) 21023 Geyserville Ave. 857-3814.

**GEYSERVILLE LODGING:**
**Campbell Ranch Inn** ($$) 1475 Canyon Rd. 857-3476; **Geyserville Inn** ($$) Canyon Road Off-Ramp, 21714 Geyserville Ave., 857-4343; **Hope-Bosworth House ($$$)** 21238 Geyserville Ave. 857-3356; **Hope- Merrill House ($$$)** 21253 Geyserville Ave. 857-3356; **Isis Oasis Retreat Center** ($$) 20889 Geyserville Ave. 857-3524.

**WINE TASTING: See Winery Map Page 156 and Listings Page 217.**
**Canyon Road. Cellars / Nervo, Chateau Souverain, Clos Du Bois, Geyser Peak Winery, Lake Sonoma Winery, Murphy - Goode Winery, J. Pedroncelli Vineyards and Trentadue Vineyards all have Tasting Rooms.**

## GEYSERVILLE INN and HOFFMAN HOUSE WINE COUNTRY DELI

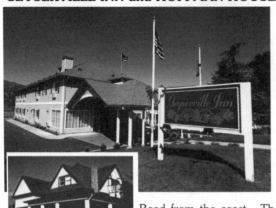

Hoffman House is a charming old ranch house that has been converted into a delightful deli, located in Geyserville in the heart of the Alexander Valley Wine Country. Next door is the newly built Geyserville Inn. The Christensens, who were born and raised in Sonoma County, provide a hospitable and quaint destination for guests traveling on Highway 101, or those traveling over Skaggs Springs Road from the coast. The indoor/outdoor facilities are a perfect stopping point, and with 2 dozen nearby wineries, this makes the Inn and Hoffman House a natural place to lunch and relax. Room amenities include fireplaces, private baths, hair dryers, ironing boards and continental breakfast ($99/2). There is also a swimming pool and jacuzzi. The knowledgeable staff is proud to host passerby's and locals as well as small groups. The inn also has an event facility, small conference room and group picnic ground on a grassy knoll in the shade of majestic trees. You will enjoy the country ambience of the Inn and the Hoffman House so be sure definitely put it down as a destination.

*$$ GEYSERVILLE INN          Canyon Road Exit, 21714 Geyserville Ave.,*
*Bed & Breakfast Motel & Deli  Major Credit Cards  Geyserville, CA. 95441*
*Fax: (707) 857-4411            (707) 857-4343  Reservations Advised*

## ISIS OASIS LODGE & CULTURAL CENTER

A magical retreat center, Isis Oasis, is located in Geyserville on ten lush acres with an ornate Egyptian Temple dedicated to Isis, the Goddess of nature. A stained glass redwood theatre, a sparkling pool, spa and sauna within a secluded garden with waterfalls, a swan pond, exotic cats and birds and an enormous 500 year old fir tree are yours to enjoy. Accommodations range from a classic lodge with twelve private rooms, plus a large carpeted meeting room, to houses of various sizes for smaller groups, some with hot tubs and fireplaces. A tower, wine barrel room, yurts, a dome teepee and pyramid are interesting alternative overnights. The pavilion is a gathering place where guests engage in fascinating conversations while partaking of healthful breakfasts each morning. Delicious creative meals are cooked to order for groups. Prices range from $45/2 in the tipi to $130/2 in the enchanted cottage.

Loreon Vigne, the proprietress and Priestess of the Temple offers month long programs, teaching participants to "Know thyself, know they heart, know thy soul, and know thy purpose," as was inscribed on ancient Egyptian temple walls. Visiting instructors make certain each retreatant has a transformational journey. For $3000 per month, you may have a private room, partake of colorful cuisine and have a profound learning experience with other seekers of wisdom.

*$$-$$$ ISIS OASIS LODGE   20889 Geyserville Ave., Geyserville, CA 95441*
*Groups and Individual Retreats  isis@saber.net/  isisoasis.org   800-679-7387*

The J. Pedroncelli Winery tasting room facilities on Canyon Road just west of Geyserville.

## J. PEDRONCELLI WINERY

Some old time wine growers believe that it is the struggle to survive which has produced the strikingly distinctive flavor of the grapes which produce the famous J. Pedroncelli wines. Climbing along the hillsides of Canyon Road, the Pedroncelli grapevines battle the rugged slopes of the hills to produce a small but potent crop of grapes rich in nutrients, flavors, and potential esters which are the significant trademark of the Pedroncelli wines. The distinctive flavor of their wines comes from these mountain grown grapes, and the table wines bearing the Pedroncelli label all carry this hardy flavor and legacy of merit.

Grapevines are rarely planted on hillsides anymore because the crop yield, though far richer in quality, is less in quantity, than that of the flatlands. Yet John Pedroncelli Sr. was determined in 1927, to found his winery on a site reminiscent of his native Lombardy, and proceeded to develop quality table wines which proudly bear the fact that it was well worth the effort.

Jim and John Pedroncelli Jr. run the winery today, and they carry on the family tradition of respect for the hardy grape which has so steadfastly proven that quality far exceeds quantity when it comes to producing fine wine. The Pedroncelli, Pinot Noir, is considered a classic example of a high quality California Red Burgundy; it's rotund flavor proves the worth of the hill-grown grape. The Pedroncelli Sonoma Red wine is distinctively a northern Sonoma wine, rich with depth.

Come to the Pedroncelli tasting room and let the colorful tasting room host offer you samplings of the hardy hill grown Pedroncelli wine. It is a wine tasting experience you won't easily forget.

*$$ J. PEDRONCELLI WINERY  1220 Canyon Rd., Geyserville, CA. 95441 Tasting, No Tours, Varietal Wines  Open 9am - 5pm daily  (707) 857-3531*

## DRY CREEK VINEYARD

Founded in 1972 by David S. Stare, Dry Creek Vineyard is one of California's leading producers of fine wines. With an annual production of more than 100,000 cases, Dry Creek wines are available nationally and in selected overseas markets. Grapes are harvested from 46 different vineyards, including 100 acres of estate vineyards. In the European tradition, Dry Creek wines are blended by taste, not formula, to ensure consistency, vintage after vintage. The winery's proud record of more than 1,000 awards for excellence tells the story of Dry Creek Vineyard's quality and consistency.

Patterned after a small chateau winery in France, Dry Creek Vineyard appears to have been here for many years, thanks to careful and extensive landscaping. A small courtyard in front of the winery offers picnic facilities. The winery offers an exceptional tasting and hospitality room staffed by a friendly and informative staff. Retail sales and tastings daily, 10:30am to 4:30pm.

*$$ DRY CREEK VINEYARD 3770 Lambert Bridge Rd., Box T, Healdsburg,*
*Tasting & Retail Sales Daily      CA.95448.    MC & Visa, Picnic Area and*
*Dry Creek Store nearby.              Fax: (707) 433-5329  (707) 433-1000*

## DRY CREEK GENERAL STORE & BAR

Located on Dry Creek Road at the junction of Lambert Bridge Road is the large drive-under porch of the historic Dry Creek General Store & Bar (circa 1881). Susie Durler, her sons and family own and operate both the store and the bar, and are second and third generation residents who grew up in the Dry Creek Valley. Inside the historic antique filled store is a nice

selection of sandwiches, homemade soups, imported and domestic beer and vintages of local premium wines are poured by the glass in the antique bar. Out back is a landscaped wine and beer garden with picnic tables underneath a shade tree. Fishermen find the bait and tackle shop a great place to buy live bait or satisfy their tackle needs. The store is open daily from 6am.

*$-$$ DRY CREEK GENERAL STORE & BAR   Durler - Alves Company, Inc.*
*General Merchandise, Wine Bar, Fishing Center, Bar and Deli*
*3495 Dry Creek Road, Healdsburg, CA 95448; (707) 433-4171 Information*

## PRESTON VINEYARDS

Situated in a remote corner of the Dry Creek watershed and bordering the coastal ridgelines of the Sonoma County Wine Country and at the end of the road is Preston Vineyards. Under the direction of Lou and Susan Preston the winery has become renowned for its Zinfandel and Sauvignon Blanc as well as for innovative blending of other estate grown varietals.   In this idyllic setting with overhead red tailed hawks and jack rabbits in the vineyards, guests can savor half a dozen premium Preston vintages in the new tasting  room overlooking the colorful Italianate kitchen gardens.    In addition to the long list of unusual grapes, the Prestons grow several Italian olive varieties and produce their own estate grown virgin olive oil.  From the wood fired brick oven fresh baked loaves of bread are baked and sold exclusively at the tasting room.    "We bottle our own wine from vines grown entirely on our estate, bake our own bread, press our own virgin olive oil and then celebrate with a game on our bocce courts", states Lou.  In my opinion life doesn't get any better than this.

A creative staff at Preston Vineyards has pooled its talent and tastebuds to guide the grapes in the production of delicious and stylish wines at a fair price. The 115 acres of grapes are managed without the use of insecticides.  Preston's signature wines are Zinfandel, harvested from turn-of-the-century vines, and a Sauvignon Blanc blend called "Cuvee de Fume'.  A major emphasis is the development and production of Rhone-style wines including Syrah, Viognier, Marsanne, Mourve'dre and a proprietary blend, "Faux".  Barbera and Semillon are also available.  Be sure to ask about the monthly surprise release. You'll find Preston Vineyards to be a wonderful pause in your north coast adventure.

*$$ PRESTON VINEYARDS*
*Tours by appt. Picnic tables.*
*Retail sales daily.*
*9282 West Dry Creek Rd,*
*Healdsburg, CA. 95448*
*(707) 433-3372*

## LAKE SONOMA RESORT & MARINA

Everything you need for a fresh water vacation is at Lake Sonoma Marina. Built above 53 miles of shoreline, the beautiful Marina offers a well stocked general store where you can pick up a delicatessen sandwich along with camping, fishing and boating supplies. There are two acres of lush lawn and patio to dine or picnic on; a patio bar with beer & wine garden, volley ball or swimming area.

Dozens of boat rentals include houseboats ($135/ 4 hrs), competition waterski boats ($225/ 4 hrs), cruisers ($105/ 4 hrs), jet skies ($75/ 4 hrs), fishing boats ($45/ 4 hrs) and sailboats and canoes ($30/ 4 hrs). Whats really special is to rent a 40 foot houseboat that sleeps up to 10. Imagine yourself floating like royalty on placid waters behind the dam, while savoring award winning wines gathered from a choice of 26 nearby wineries. How does a wonderful BBQ with loved ones beneath the warm Sonoma sun followed by star gazing into a uninterrupted heavenly sky. Houseboats are completely equipped with all the amenities of a modern luxury home including TV-VCR, stereo, full bath, refrigerator / freezer and 110 volt AC generator. All you have to do is bring your favorite bedding, linens, toiletries, food, kitchen cleaning products and garbage bags. Remember - here you are *luxuriously* surrounded by miles of wilderness, teeming with wildlife. Springtime cascading creeks refill the reservoir. The Marina is open daily 10am - 6pm. MC & Visa.

*$$ LAKE SONOMA RESORT   Hwy 101 N to Healdsburg, Exit at Dry Creek Rd, Boat Rentals, Marina & General Store   Follow Signs to Marina. (707) 433-2200*

# LAKE SONOMA Warm Springs Dam Recreation Area

Located in the beautiful coastal foothills of Northern California is Lake Sonoma. Lake Sonoma is surrounded by vineyards, rolling farmland and steep wilderness ridgelines teeming with wildlife. Warm Springs Dam, which forms Lake Sonoma, was built by the U.S. Army Corps of Engineers in 1983. This compacted earthfill dam serves as a deterrent to disastrous floods, stores water for irrigation and municipalities and creates a large lake for recreation. An on-site fish hatchery for rearing salmon and steelhead enhances California fisheries. The Dam is 319 feet high, 3,000 feet long, and creates a lake capacity of 381,000 acre feet (120 billion gallons) of fresh water.

Lake Sonoma extends in narrow fingers 9 miles up Dry Creek and 4 miles up Warm Springs Creek. There are many small coves along the 2,700 surface acres of water to explore by canoe, sailboat or motorboat. Water skiing is allowed in certain areas. Free boat launching is provided at the public boat ramp on the west end of Warm Springs Bridge, and at Yorty Creek Recreation Area off Hot Springs Road (car top only).

Trees have been left in the upper stretches to provide an underwater habitat for fish. As a result, Lake Sonoma provides some of the best bass fishing in the state. Other game fish include Sacramento perch, Channel catfish and Redear sunfish.

A real treat is to tour the State Park Visitors Information Center where guests are greeted by elaborate displays of the dam and wildlife, as well as a variety of audio-visual and ranger led programs. Afterwards you can visit the hatchery and view thousands of baby and juvenile salmon and steelhead. Whether you prefer the seclusion offered by primitive boat-in camp sites, or the convenience of a campsite in a developed campground, Lake Sonoma makes for an excellent destination. Several primitive sites are accessible along 40 miles of hiking and equestrian trails. Backcountry camp permits are required and are obtained at the Visitor Center without cost.

*$ LAKE SONOMA 3333 Skaggs Springs Road, Geyserville, CA. 95441*
*Recreation Area & Visitors Information Center          (707) 433-9483*

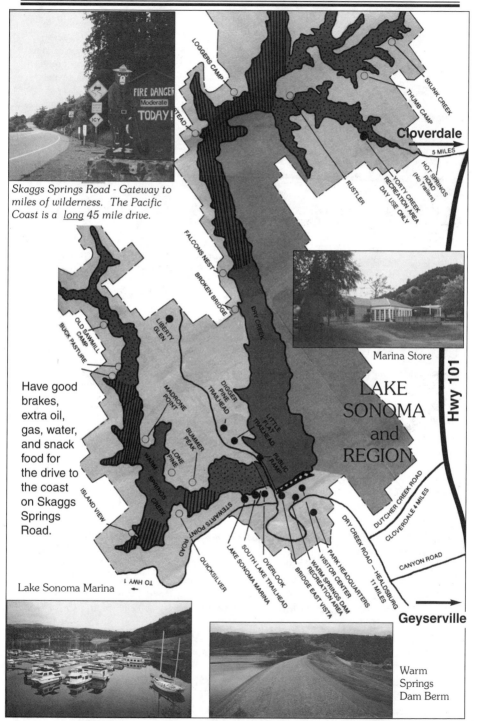

Skaggs Springs Road - Gateway to miles of wilderness. The Pacific Coast is a _long_ 45 mile drive.

LOGGERS CAMP

HOMESTEAD

SKUNK CREEK

THUMB CAMP

**Cloverdale**

5 MILES

HOT SPRINGS ROAD (No Trailers)

RUSTLER

VORTY CREEK RECREATION AREA DAY USE ONLY

FALCONS NEST

BROKEN BRIDGE

DRY CREEK

OLD SAWMILL CAMP

BUCK PASTURE

LIBERTY GLEN

Marina Store

MADRONE POINT

DIGGER PINE TRAILHEAD

LITTLE FLAT TRAILHEAD

**LAKE SONOMA and REGION**

**Hwy 101**

Have good brakes, extra oil, gas, water, and snack food for the drive to the coast on Skaggs Springs Road.

BUMMER PEAK

LONE PINE

WARM SPRINGS CREEK

PUBLIC RAMP

ISLAND VIEW

STEWARTS POINT ROAD

TO HWY 1

QUICKSILVER

LAKE SONOMA MARINA

SOUTH LAKE TRAILHEAD

OVERLOOK

BRIDGE EAST VISTA

WARM SPRINGS RECREATION AREA

VISITOR CENTER

PARK HEADQUARTERS

WARM SPRINGS DAM

DRY CREEK ROAD — HEALDSBURG

DUTCHER CREEK ROAD

CLOVERDALE 4 MILES

CANYON ROAD

CLOVERDALE 4 MILES

HEALDSBURG 11 MILES

**Geyserville**

Lake Sonoma Marina

Warm Springs Dam Berm

It is not uncommon to spot a 50's or 60's vintage car cruising the streets of this fun loving wine country town. Since the freeway by-pass, Cloverdale has whole heartedly recreated itself - replacing the conjestion and freeway pollution with a community spirit.

The heart of Cloverdale has been landscaped into a lovely park and gathering place. Cloverdale is a great small town to spend the night in due to the Highway 101 (Redwood Highway) By-Pass. Take the Citrus Drive Exit and drive to the heart of this small town to what used to be the 1st red light on Highway 101 north of San Francisco. Nearby you'll find restaurants, bed and breakfast inns, shops, galleries and motels to serve you.

# CLOVERDALE
## Gateway to the Wine Country and the Redwoods

**CLOVERDALE DINER'S CHOICE: Telephone Area Code is (707).**
**Breaking New Ground ($)** 212 N. Cloverdale Blvd. 894-9071; **Canton Restaurant ($)** 132 N. Cloverdale Blvd. 894-9188; **Hamburger Ranch & Pasta Farm ($)** 31195 Redwood Hwy North 894-5616; **La Hacienda ($$)** 134 N. Cloverdale Blvd. 894-9365; **Papa's Pizza Cafe ($$)** 117 East 1st Street 894-4453 / 4454; **Pick's Drive-In ($)** 117 South Cloverdale Blvd. 894-2962; **Quinlan's ($)** 219 North Cloverdale Blvd. 894-4788; **The New Owl Cafe ($)** 485 S. Cloverdale Blvd. 894-8967.

**ACCOMMODATIONS: Abrams House ($$-$$$)** 314 N. Main 894-2412; **Cloverdale Wine Country KOA ($$)** Box 600 894-3337 / 1-800-368-4558; **Mountain House Winery & Lodge** ($$) 33710 Hwy 128 894-5683; **Naco West Russian River Resort ($$)** 33655 N. Redwood Hwy 894-3184; **Oaks Motel ($$)** 123 S. Cloverdale Blvd. 894-2404; **Shelford House ($$-$$$)** 29955 River Rd. 894-5956. **Vintage Towers ($$-$$$)** 302 N. Main 894-4535;

**ATTRACTIONS: Cloverdale Citrus Fair ($)** At the Cloverdale Fair Grounds in February ; **Cloverdale Museum ($)** 221 Matheson St. 431-3325.

**HEALTH & FITNESS: Cloverdale Cyclery ($$)** 125 N. Cloverdale Blvd.. 894-2841; **In the Pink Health Foods ($$)** 228 S. Cloverdale Blvd 894-3164; **Warm Springs Dam Recreations Area ($)** 3333 Skaggs Springs Rd. 433-9483.

## PICK'S DRIVE-IN

One of the most historic Drive-Ins still in operation (established 1923) along the Redwood Highway is Pick's Drive-In in Cloverdale.  After the Golden Gate Bridge was finished in 1937, the wild west frontier of the remote Redwood Empire opened up and a network of what used to be stage coach stops gave way to drive-ins where travelers could recover from the bumpy dirt roads of the era, clean up and make repairs on their vehicles.

Proprietors Claudia and Russ Clow, 4th generation native Californians, purchased Pick's in 1990.  Super burgers, special sauces, the garden burger (a vegetarian delight) is served along with grilled chicken breast sandwich, giant double cheese burgers, hot dogs, French fries, hot chocolate, tea and coffee.  A variety of ice cream sundaes, floats, fruit freezes, old fashioned root beer, shakes, malts and hot fudge sundaes remind us of a less hurried era.  Pick's is open year 'round every day but Thursdays from 11:30am - 8pm and is closed the two weeks before Christmas and during the month of January.

*$ PICK'S DRIVE-IN    117 South Cloverdale Blvd., Cloverdale, CA  95425*
     *American*                   *(707) 894-2962   Sit Down or Orders to Go*

## PAPA'S PIZZA CAFE

This friendly All-American small town pizzeria is where locals and travelers dine on a quantity of quality food at a fair price.  The crispy fresh salad bar and wide screen TV add to the homeyness at   Papa's   Pizza   Cafe. Chef/owners Denaire and Michael Nixon, who were born and raised in Cloverdale, run a classy yet unpretentious restaurant where piping hot pizzas and calzone are baked the old fashioned way in a brick oven.  Delicious bread sticks,  Italian sodas, coffees, espresso, chilled juice, hot chocolate, sodas, beer, wine, and mineral water are served while you wait for your pizza or pasta entree.  Homemade pasta dinners (spaghetti and lasagna) are served with homemade soup or salad and garlic bread. Small, medium and large pizzas (12", 14" & 16" wide priced from $9 to $20) with choice of 18 toppings are made from the freshest ingredients; special blended sauce, mozzarella and parmesan cheese, olive oil and homemade hand-spun dough (regular or thin crust) and then popped into the hot brick oven.  Generous servings mean tasty snacks to enjoy later in the day or evening.  Open Mon-Thurs 9am-9pm, Fri 9am-10pm, Sat 12-10pm & Sun 12-9pm.  Papa's Pizza is definitely worth your time and money.

*$-$$ PAPA'S PIZZA CAFE       117 East 1st Street, Cloverdale, CA 95425*
*Italian and American      MC & Visa, Beer & Wine, (707) 894-4453 / 4454*

## LA HACIENDA

"Welcome! Mi Casa es su Casa", state Delia and Victor Calderon, who gracefully serve their guests at their Cloverdale restaurant La Hacienda. The spacious and festive interior is a popular destination for Cloverdale residents who respond well to large platters of Mexican cuisine served at fair prices. Delia and Victor place great emphasis on personal service and entertainment. Famous singers and Mariachi musicians perform at La Hacienda. Hints of Old Mexico are part of the decor along with a contemporary potpourri of nic-nacks, creating an unpretentious dining atmosphere where you can really enjoy the salsa & chips, imported Mexican beer, California wine, quesadillas, nachos and large margaritas. House specials (from $8.95) include the La Hacienda enchilada (large flour tortilla filled with chicken, sour cream and guacamole) or Pancho Villa's plate (2 grilled steak soft tacos and grilled green onions). Platillas del Mar de "La Hacienda" (seafood) include Crab enchiladas, large shrimps cooked in a hot and spicy red sauce with refried beans or deep fried fish with rice, salsa and tortillas. Complete Mexican dinners, Fajitas, combination plates and grande combinations are also served.

*$-$$ LA HACIENDA        134 N. Cloverdale Blvd., Cloverdale, CA. 95425*
*Mexican Cuisine & Live Entertainment  Full Bar, Beer & Wine.  MC & Visa*
*Open daily from 11am to 9pm,          (707) 894-9365  Sit down or to go*

## MOUNTAIN HOUSE WINERY & LODGE

Situated in a country setting on State Highway 128 7.2 miles <u>west</u> of Cloverdale is the luxurious Mountain House Winery and Lodge. Mike & Arlene Page moved from Santa Rosa to pursue their dreams in the rolling hills and ranches where they built their stone and wood mountain retreat. With the addition of the new deli and giftshop, the Mountain House Winery & Lodge is a self contained destination getaway with facilities to accommodate weddings and corporate events for up to 200 people. Lodging includes four spacious cottages on the lake or meadow with fireplaces, full kitchen or kitchenettes; one cottage with two bedrooms and whirlpool tub. Six suites are located in the main lodge and winery with wood stove and fireplaces. Guests enjoy an extended continental breakfast and if your heart desires a walk amid nature. Take Hwy 101 north to Hwy 128 west. Watch for the Mendocino County line sign and continue 2 miles west on Hwy 128.

*Mountain House Winery, Lodge, Deli & Giftshop*
*Private Cottages & Suites             33710 Hwy 128, Cloverdale 95425*
*www.mtnhousewinery-lodge.com   (707) 894-5683 Reservations Advised*

## CLOVERDALE WINE COUNTRY  KOA

Cozy Kamping Kabins and fish pond at the Cloverdale Wine Country KOA. A recreation room and cafe, snack bar and front entrance office and general store serves guests from around the world.

Located a thousand feet above the picturesque Alexander Valley in a remote and pristine environment with thousands of stars visible in the clear evening sky is the Cloverdale Wine Country KOA.

Natural experiences are invaluable resources we can fall back on throughout our lives. Here Al, the camp naturalist teaches a youngster how to "catch that big one".

This 60 acre camping and RV resort with wooded tent and full hook-ups combined with charming Kamping Kabins, makes for an ideal location to set up your base camp while you visit wineries, canoe, fish, marvel at the towering redwoods or explore the nearby coastline.  The Golden Gate bridge is only 80 miles to the south on Highway 101.  Sunny days and cool starry nights, hungry fish (in the catch and release fish pond) and nearby Russian River, a well stocked country store, mini-golf course, ball court, recreation hall, nature trails and large swimming pool add to a long list of amenities.  Rates are reasonable for tent sites with water & fire pits and hot showers from $25.00/night for 2 and RV sites with full hook-up (water, electricity and sewer) $28.00/night for 2 people and 2 vehicles.  A stay here means stress-free leisure time for seniors or those with busy lifestyles to empty out and detox from hectic unnatural environments.  The altitude and clear air reveals a dazzling array of constellations and meteors in the night time sky so bring your telescope or binoculars.  It is no wonder that many who come for a day end up staying a week at the Cloverdale Wine Country KOA.  Pets are also welcome.  Call or write for a free brochure.

*$-$$ CLOVERDALE WINE COUNTRY KOA*
*Camping, RV Sites & Kamping Kabins   Box 600, Cloverdale, CA 95425*
*Major credit cards are accepted.        (707) 894-3337, 1-800-368-4558*

# MENDOCINO COUNTY: Highway 101 / HOPLAND
# Crossroads to the Coast, Redwoods & Wine Country

Hopland is a crossroads community. To the east lies California's largest natural lake, Clear Lake. To the west the Pacific Ocean. To the north the tallest trees in the world and to the south the thriving cities of Santa Rosa and San Francisco. It is surrounded by vineyards and famous wineries. Hopland is also home of the first brewpub to open since prohibition, the Hopland Brewery. Exceptional restaurants, lodging, winery tasting rooms, grocery stores offering fresh produce and snacks, art & craft galleries as well as specialty shops are all within an easy stroll.

**HOPLAND DINER'S CHOICE: Telephone Area Code is (707).**
**Bluebird Cafe** ($) 13340 S. Hwy 101  (707) 744-1633;  **Cheesecake Lady** ($) 13325 South Hwy 101, 1-800-CAKE-LADY; **Hopland Brewery** ($) 13351 S. Hwy 101, Box 400  744-1361; **Munchies Gourmet To Go** ($) 13275 S. Hwy 101 (707) 744-1633; **Thatcher Inn** ($$-$$$)  13401 S. Hwy 101  744-1890.

**GROCERY STORES & SERVICE STATIONS:   Big Five Mini Market & Gas** ($)   13600 S Hwy 101  744-1948; **Hopland Farms** ($)  13501 S Hwy 101  744-1298;  **Hopland Superette & Liquor** ($)  13400 S Hwy 101  744-1711; **The Keg** ($) 13499 S Hwy 101  744-1070; **Sanel Valley Market** ($) 741 Hwy 175 (Old Hopland)  744-1724.

**LODGING:  Fetzer's Valley Oaks Food & Wine Center** ($-$$)  13609 Eastside Rd. (off Hwy 175) 744-1250;    **Mountain House Winery & Lodge**    ($$)  33710 Hwy 128  894-5683/2238; **Thatcher Inn** ($$-$$$)  13401 S. Hwy 101  744-1890.

**WINERIES:  Brutocao Vineyards & Winery** ($-$$)  13500 S. Hwy 101  744-1320; **Fetzer Vineyards Tasting Room** ($-$$)    13609 Eastside Rd. (off Hwy 175) 744-1737; **Jepson Vineyards** ($)  10400 S. Hwy 101  468-8936; **Mc Dowell Valley Vineyards** ($)  3811 Hwy 175  744-1053; **Milone Family Winery** ($) 14594 S. Hwy 101  744-1396; **Zellerbach Winery**  ($-$$) 13420 S Hwy 101 462-2423;
**ATTRACTIONS:  Fetzer's Valley Oaks Food & Wine Center** ($-$$)  13609 Eastside Rd.  744-1250;  **Real Goods Solar Living Center** ($-$$$)  13771 S. Hwy 101  744-2104.
**TOURIST INFORMATION:  Hopland Chamber of Commerce,** Box 677, Hopland, CA. 95449  (707) 744-1171 or 1-800-266-1891.

## MENDOCINO BREWING COMPANY
## and HOPLAND BREW PUB

The hardy pioneer spirit Mendocino County is known for is alive and well in the tiny community of Hopland. Here, California's first brew pub since prohibition opened on August 14, 1983 and has since put down deep roots under the direction of Michael Laybourn, Norman Francks, Don Barkley, Michael Lovett and John Scahill. Fine beer and ale is brewed on the premises and sold at the tavern bar or over the counter to the increasing number of beer enthusiasts who are seeking out the best beers in America today.

Currently available are brews of popular Red Tail Ale, Peregrine Ale, Blue Heron Ale and Black Hawk Stout by the glass or pitcher tavernside or in attractive bottles to go. Seasonal gold medal winning ales are also available including Eye of the Hawk. In addition there is a restaurant where fresh seasonal produce, meats, poultry and fish are served with hearty soups and garden fresh salads. Live entertainment is hosted on Saturday night so bring your dancing shoes.

*$-$$ MENDOCINO BREWING COMPANY   Ales & Beers on tap & off-sale*
*and HOPLAND BREW PUB            Retail gift sales from the Brewery*
*13351 S. Hwy 101, Box 400,    Restaurant, Beer Garden & Live Music*
*Hopland, California  95449    (707) 744-1015 Office / 744-1361 Tavern*

### THATCHER INN

For the weekender seeking a change-of-pace escape, or the mid-week business traveler, the Thatcher Inn's unique setting makes it a very special destination. Period furnishings, late 19th Century decor, A comfortable Fireside Library - where a guest may curl up with a good book - and the Grand Dining Room, which features breakfast, lunch and dinner seven days a week are all a plus. Outdoor patio dining and a garden pool provide a welcome respite during warm weather months. The classic California-Continental cuisine and fine wine selection have established the Thatcher Inn as one of the quality dinner houses in the Redwood Empire. Its a perfect setting for a wedding or reception.

Twenty rooms await you. All have private baths and occupy the 2nd and 3rd floors of the Inn. Mornings are a less hurried time. You can choose from a variety of traditional and gourmet breakfast items from the fixed menu. During breakfast your eyes begin to run along the 14 foot walls and you begin to appreciate the original Victorian style that is the Thatcher.

*$$ THATCHER INN        Hours subject to change on a seasonal basis.*
*Dinner/Lodging: California Continental   Full Bar & Espresso  MC & Visa*
*13401 S. Hwy 101, Hopland, CA. 95449      (707) 744-1890 Res. Rec.*

## BLUEBIRD CAFE

The morning sun rises above the mountains east of Hopland, climbing above main street and reaching inside the dining room windows of the Bluebird Cafe. Faces illuminated by the early morning light beam over breakfast. The bright and cheery dining room with old fashioned soda fountain bar and simple slogan - *"quality food, big portions and reasonable prices"* bring the locals and travelers in by the throngs. Great Chefs of Mendocino Stephen Yundt and Robin Paul not only utilized the finest seasonal produce they can buy, but also showcase and sell a variety of Made-in-Mendocino sauces and spreads, salad dressings and locally grown organic herbs.

Evening time means romantic candlelight and flowers as the dining room takes on a soft hew and the enamored eyes of lovers become inspired by the ambiance. Appetizers (from $4.95) include smoked salmon. Complete dinners (from $7.95) such as grilled teriyaki chicken breast, pasta primavera, steaks, chops, fresh fish and vegetarian entrees come with homemade soup and garden fresh salad. Delicious desserts, ice cream sundaes, banana splits and soda fountain beverages are also served. The Bluebird Cafe' specializes in breakfast and weekend brunch.

Across the street from the Bluebird is Munchies Gourmet To Go which extends the Bluebird's menu into more quality fast food to go. Gourmet sandwiches, organic espresso and cappuccino, homemade pastries, cookies, pies, breads and ice cream specialties are served indoors or on the outdoor patio. Not only can you wine taste next door, but you can purchase all your picnic supplies at Munchies. Rent a bicycle and receive a free map to the quaint backroads around Hopland. It is the dream of Stephen and Robin to offer a gourmet grocery store where the talent and products of Mendocino's Great Chefs can be showcased and sold.

| | |
|---|---|
| *$-$$ BLUEBIRD CAFE* | *$-$$ MUNCHIES GOURMET TO GO* |
| *American Cuisine* | *Gourmet Food to go & Picnic Supplies* |
| *13340 S. Hwy 101, Hopland, 95449* | *13275 S. Hwy 101, Hopland, 95449* |
| *Open 6am to 2pm daily, Wknds 8am to 8pm* | *Open 9am to 6pm daily* |
| *www.mendofood.com/mendo/gcm* | *(707) 744-1633 Sit down or to go* |

## BRUTACO CELLARS and the SCHOOLHOUSE PLAZA

Located in the historic Hopland School is Brutaco Cellars and a small complex of art and craft shops to please the eye and appetite. The winery tasting room is located on the first floor. Behind the complex are fields of lavender and roses making Schoolhouse Plaza a lovely stop for a picnic or bite to eat.

*($-$$) BRUTACO CELLARS  13500 S. Hwy 101, Hopland, CA  744-1320 INFO.*

The Sonoma Thunderbirds car club often cruises up the redwood lined corridors of the wine country and along the coast. Here they pause at the Valley Oak Wine and Food center in Hopland, which is just 14 miles north of Cloverdale in Mendocino County.

## FETZER WINERY TASTING ROOM and RETAIL SHOPS

Fetzer Vineyards tasting room is lodged in Hopland's old schoolhouse. Here is a warm, friendly atmosphere within which to buy, taste and talk wine. There is also a unique selection of gifts and local art, a wine museum and delicatessen for picnickers. Nearby is the Fetzer Valley Oaks facility where wines, herbs, organic vegetables, fish and meats are combined to create some of the most delicious dishes in the world and overnight bed and breakfast accommodations are available. Inquire at the tasting room about special winemaker dinners and events.

The Fetzer family founded their vineyards and wine operations about 30 years ago and today their full line of fine red and white varieties including Cabernet, Zinfandel, Petite Sirah, Chardonnay, Johannisberg Riesling and Gewurztraminer are found wherever premium wines are sold.

*$$ FETZER TASTING ROOM    Box 333, Highway 101, Dntwn Hopland,*
*Tasting Room and Retail Shops   CA. 95449  (707) 744-1737 Information*

## The CHEESECAKE LADY

The famous Cheesecake Lady Bakery and Cafe is one of the best reasons to stop in Hopland. For an early morning break for coffee or a lunch destination, you can enjoy sinfully delicious cheesecake on the hottest of summer days in the air conditioned dining room. The red brick floor, colonial windows and toasty stove warm rainy chilly winter days.

Founded by Robin Collier in 1982 and now under the direction of Paul Levitan, word of the legendary and award winning Philadelphia style cheesecake has spread coast to coast. Pies, cakes and desserts can be purchased by the slice, the whole cake or in mini-dessert form.

The best news is that the Cheesecake Lady desserts are served at 100's of California's finest hotels and restaurants. Even better news is that they ship these fluffy clouds of ecstasy by overnight Express Mail! Just pick your telephone up and call 1-800-CAKE-LADY. Fresh berry, pineapple macadamia nut, espresso, chocolate swirl, chocolate grand marnier and the original sour cream are yummy! The next time you are in Hopland stop by The Cheesecake Lady Bakery and Cafe for a taste of some of the most delicious cheesecake on earth.

*$-$$ The CHEESECAKE LADY     13325 South Hwy 101, Hopland, CA.*
*Bakery and Cafe     Open wk days 7:30am - 6pm, wk ends 9am-6pm*
*Available by Federal Express Shipment  800-CAKE-LADY (707) 744-1469*

# Guide to

# Recreational Transformation

## It is the nature of things to grow.

It is the nature of things to grow. Like the mighty oak tree, it is also our nature to reach for the sunlight. Our daily choices are rooted somewhere between Love and Fear. At the end of each years growth, we produce our acorns for the next season. We sincerely hope this section is an introduction for you to physical, mental, emotional and spiritual health, abundance and growth.

Photograph by Richard Gillette

Love
Sunshine
Nutrients
Growth

*" Along lifes path tiny acorns*

*are transformed  into mighty oaks."*

# TABLE of CONTENTS
## Re Creational Transformation

# Introduction to Recreational Transformation

Recreational Transformation, as I have defined it is, you might say, a conscious vacation. Many people are on a spiritual or healing path to expand their awareness of who they are, the purpose for which they were born and the greater possibilities that life has to offer. Whether you are a beginner or a veteran on the spiritual path, this journey, on both the inner and outer levels, has something for everyone. That's why I have outlined certain people, places and things to connect you with along your way. Who knows what new doors will open to offer a solution to a problem or an answer to a prayer. Besides a backpack or a suitcase, the only other essential ingredient to a journey of this kind is an open mind. Let me also say that this path does not cater to any particular "spiritual persuasion". It is as each needs it to be for herself or himself. To be a successful traveler on this path however, one must honor the mystery and what treasures unfold one moment at a time. Learn to listen and follow your intuition and inner guidance to guide you to where you need to go, who you need to meet and what you need to do. A balance of being well planned and organized and also being free, unstructured and spontaneous will add to the richness and fullness of your experience. So, wherever your journey may take you, may it be a healing, transformative and exciting adventure!

## The Facets of Healing - An Integrative Approach

Because the world is out of balance due to the over-population of humans living out of balance, everyone needs healing. The master healer is God in nature. The master role model is God in nature in balance. All healing is based on this concept. What most people don't realize, is that as well as having a physical body, we also have an emotional, mental and spiritual body. They are also known as the subtle bodies, because it takes a greater degree of awareness to sense them. I will be discussing each of these facets in the following section. More and more in today's world, healing is taking a more wholistic approach. People recognize the value of this and want those results more than ever in their daily lives, for themselves and their loved ones. They are more interested in the quality of life, not just the quantity. They are not satisfied with archaic models that only deal with their physical bodies and ignore their souls. For optimum health and well-being on every level, people recognize the need for the integration of the physical, emotional, mental and spiritual aspects of their being. That's why I have outlined an introduction to a very special group of healers and healing centers for you to explore and utilize. They are thrilled to serve you!

## The Physical

Physical health is more than running on the beach or pumping iron at the local gym. It is more than just eating three meals a day, or getting the allotted eight hours sleep a night. It includes an intelligent analysis of the uniqueness of each person's body and life situation and their own particular needs. Deborah Burkhart of the Health Options Center in Santa Rosa, California, educates and facilitates people in mastering the balance of their 16 different body systems, including the acid/alkaline ph balance of the body. With a specific analysis of these systems, plus other health enhancing modalities such as chiropractic, acupuncture, ayervedic and herbal medicine, therapeutic massage and an appropriate excersize program, people can come into higher levels of optimum health. The healthiest people drink purified living water, breathe rarified air full of negative ions and eat living organic foods from the garden. They also pay attention to the quality of environment they live in. Oxygenation is also extremely important. Deep breathing, breatherapy or running on the beach are ways of taking in the oxygen that we need to prevent illnesses such as cancer or heart disease. But remember, the whole is greater than the sum of its parts. Humankind cannot live on bread alone. We need more to sustain us than the obvious. We need the subtleties that enhance our emotional, mental and spiritual well-being as well.

## The Emotional

Emotional well-being has to do with the health of our heart. Not our physical heart, but the heart of our feelings. Feelings are something a lot of us get are "not okay" by our families or the society and culture in which we live. They are suppressed and repressed as a way to make us think we are "in control". But all the suppression of our feelings does is diminish our life force and oppress our creative energy. There are very few role models that teach us how to effectively and graciously deal with our emotions in order to feel better, literally, and produce positive results, particularly in our relationships, work and creative life. Whether we like it or not, human beings are feeling people. That is one thing that makes us unique, and yet it also binds us together as one. We all have the same "range of emotions". The only thing that may differ is the degree we allow ourselves to feel those emotions. All emotions come from love or a lack of it. Love, joy, anger, sadness, pain, pleasure, sorrow, happiness, etc., are different colors of the same rainbow. What matters is our ability to respond (or our responsibility) appropriately, effectively and maturely to the emotions we're feeling and the situation we find ourselves in. Emotional health starts with loving and accepting ourselves first and then extending that loving-kindness to others equally. Emotional healing is the way to a happy heart.

# The Mental

Mental health is inextricably connected with the health of the rest of us on every level. It is very much like the "chicken and the egg" conversation. Which comes first? Does the mind affect the body and one's life, or does one's life and body affect the mind? In integrative medicine, it is being revealed that it is all one. Our thoughts affect everything in our reality - our emotions, body, work/career, relationships, spiritual life and creativity. One of the ways to enhance mental health is through understanding the nature of the mind. A classic and very effective way of doing this is through meditation. It allows the mind to become quiet and clear. Where the mind goes, the body follows. All memory is stored somewhere in our systems. Traumatic events, if not fully processed, lodge themselves in different places in our psyche and our body. That's why different forms of body work, work the memories out of the muscles to allow our bodies to regenerate and transform. The mental body, as it is called, is the most stubborn and difficult to change. It wants to hold on to its old ideas, attitudes and beliefs, particularly if it feels its survival is threatened. Once we breakthrough into new ground, our imagination becomes "more important than knowledge", as Einstein said. We open our minds and become aware of our choice to flow our energy in a positive or negative direction. A positive direction always opens up doors; a negative direction will close them. The mind is a very powerful tool. With wisdom and discernment, we can do amazing things that uplift ourselves and the world. What you can imagine you can create, and the possibilities are endless.

# The Spiritual

Wow, what a big subject! The world seems more ready for a spiritual awakening now than ever before. Everyone feels a stir inside themselves that something significant is occurring and about to happen. More and more people feel drawn to work on themselves, to explore and delve deeper into the mysteries of life itself. They want answers to questions that conventional religions have not, perhaps up until now, been able to address. Many are finding out who they really are and their greater connection with the Universe. They are exploring their greater potential for the purpose they were born. Humankinds eternal search for the value and meaning of life drives people forward. Without that, life can feel very dry and empty. That's why spiritual pursuit, in whatever way is appropriate for each individual, is becoming increasingly important. Attention to our souls, is just as important as our attention to our physical, emotional and mental aspects of being. It is said that there are as many paths to God or Spirit as there are people on the planet. I believe this is true. And when we honor each person's unique choice of that path, we are honoring spirituality in the greatest way. So, on the following pages are people who are skilled teachers, mentors, counselors, consultants, therapists, doctors and energetic healers who can help you heal and gain a larger perspective of who you are, why you're here and why you have experienced the life you have.

# Spiritual Partnership
## The Road to Enlightened Relationships:
by Jenifer Todd and Robert W. Matson

Artwork by Wolfgang Gersch
P.O. Box 698, Point Reyes, CA. 94956

We have all gone on vacation to reclaim that which we have lost in relationship with ourselves, our loved ones, our work, our world, the Universe. We have traveled to special places to reward ourselves or rekindle our relationships with those that mean the most to us. We have looked for answers in the four corners of the world. On the journey to enlightened relationships, all too often we come across roadblocks that get in our way of creating that which truly uplifts and nourishes us in all our partnerships, both personal and professional, as well as being something that serves and contributes to the world. Traditionally, we have had few if any role models to teach us the skills and tools that can guide our way on this path. It is to this end that the organization The Institute for Spiritual Partnership and Higher Alignment is dedicated.

Larry Byram, the founder of this organization has pioneered a conversation that is guiding people into this new possibility since 1986. With a phenomenal realm of information and practical application for the integration of this incredibly rich material, thousands of people are learning how to make this a reality in their own lives. The spirit of this work reaches out to all relationships everywhere on all levels; from one's relationship with one's self - our primary relationship, to one's significant other or spouse, work partners or associates, as well as to one's community and the world. Spiritual Partnership touches all facets of this important arena.

Centered in northern California, it's success is reaching out to other regions as well, such as Boulder, Colorado, and plans to expand from there. The Institute gives comprehensive, enlightening, informative and fun courses and workshops that broadens one's horizons for fulfilling relationships of all kinds.

This is the kind of work that can truly enhance not only your personal travels, but your overall journey through life . . . May it be beautiful.

*For information on classes and current curriculum, visit their website at www.higheralignment.com, or call the 24 hour info. line: (415) 461-5337*

## A New Kind of Renaissance is Occurring

Riane Eisler talks about the partnership model in her book, "The Chalice and the Blade". She notes that we are evolving from the dominator model that took effect about 3,500 B.C. back into the partnership model which was in effect from 30,000 B.C. to 4,000 B.C. Her basic premise is that we are moving from a patriarchal paradigm of society back into a balance between the patriarchy and the matriarchy. When people begin to balance the masculine and feminine aspects of themselves, the culture will evolve into a more integrated and healthy state, and true partnership will become the relevant model.

Men and women have been re-evaluating what relationship means to them for the last 30 years, and many are seeking a new way, a more deeply satisfying and authentic way to be themselves, not their "roles" in their partnerships. For the partnership model to truly work, <u>both</u> men and women must heal from centuries of "dominator imprinting". The idea that partnerships can actually work and be highly compatible, as well as spiritually uplifting and socially contributing is a relatively new concept. Let's hope that most of us have the courage to live this new possibility.

In ancient Greece the women would try to lighten up their husbands by taking their sword away from them and dancing with it. Men and women both need to heal from their dominator imprinting which they have received intergenerationally and from modern societal programming and shift back to the Partnership Model.

# Introduction to HEALING, WORKSHOPS & RETREAT CENTERS

Northern California is a haven for alternative health care workes as well as healers and teachers who facilitate the heart - mind connection and help students and patients restore the balance between the physical, mental, emotional and spiritual bodies. Here are a few of the finest. Pictured is Tai Chi master and visionary artist Maire Palme who facilitates prayer circles, spiritual astrology readings and soul retrival at the Opened Heart bookstore in downtown Santa Rosa.

## WORKSHOPS and RETREATS

I would like to recommend you pick up a free copy of Bay Area Naturally, Common Ground, Open Exchange or the Share Guide for the latest quarterly listings of Retreat Centers and Workshops in the San Francisco Bay Area and Northern California. These excellent publications are widely distributed in the Bay Area and Northern California. Call or check out their websites. Don't forget to view our website at www: seawolfpublishing.com or call (707) 522-0550 for info on a variety of retreat centers.

BAY AREA NATURALLY
(415) 488-8160    www.bayareanaturally.com
COMMON GROUND
(415) 459-4900    www.commongroundmag.com
OPEN EXCHANGE
(510) 526-7190    www.open exchange.org
SHARE GUIDE   (707) 829-0260  www.shareguide.com
Tune in to KEST 1450 AM   (415) 978-5378

## THERE ARE NUMEROUS RETREAT CENTERS

Here is a tiny sampling of the healing, meeting and retreat centers in Marin, Sonoma and Mendocino Counties.

| | | | |
|---|---|---|---|
| **Fred's Place** (707) 544-FRED | **Saint Orres** | (707) 884-3303 |
| **Isis Oasis** (707) 857-3524 | **Sea Wolf Lodge** (707) 522-0550 |
| **Jenner Inn** (707) 865-2377 | **Spirit Rock** | (415) 488-0164 |

Don't forget to check out the **Health and Harmony Fair,** which is usually held in June of each year and is the largest alternative health care fair on the West Coast.        *(707) 575-9355    Website: www:harmony@wishwell.com*

## EAST-WEST HEALING ARTS and SCIENCES

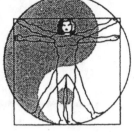

The Sonoma-Mendocino coast is a powerful magnet for self-discovery, healing and healer. Having been a student of preventative medicine and a patient of both Western and Eastern medicine, I was most impressed with Dr. Bill Schieve. He established East-West Healing Arts & Sciences, a multi-interdisciplinary health care practice, in Gualala in the fall of 1989.

He is licensed as a Chiropractic Physician and Licensed Acupuncturist. Dr. Schieve offers an integrated multi-disciplinary approach to health care for his patients, coordinating his services with other health care professionals to provide the most effective approaches necessary for the particular nature of the patient and his or her particular condition. Bill is in touch with the health realities of each situation on every level and works accordingly. Dr. Schieve has worked closely with general practice M.D.s, orthopedic surgeons, oncologists, neurologists and internists as well as homeopaths, massage therapists, physical therapists, energetic and body workers. His services include chiropractic, acupuncture, herbal supplementation, dietary counseling, Tai Chi, Yoga and exercise therapies. Personal balance on every level is the key to longevity and excellent health.

*$$ EAST WEST HEALING ARTS & SCIENCES  Box 2571, Fort Bragg, 95437*
*Multi-Interdisciplinary Health Care  (707) 884-4805/961-1472 for appointment*

## AMAZING FENG SHUI with Meredyth Yates

Feng Shui is the ancient Chinese art of placement, technically known as geomancy. With the proper understanding of Qi (ch'i), and the science of balancing and harmonizing this vital lifeforce energy within any environment, one can, with intention, increase health, happiness, prosperity and peace of mind. Meredyth has been helping transform people's lives with Feng Shui for the past 33 years. With her knowledge, skill and expertise, she can create *magic* in your home, your office, your life!   *MEREDYTH YATES - AMAZING FENG SHUI:*
*For a consultation, call toll-free: 1-877-711-7711, Santa Rosa, CA.*

## MASSAGE THERAPY  *Soft Shell, Michelle Wellington / Certified Massage Therapist   18 Kentucky Street, Petaluma, CA.94952   (707) 773-4950*

## PSYCHIC READING and DREAM ANALYSIS   Inner Light Foundation:
Psychic reading and dream analysis teacher Betty Bethards. (707) 765-2200

## ONTARIO - Psychic, Healer, Astrologer

Every once in a while you run into a person who has genuine gifts and insight; one who is dedicated to the purpose of the spiritual upliftment and healing of human-kind. Ontario is such a person. In a very safe and confidential environment, Ontario can help facilitate you through the changes your soul is asking you to go through - for your greater evolution. He brings light to your darkness, healing to your wounds and comfort to your soul. If you feel so guided, trust your intuition. *ONTARIO: 707-935-3948   www.thekai.com*
*e-mail: stars@thekai.com    Sonoma, CA.*

## MASSAGE THERAPY

Located just north of town in the new Cypress Village complex is the first of Mendocino Coast's famous healing arts centers. A visit here will help to harmonize your body and your vacation. At the Healing Arts Massage Center Judith Fisher and Jo Ann Dixon will put you in touch with potential health problems and help you gently and safely eliminate them from your life.

Judith is a certified massage therapist who has a large following of locals and returning visitors who place great value on the wholistic nurturing massage and transformational body work she gives to them. The same is true for Jo Ann who uses an ancient and highly effective way to balance the body's energy and release pain and stress by applying the healing art of Jin Shin Jyutsu. The two healers used in combination with each other through back to back appointments produce powerful and meaningful sessions of healing and increased self awareness.

Jin Shin Jyutsu is an ancient Japanese healing art form similar to acupressure, utilizing energy focus points. It is a fascinating application which works with the three main energy flows that descend and ascend within the body. Flowing and spiraling in and out of these Main Energy Flow Patterns are 12 individual Organ Flow Functions. Safety Energy Keys - 26 in all - can get locked and shut down due to out of balanced living. Gently using her hands "like jumper cables" Jo Ann helps you unblock the energy and restore life giving balance. Thus, Jin Shin Jyutsu releases accumulated tension along energy pathways and reminds the body of it's natural balance and harmony, which are necessary for good health. Disharmony or tensions are a result of our "individualized" daily eating and physical habits, mental and emotional anxieties, hereditary characteristics, and/or accidents causing injury to the body. Jo Ann's treatment is performed by gently holding energy points to reopen blocked areas. As points open, energy circulation resumes. This results in deep relaxation with a sense of wholeness, well-being and renewed vitality. A balanced, tension free body is the foundation of good health.

Judith's massage therapy relaxes, nurtures and re-vitalizes the body with the integrated long strokes of Swedish-Esalan style massage. She also uses craniosacral therapy to assess and gently release restrictions associated with the spine and skull. This therapy relies to a large extent on the body's natural ability to correct itself.

After a session you'll return to the reception area and out the lofty windows a broad expanse of sea and sky awaits. Your day has been renewed. What will you do now? There are many paths yet to explore, both inner and outer. Let the healing touch of Judith and Jo Ann revitalize you and give you strength and energy to continue on your journey home.

*$$ HEALING ARTS MASSAGE CENTER     39000 S. Highway 1, Gualala,*
*Massage & Transformational Bodywork  CA. 95445   10am - 6pm Mon. - Sat.*
*Appointments and Information  (707) 884-4800*

## OSMOSIS

Osmosis is a wonderful refuge for tranquility and renewal.  In this sanctuary the busy outside world disappears as you stroll in a Japanese Garden, emerse yourself in a rejuvenating enzyme bath, enjoy a healing Swedish/Esalen massage or relax in the peaceful Pagoda amid the nature sanctuary and soothe your soul.

Osmosis was founded by Michael Stusser who first brought the healing effects of the Japanese enzyme baths to northern California in 1986.  The action of over 600 active enzymes produces a special quality of heat that improves circulation and metabolism, helps the body to break down toxins, and thoroughly cleanses and beautifies the skin.  The bath often relieves aches and pains, and is especially beneficial for people suffering from tension, fatigue and high stress.  Following the bath highly professional and certified massage therapists, who have been chosen for their gifted touch, will help transport you to a energetic level of deep relaxation.  Your guided tour to "deep re-creation" almost always produces the desired results - inner questions and truths about yourself are asked and answered effortlessly.  This little slice of heaven is located only a few minutes off State Highway 1in the historic community of Freestone.  Open daily from 9am to 9pm.

*$$ OSMOSIS*                          *209 Bohemian Hwy, Freestone, CA. 95472*
*Health Spa, Enzyme Baths & Massage Therapy*                 *MC & Visa*
*http://www.osmosis.com*        *(707) 823-8231 Reservations Suggested*

# THE
# HEALING

## HEALING LOFT

Open your heart and spread your wings - optimum health can be yours when you choose so.  However, you'll need a solid team of sensitive and knowledgeable health practitioners to help you along the path and that is where the team at the healing Loft comes in.  Founded in 1996 by Elizabeth Kraatz to provide a unique combination of healing services including massage, chiropractic, acupuncture, physical therapy, yoga and educational workshops that promote and support wholeness, wisdom and wellness.  Her vision comes true on a daily basis as patients are treated by Bay Area - even nationally known doctors, massage therapists, healers and workshop leaders.  As the staff at the Healing Loft alleviate your stress and help you heal your injuries you begin to remember your self-healing abilities and bring balance to your body, mind and spirit.  Healing into Spirit is at the heart of wholeness."

Call or write for a seasonal calendar of events or the "Well In Hand" newsletter.  The "angels" at the Healing Loft are located upstairs overlooking the heart of main street Sebastopol.

*$$ HEALING LOFT*              *165 North Main St., Sebastopol, CA. 95472*
*Center for Healing, Education and Yoga   (707) 824-0790 Appts. & Info.*

### SATAYA

Located near Sonoma Mountain in a tranquil setting where small groups of up to 25 people come to celebrate life and spirit is Sataya. Sachi's vision was to create a sacred space where groups come together for classes, rituals, celebrations, meditation and movement in order to do transformational inner work while being nurtured and inspired by the peaceful healing spirit of the space and surrounding gardens. Amenities include a state of the art sound system, spectacular 1,000 sq. foot meditation room and gardens with Koi fish pond. Sachi is also a Reiki Master. Only one hour from SFO and 10 minutes from Santa Rosa. Please call or write for more information and day use rates between 9am to 10pm.

$ *SATAYA by the Mountain*          *www:sataya.com*
*Group Meditation, Yoga and Dance*    *(707) 585-0521 Information*

### STILLPOINT FAMILY HEALTH SERVICES *MICHAEL J. LIPELT, DDS, ND, L.AC. (707) 829-2737*

*523 S. Main Street, Sebastopol, CA 95472*

Dr. Michael J. Lipelt integrates Traditional Chinese Medicine, Naturopathic Medicine and Biological Dentistry into treatment plans that emphasize a partnership in healing. He relies on his intuition, clinical skills and experience to find underlying causes of disease imbalances. Dr. Lipelt looks at the big picture regarding the body and its entire ecosystem. His perspective is looking at daily activities, habits and food choices to enhance high level wellness. His foundation of assessment is evaluating the structural, biochemical, emotional/spiritual and environmental components. He utilizes functional diagnostic tests when needed and many "high tech" European medical diagnostic and treatment machines. He also focuses on clearing the "obstacles of cure" like environmental stressors, mercury fillings and chronic jaw bone infections. Dr. Lipelt promotes mercury-free dentistry and is quick to point out that the E.P.A. and W.H.O. treat mercury as one of the most toxic metals on earth. So, what is it doing in our mouths? Dr. Lipelt is a doctor of naturopathic medicine and graduated with honors from Bastyr University of Natural Health Sciences. He is certified and licensed by the Board of Naturopathic Medical Examiners in the state of Hawaii as a naturopathic physician. He graduated from Meiji College of Oriental Medicine with honors and is a licensed acupuncturist, certified by the state of California Acupuncture Committee.

## PREVENTIVE HEALTH CARE CLINIC
*Dr. Harvey Eckhart and Esther Thaler-Eckhart*
*327 College Ave., Santa Rosa, CA. 95401*
*(707) 579-9355*

Conveniently located two blocks off Highway 101 at the College Avenue Exit is the Preventive Health Care Clinic. Doctor harvey Eckhart and his staff pay careful attention to helping individuals achieve structural balance between the spine, nervous system and musculoskeletal system.

Utilizing state of the art physical therapy equipment, the clinic has great success with conditions such as sciatica, low back pain, rotatercuff/shoulder syndrome, carpel tunnel, headaches and many other pain syndromes. Each treatment also includes massage therapy to relax the muscles and prepare the body to receive the proper alignment.

Here is what some of Harvey's patient's are saying about their experience at the clinic. "Dr. Eckhart's office is a healing place and I received a lot of caring and support from all the staff." states one patient. Another patient comments, "My own Medical Doctors in Colorado were so impressed with my recovery without drugs working with Harvey and Esther that they went back to school to learn more about nutrition." "From our smallest to our eldest you help keep us well," concludes a third.

Harvey points out that some insurances are accepted. If you are in pain and stress relief then please call now. Don't deny yourself or your loved ones the health you could be enjoying with them.

## WENDY THAYER LICENSED ACUPUNCTURE
*343 College Ave., Santa Rosa, CA. 95401*
*Acupuncture, Herbs and Homeopathy*
*(707) 575-9443*

Over the centuries billions of people have had their lives rebalanced and revitalized by the ancient healing arts of acupuncture, nutrition, homeopathy and Chinese, Native American and Western herbal medicine. Wendy Thayer on College Avenue in Santa Rosa enhances our recuperative powers, immunity and the capacity for pleasure, work and creativity. Ancient roadmaps and body vital signs help doctors, nurses and practitioners direct your body to balance and optimum health. Chinese medicine looks at the body as a self-sufficient eco-system affected by the four elements much like a garden would be. All illnesses can be cured - all body's can be made well again if the patient is willing to co-operate with the healer. Relief from lower back pain, migraines, PMS, sciatica, heart blood deficiency, poor memory or concentration can be only a few hours or few weeks of treatments away. Over 200 of the finest quality herbs in the world are also prescribed.

## OPTIMAL HEALTH CENTER and LIFE EXTENSION CLINICS
2456, 2462 & 2464 West Third Street (at Fulton in the Big Oak Plaza)
Santa Rosa, CA. 95401   (707) 570-2700

The Optimal Health Center is the largest alternative medicine center in Sonoma County offering over 25 specialties in alternative health.    Personal miracles can happen at Optimal Health Center and Life Extension

*Jody Potiker C.C.H.*          *Debbie Burkhart R.N.*          Clinics.  Bright eyes,

sharp minds and open hearts lead the way.  Experienced and gifted practitioners empower you to create personal breakthroughs in well-being.  A new outlook, and true wellness and vitality begin at this center.

What can you do about your health problems, irritating symptoms or high stress levels?  When underlying core problems are addressed, the body responds, and renewed energy and deep re-balancing occurs.  Our goal is to be on your side to optimal health.    Seventeen experts in alternative medicine make this an excellent choice to receive your health care, to ask questions and to be heard.

**Deborah Burkhart, R.N., (707) 570-2020,** helps restore your energy and health through a 17 system body evaluation, food sensitivity analysis and individualized nutritional programs.  Detailed testing directs your unique program, which promotes deep cleansing, detoxification, rebuilding and weight loss.  Deborah is a specialist in rejuvenation and has written a detailed handbook on the subject.  **Jody Potiker, C.C.H., (707) 579-9479,** performs deep clonic irrigations and colon hygiene to relieve a wide range of symptoms and health concerns.  **Dr. Rebecca Potter, D.C., (707) 570-2501,** practices gentle chiropractic, including craniosacral, and Network Spinal Analysis for emotional, physical and spiritual harmony.    **Dr. Ron Kennedy  (707) 576-0100,** director of Life Extension Clinic authored the book *A Thinking Person's Guide to Perfect Health.*  He offers Human Growth Hormone (HGH) treatments, intravenous chelation and H2O2 therapy.  **Christine Cress, R.N. (707) 322-1567,** brings professional nursing skills to her A+ therapeutic massage, aromatherapy and reflexology practice.    **Joyce Higgins, M.A., MFT (707) 522-0402,** a licensed marriage family therapist offers hypnotherapy as an effective tool for healing emotional wounds and enhancing health and relationships.    **Deborah Myers (707) 538-3738,** an acupressure instructor and practitioner provides gentle bodywork techniques to reduce stress, relieve pain and restore balance.  **Linda Marshall, P.T., (707) 569-8204,** provides craniosacral therapy, myofascial release and energy healing for adults, children and infants.    **Phillip Henderson, (707) 538-0710** uses Upledger style craniosacral therapy, somato-emotional release & therapeutic massage to facilitate self-healing processes.

**Elaine Miller, M.M., (707) 578-0227 or (707) 578-4346,** performs live and dry blood cell and hair analysis. See what your blood reveals on a large-scale video monitor with explanation. **Dr Cindy Zafis D.C., (707) 527-7710,** specializes in allergy elimination by

*Rebecca Potter D.C.*          *Ray Wilbur  D.C.*

using a gentle acupressure technique to deal with food, chemical & pollen allergies, as well as addictions. **Jim Berns (707) 823-8067,** performs a gentle painless body therapy called Ortho-Bionomy, which results in deep relaxation and aliveness. **Judith Blackbird Joinville, M.A., MFT, (707) 824-9884,** uses psychotherapy, counseling, and biofeedback to help with trauma, depression, family of origin and relationship issues. **Ray Wilbur D.C., (707) 579-BACK (2225),** utilizes a drug free approach to the treatment of pain, backaches, headaches and trauma using preventative wellness care and sports medicine. **Paul Saure', (707) 568-5425,** uses his experienced hands to perform deep neuromuscular therapy & fitness training. **Giselle Reeves  (707) 539-6389,** skillfully uses essential oils to enhance health, eliminate dis-ease and increase overall vitality.

### Symptoms commonly addressed at the Optimal Health Center:

*Headaches
*Fatigue or low energy
*Irritability
*Sugar and other food cravings
*Allergy symptoms
*Fluid retention
*Poor digestion
*Bloating and gas
*Premenstrual syndrome (PMS)
*Back pain
*Mood changes
*Respiratory problems
*Poor memory or concentration
*Dizziness

*Bad breath
*Coated tongue
*Dry Mouth
*Chronic insomnia
*Aggression
*Asthma
*Anxiety or paranoia
*Arthritis/joint pain
*Psoriasis, acne, eczema, rashes
*Athlete's foot
*Toenail problems (yellow or thickened)
*Fingernail or toenail ridges
*Depression

Check which symptoms you have experienced. Find out what your symptoms really mean and what can be done about them. **Feel free to call the general center number for other specialties (707) 570-2700.**

## A SIMPLE TOUCH SPA

This lovely day spa is located down an inviting pathway, just off the Healdsburg Plaza on Center Street.  As you enter the reception area you are greeted by a team of dedicated massage therapists, whose focus is on creating an experience of complete comfort and relaxation.  The ambiance, with its Tuscany murals depicting water nymph's, soft lights and a bubbling fountain, begin to assimilate you towards releasing the outside world and embracing a moment just intended for you.  Three private treatment rooms (two with a single and one with two massage tables for couples) and a Jacuzzi tub room, are quiet and cozy.  You will have your choice of several wonderful treatments; they offer mud, mustard, rose whey and sea salt baths.  Other special treatments include herbal facials, salt scrubs, rose herbal and mud wraps.  The staff are not strangers to alternative healing.  They have a strong background in a variety of integrative therapies, ranging from deep tissue through reflexology, with a clear focus on meeting each clients individual needs.

*$$ A SIMPLE TOUCH SPA   239 C Center Street, Healdsburg, CA. 95448*
*Fax: (707) 433-6873  www.asimpletouchspa.com    Appts:  (707) 433-6856*

## HEART to HEART MEDICAL CENTER

Heart to Heart Medical Center is a clinic specializing in alternative medicine, including acupuncture, osteopathic manipulation, nutritional medicine and cranial therapy among others.  The staff is headed by Shiroko Sokitch M.D., with Jason Liles as business manager and includes four other physicians that specialize in alternative medicine.  The treatment rooms are color coordinated with murals and plants to promote a lovely feeling of hope and well being.  All their doctors believe in spending time with patients and all offer a free fifteen minute consultation.

*$$-$$$ HEART TO HEART MEDICAL CENTER        Fax: (707) 524-9649*
*175 Airport Blvd., Santa Rosa, CA.  Office:(707) 524-9640   www: hth@liles.net*

## SOBAGARA ENTERPRISES

Almost half of our life is spent in relaxation and sleep.  Not only is support for our neck and head important during sleep, but also support for our dream state.  You can rest on a cotton lined Sobagora Pillow filled with flax seed, herbs and essential aromatherapy oils which smell wonderful and help you create the dreams of a lifetime.  Titania Numa's dream was to create a business that would enhance the qualtiy of life by helping people stay in touch with their well-being.  I hope you have the time to call or write Sobagora or stop by their location in Healdsburg.  They are dedicated to giving you the best rest you've ever had.

*$$ SOBAGARA ENTERPRISES 70A West North St. Healdsburg, CA. 95448*
*Therapeutic Pillows & Accessories    800-369-2000  Fax:(707)433-9601*

## WINE COUNTRY SPA

I like to think of this healthful destination as a little corner of heaven on earth. The cool, quiet reception room is just the beginning of the tranquility you'll experience here. Proprietors Edie and Tom Happ truly dwell in their hearts. They and their staff are totally dedicated to your health. Ladies and gentlemen leave with a lovely glow about them - their hearts open to the world they will interact with for the rest of the day - even the whole week before instinct returns them to the Wine Country Spa.

Of special significance are the body and skin care products showcased in the reception area. The creams, lotions and make-up are all natural and completely organic (no harmful chemicals or pesticides). Please inquire about Edie's cosmetic creations which can be mailed direct to your home.

Spa treatments include facials, massage therapy, water therapy, body treatments, make-up, lashes and hair removal with wax. Gentlemen, remember the Wine Country Spa is not just for the ladies, but a great destination for you to reduce stress, revitalize your look, your skin and increase your performance and longevity.

Spa packaged treatments are carefully chosen combinations that create synergy. The effects of each individual treatment are enhanced by the others and give a greater overall result. Everybody receives pampering and professional service. All products used are natural and pure, coming from the earth, the plants and the oceans. Spa packages include Radiance, Antidote for Stress, Revitalizer, Aromatica, Il Makiage, Rejuvenescence, Serenity and Beautifier. A favorite of the ladies is Radiance which includes a European facial, full body massage and salt glow. It is the Wine Country Spa's Signature package and by far the most popular. It will give you total cleansing, exfoliation and hydration of your skin. This package is very beneficial, relaxing and aromatic. You will leave feeling silky and radiant. Treatment time approximately 3 hours and 45 minutes. Cost $175.

A good introductory Spa package for men is Serenity which includes a aromatherapy facial, stress reliever massage and seaweed bath. This package is a balance of essential oils for stimulation and clearing of your senses. Calmness and clear thought is a benefit of this service. Treatment time approximately 3 hours. Cost $130.

I hope you will open yourself to a much better lifestyle by visiting the Wine Country Spa. We never know what the day may bring or how long we will live. One of life's personal promises should include a visit to a spa like the Wine Country Spa, which opens you to the path of less stress and greater longevity.

*$$-$$$WINE COUNTRY SPA   1601 Terrace Way, Santa Rosa, CA. 95404*
*Body Care, Massage, Lotions and Cosmetics   MC & Visa    Open Daily*
*Fax: (707) 545-4675     Reservations and Information: (707) 545-8390*

## THE EIGHT STAR DIAMOND

The eight star diamond is truly the most perfectly cut and brilliant diamond on the planet.. It takes diamond cutters approximately 100 times as long to make Eight Star diamonds as it does to fashion them with a "commercial" grade of cutting. These miraculous gemstones are not only spectacular to look at, but also have highly tuned healing abilities if matched to the resonance of the buyer. It is the healing and balancing abilities of the Eight Star diamond that make them so attractive.

The quest for the perfect diamond is probably an eternal journey. The descriptive label *ideal,* applied to diamond cutting evokes a set of mathematical boundary lines which extend from gemological laboratories to diamond polishing factories around the globe. In 1917 an American physicist, Marcel Tolkowsky, attempted to mathematically codify standards which, according to his calculations, had to be incorporated into the fashioning of any given diamond in order that it be considered "ideally" polished; roundness, symmetry and conformity to critical angle, path-of-light geometric models. Without these criteria, Tolkowsky claimed, it was not possible for a diamond to put on its maximal light show, it was not, therefore, ideal.

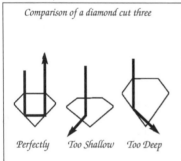

*Comparison of a diamond cut three*

*Perfectly    Too Shallow    Too Deep*

The Eight Star diamond was eventually created by people in Japan who wouldn't settle for anything less than perfection. One day in 1977 a gentleman who purported to be selling ideally proportioned diamonds presented some for sale to a successful businessman, Mr. Takanori Tamura, who had built a large distributorship of electronics products. The salesman had never expected to prove that any of his diamonds were actually within the prescribed parameters of the Tolkowsky theory. Mr. Tamura had developed a seasoned perspective from his two decades of operation of a celebrated Sony distributorship so asked the salesman, "With only the appearance of the diamond to go on, how could I be sure there really was something different, something special about any particular stone?" The gentleman was told to return again when he could prove his statements.

Seven years later, the same gentleman seller of diamonds returned with a device allowing.. the viewer to see the path of light through the diamond. What appeared red indicated reflection; white indicated leaked light. The scope became known as the FireScope and Eight Star diamonds can be viewed locally at E.R. Sawyer Jewelers in downtown Santa Rosa.

*The spiritual symbol of the Buddhist Tao (left)*

E.R. Sawyer Jewelers, founded in 1879, is the oldest jewelry store in Sonoma County. Gemstones, rings, bracelets, necklaces, watches, Tiffany & Co. gifts and fabulous Eight Star Diamonds are showcased here. Pictured are owners Douglas (left) and Robert Van Dyke.

## E.R. SAWYER JEWELERS

Located in the heart of downtown Santa Rosa, E.R. Sawyer Jewelers is Sonoma Counties oldest jewelry store having been founded in 1879. E.R. Sawyer Jewelers offers a pleasant and secure showroom from which to explore your dreams and make loving commitments for the future. The celebration of life would not be complete without the inclusion of a fine gemstone, ring or necklace into your life.

At E. R. Sawyer Jewelers you can peruse attractive showcases of diamonds, sapphires, rubies, emeralds, pearls and all gemstones including the fabulous Eight Star Diamond. Tiffany & Co. crystal and gifts, fine watches including Omega, Baume & Mercier, Tag Heuer, Rado, Accutron and Bulova are also displayed. In addition designers and goldsmiths work on the premises to help you with special requests, custom designs and restorations.

Of special note is the Eight Star Diamond, which can be viewed in the Firescope at E.R. Sawyer Jewelers. The Eight Star Diamond is the most perfectly cut and brilliant diamond in the world. Many who buy and wear the Eight Star Diamond claim it helps to balance their body promoting health and abundance.

*Commercial diamond - note light leaks*    *Eight Star diamond with perfect pattern*

Originally founded by Frank T. Sawyer in 1878, the business prospered under the direction of his son Elbert R. Sawyer who transferred ownership to a partnership shared by Allan and Virginia Flood and Orrin Magoon in 1949. In 1962 Robert Van Dyke assumed proprietorship of the jewelry store, having learned his fine craft from the previous owners. Today 4th and 5th generation family members Robert and Douglas Van Dyke continue E.R. Sawyer Jewelers fine tradition of serving residents and visitors to the Redwood Empire. E.R. Sawyer Jewelers is open from 10am - 5:30pm Tuesday - Friday, and on Saturday from 10am - 5pm.

*$$$ E.R. SAWYER JEWELERS 638 Fourth Street, Santa Rosa, CA. 95404*
*Jewelry, Gemstones, Watches & Tiffany & Co.*        *AX, Dis., MC, Visa*
*(707) 546-0372        Website: ersawyer.com        Fax: (707) 546-0305*

# HERBS & NATURAL MEDICINE
## Gardens, Schools & Suppliers

Photo Occidental Art & Ecology Center

### SONOMA COUNTY HERB ASSOCIATION
This is a very dynamic and talented group dedicated to growing, producing, processing and selling herbs, produce and products in a sustainable, ethical and responsible fashion. The Sonoma County Herb Association helps to ensure the quality of herbs and produce, reduce the impact of wildcrafting herbs, create "islands of diversity" and keep the local economy healthy. Our little friends in the plant family empower small growers and herbalists to produce wonderful medicinal cures to disease and to feed the hungry. The Harvest for the Hungry Garden provides hundreds of pounds of fresh locally grown produce to groups who distribute food to the needy. The S.C.H.A. is the source for your Secret Garden or personal edible-medicinal home garden. S.C.H.A. is an information resource to fresh & dried herbs, herbal creams & salves, nursery plants, herbal crafts, herbal extracts, natural remedies, herb walks, kid's activities, workshops on Aromatherapy, Animal Health Care and many other topics. Meetings are monthly. Call (707) 522-8500 for info. as well as packaged seeds and live plants. Also: *e-mail: momshead@ap.net    Fax: 707) 585-1264,    (707) 585-8575*
*SONOMA CO. HERB ASSOC. & ORGANIC GARDEN & NUTRITION CLUB*

### SOURCES of SEEDS  and HERBS (See Page 58 for SEED BANK INFO)
See the Back Index of this book under "Farms, Ranches and Gardens"
Bioneers  www.bioneers.org  Education, research and information clearing house.
Harmony Farm Supply & Nursery
Box 460, 3244 Gravenstein Hwy N., Sebastopol, CA. 95472 (707) 823-9125
Horizon Herbs (also live roots)     Box 69, Williams, Oregon 97544 (541) 846-6704
Occidental Arts and Ecology Center  Fax: (707) 874-1557  or Call (707) 874-1557
15290 Coleman Valley Rd., Occidental, CA. 95465  Ask about the Mother Garden
Seed Savers Exchange  Send $1 for color brochure. 1,000's of rare & unusual vegetables and herbs for trade or sale. 3076 North Winn Rd., Decorah, Iowa  52101
Territorial Seed Company Fax: (503) 942-9881 (503) 942-9547
Box 157, 20 Palmer Ave., Cottage Grove, OR 97424
Trinity Herb  P.O. Box 1001, Graton, CA. 95444  email:info@trinityherb.com

## CALIFORNIA SCHOOL of HERBAL STUDIES

Founded in 1978 by Rosemary Gladstar, the California School of Herbal Studies (CSHS), is recognized as one of the nation's leading centers of herbal education. Class curriculum is rooted in earth's earliest history and founded on the simple laws of nature. Having learned plant skill, the

herbalists knew the passing of the seasons, the ebb and flow of life's tides, had knowledge of the foods and medicines of the earth, and in these found balance. The highly regarded CSHS was created as a place where the art and science of herbology would be perpetuated, a place of fellowship amongst herbalists, a center emphasizing Earth awareness and self-health care.

The school has become a meeting ground for some of the best minds in modern herbalism. In the classroom, facts and opinions are shared. In the field your hands-on experience will yield different lessons of heart and soul. Programs include Foundations & Therapeutic Herbalism, a nine month / 480 hour intensive program for beginning to intermediate students focusing on herbs for health and well-being; (rates vary from year to year but are approximately $2,600-$3,000 per semester). Therapeutic Herbalism, is a 240 hour intensive program focusing on clinical use of medicinal plants, and The Essence of Herbalism - a great weekend course including a field trip, plant identification, gardening and wildcrafting. Other retreats & workshops include 6 months of weekend courses ($475), 1 day workshops ($30 - $50) and 1 day evening workshops ($25) in Herbal Medicine Making, Herbal Cosmetics, Seaweed as Food & Medicine, Introduction to Wild Mushrooms, Special One Day Workshops and Community Events throughout the year.

Located on a beautiful 80 acre ranch in Sonoma County, Emerald Valley provides that "peaceful country setting" conducive to the study of herbs. The facilities include a large classroom, kitchen, library, herb lab and drying room, spring fed swimming pond, sweat lodge, and favorite teaching sites - the herb gardens, hills, valleys and meadows.

*$$-$$$ CALIFORNIA SCHOOL of HERBAL STUDIES (CSHS)*
*For a complete calender list send $2.00 to CSHS, Box 39, Forestville, Ca. 95436.     http:www.cshs.com  Or call (707) 887-7457 for information.*

**Combining Forces Herbal Education:** For over 20 years Catherine Abby Rich has been leading herbal walks and classes along the Marin and Sonoma Coastline. Her students learn herbal medicine making, flower essence training, and wild beauty spa skin and hair care with cosmetic herbs. For a class schedule and product line information call (415) 924-5961 or write 201 Hawthorne Ave., Larkspur, CA. 94939

## MOM'S HEAD GARDENS

Located on the southwest side of Santa Rosa is a dash of Hollywood, a dash of Watershed Down and a slice of the Secret Garden. Intrigued? You should be, for here are the answers many of you have been looking for.

Mom's Head Garden is a whimsical organic garden where rare medicinal and culinary herbs from around the world are carefully grown. It is the brain child of two motion picture film editors - Vivien Hillgrove and Karen Brocco. Children and adults are entertained and educated by the wonderful qualities of the plant kingdom. You will enjoy the guided or self-guided tours, classes and special events and hundreds of herbs all waiting for you to discover. You can see herbs drying in the rare vintage Santa Fe caboose. I highly recommend you invest in your health by visiting Mom's Head Gardens. Call for directions to this precious destination. You can also write for a newsletter (for $5 per year) that has information about herbs and zany anecdotes about the garden.

*$ MOM'S HEAD GARDENS  4153 Langner Ave., Santa Rosa, CA. 95407*
*Medicinal and Culinary Herbs and More!*
*Open Sundays 11am - 5pm  May - October    e mail: momshead@ap.net*
*Fax:  707) 585-1264,            (707) 585-8575 Directions & Information*

## CALIFORNIA FLORA NURSERY

Those seeking to expand their ornamental or medicinal landscapes will enjoy a visit to California Flora Nursery, which lies practically hidden at the end of D Street in Fulton. This delicious "lost world", or Calflora for short, is carefully tended by Sherrie Althouse and Phil Van Soelen. Time permitting they give visitors brief tours and explanations of the merits of the miraculous California native plants, perennials, shrubs, grasses and vines they grew from seed, cuttings and propagation techniques which allow them to offer many exceptional plants that you are unlikely to find elsewhere. Those who add native California plants to their office or home garden take great delight in the chorus of native birds and beautiful butterfly's who come to visit. Calflora serves both the retail and wholesale public from near and far. Summertime open M-F 9am-4pm, Sat & Sun 10am-4pm, Winters open M-F 9am-5pm, closed weekends. From Santa Rosa or the Bay Area take the Hwy 101 River Road exit, go west one mile to one block before the stop light in Fulton, turn left on Somers Street, and go east to D Street (just before the railroad tracks) and you'll find Calflora.

*$ CALIFORNIA FLORA NURSERY (CALFLORA)  2990 Somers at D St.,*
*California Native Plants        Fulton, CA. 95439  (707) 528-8813 Info.*

## HERBAL MAGIC

Master Herbalist, Nutritionist and National Speaker Renee Ponder commenced her herbal journey over 20 years ago leading to the founding of her own high quality herbal company, **Herbal Magic** in 1981. Renee  is a pioneer in the field of Herbal Nutrition for Cancer, HIV/AIDs, Epstein Barr, Menopause, Cleansing and Detoxification by creating individual diets and herbal programs which can positively transform your life.

Renee refuses to mass manufacture or warehouse her herbal remedies. Each order is prepared from scratch with potent fresh organic herbs, some of which are grown locally. As soon as you open a bottle you can smell the difference. Renee and her health conscious staff ethically avoid all that is "high-tech" and say no to machinery and metal, preferring natures more gentle and nurturing ways of harvesting and preparing **Herbal Magic's** fresh organic herbs gently and lovingly.

If you have the opportunity to meet Renee or attend one of her lectures, she will leave you informed and optimistic about your future health with herbs. The next time you are out on a walk, take the time to say hello to the members of the herbal community before you. You can order **Herbal Magic** directly from Renee by writing or calling for a free brochure and information packet from her Marin County, California offices.

$$ **HERBAL MAGIC**          *P.O. Box 70, Forest Knolls, CA. 94933*
*Herbal & Medicinal Products  Fax: (415) 488-1057  Office: (415) 488-9488*
*To Order or Ask Questions;  CALL  1-800-684-3722*

Rosemary's Garden is like gazing through a beautiful kitchen window upon a full spectrum of herbal and medicinal plants. It is also the location of an exhibition garden where gentle adult and child browsers can see many kinds of herbs and flowers growing. Visitors will take great delight in the herbal tea garden.

Rosemary's Garden has Sonoma County's finest selection of 350 culinary & medicinal herbs. You'll discover herbal tinctures, homeopathic remedies, chinese herbal preparations, flower essences, aromatherapy and herb/health books. Trained herbalists are on staff to serve you. Quality natural bodycare products & gift items - crystals, jewelry, essential oils, potpourri, medicine bags, cards - and a continuous influx of craftwork by local artisans will treat the mind, body and spirit of all age groups.

A visit to Rosemary's Garden promotes mental clarity as well as inner and outer beauty. The staff is most helpful. Ask about the calendar of on-going workshops and lectures.

*$-$$ ROSEMARY'S GARDEN    132 N. Main Street, Sebastopol, CA. 95472*
*Herbal &  Health Care Products               (707) 829-2539 Information*
*Open: Mon - Sat 10am - 6pm,   Thursdays till 9pm and Sunday  11am -6pm*

# HEALTH FOOD
## Restaurants, Markets & Bakeries

### FRESH SQUEEZED VEGETABLE & FRUIT JUICE BARS

Cloverdale: In The Pink     Cotati: Oliver's  Redwood Cafe
Healdsburg:  Center Street Deli & Cafe,   Healdsburg Natural Foods
Petaluma: Copperfield's Cafe   Petaluma Natural Foods  Food For Thought
Santa Rosa:   All Ways Healthy / Coddingtown, Alverado Street Bakery,  Community
Market,  Country Store Health Foods / Montgomery Village,  East West Cafe,   Food
For Thought,  Juice Shack,   Lotus Bakery,  Organic Groceries,  Squeezer's Juice Bar
Sebastopol:  Food For Thought

### EAST WEST CAFE

The best of the East and West truly meet at the East West Cafe and Restaurant in Santa Rosa and Sebastopol.  Proprietors Sam and Lena Shaboon in Sebastopol along with Maen, Cheryl and Nawar Laham in Santa Rosa bless us with nutritious and delicious International cuisines woven together with the flavors of the Middle East. It is the custom of the Middle East people to always bless the food, then sit down together to talk and feast.  Once inside the door you'll soon discover why so many health oriented people dine at these oasis's.  The East West Cafe uses the finest, most natural ingredients mother earth has to offer.  The wholesome pancakes are prepared with organic flour, blue corn and served with Canadian maple syrup.

Appetizers, soups, salads, sandwiches, vegetarian, chicken, and pasta entrees along with the catch of the day are served with a variety of hot and cold drinks, fresh squeezed fruit juices, smoothies, tea, beer, wine and organic coffee drinks.

I particularly enjoy the light summer or hearty winter vegetarian soups (no oil, no dairy & no meat) and colorful garden fresh salads.  Soup and salad ($6.95) along with homemade pastries, muffins or Baklava and a piping hot cup of organic herb tea really hits the spot.  The Wraps are especially popular - four types - burrito ranchero wrap, macro wrap, garden wrap and terriyake chicken wrap.   Another favorite is the Mediterranean Platter of Homus, Baba ghanouj, tabouleh, dolmas, yalanji, falafel patties and whole wheat pita bread.  If you have special dietary needs be sure to let the staff know when ordering.  The East West Cafe is a good bet for the early morning working person's breakfast or a long drawn out weekend brunch for lovers.

*$-$$ EAST WEST CAFE*
*International & Vegetarian Cuisine    MC & Visa, Smoothies, Beer & Wine*
*Open: Mon - Sat 10am - 6pm, Thursdays till 9pm and Sunday 11am -6pm*
*128 N. Main, Sebastopol, CA 95472   Sit down or to Go  (707) 829-2822*
*2323 Sonoma Ave., Santa Rosa, CA. 95402                    (707) 546-6142*

## RECOMMENDED BAKERIES and NATURAL FOOD MARKETS

Sonoma County is blessed with a number of award winning bakeries. **ALAVARADO STREET BAKERY** sells their baked breads, bagels and specialty items to a number of grocery stores in the north bay as does **BROTHER JUNIPERS** which was founded by Brother Peter and Sister Susan Reinhart.  They are nationally famous Straun 5-Grain Bread, which is a highly nutritious Celtic bread that travelers used to pack with them for long trips.  You'll want to try more than the breads, bagels and pastries at the **LOTUS BAKERY.** The Spirulina Bee Bar is a delicious mixture of oats, spirulina and bee pollen and is great for snacking, camping or survival food.

*ALAVARADO STREET 500 Martin Avenue, Rohnert Park (707) 762-9352*
*BROTHER JUNIPERS  463 Sebastopol Ave., Santa Rosa  (707) 542-6546*
*LOTUS BAKERY       3336 Industrial Drive. Santa Rosa  (707) 526-1520*

### FOOD FOR THOUGHT

Sonoma County's first and largest natural food chain will enrich your life with health promoting natural foods, vitamins,  supplements, cosmetics  and child safe household products.  A natural line of medicines and pet care products are also stocked.  The vital and alert staff are usually quick to answer questions regarding their products and can  help you plan a high energy picnic for the beach or great outdoors of Sonoma County.  Local products include fresh certified organic vegetables, fruits & herbs,  roasted coffees, herbal teas, premium wines, micro-brewed beers, honey cider, jams and jellies, cheese's, herbs and seasonings, smoked fish, baked goods, and diet & nutritional supplements.  Food For Thought is dedicated to your health and well being.

*$$ FOOD FOR THOUGHT     Natural Foods, Medicines & Cosmetics*
*ATM, Approved Checks, MC & Visa     Open from 9am - 9pm daily*
*Petaluma:     621 E. Washington Ave.     (707) 762-9352*
*Sebastopol:  6910 Mc Kinley          (707) 829-9801*
*Santa Rosa:  1181 Yulupa Ave.  Catering: 546-8121  Mkt: 575-7915*

### OLIVER'S MARKET

As soon as you walk in the door you notice the interior is friendly and open and it truly feels good to be in Olivers.  Owner proprietor Steve Maass started his career in Forestville by selling garden fresh produce out of the back of a truck to travelers interested in fresh unsprayed foods.  A knowledgeable staff at Olivers answer health food questions and host special store events.  Those on the go can enjoy a international selection of vegetarian, pasta, seafood and meat dishes in Oliver's Delicatessen.   Oliver's is open from 7am to 11pm daily and is located just 4 blocks east of downtown Cotati and 1 mile west of Sonoma State University.

*$$ OLIVER'S MARKET          546 E. Cotati Avenue, Cotati, CA 94931*
*Juice Bar, Delicatessen & Bakery.     MC & Visa, Travelers & Personal Cks*
*Fresh Produce, Natural & Gourmet foods, Beer, Wine and Gift Items.*
*Fax: 795-5277     Store # (707) 795-9501 Info*

"People and Nature have inherent worth and deserve our respect. We're dedicated to providing a unique, diverse atmosphere based on social responsibility. We believe we can be financially successful through providing local and environmentally sensitive products to enhance our community and create greater social change."

**Community Market Staff**

## THE COMMUNITY MARKET

This fine tuned gemstone of a community natural foods market is the only not-for-profit market in Sonoma County. That means less emphasis on creating a hierarchy of corporate gouging with high profits on health food as the goal and more emphasis on creating a fair and sustainable economic environment for the workers and their customers. It also means CCOF and Cruelty Free products are sold there. Go there and shop; the prices are right and the vegetarian ethics and quality are high.

The entrance to the Community Market is located to the rear of Higher Grounds Cafe in a parking lot off Clement Street, 1 block north of Santa Rosa Junior College. The well organized interior overflows with life promoting products. Just inside the door is the fresh produce department stocked with California Certified Organic Foods (C.C.O.F.) vegetables, fruits and herbs. Up the first aisle are coolers full of smoothies, fresh squeezed juices, mineral water, yogurt with natural bacteria to improve digestion, tofu and dairy products. In the bulk foods section are chips, grains, seeds for sprouting, pasta, cooking oil, granola, freeze dried survival food and candy. There is a great selection of ready to cook frozen meals. CCOF bulk edible and medicinal herbs can be purchased by the ounce. Pet food, biodegradable and non-toxic cleaning aids, recycled paper products and purified water are stocked to the rear of the Community Market. In the middle of the store are all sorts of packaged health foods, coffee, organic juices and herbal teas. On your way to the check-out stands scope out the health books, note cards, natural bath scrubs and a wonderful selection of natural cosmetics. Complementary newsletters, magazines and tabloids profile the thriving New Age and Healthy Lifestyle movement in Sonoma County. The Community Market is open from 9am to 9pm Monday thru Saturday and from 10am to 8pm Sundays.

*$-$$ COMMUNITY MARKET    1899 Mendocino Ave., Santa Rosa, CA. 95401*
*CCOF Produce and Health Promoting Products    (707) 546-1806 Information*

## JUDY'S BREADSTICKS

Award winning baker Judy Griswold and owner / marketing wiz Lynda Najarian get rave reviews about the delicious homemade breads baked in Marin County. The local paper says "cupid's arrow lurks in every sack". Judging from the sales, I'd say they have inspired the cupid in millions. What makes the product so wonderful is the handmade uniqueness, the taste, size and texture. Considered Vegan, the "Lovestick" is 12 ounces in weight, 12" in length, hand rolled in either sunflower or sesame seeds, baked to a deep golden brown and come in a brown waxed bag with the above label on the bag.

North coast adventurers enjoy packing the "Lovesticks" as they are also known in their backpacks and as a picnic treat. I personally find this lbread to be alive and full of Chi for the active explorer! Homemakers know what a hit Judy's Breadsticks make with wine and cheese. Available at high end gourmet stores or call for the location of a store near you.

$ *JUDY'S BREADSTICKS*          P.O. Box 5, Mill Valley, CA. 94942
  *Bred from the Heart*          (415) 388-3274 Information

## BILL'S FARM BASKET

Bill's Farm Basket country store is located on the left hand side of Bodega Highway approximately 3 miles west of Sebastopol on the way to Bodega. It's like an optical illusion, because when new customers come in they are surprised to see how large the interior is, in fact, your whole shopping list can be fulfilled here. You can pick up anything from Rocky Chickens, to the best local organic produce. The organic salad mix is picked every day, and brought by local organic farmers. Bill's carries the best of local products that range from Flour Creations scones, Heart Desires truffles, to Bodega Goat Cheese. Visitors are amazed at the large selection of pastas, dried sulphered and unsulphered fruits and nuts, local honey and pollen, and wheat free products. "Our specialty is customer service, because we want to, not because we have to", states owner Debbie Martinez. "We (Cathy, Oscar, Gloria, Alex, Tara, Jim and Debbie) love our customers." Bill's breathes and lives on it's own. It smells good and feels good. The prices are reasonable, and the products outstanding, but most of all this down home country/health food store can feed more than your stomach.

$-$$ *BILL'S FARM BASKET*          10315 Bodega Hwy, 3 miles west of
*Farm Fresh Produce & Drinks*   Sebastopol, CA  95472   (707) 829-1777

## ANDY'S MARKET

One of Sonoma County's best kept secrets is Andy's Produce which is located just north of Sebastopol on Highway 116 in the heart of the Gravenstein apple country. Locals and visitors are so lucky to have a one stop destination to shop in where a myriad of lush produce and farm and garden products are sold under one roof.

This expansive family run produce stand and market started out small in 1964 when Andy and Kathrin Skikos moved here from Utah. Andy told Kathrin, "I've found God's Country and we are moving there!" They started with one small produce stand in Santa Rosa 35 years ago and slowly built the business up as they raised a family of three daughters and two sons.

Because Andy's own their own trucks they scout the entire West Coast for the highest quality organic foods and best buys for their loyal family of customers.

Tall trees, apple orchards, fresh country air and a spacious parking lot big enough for RV's, trucks towing boats, the family car or a bicycle touring group makes a stop at Andy's inviting. The **Coffee Coral** which is located under the big awning out front is a great start for a fresh made coffee latte, espresso, mocha, fruit or veggie smoothie, hot dog or snack.

In the **Wholesale Bulk Foods** section you'll find showcased all the grains, freeze dried soups, cereals, vegetables, fruits, vitamins and mineral supplements including bulk spirulina, vitamin C and bee pollen. Andy's makes it easy to stock up the home pantry or emergency food supply for your RV, fishing boat or getaway rental home.

The **Retail Gourmet Foods** customers enjoy filling their shopping carts in the voluminous isles overflowing with fresh fruits, vegetables, herbs, extensive gourmet cheese section, premium California wines, selection of micro brewed beer, canned goods, breads, fresh squeezed fruit and vegetable juices. Look for Andy's high quality personally endorsed and labeled products.

This big hearted and big spirited family is in partnership to provide you the best organic produce at very fair prices. Andy and Kathrin, sons Jim and Chris, daughters Kim, Julie, and Shelley and Uncle Dee plus Frank, Jane, Jack and the 19 grand children invite you to visit Andy's Produce rain or shine any day of the week from 8:30am to 7:30pm.

*$-$$ ANDY'S PRODUCE   Box 870, 1691 Gravenstein Hwy, 3 miles north Farm Fresh Produce & Drinks  of Sebastopol, CA  95472  (707) 823-8661*

## FOOD FOR HUMANS

Health minded travelers are always looking for a natural food store that is conveniently located along their route. Such is the case with Food For Humans, which is located one block off Guerneville's Main Street, on 1st Street next to Safeway. Natural Food Store proprietors are often not only the picture of health, but are very concerned about the environment and making sure store

patrons get the freshest and most nutritious "full of life" foods possible. The coolers and store isles overflow with strictly organic fresh produce (from local farms), a comprehensive bulk foods section including culinary and medicinal herbs, fresh squeezed juices, and fresh made health food snacks and sandwiches to keep you strong and alert whether biking or driving. There is also a corner of the store devoted entirely to natural body care and vitamins as well as an expanding eco-gift shop.

Biking and hiking enthusiasts will appreciate the high energy snacks as well as scenic biking and hiking routes the Sonoma Coast offers. Body care products are also carried to help keep you healthy, strong and lookin' good! Travel and health care questions about the store's products are cheerfully answered. The choices you make today affect your health tomorrow. Make the right choices and get out there and shine!

*$-$$ FOOD FOR HUMANS*      *16385 First Street, Guerneville, CA. 95446*
*Full Service Natural Food Store*          *(707) 869-3612 Information*

## SLICE of LIFE Vegetarian Restaurant

At the Slice of Life chef/proprietor David Burns has created a menu that strives to meet the needs of a conscious society for nutritious and flavorful vegetarian and vegan foods. David has created a menu that uses no animal products (except dairy cheeses) and offers fat free, low fat, and dairy free choices. All the ingredients are of the highest quality, with many grown organically and locally to support your healthy lifestyle.

Dining is "al fresco" under umbrellas or inside a narrow dining room amid inspirational art amd an occassional solo musician. You can create the pizza of your dreams from a combination of 13 cheese and vegetarian items. Other dishes include veggie burgers, vegetarian hot dogs, grilled tofu and tempeh or seitan sandwiches. Italian and Mexican entrees include fresh pasta of the day, mock meat balls, lasagne, tostada muy grande, and quesadilla suprema. McDougall and Vegan burritos, salsa and chips, dairy free soups, garden fresh salads (with choice of dressings) and steamed seasonal vegetables bring depth to the selection. Fresh squeezed fruit and vegetable juices, smoothies, date shakes and Hi Pro malts as well as chilled mineral water, hi or no caffein coffee drinks, beer and wine are served. Homemade desserts include berry tofu, cheesecake, chocolate brownies and assorted muffins. The Slice of Life is located across from the Sebastopol Plaza next to the Food for Thought Market on Mc Kinley Street. *Conclusion: Old Hippies Never Die - They Just Ascend To A Higher Level.*

*$-$$ SLICE OF LIFE*        *6970 McKinley Street, Sebastopol, CA 95472*
*International Vegetarian and Vegan Cuisine (707) 829-6627 Sit down / to go*

# SUSTAINABLE TRAVELER
# SUSTAINABLE COMMUNITY
# SUSTAINABLE WORLD
## by Suzanne Rosso

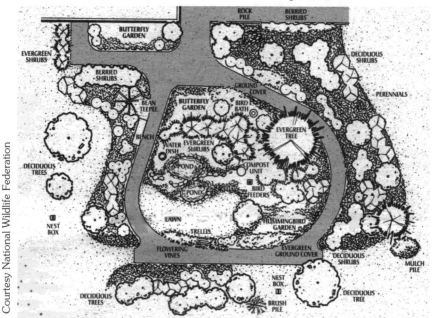

Courtesy National Wildlife Federation

The backyard garden/wildlife habitat encourages the honey bee, dragonfly, hummingbird, the butterfly and our inner child to take real joy in sustainability.

One of the joys of traveling is the time to step outside of our regular habits and thought patterns and take the opportunity to recognize, contemplate and experience our natural rhythms, as well as new ideas and new ways of being.

As travelers and planetary, cosmic citizens on spaceship Earth, *"The choices we make every moment, every day move us away from or toward sustainability."* As travelers, we are consumers. In fact, we as human beings are consumers. As individuals, what and how we choose to consume physically, mentally, emotionally and spiritually will determine whether we continue to travel on this planet as a sentient human species. We are responsible for each feeling and thought we give energy to.

We know scientifically and biologically that all living things are driven by the need "to get energy" on a very basic survival level (2nd Law of Thermodynamics). We are aware that as humans we have the ability to think, to pause, to reflect and therefore can realize when our basic needs are being met and can shift our drive "to get energy" (biological survival) to our need "to get sustainability", (species survival). Until recently, sustainability was not a generally understood concept or idea.

Sustainable Sonoma County, an organization of local citizens, has identified several means to measure and indicate where we are on the sustainability continuum. For example, what is the carrying capacity of the geographical boundaries of Sonoma County's square land base? An evolved and sustainable society secures quality of life for all of humanity, other species and future generations within the means of nature.

Sustainability, simply stated is the ability to continue over time. *Sustainable Communities are and will continue to be created by cooperative human beings, in meaningful relationship to all life, making individual "informed conscious choices".* The cycles of time and the circularity of nature insure that every molecule on this planet does some traveling; therefore all our choices must be viewed from a global perspective while acted upon locally. Living in the Information Age gives us the ability to be informed and empowers us to be able to create changes in our lifestyle habits. As travelers we can visit and learn from existing "sustainability systems".

## WHAT IS and WHAT CAN BE

At the Community Learning Center and Institute, nature is everywhere. In the design structure of buildings, in habitat and healing gardens, in the International Peace Park and Sculpture Garden, in the playgrounds and in the ponds, springs and lake. All buildings are representative of state of the art building practices using appropriate technology and have influenced the changing of building codes to incorporate sustainable building practices. Waterways and water sources are models of restoration projects and water purification systems. All the herb, flower and vegetable gardens are ongoing experiments in sustainable gardening and farming methods, recognizing the critical need to use heirloom and open-pollinated seeds. Seeds are shared regularly during Seed Exchange gatherings and are available by mail. Seed saving and plant saving kits are also available through the center. Feel free to stroll through the edible landscaping and graze as you go. Watch the dragonflys, butterflies, bees and birds and how they interact with the plants. The Web of Life is everywhere. Life in balance insures sustainability and the kind of world we want to create for future generations.

Meet other international travelers and bioneers at the Herb and Healing Gardens Tea Room and Restaurant and share a magically alive and delightfully delicious meal. (What else would you expect from Findhorn type gardens?) Enjoy the Visual and Performing Arts Center which hosts local and visual, literary and performing artists providing heartfelt soul food for the spirit. Great fun and great shopping! Attend one of the Center's ongoing trainings, seminars and workshops which recognize the collective heritage of the cultural and genetic diversity of the Earth as the living treasure of the World. All Center resources are available to the pre-school and K-12 school which are utilized by the children of the Center's staff and interested community members. Sustainability education kits and models are available through the Center. The center offers a summer learning Intensive for young people in 7th - 12th grades.

East meets West at the Center's clinical and teaching and health center located on a working farm, where students participate in developmental research on the efficacy of herbs. Individual herbal preparations are made each day for health center clients who actively participate in their own healing through meditation, prayer, Chi Gung, Tai Chi, Yoga, massage, storytelling, drumming, dancing, singing, creating imagery and art and learning about dreamtime. Many traditional and non-traditional healing modalities are utilized, researched and studied at the center. Participants are learning to experience themselves as a part of the environment and experience time in patterns, cycles and rhythms. All learn that we must be stewards of our worlds, thoughts, actions, for they all have the power to make sick or to heal. The Center collaborates with other programs, projects, organizations and Institutes working on similar research. Apprenticeship and work/study positions are available for projects and programs.

As you reach the commons, you are likely to encounter a group of people heartily discoursing on the pros and cons of a newly proposed project, working towards consensus. Throughout the Center, young and old watch as the sun comes and goes each day at sunrise and sunset. Birth and Death (transformation) are experienced as a part of the Life cycle. Many traditions are practiced, depending on cultural background; all recognizing reverence for Life and Death. All are learning to remember another way of knowing, learning about relationship and the kinship of all life. That we are a part of all life. A visit is well worth the trip. There are a few places you can visit covered on the pages of this book where bits and pieces of the Community Learning Center and Institute exist (see next page for more information). Some elements of this center are already in existence in our geographic watershed region. Some elements are in development and some are yet to come.

## WHAT YOU CAN DO

As we journey we often look for gifts for loved ones, or gifts to ourselves that will serve to enrich our lives and provide us with memories. As we give gifts instead of buying "things", we make an impact. As travelers, we can contribute to sustainable communities wherever we go. We contribute our ideas, feelings, words, thoughts and our dollars and we can participate in a *"buycott"*. A *"buycott"* is when you make a conscious choice to buy products, services and goods from a business because you support their values and business practices. A tiny example of a "buycott purchase" might be a ceramic or clay coffee cup made by a local crafts person. This cuts down on wasting paper or styrofoam cups and supports a local artisan. Another purchase might be the acquisitions of $100 in Community Cash (see page 295). Purchase a low cost portable water filtration system and know the quality of your water while reducing plastic garbage (See WETech page 277).

Ask questions before you exchange your dollars and energy for products, goods and services. Will the dollars you exchange contribute to the economy of the local community your visiting, or will they go to a multi-national corporation? What is the quality of the business' relationship with people and the Earth? How does their mission statement read? You can add your own questions and make it fun, educational and enlightening. Above all, make it count!

Nature is the map, simplicity is the key, our desire to live sustainably is the compass. One small choice of action today can have a multiplied effect over our experience of time. Everybody lives up wind and downstream - choose wisely.

## GIFT GIVING IDEAS FOR YOURSELF AND OTHERS

Use the resources in this book.  Shop at locally owned and operated businesses.
Buy and use locally made products, goods and services.
Visit Sonoma County Nurseries and bring home some new plant friends.
Shop on Farm Trails and Art Trails.  Have a fun trip through the country.
Participate in a workshop, community event, community program, garden work,
day and/or retreat eco-adventure.  Get involved in a watershed restoration project.
Buy a book from a local bookstore - read and reflect.
Purchase a low cost water filtration system (see WETech).
Give the gift of increased intelligence to your young ones.  Read books like those
of Joseph Chilton Pearce, especially "The Magical Child" and "Evolution's End".
Contemplate and act on the "Aborigine Message From Forever", by Bee Lake in
"Message From Forever" by Marlo Morgan.
Feed your Body, Mind, Heart and Spirit with culture and relationship in
community with Storytelling, Dance, Drumming, Music, Song and Laughter!

## FOR MORE INFORMATION

**Bodega Bay Marine Lab**  Box 247, Bodega bay, CA. 94923 (707) 875-2211
**The Occidental Arts and Ecology Center**
**Real Goods**  13201 S. Hwy 101, Hopland, CA. 95449  (707) 744-2100
**New College of California**  www.newcollege.edu  (707) 568-0112
**The Natural Step** developed by Dr. Karl-Henrik Robert of Sweden
www.naturalstep.org
**Ecological Footprint:** www.ecouncil.ac.cr/rio/focus/report/english/footprint/
**Sustainable Sonoma County** Box 558, Graton, CA. 95444 (707) 829-1224
Check out the **Bioneers Conference** and the **Collective Heritage Institute** at
www.bioneers.org.  (505) 986-0366 OR 877BIONEER
**Seed Savers Exchange,** 3076 North Winn, Decorah, Iowa 52101
**National Wildlife Federation,** Backyard Wildlife Habitat Program at
www.nwf.org or call (703) 790-4000  (see illustration on page 274)
**Eco-Regional Restoration Alliance,** P.O. Box 2075, Sebastopol, CA. 95472
or call (707) 829-3835
**Community Learning Center Institute:** CLCI@monitor.net
**WE Tech Water Efficiency Technology 888-822-9724  www.earthcrew.com**

The pebble in the pond
creates ripples of
change. . . . .

# SELF SUFFICIENCY

Since our origins, humankind has connected with energy around a campfire, staring into the flames and watching the effect this energy has on other matter. Since this historic event, the nature of humankind was to create ways to transform energy from dormant things into movement and life. From the garden of Eden, we create a variety of foods that sustain and nourish us in more ways than one. These plants not only fuel our bodies, they can be used as another source of energy as well. One that is far more effective and efficient than current sources of fuel, as well as far less destructive to the planet we live on and need to love. These plants can be transformed to create ethanol fuel to power vehicles, provide paper for the Information Age we live in and building materials for homes and automobiles which are ten times stronger than steel! We no longer need to be dependent upon the whims of greedy oil barons and their droid investors who feast on our life force energy, while destroying our planet and precious natural resources.

A variety of crops can be grown to create ethanol. Corn and hemp are two of the most promising. Paper is traditionally made from trees, but we have all seen the devastating effect clear cutting of forests has had on the planet. Hemp, which actually rebuilds the soil as it grows, can yield 4 times the pulp per acre of traditional forests and grows to maturity in only 110 days, as opposed to hundreds of years. Building manufacturers utilize hemp in the construction of particleboard, which is many times stronger than wood products. In 1938 Henry Ford actually built a car out of hemp. He pointed out that he could "grow cars" from the garden and power them with ethanol fuel, (see picture at right). Information on the carbohydrate economy can be attained from the Institue for Local Self Reliance at www://grn.com/grn/org//ilsr.htm or (612) 379-3815.

So what is the problem with shifting away from oil dependency and into self-sustainability using biomass? It's very simple. We are a product of mind-control from corporations including the media, oil companies, and corporate government. We

In 1938 visionary Henry Ford demonstrated the strength of his car "grown" from a combination of hemp and other annual crops, and designed to run on hemp fuel. Photo from collections of Henry Ford Museum and Greenfield Village.

have the tools (see Sovereignty article) and people to create a parallel society based on sustainability and self-sufficiency.

There are numerous devices that have been created including super efficient heat pumps that provide 80% of the energy for a house. Cars have been invented that run on water (yes, H20 - hydrogen fuel cells) as well as electricity and ethanol. Oil companies and their corporate government lackeys have successfully squashed small groups, but there's no way they could stop a movement of millions. Many are quietly living the dream and perhaps this is the smartest way, but there are also millions who are protesting the dependency on oil and working hard toward creating a sane and sustainable alternative. Universally the most promising appears to be the hemp plant, which if properly utilized could save the world from humans who live out of balance.

Hawaii and Idaho are among the first to grow hemp for fuel, paper pulp, construction and medicinal purposes. The people in California are also organizing, and hemp cultivation will no doubt follow. The product potential is limitless - the opportunities for the little to big grower, enormous. But first we have to eliminate opposing forces of media mind-control, corporate government hit squads and corporate monopolies. Hemp grows wild and requires no expensive drilling equipment to harvest, or high-tech cruise missiles to protect the supply of it to refineries. Anyone can grow hemp and it can be turned into ethanol at any small farm, much like home brewed beer or wine can be made at home. It truly is a source of fuel to get to work, or to the beach to go surfing, as well as attend those all-important sustainable community or sovereignty meetings.

## HISTORY REPEATS ITSELF: A Hemp Renaissance is Happening

The most important document ever printed in America was the Constitution. Many prominent American revolutionaries including George Washington and Thomas Jefferson were hemp farmers. Indeed, hemp farmers financed the American Revolution of 1776! It wasn't until Henry Ford "grew" the first automobile using hemp resin and powered it with ethanol fuel made from hemp pulp in 1938 that the big three corporate forces united to make the growing of hemp difficult and eventually illegal. They were George Rockefeller (non-sustainable oil and timber interests), Lammont Du Pont (non-sustainable petrochemical and plastics production) and the mind-controlling hatchet man, William Randolph Hearst (non-sustainable timber for his newspaper chains). These three, plus, then Secretary of the Treasury and owner of Gulf Oil, Andrew Mellon, and a hand-full of crooked district attorneys and politicians, pushed through the Marijuana Tax Act, which effectively made it impractical for small and large farmers to grow hemp.

It should be noted that hemp has a low THC content, while marijuana has a high THC content, which is what gets people "high" or "stoned". They are two completely different plants and are like comparing a male (hemp, which is tall and stalky) to a female (marijuana, which is short and bushy). They are not the same.

Legalizing the growth and conversion of hemp biomass for meaningful purposes and regulating the use of marijuana for *medicinal purposes only* would be a boost to the American economy and a significant step to healing the planet by creating a sustainable society no longer dependent on oil and "Old World Order".

## ZAP

In Sonoma County we are fortunate to have ZAP (Zero Air Pollution), electric bicycle and scooter company. Founded in 1994, and now a publicly owned stock, ZAP produces an excellent electric cruiser for the house wife or busy executive to get around town in style. Luggage racks, baskets, reflectors, lights, solid steel frame and electric motor/generator with rechargeable battery can last for up to 15 miles between charges. To conserve the battery you can peddle the bike anytime you want to. In addition there is a recreational scooter model that kids and students, K through college love. To recharge the battery you can plug a recharger into your home 120 VAC line. Price is moderate from $500 and up, and think of all the money you are going to save on gasoline. You can tour the Sebastopol Factory and test drive a ZAP bike or scooter, or rent an electric bike, scooter, motorcycle or even a new neighborhood electric car. Also, tour their website at www.ZAPWORLD.com.

$$-$$$ ZAP       · One ZAP Drive - 117 Morris St., Sebastopol, CA 95472
*Electric Bikes, Cars & Accessories  tel: (707) 824-4150) fax: (707) 824-4159*
*e-mail: zap@zapworld.com*                        Stock Symbol: ZAPP

## REAL GOODS Store and Solar Living Center

There are many who reside in the remote coastal mountains and valleys of northern California where utility power lines and telephone lines end miles from their doorstep. Many have economically fashioned their homes simply yet elegantly out of recycled materials. They often live where the air is crystal clear, the water pure, and the evening stars have that unmistakable twinkle of the most pristine of environments. They have turned to the sun for their needs and created a quality of life unimaginable to many Americans who fear living "off grid".

Most of us are too soft - accustomed to turning on a switch and paying for electricity that is generated from hundreds of miles away. Its convenient - too convenient - and when the grid goes down we are often without hot water, lights, computers, hair dryers, radio etc. Many have taken control of their energy needs and source electricity from batteries, solar panels, wind generators and heat pumps. The showcase at Real Goods Solar Living Center in Hopland will reveal outdoor displays of solar panel arrays, gardens, water supply and purification systems, and indoors, a spacious retail sales room where a myriad of products are sold, seminars and classes are held, and a knowledgeable staff trained in alternative energy technology answers your questions. Your R.V., home, ranch, school or complex of buildings can become energy self-sufficient. Real Goods has helped people who live in the middle of San Francisco, as well as those who inhabit remote islands. They have helped thousands become comfortably self-sufficient and secure, and they can help you too.

Real Goods was founded by such people who courageously chose the freedom to take responsibility for their lives by creating their own homes and becoming their own power and water company. The Real Goods showroom and Solar Living Center boldly validates such lifestyles for those who desire a simple and inexpensive way to live, absent the stress of large communities where people are forced to give their power away to organizations and companies who make up the rules they should live by and then feed on their dependency. Stop by or write for the Real Good's "Everything Under the Sun" Catalog. You'll be glad you did.

*$-$$$ REAL GOODS Solar Living Center 13201 S. Hwy 101, Hopland, CA*
*Tools and Products for Energy Independence and Sustainable Living*
*Open daily 9am to 6pm Fax: (707) 744-1342 Telephone: (707) 744-2100*

## HEMP SOLUTIONS

Hemp Solutions is a showcase of practical applications for the miraculous Hemp Plant - a plant that if properly utilized would solve air pollution, transportation problems, help cure medical ailments, provide clothing for the needy to the affluent, make sails and rope for recreation and work and totes to carry our

Photo Hemp Solutions

belongings. Hemp Solutions opened in 1998 to the applause of a spirited community with practical and courageous solutions to creating sustainable communities. One acre of hemp produces as much cellulose fiber pulp as four acres of trees for paper production. Prior to 1883 over 70% of all books, maps and parchments were printed on Hemp including the original draft for the Declaration of Independence and the Bill of Rights. Henry Ford created a car made of hemp and vegetable composite resin and powered by Hemp methylene, which after combustion breaks down to water and hydrogen (ending automotive air pollution). In the Hemp Solutions showroom you can check out the dresses, hemp silk, jumpers, pants, overalls, jeans, hats, back packs, bags, string, rope, curtain fabric, hammocks, magazines and books. Hemp is a true friend that brings years of pleasure. There is nothing like lounging in a sturdy and comfortable hemp hammock while swinging in the breeze and experiencing an all natural high connecting to Mother Earth. I'm glad I'm doing my part to support a sustainable economy for mine and the next seven generations. I hope you do too.

*$-$$ HEMP SOLUTIONS 641 Fourth Street, Santa Rosa, Ca. 95404*
*Clothing, Luggage, Fabric & Gifts Fax: (707) 542-1667 (707) 542-HEMP*

# RETAIL OUTLETS
# Promoting Recreational
# Transformation and Well Being

## SEA TRADER

Our need to meet the requirements of a stressful and ever changing world often leads us to search outside the traditional realms of science and logic. To look inside and trust one's own intuition and become New Age literate is a growing priority among many.

The Sea Trader is a window into the holistic world where an array of high quality crystals and gemstones glisten amid a metaphysical theater with an ocean view. Proprietress Kathy Kopfer's desire and dedication to seek the answers of the spiritual side of the world we live in lays the foundation of this playground for personal growth. An expanded selection of New Age musical CD's & tapes, tarot cards, greeting cards, metaphysical books, jewelry, aromatherapy, oils, candles and incense are among the many items of interest displayed at the Sea Trader. There is also a large selection of handcrafted gifts that please and enlighten. The Sea Trader is open from 10am - 5pm daily. Visitor information is also available. AE, MC, Visa & Novus honored.

*$-$$ THE SEA TRADER   38640 North Hwy 1 (1/2 mile north of Gualala)*
*Gift Shop and Gallery       Gualala, Ca.  95445  (707) 884-3248 Info.*

## THE CRYSTAL PEOPLE SPIRITUAL CENTER

The Crystal People Spiritual Center is a combination retail store and healing center. It showcases light quality crystals, minerals, gemstones and metaphysical books and literature, as well as other delightful and uplifting gift ideas. The proprietors Chris and Diane Loukas host meeting circles and lectures where people of all spiritual paths come to explore and support each other. Chris and Diane are inspiring examples of personal transformation and healing. Chris recovered miraculously from a near fatal car accident and now translates his experience into an energetic healing practice in the store. His sessions are awesome and to avail yourself of this opportunity to work with him is a true gift. The Crystal People Spiritual Center is full of treasures, both inner and outer, that will gratify your heart, mind, body and soul and let your spirit soar.

*$-$$ THE CRYSTAL PEOPLE   313 N. Main Street, Sebastopol, CA. 95472*
*Crystals, Gemstones, Spiritual Events & Seminars MC & Visa (707) 823-2663*

## EARTHWOOD Crystals - Books - Music

A mountain stands before you. There are many paths to the summit. Which path is best for me? Indeed, there are many hallways to explore and many doors to open.

Life's journey is fortified with friends and relatives, knowledge applied wisely and joyful events. At Earthwood proprietors Diane Novak and JoAnne Ingerson have assembled many meaningful tools to help us remove the roadblocks to spiritual enlightenment. Her unique perspective and insight into the fears and karmic challenges we face empowers us to expand our comfort zones beyond what we thought possible.

A New Age book and tape section showcases the knowledge and experience of some of our more successful ancient and contemporary explorers. Display cases of fine jewelry and walls lined with works of art bridge the gap between the physical and the divine. Gifts include incense, candles, angels, spiritual totems, dream catchers, stained glass, cards and calendars. Earthwood is open daily from 10am to 6pm and is a must stop for those who realize that the greatest journeys begin within, before they manifest in the physical world.

*$-$$$ EARTHWOOD   #15 Petaluma Blvd. North, Petaluma, CA. 94952*
*Crystals, Books & Music        MC & Visa   (707) 763-6155 Information*

## The LAPIDARY CENTER

Rocks inspire us. Those who have a corner of their home filled with a intimate collection of rocks, minerals and gemstones are rich indeed.

At the Lapidary Center in Petaluma you can see and touch tiny fragments of the building blocks of the Universe. It is very exciting. Proprietor and avid collector Richard Brosamle showcases thousands of rocks, minerals and gemstones from around the world. In addition they sell jewelry, jewelry making supplies, gold and silver findings, cut and rough stones, natural stone beads, pearls, sea shells, petrified wood, prehistoric scenes, meteorites, rock-hound tools and equipment, Native American artifacts and technical guide books and maps. Like puppies and kittens in a pet store, some of the stones and minerals will pull on you. Some will actually enhance your physical and emotional well-being and you should purchase them for your home collection.

*$-$$$ THE LAPIDARY CENTER                    AE, MC & Visa*
*Rocks, Minerals, Gemstones & Jewelry  316 B St., Petaluma, CA. 94952*
*Open 10am - 5pm Tues. - Sat.              Information: (707) 762-6886*

## PASTORALE

Surrounded by rolling hills in the lush Freestone Valley of Western Sonoma County is a place called Pastorale. Owners Lary and Nancy Rowinsky describe it simply as a ;natural fiber clothing workshop and retail showroom, but to its many devoted customers Pastorale is a rare and unforgettable experience in country shopping at its best.

What makes Pastorale so distinctive and memorable is its unique blend of hand made products, its relaxed, homelike interior setting, its emphasis on fine quality women's clothing made in the Pastorale Workshop, and its dedication to customer service.

Browse through the Pastorale showroom for treats at every turn: women's casual-to-dressy clothing, rugged shirts and jackets for men, a great line of sheepskin boots and slippers and a large collection of men's and women's sweaters, locally made leather products, hand crafted boxes and a fascinating selection of jewelry and accessories.

Pass through the showroom door and you're in the Pastorale Workshop. Visitors are always welcome.  Under the careful supervision of designer Yeunny Mears, the Workshop produces limited-edition separates, dresses, jackets and coats for women.  The fabric seleciton is impressive: specialty silks, unusual rayons and fine wools in a variety of seasonal colors and weights.  Because all fabrics are purchased in limited quantities, Pastorale wardrobes will always be unique. Also unique is the experience of meeting the designer, selecting the fabric of your choice and knowing that these clothes were created just for you.  Prices on Workshop fashions are surprisingly moderate, with a slightly higher charge for custom sizing.

*$$-$$$ PASTORALE        12779 Bodega Hwy, Freestone, CA. 95472*
*Hand Crafted Clothing        Open daily from 9:30am to 5:30pm*
*Turn on Bohemian Highway from Bodega Highway, then left after 100*
*yds. on El Camino Bodega.  Pastorale is the 2nd building on the left*
*Information:  (707) 823-0640*

# CRYSTAL CHANNELS

Our need to meet the requirements of a stressful and ever changing world often leads us to search outside the traditional realms of science and logic. To look inside and trust one's own intuition and become New Age literate is a growing priority among many.

Crystal Channels is an experience into the holistic world where an array of high quality crystals, gemstones, jewelry and artifacts glisten amid a metaphysical theater of beauty, light, fragrance and sound. Crystal Channels is a gentle and beautiful reminder for the inquisitive mind to explore new paths and remember there is much more to life on earth than meets the eye. We have all experienced a glimpse of something not quite clear - just out of range of touch, sight and sound. Perhaps the answer you seek lies in the library of books, magazines and videos at Crystal Channels. Inspirational gifts such as dream catchers, affirmation and divination cards, sacred candles, incense, music (CD's & cassettes), earrings, necklaces, American Indian art and note cards are attractively displayed. Give yourself the treat of enchantment and visit Crystal Channels. It will delight your heart and inspire your spirit.

*$-$$$ CRYSTAL CHANNELS 1301 C Cleveland Ave., Santa Rosa, CA 95401*
*Crystals, Gemstones, Jewelry, New Age and Native American Artifacts*
*Open daily 11am to 6pm / Sunday from 12 to 6pm          (707) 578-LOVE*

# PETRIFIED FOREST

3.4 million years ago Mount St Helena, which is located in the northern end of the Napa Valley, was formed by a volcanic eruption which spewed ash over a 10 mile wide circle. The eruption's explosive force was only a fraction of the 1980 eruption of Mount St Helens in Washington, yet huge virgin redwood forests were knocked over and

covered with volcanic ash. In 1880 pioneer, Charlie Evans, while clearing fields for his cows, discovered the "Petrified Forest" and started conducting tours. Today a splendid tour awaits the novice who wants a glimpse into the geological history of a catastrophic event of the past. Well maintained trails meander through excavations of ancient trees - now solid as rocks. In the giftshop you can purchase a souvenir of petrified wood, crystal minerals, or artifact of the paleosoic era when giant insects, dinosaurs and winged reptiles hunted in the sky's above today's redwood forests and vineyards. Tours take 20 minutes and cost $5 for adults. Open year around from 10am - 6pm summertime and 10am - 5pm winters.

*$ PETRIFIED FOREST     4100 Petrified Forest Rd, Calistoga, CA. 94515*
*Tours and Giftshop    Major Credit Cards    (707) 942-6667 Information*

## TIBETAN CULTURE HOUSE

As soon as you enter the cozy Tibetan Culture Houses in downtown Santa Rosa or downtown San Rafael you are overcome with the spirit of the Dalai Lama and Tibetan Culture.  Both shops are most inspirational. Jamyang Lama, the proprietor, is a former monk who specialized in the study of Tibetan Buddhist philosophy. In these stores customers can ask questions about Tibetan culture and traditions, as well as purchase authentic goods from Tibet, Nepal and India.  The retail stores showcase the works of exiled Tibetans and Himalayans and include fabulous silk scarves and clothing, wool handicrafts, handmade paper stationary, religious artifacts, masks, household decorations, jewelry, books and musical instruments as well as American made tapes and CD's.

The Buddhist tradition seeks to end all suffering on earth and elsewhere.  I hope you'll visit the Tibetan Culture House and bring new meaning to your home or workplace as well as your life's path.

*$-$$ TIBETAN CULTURE HOUSE  Specialty Gifts from Tibet, Nepal and India*
*Open 11 - 6 Mon - Sat  1223  Fourth St., San Rafael, CA. 94901  (415) 485-1244*
*631 Fourth St., Suite #10, Santa Rosa, CA. 95404*             *(707) 545-0901*

## The OPENED HEART BOOKSTORE

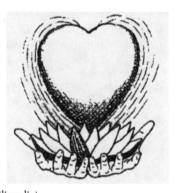

Those who feel there is much more to life than meets the eye will truly cherish a visit to The Opened Heart Bookstore.  Proprietors Elena and Christopher Starbuck have created a wonderful showcase of gifts for the Inner Child in all of us. The meditation room in the back of the store is a powerful sacred space in which to recenter ourselves or ask our inner guides for direction. You can also attend one of the special events or lectures designed to open one to endless possibilities - be sure to check the Opened Heart's calendar of events or ask to be included on the mailing list.

Besides a complete selection of New Age, Metaphysical and Personal Growth books, cards and tapes, you'll be able to touch and hold a gallery of precious gemstones and minerals to determine exactly which one feels right for your heart or a loved ones.  The gemstone meditation fountains are the most beautiful and inspirational I have ever seen.  A nice selection of dream catchers, incense, herbs, aromatherapy oils, and candles helps you create your personal car or at-home alter.   Elena and Christopher and friends are most knowledgeable at helping us find the rights tools to assist us in opening our heart to our life's choosen path.

*$-$$$The OPENED HEART BOOKSTORE    619 Fourth Street, Santa Rosa*
*Gifts for the Inner Child  Open from 10am  AE, MC & Visa  (707) 547-4847*

# SOVEREIGNTY

Sovereignty is the pathway to true choice, personal power and real freedom. The dictionary definition of Sovereignty is defined as: Free, supreme power over a body politic or corporation; self governing, having undisputed ascendancy, freedom from external control; autonomy, independence. The need for freedom of movement is tantamount to exploration from conception. Freedom of movement is necessary for a human being to grow and develop on every level. As travelers and tourists we all want to feel free to enjoy the roads. For example, the right to travel on public roads is a god-given right, not a privilege, as state issued driver's licenses would imply. Yet, there are those who would inappropriately attach themselves to us, inhibiting our freedom and basic right to explore the planet unencumbered unless we pay them money for licenses, fines, fees, registrations, inspections and forfeitures. Corporate government has

---

**CHART A    FORTY-FIRST CONGRESS Sess III Ch.61, 62. 1871
(formation of the District of Columbia Corporation)**

appropriated.
APPROVED, February 21, 1871.

CHAP. LXII.— *An Act to provide a Government for the District of Columbia.*     Feb. 21, 1871.

*Be it enacted by the Senate and House of Representatives of the United* Vol. xvii. p. 16.
*States of America in Congress assembled,* That all that part of the terri- District of Co-
tory of the United States included within the limits of the District of lumbia consti-
Columbia be, and the same is hereby, created into a government by the porate for muni-
name of the District of Columbia, by which name it is hereby constituted cipal purposes.
a body corporate for municipal purposes, and may contract and be con- Powers, &c.
tracted with, sue and be sued, plead and be impleaded, have a seal, and
exercise all other powers of a municipal corporation not inconsistent with
the Constitution and laws of the United States and the provisions of this
act.

SEC. 2. *And be it further enacted,* That the executive power and au- Governor, ap-
thority in and over said District of Columbia shall be vested in a gov- pointment, and

---

A few events that have eroded away our rights and freedoms include the above act of the 41st Congress in 1871 making our government a corporation, the formation of the IRS in 1913, the Stock Market crash of 1929 and Bankruptcy of 1933, placing all America under a state of national emergency. This has been a slow deliberate process by smart people in high places who know how to create and manage a force of corporate employees to do their dirty work.

It is important to notice the difference between the united states of America and the United States (Corporation), as it is written. The united states of America is a Republic; whereas the United States Corporation headquarted in the District of Columbia (Washington D.C.) was formed on February 21, 1871, and created the "Color of the Law" and functions as a Democracy. The United States Corporation was created on the ashes of the Civil War, which is a story in itself. If you remember your history, the South wanted to be Sovereign from the North because it was being hit with unfair tariffs and taxes. As a result of the North's victory, every American citizen (black and white) became a slave of involuntary servitude to the fraudulent taxation system we have today. Deception has always been used by the heirachy to rip off the general population.

cleverly postured themselves by placing an invisible layer of law between us and the land, the roadways and even each other. They are called parasites. There are many, but the few that will be focused on here that suck our very life force energy materially, energetically and psychicly include the U.S. Corporation, whose headquarters is in the District of Columbia, the IRS, the DMV and the FDA. These are surprisingly all corporations acting under the "color of the law" which will be explained later in this article.

This article was carefully researched with information, documents and proof supplied by dozens of individuals and organizations. Some of you will be very surprised and even shocked by what you are about to read. Those of you who are unconscious could become very angry because this article may shake your reality and challenge you to wake up to personal responsibility, real freedom and sovereignty. Lots of us are very happy living in a false sense of security, like cows in a herd grazing freely on the grass in a controlled environment. As long as the cows give milk or calves they are spared from their future slaughter. We all have choices, don't we?

Many of you are already well aware of sovereignty. Each of us has a very personal path to walk and we_all have choices as well as freedom of speech guaranteed under the 1st Amendment of the 1787 Constitution of the united states of America. For those of us who choose to be conscious and fully awake, the Sovereign Movement could be one of the most exciting possibilities of your lifetime. Taking all your power back from corporations masquerading as the government not only protects your personal life force energy, but most importantly also that of our future generations.

## OUR GOD GIVEN BIRTH RIGHT

We are brought into this world by an act of divine guidance. We arrive naked, empty handed and totally dependent on our mother and father. We draw our first breath and begin a life process of evolving ourselves physically, mentally, emotionally and spiritually.

### CHART B

Yet most Americans, unless we are of Native American status living on a truly Sovereign reservation or born into a Sovereign household, become involuntary slaves to a corporation at birth through an "adhesion contract", created from a corporate issued marriage license or birth certificate. That corp-oration is the state you reside in and the U.S. government or United States Corporation, head-quartered in Washington D.C. - a ten square mile area. One of the parasitic realities this creates is a shackling of debt at birth to the interest on the national debt (which is collected by the IRS). Further entanglement begins in the delivery room of the hospital with the assignment of a social security number to a newborn baby. Did this baby ask to become a slave at birth? Was its

| CHART C | Historical Time Line | u.s. of A | verses | United States |
|---------|---------------------|-----------|--------|---------------|
| Date | Type of Government | Name of Country | Citizen Status | Jurisdiction Foreigner vs Member |
| 1787 | Republic | united states of America | Native American | Foreigner to the U.S. Corporation |
| 1871 | Democracy | United States | Corporate Slave | Corporate Citizen |

naked and innocent hands capable of holding an ink pen and filling in the blanks of a social security application? This act shackles each of us to pay taxes to the IRS, a corporate trust head quartered in Puerto Rico and collection agency for the Federal Reserve. The Federal Reserve pays the interest on the national debt (set up to be an endless black hole) to the International Monetary Fund, which is controlled by the global bankers. Not one penny we pay the IRS stays in America (except for the salaries of the IRS personnel) to help one child or family. It all goes off shore to pay the global arms dealers, drug smugglers and slave traders.

The solution? Don't get a state issued marriage license. Give birth to your child at home and home school your child or put them in a private school that does not require a SSN#. Furthermore your child is not required to be immunized with questionable vaccines. All you have to do is fill out a Waiver of Religious Exemption (Vaccines) which are all available in the Global Sovereigns Handbook. (See page 292).

So where did personal freedom and sovereignty go? How did this come about and what can you do to regain your personal freedom and sovereignty?

Well, it is a simple mechanical process of rescinding your signature on the adhesion contracts that were created by your parents and you since birth. Then you can exit the jurisdiction of the U.S. Corporate Government by becoming Sovereign and reverting back to the status of a Native American. Adhesion contracts were created by you acquiring a birth certificate, social security number, state issued driver's license, registering your vehicle with DMV, business license, voter registration and signing your name on state and IRS tax forms. The definition of a Adhesion Contract is - "a contract so heavily restrictive of one party (e.g., U.S. citizen) while nonrestrictive of the other (e.g., the government corporation) that doubts arise as to the voluntary nature of the contract; take it or leave it basis; weaker party has no realistic choice as to its terms."

Making the shift to sovereignty is 80% emotional. It is entirely legal, though requires courage to create a new lifestyle and the emotional approval and energetic alignment with your relatives, loved ones, friends and clients. Sovereign individuals are sometimes misunderstood by the masses and can be discriminated against, just like any special or unique social economic group. Albert Einstein said, *"Great Spirits have always encountered violent opposition from mediocre minds"*. Also, it is a common practice for corporate individuals including judges, district attorneys, cops, IRS, DMV, FDA employees to bad mouth you because you dare to challenge their fraudulent parasitic authority and their ability to rip off your money, assets and life force energy. Believe me, many of them know exactly what they are doing, yet criminally continue to do so.

That is why millions of Americans are taking steps to create a parallel society by becoming Sovereign. The Sovereignty Movement is growing by leaps and bounds. All 50 states have s o v e r e i g n t y movements. Arizona, California, Hawaii, Idaho, Montana, Oregon, Texas, Washington and Wyoming have strong sovereignty movements.

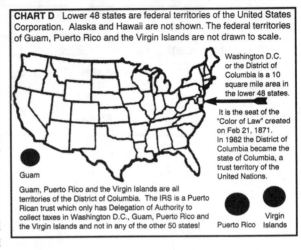

**CHART D** Lower 48 states are federal territories of the United States Corporation. Alaska and Hawaii are not shown. The federal territories of Guam, Puerto Rico and the Virgin Islands are not drawn to scale.

Washington D.C. or the District of Columbia is a 10 square mile area in the lower 48 states.

It is the seat of the "Color of Law" created on Feb 21, 1871. In 1982 the District of Columbia became the state of Columbia, a trust territory of the United Nations.

Guam

Guam, Puerto Rico and the Virgin Islands are all territories of the District of Columbia. The IRS is a Puerto Rican trust which only has Delegation of Authority to collect taxes in Washington D.C., Guam, Puerto Rico and the Virgin Islands and not in any of the other 50 states!

Puerto Rico  Virgin Islands

British author and former BBC investigative reporter David Icke states so well in his book, *The Truth Shall Set You Free*"What happens when the human race gives its mind and power away? What happens when the veil of secrecy is lifted to speed the moment when the days of domination and manipulation are over? An elite few cannot dominate and control billions of people and create wars for their advantage unless thousands of millions are willing to be used as economic slaves and cannon fodder. Collective consciousness is the accumulation of the sum thoughts broadcasted each moment by the human race. These thoughts can be negative or positive. Presently, there's an overwhelming vortex of negative thought forms and energy keeping the human collective consciousness grounded in the root chakra of fear and control. Until we take our minds back, start thinking and deciding for ourselves to live as co-creators in this beautiful universe, co-creating our own realities with the divine, we'll be subject to intense mind control and manipulation that robs us daily of our life force.

## MIND CONTROL: MEDIA, CENSORSHIP & CORPORATE AGENDAS

Every year Project Censored at Sonoma State University releases the years most censored articles that the corporate media ignores or downplays. Many of these stories that never hit the corporate press cover up the acts that affect the health and well-being of all of us. Sonoma County newspapers include the Santa Rosa Press Democrat which is owned by the New York Times, and the smaller Sonoma Independent which is a free tabloid newspaper is part of a corporate owned chain. The only true independents are The Sonoma West Times & News in Sebastopol, which covers progressive news and issues promoting community, agriculture and sustainability, the Independent Coast Observer and the Anderson Valley Advertiser. All have editorial agendas with the Press Democrat promoting status quo mind control. The "P.D." is under century owned control of the Ochs-Sulyberger families - a Trust. The most important question to ask of any news item is what's the source? Carl Jensen, the creator of Project Censored states, "Media manipulation and bias does not occur in random fashion; rather it moves in the same overall direction again and again favoring management over labor and corporations over corporate critics." He continues in his book <u>20 Years of Censored News,</u> "The media uses omission and suppression, lies, balk and repetitive, labeling, face value transmission, false balancing and framing to manipulate public sentiment one way or another."

## WHAT DO YOU NEED TO BECOME SOVEREIGN?

"David Icke states, "We are more afraid of what other people will think of us than what we think of ourselves. If we step out of the herd and go our own way, dance to the beat of our own drummer, others will notice and they might not like us anymore. If you evacuate the "hassle-free" zone and have a mind of your own, do your own thinking and come to your own conclusions, then others won't approve. You ask, "What would the other slaves think if I freed myself. Gee, mother and father won't approve. Neither will our friends, our lovers, perhaps even our children will hate us. Are we so weak, so cowardly that we cannot step out and live our own lives?". Are we people or sheeple?

After you make the emotional shift it is simply a matter of filing a series of letters and forms refuting the fraud that has been committed against you at birth and throughout your life, rescinding your signature with the appropriate U.S. corporate agencies with a pen, type writer or computer, paying some postage, attending classes or seminars, or paying coaching of experts, which can be moderate to expensive in price. You will need a support group of conscious like-minded people to help you with this transition. Don't worry, there are *millions* of us and it is a lot easier than you think!

As I said earlier, babies that are given social security numbers are indentured to the interest on the national debt at birth. This is the money paid to the IRS, which is another corporation. By rescinding your social security number and filing certain forms you will legally be out of the IRS loop forever. Beware of anyone who asks you for your social security number to open bank accounts, acquire credit, insurance or privileges. First of all it is illegal to require anyone to give their social security number in order to receive privileges. Any person who requires your SSN#can be fined up to $10,000, but you need a witness and a tape recording of said refusal.

Another parasite is the Department of Motor Vehicles, which is a corporate entity run by the state you reside in. In fact you own the roads. The right to travel is a right, not a priviledge, and you can do so without a state issued driver's license and car registration, provided you are not engaged in interstate commerce. Please reference California Supreme Court decisions: <u>The Matter of Application of Stork</u> 167Cal 294 (Cal Supreme Court 1914), <u>Bacon Service Corporation vs Huss</u> 199Cal 21 (Cal Supreme Court 1926 and finally <u>in re Schmolke</u> 199 Cal 42. You can rescind your state issued drivers license and vehicle registration for fraud and take allodial ownership of your vehicle. You can drive legally with a passport and International Drivers License (IDP) if you are of Sovereign status to the United States Corporate Government. Author of the Global Sovereign Handbook Johnny Liberty states, "Sovereign people tend to be much more responsible on America's highways." He encourages everyone to take a driving test regularly and purchase various forms of Sovereign Insurance that do not require a state issued drivers license or United States Corporate Government social security number. Good Luck!

## SOVEREIGNTY RESOURCES and INFORMATION

**There are thousands of sources who can provide physical, mental, emotional and spiritual support around Sovereignty.**

**Asset Protection, Allodial Ownership, Sovereignty**
Info at (707) 522-0550  or  (707) 573-6058.

**Cascadian Resources Center** / Global Sovereigns Handbook {see below}.

**Cop Watch:** Berkeley, San Francisco and Sonoma County,  civil rights violations & complaints against cops guilty of misconduct and lethal force.  For Cop Watch Berkeley & San Francisco contact **Sonoma Center for Peace and Justice,** 540 Pacific Ave., Santa Rosa, CA. 95403 (707) 575-8902 www.sonic.net/-peacentr

**Freedom Law School:  www.freedomlawschool.com**

**IRS Relief:**  Larry Hare 903-849-6507 works with christian patriot attorneys to put an end to the IRS.  also author Larry Schiff www.paynoincometax.com

**Project Censored** by Carl Jensen, 20 Years of Censored News:  Covers methods of media manipulation for national and global corporate agendas. Contact Project Censored at Sonoma State University, Cotati.

**Sonoma County Citizen's Watch Group:** Monitors court & judge abuse of citizen rights   http://ournameis.com/citizens_watch/

**Stolen Lives Project,** compiled by Karin Sari:  A network of civil rights groups, legal defense funds and attorneys who researched police killings state by state.

## GLOBAL SOVEREIGN'S HANDBOOK

Johnny Liberty is one of the most articulate, informed and resourceful experts on sovereignty in the world.  He created the Cascadian Resources Center in Oregon and Hawaii, with offices scheduled to be opened in the San Francisco Bay Area and northern California in 2000.

Sovereignty is the most important work on the planet.  Subjects covered include spiritual, emotional, economic, legal, and political sovereignty.  Rescinding adhesion contracts, acquiring passports and an International Drivers License, Sovereign insurance, challenging the IRS, FDA, state and other corporate entities, allodial ownership of land,  Trust asset protection, u.s.of A  verses  U.S gov't., plus visions and solutions for the Global Sovereign Movement.   *Highly Recommended!*

*Global Sovereign's Handbook   (2nd edition - 300 pages)}      $105.00*
*General Affidavits & Identity Package  (315 pages}          $105.00*
*Website & Online Catalog:  http://www.cascadian.com*
*Email & Online Orders:  cascadia@cascadian.com     1-800-299-4497*

# $ VISIONARY ECONOMICS $

## The Healing Force of Economic Generosity

Gving just 10% in Economic Generosity creates personal freedom, ends guilt and suffering, promotes "generativity" where everybody wins and peace and harmony is nurtured!

According to Marc Allen, author of <u>Visionary Business (New World Library)</u>, "there is plenty of money in the world; in cash, gold stocks, bonds, real estate, inventory, art, jewelry etc. There is no shortage of money. There is plenty of it in the world, just as there is enough of everything for everyone on the planet, because the Universe is an abundant place. If there is no shortage of money, then what is the problem? The problem is, as I see it, distribution. The money isn't getting to the people who need it the most. There is only a shortage of human values and belief to overcome fear which manifests as lack and scarcity. We need to encourage those who have money to distribute it more effectively. The solution is for a sufficient number of us - a minimum of 10% will do - to distribute at least 5-10% of our wealth around, on a regular basis. This creates a void or space in our natural ability to recreate wealth, which brings us even more abundance on a variety of levels. The solution is contained in the word, generosity. Generosity leads to "generativity", which generates more and more success in the world. When generosity is linked to creativity, creative solutions are found to the challenges that face us. It is happening already. Buckminster Fuller shared a vision of a world with a steadily improving standard of living for all. The driving forces of a new age of partnership, global in scope, has the potential to support everyone on the planet; in a way that's entirely harmonious with all life on our Spaceship Earth."

### FIRST THINGS FIRST

All people need food and shelter. If we don't have our survival needs met, all our time and energy goes into obtaining that first. It dominates our consciousness. It becomes our highest and most important priority. Once we have our most basic needs met, we can start to focus on our creativity, our relationships and on expanding our higher human potential through education and other types of learning experiences. We can start to develop our talents and contribute them to the world and start being a part of the global solution, instead of the global problem. Self-discovery now becomes available to us. We find we are filled with questions and desires and are driven to explore, learn and grow. In the world of education, we discover our passion and our focus. We may receive some kind of artistic impulse, business idea, "calling" or dream of helping others or the world in some way. We discover what we want to do with our lives, and how to do it, and hopefully are imbued with a desire to make a difference. Once we have clarity about that, we are at the top of the pyramid. This is the stage Maslow called self-actualization. We need to find creative ways to manifest our artistic projects, businesses and humanitarian dreams. These are the challenges at the highest levels of the pyramid. Creative resourcing seems to be the answer.

It's the realization that we cannot and were not meant to do it all alone. We need each other to help all of us progress and evolve, as human beings, creatively and economically. Individuals with dominator imprinting and parasitic personality disorders think that to get rich they have to keep a percentage of the population under their control or dependent upon them (i.e. controlling land, water, food, shelter and energy). Once we outgrow the"dog-eat-dog" mentally, where we fight over resources to get to the "top", then we can begin to cooperate and collaborate to co-create a greater possibility where *all* of us win, not just some of us.

## Sharing Makes A Difference

We need to understand the generative power of giving. Tithing is the art and practice of giving 10% of your income to an organization or a cause that gives you positive energy or support or is a source of inspiration, and uplifts you to a higher level in your life.

More and more of the private sector is realizing the government shouldn't do it all and is stepping in to contribute to their communities and the world. In the public sector, companies are giving people paid vacations to do volunteer work, and are taking on more and more special projects to support. In the book The Chalice and the Blade Riane Eisler talks about how we need to alleviate the impact of a system that's fundamentally unbalanced, a dominator system that constantly creates poverty, hunger and violence, by spending a large portion of the 10% we contribute to fund and encourage what she calls, new social and economic inventions. In order for the new inventions to take hold however, the overall paradigm in which those inventions would take effect would need to change. And for the paradigm to change, there would need to be a fundamental transformation in consciousness to allow those changes to truly take effect. For example, the shift from the "dominator model", in which one feels the need to have power over someone, instead of the " partnership model", where we can have power *with* another, creates the experience of mutual co-creative empowerment. In my experience, the latter approach is far more productive than the former approach.

These economic inventions need to give value to the most essential human work: caring and caretaking. Under conventional economic systems, that work isn't counted. For example, it's supposed to be done for free by women in male controlled households. That's a dominator economic assumption. A partnership needs different economic assumptions; one that honors all people and embraces equality on all levels and values the contribution of both people, while not taking it for granted. And as well as those contributions are appreciated, they are also fairly economically rewarded, creating a win-win situation. (see Community Cash)

If every person tithed 10% of their income, or at least gave what they could, when they could to a person, an organization or a worthy cause in need, whether it was money or other resources, including volunteer time and energy, that would contribute to the global solution in a very big way. Ant the point is not so much the quantity you give, but the generosity, the open and kind-heartedness from which you give it. It's that genuine giving that makes all the difference in the world. It is the light in the eyes of the one whose just received, that gives the gift to the giver. When you know the effect your goodness has on the world, it makes you just want to keep on giving, and at the same time receive the true richness of life.

## COMMUNITY CASH
### From the tiny acorn springs the mighty oak!

A new form of money!  A great way to embrace and support people in your community is to buy and utilize Sonoma County Community Cash.

Adding to the local abundance, Sonoma County's local currency, or Community Cash is catching on.  Local currency  is an idea that is being practiced all over the united states of America.  It is based on the highly successful model started in Ithaca, New York.  Local currency is legal as long as it appears distinct and separate from Federal Reserve notes and isn't used for interstate transactions.  Community Cash has value to us locally because it represents our time, not gold stored by the federal government.  When we use Community Cash our wealth is being continually flowing within our community, not being diverted to individual with no connection to our neighborhoods.

The bills are printed from recycled U.S. currency and feature an oak tree, farmer's market and the phrase, "Building a Community While Making a Living."  People sign up, list three goods or services they would be willing to provide in exchange for local currency, and then are listed in a directory.  A person who signs up is issued 5 Hours of Our Community Cash, and may begin trading with anyone else in the directory.  For more information, call (707) 573-0853, (707) 763-1419 (Community Time) or check out the website www:sonomacash.bellanet.com.

# CHARITY:
# Recreational Transformaiton

We have all seen the eyes of a child reflect our love, the hand of a less fortunate gain strength in ours and a puppy or kitten tremble with joy at being held for the first time by its' new caretaker. Give, Give, Give, - Open your heart for someone's world can't wait a minute longer. Let your genius, your generosity and your heart radiate love by where you direct your eyes and your hands. In the photo, the Big Hand of God and Charity protects the children andinspires us to give.

Children light up to the encouragment of Monsignor Thomas J. Keys who founded the Script Center in Petaluma, California in 1978. The wealth of a nation can be judged by the spirit, conviction and thoughful resourcefullness of its youth. We are all role models who can teach generorsity, light heartedness, kindness, loyalty and positive prayer.

## CHARITY: The 1st Law of Abundance. It Is Better To Give Than Receive. "YOU CAN CHANGE THE WORLD!"

**Catholic Charities** was established in 1954, and began with one counseling program. Today they operate 22 programs and services, and assist more than 40,000 people annually - the homeless, the hungry, the sick and the mentally challenged. They are the largest provider of homeless services between the Golden Gate Bridge and the Oregon Border. One 120-bed facility helps an estimated 760 people annually. Sixty percent of the residents are children. In addition they operate Sonoma County's first day center for homeless individuals, where showers, lockers, food and counseling toward self-sufficiency is provided.

For questions about Catholic Charity Programs you may call (707) 528-8712. To make a donation, please make all checks to Catholic Charities. For information on giving options call (707) 528-8712, ext 27.

**Computer Recycling:** Benefits Public and Non Profit Schools
3249 Santa Rosa Ave., Santa Rosa, CA. 95407
Recording: 570-1600 Office: 570-1190 Steve Wyatt Pager # 325-2298

**Computer Thrift Store:** Donated Computers that are Resold
Santa Rosa, CA. 526-4900

**Face to Face Annual Art for Life Auction** benefits Sonoma County AIDS
patients. Held every September at Friedman Center, Santa Rosa.

**Redwood Gospel Mission:** Feeds and Lodges the Homeless
101 6th Street, Santa Rosa, CA. 95401 Prayer and B,L & D daily.

**Salvation Army,** 1059 Second St., Santa Rosa, CA. 95404 (707) 542-0981
Ask about Youth Children, Senior & Adult Programs, Bible Study & Worship

**S. E. E. Green** (**S**ocial, **E**nvironmental & **E**conomic) You have to be a charity
business, environmentally and economically in integrity to be a member of this
organization.

**Sonoma Center for Peace and Justice,** 540 Pacific Ave. Santa Rosa, CA.
95404 (707) 575-8902 Fax: (707) 575-8903
email: peacecentr@sonic.net www.sonic.net/-peacentr

**Sonoma County Conservation Council** 632 Fifth Street, P.O. Box 4346
Santa Rosa, CA. 95402 (707) 578-0595

**West Sonoma County HIV/AIDS Ministry Fund**
Contact Food for Thought Grocery Stores

**YES! CAMPS** Ocean & Michelle Robbins Environmental Youth Camps
1295 Brisa Del Mar., Santa Cruz, CA. 95060
email: yes@yesworld.org (408) 454-9970

ALSO SEE **WILDLIFE RESCUE SERVICES** on Page 299

---

Remember the story of the fish and the fisherman? I would like to change that to: "give a person garden produce and they will be hungry tomorrow. Teach a person to grow a garden, and they will hunger no more". What is your favorite charity where you want to teach people to grow a garden for themselves?

# WILD HEARTS in LONELY PLACES

All of us must one day face the end of the road. I shall never forget the perfectly undisturbed deer skeleton I discovered in a creek bed on the Sonoma Coast. This deer had the simple dignity of knowing where to lay down and die - and all of nature honored his last wish. There he laid, perfectly undisturbed in a canyon of lush ferns and majestic redwood trees - beams of sunlight filtering down on his skeleton - not a bone was out of place. Every living thing deserves the same dignity.

For some wild animals death can be extremely slow and brutal. A raccoon had suffered a brutal near-death on Highway 1. Two of her babies were hit and slowly mangled by the relentless flow of cars and trucks - all just a few feet from where their mother lay semi-conscious and unable to move at road's edge. Had I not stopped to remove her body to the ditch I would have never known she was still alive. As I approached, her legs slowly started to move. My God - she was still alive and wanted to live! She had laid beneath torrential winter rains for almost two days. No food - no help and no hope but for me and divine guidance. What should I do? I have bills to pay and places to be. Suddenly nothing else in my world mattered more than that helpless raccoon mother's life. I wrapped her in a towel and put her in the car.

Thank God for Richard HoJohn at Timber Cove Inn who had the telephone number of a Wildlife Rescue Center. "My God, you mean that raccoon is still alive!" screamed a guest he had been talking to, "We saw her laying there yesterday!"

I re-wrapped the mother raccoon in native grass and laid her on the passenger floor with the heater on low. I pointed the nose of the Miata into the fog and down pour and 700 foot cliffs above the crashing surf and headed for Santa Rosa. On the way in I remember the story of "Harley the Fawn". A biker had found her almost dead along the road and had taken her on the back of his Harley - all the way to veterinarian Dr. Grant Patrick. Grant saved her and she fully recovered at Fawn Rescue in Glen Ellen to be released into the wild.

My PTSD mixed with the ridgelines, fog and rain and I began having flash-backs of Med-a-Vac Choppers in the monsoons of Vietnam. I surrounded the car, raccoon and road ahead of me with white light. We were guided and blessed. We were unstoppable. At 6:30pm I called Dr. Patrick. In the rush I had left his phone # at Timber Cove Inn. "Operator I'm not sure of the name of this Vet that is waiting to treat a injured raccoon I have in my car - can you help me." Click - she hung up. I couldn't believe it - what a cold hearted thing to do. (Later I found out that information operators are only allowed to stay on the line for so many seconds - then hang up or face possible firing - all so the Pacific Bell investors can get a higher return on their corporate investment. This type of greed is the most repulsive).

Thank God for Dr. Grant Patrick who waited past closing time at the Montecito Veterinary Clinic to receive her. She was in a comma, had a bad burn on her shoulders from being dragged under the car, had a broken leg, was in shock and hypothermic. He saved her life. For five days she slowly recovered Because it was just before Thanksgiving - I named her Thanksgiving. Members of my church circle prayed for her - so did many others. I called anybody who I thought could help her and support Dr. Patrick and his staff. On the fifth day a specialist treated her and said she would choose to totally recover or transition within the next 12 hours. She transitioned in the night, but not without experiencing an outpouring of love from dozens of humans who dared to make a difference. I hope that in sharing this story some of you will also dare to save a wild heart in a lonely place.

Thanksgiving the racoon was slowly recovering from internal injuries and a comma after being hit by a vehicle on Coast Highway 1 north of Jenner. She was being treated by Dr. Grant Patrick (left) at Montecito Veterinary Clinic in Santa Rosa. The author, Robert W. Matson (right), discovered her incredible will to live and drove her to Dr. Patrick in Santa Rosa.

**Don't be afraid to get involved. The spiritual rewards are enormous when you take the time to help an injured animal. Here are tips on transporting wild or injured animals to the hospital.**
Use a thick towel, blanket or coat when lifting them. Duplicate their native environment - wrap them in grass so they smell nature - not your human scented car or truck. Keep them quiet. If possible put them in a box or wrap them in a blanket or towel. Keep them away from your pets or anything that would stress them. No loud music or hot heaters on them. Wash or shower after handling them. Pray for their recovery. Pat yourself on the back for making a difference.

## VET'S with HEARTS

Dr. Grant Patrick at Montecito Veterinarian Center    Specialty: Wild Mammals
4900 Sonoma Hwy (Hwy 12), Santa Rosa, CA.    (707) 539-2322
Dr. Long at Forestville Veterinary Clinic    Specialty: Dogs & Cats
5033 Gravenstein Highway N., Forestville, CA.    (707) 887-2261
Dr. Vince Pedria at Animal Care Center  (24 Hours)    Specialty: Dogs & Cats
6620 Redwood Drive, Rohnert Park, CA.    (707) 584-4343
Dr. Leslie Miller at Petcare Emer. Hospital (24 Hourss   Specialty: Dogs & Cats
1370 Fulton Rd., Santa Rosa, CA.    (707) 579-5900

## WILDLIFE RESCUE SERVICES

Bats Unlimited
Marine Mammal Center      (415) 289-7325
Fort Cronkhite, Sausalito, CA.
Sonoma County Wildlife Rescue      (707) 526-WILD (9453)
Box 9360, Santa Rosa 95406
Wildlife Center   Box 670, Kenwood, CA.      (707) 575-1000
Wolf Lifeline Inc.      (707) 573-9653

**DONATIONS:** Don't forget to donate to one of the above organizations. Make checks out to the name of the organization and mail to listed address. I personally checked each veterinarian and organization. Not only are they incredible, they are Heroes!

# ANGEL DOGS AMONG US - My Beloved Karma

Painting by Scott Kennedy

*They come to us at all times of the day and night. They are born in wood piles, in the back of pick-up trucks, in cabins atop mountains, beside rushing streams, on farms, in apartments and mansions in small towns and major cities, in castles by the sea and in the bedrooms and garages of suburbia. As their mothers gently bring them into this world, their fathers and human caretakers guard the den as this new miracle of life breathes its first breath. A sweet motherly kiss is followed by a first gasp of cold air as tiny lungs fill for the first time. A fertile nipple and the warm flow of milk is their first experience with the unconditional love of their mother.*

*She was born during a thunder and lightning storm in Mendocino, California on Halloween night in 1987. I knew we had a path to walk together the moment I first picked her up - her little legs straddled my forearm - her chin came down on the wrist of my left hand and then up - she had claimed me as her's. Panda and Zeke had created a beauty. From that moment on our spiral of life began a path that would bring us into contact with thousands of animals and people over thousands of miles of travel in the 11 years we would be together. I named her Karma.*

*One day in the Trinity Alps I made a vow to always be there for her - to never abandon her. The next day we were in a earthquake. I resolved that even if their was a great earthquake and biblical flood, and the helicopter came to pick us up, and they didn't take dogs - I would stay behind with her. She gave and taught me unconditional love. She became my telepathic spiritual partner and still is. I lovingly embraced her as she breathed her last few breaths. Just before I buried her I saw the sky fill with the lights of her ancestors. Her mother Panda, father Zeke, daughter Meesha, aunt Sheba, great great grandfather Timberline and others in her soul pack reunited and ascended in a spiral with her. My Angel Dog Karma is often in my thoughts and is my spirit guide.*

Canine Companions for Independence  *ANGEL DOGS AMONG US*

> *They serve the physically dependent at all times of the day and night. They give the physically challenged hope, unconditional love and animal ali companionship at the deepest level. They are our brother and sister Canine Companions for Independence.*

We are fortunate in northern California to have a large facility dedicated to training assistance dogs for people with disabilities other than blindness. The Canine Companion facility is located in the southeast area of Santa Rosa. Tours are available Monday/Wednesday at 10am and 1pm, or by appointment. As a bonus, you might qualify to raise a puppy for the year, before its advanced training at the facility and placement with one of CCI's student applicants.

Many teary, yet joyous moments, are experienced as "puppy" moves to maturity through training and experiences you and your family impart as the day moves toward the goal of becoming a working team partnered with someone with a disability.

These "angel dogs" create a bond of love and raise our spirits to unbelievable heights. They sacrifice and give us hope and guidance in the most loving way imaginable. Canine Companions has been a pet project of Jean Schulz, wife of Charles Schulz, creator of the Peanuts comic strip (or if you prefer: of Charlie Brown, Snoopy and Peanuts Gang). The Schultz's also created and operate the Redwood Ice Arena in Santa Rosa where children and families can enjoy quality recreation in a safe, supervised, and "cool" setting.

Information on general sessions, lessons, special events and merchandise in Snoopy's Gallery and Gift Shop is available by phone or on the Web.

*CANINE COMPANIONS for INDEPENDENCE*
*2965 Dutton Ave., Santa Rosa, CA 95402*
*(707) 577-1700  www.caninecompanions.org*
*$-$$ REDWOOD ICE ARENA*
*1667 W. Steele Lane, Santa Rosa, CA 95403*
*(707) 546-7147  www.snoopy.com*
*Snoopy's Gallery (707) 546-3385*

## MONTECITO VETERINARY CLINIC

Good veterinarians with big hearts are hard to find - especially if you are on a trip to northern California and you don't know who you can trust. Though everybody has their favorite veterinarian I have found Dr. Grant Patrick and the Montecito Veterinary Clinic to be one of the best for your dog or cat. Alert and enthusiastic he is a favorite of many north coast residents. Open from 9am to 6pm Monday thru Friday and till noon on Saturday, Grant and his fine staff are capable of handling most emergencies, surgerys, X-rays, dental work or routine examinations and check-ups. Time permitting, Grant is one of the few veterinarians who will administer emergency treatment to wild animals such as raccoons or deer. He has a high success rate and a big heart. He treated a raccoon for me that had been hit by a car and he and his staff saved my dog Karma's life. I would recommend Grant to anybody who loves their dog or cat.

*$-$$ MONTECITO VETERINARY CENTER  4900 Sonoma Hwy, Santa Rosa*
*Dog and Cat Veterinary Hospital        MC & Visa        (707) 539-2322*

## BAR ALE FEED & PET STORE

Founded in 1911, Bar Ale is a name synonymous with food, shelter and service to farmers, ranchers and pet owners in northern California. The huge warehouses of Bar Ale line the Petaluma River at the D Street draw bridge. It is not uncommon for hundreds of birds to sit on the wires outside the Bar Ale Feed and Pet Store entrance. Inside the store Don Benson and his staff are helping pet owners with all their needs as well as dreaming up new ways to meet their future needs. "We feed crickets to elephants", states Don.

Inside the store are isles lined with food, vitamins, environmental comforts and gifts to keep your dog, cat, bird, horse, rodent or lizard happy and healthy. Watch for exciting changes at the Bar Ale Feed and Pet Store as the owners and staff shift gears to host educational programs to help you with the physical, mental, emotional and spiritual needs of both pet and caretaker. There is no greater satisfaction than to gaze into the eyes of unconditional love of your pet and know in your heart that you are being the very best caretaker you can be.

*$-$$ BAR ALE FEED & PET STORE    201 First St., Petaluma, CA, 94953*
*Food Supplies and Lifestyle Enhancement for Pets from A-Z*
*AX, Discover, MC & Visa  Fax: (707) 763-9486  Info: (707) 762-4505*

## FRIZELLE ENOS CO. and PENNGROVE HAY & GRAIN

Much more than a pet and feed store, Frizelle Enos has always been a fun shopping experience for the home maker, farmer and rancher in all of us. The two cavernous warehouses and attractive retail showrooms work well together in Penngrove at the Penngrove Hay and Grain and in Sebastopol at Frizelle Enos. Owners Linda and Tenny Tucker offer a practical destination where pet and farm owners can load their truck or car with hay and grain, shavings for the floor, salts and a range of economically priced to expensive pet foods and supplies for dogs, cats, horses, birds and fish. Wood stoves for heat or cooking, gourmet foods, books on gardening and farming, chickens, ducks, trout and catfish are also stocked. In the retail show rooms there are saddles, boots, all-weather and Country Western clothing for work around the farm or ranch as well as Saturday nite dancing clothes. Both stores support grounded lifestyles based on hard work and fun with *all* our special friends.

*$-$$$ FRIZELLE ENOS CO.*          *$-$$$ PENNGROVE HAY & GRAIN*
*Full service pet stores with retail country store show rooms & giftshops*
*265 Petaluma Ave., Sebastopol, 95472   10035 Main St., Penngrove,  94951*
*(707) 823-6404*                 *Fax: (707) 795-5748   (707) 795-5712*

## WESTERN FARM SUPPLY

Located on the west side of Highway 101 near Railroad Square in Santa Rosa is Western Farm Center, the largest pet food and supply general store in Sonoma County. Whether you live here or are visiting, at Western Farm you'll find highly nutritional food and lifestyle enhancement for dogs, cats, horses, birds, fish and wild and domestic animals from A - Z. Owners Larry and Louie Bertolini grew up on a truck farm a few miles from where their office and store is today. They state, "Our goal is to serve our public with the best supplies, backed by knowledgeable and friendly people. We are constantly searching for new and better products for our clients." Bulk vegetable seeds, a complete line of bee supplies, including candle making supplies, dog houses, kennels and a year round supple of baby chicks, rabbits, birds and cut little guinea pigs are also stocked. Western Farm Store has been honored many times for its work with local agencies and has been selected best pet shop in Sonoma County, best retail store feed store in California and has been honored as National Retail Feed Store of the Year. Open: Mon. - Sat. 8am - 5:30pm & 9:30am - 4pm Sun.

*$-$$ WESTERN FARM SUPPLY  21 West 7th Street, Santa Rosa, CA. 95401*
*Food Supplies and Lifestyle Enhancement for Critters from A - Z.*
*AX, Discover, MC & Visa   Fax: (707) 545-4302   Info: (707) 545-0721*

## STAR WATCH and DREAM

Since the beginning of time we have looked to the heavens for inspiration and answers. One wonders how many curious souls have climbed to the top of a tree or a mountain to catch a twinkling star in their hand. To ancient hunter gatherers the stars must have seemed like campfires in the sky.

As the earth rotates clockwise around the sun different stars appear in the eastern sky as the evening progresses. Each month a new set of constellations appears in the nighttime sky marking the beginning and ending of important seasons and growing cycles. Shepherds, mariners and early astronomers looked up and named constellations, which reassuringly appeared each night on their journey across the heavens. Sight unseen, cosmic events of a grand magnitude unfold in the universe around us as we toil in our daily lifestyles. Occasionally we sense something much bigger than ourselves and become frustrated when we can't fully comprehend what we intuitively feel happening somewhere else around us.

Ancient tablets and carvings show that the movement of planets were understood before 3000 B.C. The Egyptians placed their pyramids with reference to the stars. The circles of stone at Stonehenge may have been used to keep track of lunar eclipses. With the invention of the telescope in China in 1100 AD new stars and planets were discovered and the heavens moved much closer. Like ourselves each star has a birth, life cycle, color, temperature and death. Everything on earth is made from stars. Throughout history the greatest minds and most wonderful lovers all watched and dreamed beneath the stars.

There is a mathematical harmony to the universe that reminds one of the most beautiful symphony imaginable. For the experienced observer stars can tell you time, direction and position. For example, two of the stars in the bowl of the Big Dipper, which is prominently displayed in the northern California sky, point toward the north star Polaris. Annual first time appearances of constellations have significant meanings for those who are tuned in. Roughly the time that the Pleiades (Seven Sisters) first appears in the eastern nighttime sky the first salmon begin their migration up north coast rivers. With the emergence of the bright star Arcturus in the early evening it is evident that Spring is near.

**Star Watching:**  It is important to get well away from all forms of atmospheric pollution including electric lights, electromagnetic fields, smoke and engine exhaust. Put your back against a tree trunk, a mountain boulder or rest against a sandy knoll at the beach. Get earthy before you get heavenly. For some, to be beneath a darkened sky full of stars far away from cities and street lights may seem frightening. This is so only because you have been cut off from a very beautiful and natural part of being human for too long. There is nothing to fear. With time you will "remember" and a new found love will fill your being as the stars work their magic on your soul.

Dress for the season. Dark, still and cool nights are often the best for star watching. A 6 to 8 power pair of binoculars will reveal the moons of Jupiter, craters on earth's moon and nebulae. Jenner north to Gualala is great viewing on the Sonoma Coast. The Milky Way is particularly vivid from June through October. It is as if the creator took a paint brush full of stars and made a giant swath across the heavens above us. The hillsides east and west of Cloverdale are also excellent observation points as are the wilderness ridgelines around Lake Sonoma and west to the coast on Skagg's Springs Road. We are blessed indeed. There are also several planetariums and observatory's you can visit in northern California which offer public showings. Personally I like Hood Mountain or Sugarloaf State Park for viewing opportunities.

### PLANETARIUMS & OBSERVATORY'S Which Offer Public Viewing

Cabrillo College Planetarium / Aptos (near Santa Cruz) (408) 688-6466
Lawrence Hall of Science / UC Berkeley William K. Holt Planetarium (415) 642-5132
Morrison Planetarium / San Francisco (415) 750-7127 Recording: (415) 750-7141
Santa Rosa Junior College Planetarium / Santa Rosa (see page 187) (707) 527-4465
Sugar Loaf State Park Observatory (707) 833-5712
Taylor's Observatory / Kelseyville in Lake County (707) 279-8372

**Great Dates** and hot tubs helped contemporary humankind rediscover the stars! Under the phase of the new moon, meteor showers are extremely visible. It is a time for new beginnings and planting seeds. The best viewing times are between midnight and dawn. One of the best times to make love is beneath a blanket of nighttime stars.

**Major Meteor Showers** include the Quadrantids (@ - around ) January 3, Lyrids @ April 21, Eta Aquarids @ May 4, Delta Aquarids @ July 28, Perseids @ August 12, Orionids @ October 21, Leonids @ November 17 and Geminids @ December 13. Over 50 meteors per hour fall during the Perseids and Geminids shower. Check with the SRJC planetarium for annual dates and star parties.

**Heavenly Treasures:** We are never alone beneath the twinkling starlight. Curious souls in other galaxy's must look toward earth and get a reassuring feeling that life exists here. What would they think of us if they could visit California? What would they think if they could visit you? Stars are in integrity with the universe. They are sovereign. They obey all natural laws and exist as a stellar community in a vast expanse of space. Above us and all around us they silently work their magic on the human psyche. Each night they reassure us with their presence. As we turn with the earth our eyes made of star dust scan a never ending treasure of twinkling constellations above us.

# SUMMER NIGHTIME SKY

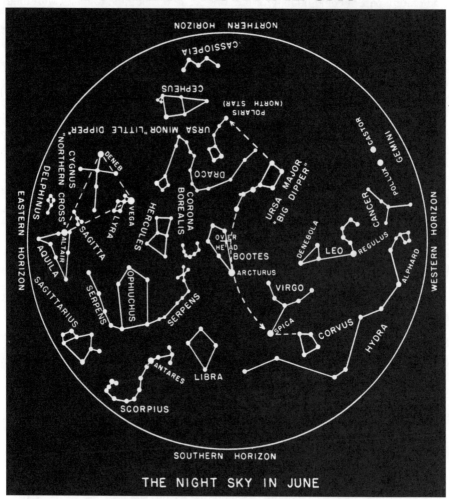

THE NIGHT SKY IN JUNE

The summer sky above northern California offers views of the Big Dipper (Ursa Major), the Little Dipper (Ursa Minor) and the North Star (Polaris). **You can always find true north by locating the Little Dipper.**

On any given night up to 15,000 stars can be viewed in a sky unhampered by outdoor lighting. Only about 10% of the us of A population experiences these conditions regularly. Protecting dark skies is as vital as protecting clean air, pure water, wildlife and the sounds of nature. Our bodies and souls need these connections to heal and restore sanity. Everyone should be able to see the stars and planets at night. It lessens our fears and promotes good will. Over the past 40 years millions of lights in cities and even in the countryside cause problems for

# WINTER NIGHTIME SKY

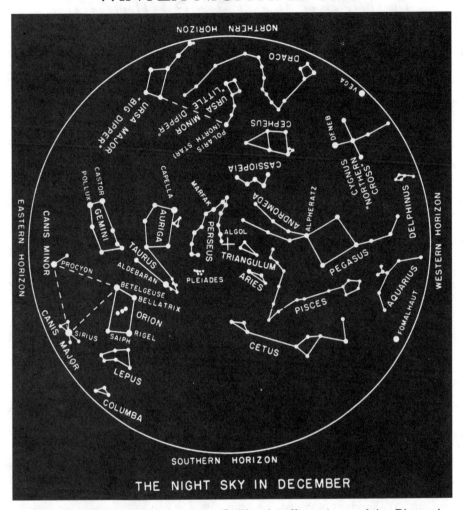

THE NIGHT SKY IN DECEMBER

The winter sky above northern California offers views of the Big and Little Dipper as well as the North Star. A special winter time treat is a view of the Pleiades (the Seven Sisters) and Orion.

star watchers. Corporations that promote fear make millions of dollars blocking out the night time sky. We all have choices about what we see or don't see. If you want to promote a love of viewing twinkling stars against a darkened sky at night, then simple encourage your neighbors and communities to install outdoor lights that face downward. There are a number of highly spirited astronomical organizations and movements that can help you. A vigorous leader is the British Astronomical Society and their Campaign for Dark Skies. An example of a small community that lives with dark starlight skies at night is the historically preserved seaside town of Mendocino.

# *A Vision For The Millennium*

"Seedling" by Roy Thompson

## Love is the vision for the Millennium

The Millennium Citizen is all about LOVE. Unconditional love. Unconditional love in partnership with your mate, your family and your community. You are unstoppable and inseparable by any of the negative or challenging influences on our planet or in our galaxy if love is your first and foremost reason for being here and now.

In Chapters 1 and 2 you read about the physical goodies that are located is this garden of eden setting north of San Francisco. Children and adults had the opportunity to read about the Web of Life and secret victory gardens. Not only did you discover great destinations to dine at and spend the night, but you also discovered a vast network of farms and gardens as well as sacred sites and energy vortexes.

In Chapter 3 you have read about balance of the physical, mental, emotional and spiritual aspects of ourselves. Spiritual partnership and relationship tools are a key to recognizing and building relationships that last

# A Vision For The Millennium

as opposed to the old dominator model which always comes to an end when health and balance are a priority. You have been introduced to a variety of techniques and individuals who can help you achieve balance in your well being. Culinary and medicinal herbs grown naturally with living soil and living water promote health as do shopping at superior health food stores and dining at health food restaurants. You learned about sustainable communities and self sufficiency. You have been introduced to community based "mom and pop" businesses that showcase a variety of health promoting products. You also learned how to get rid of parasites that steal your life force energy in the Sovereignty article. The emotional shift to Sovereignty is 80% of the work to transform paralytic fear to self love to achieve your goals and real freedom. Now that you have some extra "community cash" you can practice Visionary Economics. Don't forget that Charity is the first law of abundance. Please honor the plants and animals you share the planet with. Last but not least, look up at night and witness the awesome majesty of the star studded galaxy you were born into. Feel your heart beating in step with the pulse of the Universe and the loved ones around you. Happy Millennium!

*At the end of all the ages, a knight sat upon steed, tired of fear and separation. 'Lo and behold' said knight to steed, as he loosened the reigns and charged into infinity . . . . . . And finally, silence did silence remain. Then. amid the rest and twinkle, the spark of creation gave birth to a brilliant unyielding wave of love which spiraled outward creating Oneness throughout the Universe.*

## SONOMA COUNTY INLAND VALLEY RESTAURANTS

Special thanks to Jenifer, Suzanne, Jan & Ken, Lendon, Monsignor Thomas Keyes, Glenn, Jeff, Randy, Ted, David and Sharon. Artists: John Boskovich Jr., Roy Thompson, Anthony Rees, Mike Gray, Jack Haley, Richard Gillette, Wolfgang Gramatzki and all the artists, writers and photographers so noted throughout this book. Its Incredible! Thank You! To all the kindred spirits I met along the way who believed in this book. May the information on these pages help set you free.

Thanks to my Old Soul Animal Guides - brothers & sisters in furry suits who unconditionally loved and protected me while on the sacred path. To my Angel Dog "Karma", who touched the hearts of many and lit up the way. Blessed be to all those who retreated at the Sea Wolf Lodge - our cups overflow with goodness. To my sweetheart Jenifer - I couldn't have done it without your loving support. I love you Jenifer.

Photo by Rick Hansen

*Robert W. Matson with Karma (right) and her mate Sammy.*

Robert W. Matson has been writing about the people and land north of San Francisco for over 20 years. As a resident author of Northern California, he is more capable of keeping his fingers on the pulse-beat of this vibrant region. It is part of the Garden of Eden which is very accessible, yet hasn't been completely civilized—nor will it ever be.

During much of the writing of this book Robert traveled with his friendly Samoyed, "Karma". You'll find the people warm and friendly and the land as fair as any under the sun. California's north coast is a wonderful place for Re-Creational Transformaion.

If you would like to correspond with Robert you can write him at Box G, Santa Rosa, California Republic or call (707) 591-WOLF (9653).

## ORDER FORM

The following books are in the works (or ready) and will be available at wholesale prices (20% off and no tax) to individuals who order 5 or more of one or more titles. Send no checks; terms are UPS/COD with your order, unless otherwise stated. Book retail prices are subject to change without notice.

Distributors, bookstore and giftshop owners may write for order information to:
SEA WOLF PUBLISHING   P.O. Box G, Santa Rosa, California 95402 or call the
Sea Wolf Travel Bookstore & Information Center at (707) 522-0550.
MARIN COAST - The Enchanted Coast          ($9.95)      )SBN 0-916310-04-3
SONOMA COAST,
WINE COUNTRY & REDWOOD FORESTS     ($14.95)      )ISBN 0-916310-05-1
MENDOCINO, HUMBOLDT - LOST COAST   ($12.95)      ISBN 0-916310-06-X

ROUTE 1 Series in a Library Fireside Gift Box   ($35.00)      ISBN 0-916310-03-5

HAVENS, RETREATS & HIDEAWAYS north of San Francisco  ISBN 0-916310-02-7
($15.95).   An Encyclopedia to Lodging and the Healing Arts in Northern California

The NORTH of SAN FRANCISCO NEWSLETTER
In the future, the no-nonsense, informative (and at times humorous) north of San Francisco Newsletter will be published. If you are interested in being on the mailing list then send your address to *Newsletter, Box G, Santa Rosa, CA 95402.* This more updated Big Picture north of San Francisco will cover subjects too timely or inappropriate for the book series to cover.